STALINISM IN A RUSSIAN PROVINCE

Also by James Hughes

STALIN, SIBERIA AND THE CRISIS OF THE NEW ECONOMIC POLICY

Stalinism in a Russian Province

A Study of Collectivization and Dekulakization in Siberia

James Hughes
*Lecturer in Russian Politics, Department of Government
London School of Economics and Political Science*

 in association with the
Centre for Russian and East European Studies
University of Birmingham

First published in Great Britain 1996 by
MACMILLAN PRESS LTD
Houndmills, Basingstoke, Hampshire RG21 6XS
and London
Companies and representatives throughout the world

> This book is published in Macmillan's *Studies in Russian and East European History and Society* series.
> General Editors: R.W. Davies and E. A. Rees

A catalogue record for this book is available
from the British Library.

ISBN 0–333–65748–9

 First published in the United States of America 1996 by
ST. MARTIN'S PRESS, INC.,
Scholarly and Reference Division,
175 Fifth Avenue,
New York, N.Y. 10010

ISBN 0–312–15948–X

Library of Congress Cataloging-in-Publication Data
Hughes, James (James Raymond)
Stalinism in a Russian province : a study of collectivization and dekulakization in Siberia / James Hughes.
p.   cm.
Includes bibliographical references and index.
ISBN 0–312–15948–X
1. Collectivization of agriculture—Russia (Federation)—Siberia—History. 2. Peasantry—Russia (Federation)—Siberia—History.
3. Siberia (Russia)—Rural conditions. 4. Soviet Union—Economic policy—1928–1932. I. Title.
HD1492.R92S554   1996
338.7'683'0947—dc20   95-49484
                                                                  CIP

© James Hughes 1996

All rights reserved. No reproduction, copy or transmission of
this publication may be made without written permission.

No paragraph of this publication may be reproduced, copied or
transmitted save with written permission or in accordance with
the provisions of the Copyright, Designs and Patents Act 1988,
or under the terms of any licence permitting limited copying
issued by the Copyright Licensing Agency, 90 Tottenham Court
Road, London W1P 9HE.

Any person who does any unauthorised act in relation to this
publication may be liable to criminal prosecution and civil
claims for damages.

10 9 8 7 6 5 4 3 2 1
05 04 03 02 01 00 99 98 97 96

Printed and bound in Great Britain by
Antony Rowe Ltd, Chippenham, Wiltshire

for Julia

Contents

List of Tables	viii
Preface	ix
List of Abbreviations	xii
Map of the Siberian Krai in 1930	xiii
Introduction	1
1 Capturing the Peasantry	7
2 Mobilizing Social Influence	33
3 The Search for a New Method	52
4 The Ural-Siberian Method	73
5 *Volynki*: The Russian *Jacquerie*	92
6 A Prologue of Repression	111
7 Stalin's Final Solution	136
8 *Barshchina* and *Maroderstvo*	160
9 The Great U-turn	183
Conclusion	204
Notes	217
Appendix: Documents	249
Bibliography	258
Glossary	264
Index	266

List of Tables

4.1	The *piatikratniki*: compulsory registrations and compulsory auctions of peasant property in Siberia (March–May 1929)	74
4.2	A comparison of procurement levels in Siberia in March–April 1928 and 1929	85
6.1	Compulsory grain quotas on peasants in Siberia in 1928/9 and 1929/30	123
6.2	Punishment policy under Article 61 in Siberia in 1929/30	126
7.1	Siberian OGPU statistics on dekulakization, to 24 February 1930	154
9.1	The level of collectivization in Siberia, 1 July 1929 to 1 May 1930	195
9.2	Siberian OGPU statistics on the deportation of Category Two kulaks, to 24 February 1930	200

Preface

Stalin designated 1929 the year of the 'great breakthrough' in Russian history. The cataclysm of the self-declared 'revolution from above' marked the decisive turning point where Stalin propelled the country into a dash for growth: a planned 'great leap forward' that would stake out the construction of the Stalinist state. It articulated and released the pressures for change to the status quo of the New Economic Policy (NEP) that had been building up in the Communist Party during the 1920s. The Stalinist revolution was an attempt to smash a conjuncture of economic, political and contingent constraints obstructing the realization of the Bolshevik ideal of a modernizing transformation of the Soviet Union. After the grain crisis of 1927/8, the Stalinists had come to view the existence of a market oriented free peasantry under NEP as the *main* constraint on the building of socialism. The success of a modernizing crash industrialization programme hinged on a resolution of the question of who would control the countryside, the peasant or the state. For, given the Soviet Union's backwardness, whoever won this battle would dictate the nature and pace of the development of the country.

This study is a continuation of the author's previous work, *Stalin, Siberia and the Crisis of the New Economic Policy*, that investigated the relationship between contingency, Stalin's personal experiences of Siberian conditions and the abandonment of NEP during the grain crisis. In this book the focus of analysis has been taken forward to examine the aftermath of the grain crisis and the evolution of the primary programmatic pillar of the Stalin revolution: the formation and implementation of the policies of forced collectivization and dekulakization. It was the resolution of the peasant question which shaped the entire modernization process in Soviet Russia, for collectivization subordinated the peasant economy to the demands of the state-led rapid industrialization which was the foundation of the Stalinist state.

In preparing this book I have sought to build on the strengths of my expertise on one Russian province, Siberia, as well as attempting to be responsive to criticisms of structural faults in my earlier work that focused on its non-archival source base. The revolution in historical investigation in Russia that has occurred following the disintegration of communism has been driven not only by much freer access to archives previously closed to foreign scholars, but also by the unbrokered exchange of ideas and materials through personal, scholar-to-scholar contacts. The new environment in 1990–94 allowed me to collect and incorporate in this book a massive amount of new materials, the bulk of which are from Siberian and central party archives. I would like to acknowledge my debt to the Siberian historians, Nikolai Gushchin and Vladimir Il'inykh, whose work on this period acted as an intellectual stimulus for me. I am obliged to single out for special recognition and warmest thanks Vladimir Zhdanov, formerly of the Institute of History in Akademgorodok, Novosibirsk, who was employed as a research assistant for two years during my investigations of Siberian archives. The best scholar of his generation in the region, Vladimir guided me through the labyrinthine academic Hades that exists in post-communist Russia. His friendship and our constant disagreements over the interpretation of documents enthused and undoubtedly enriched my work. There are many other Russians, whose names I would rather not cite, to whom thanks are due: from archive assistants, administrative and clerical staff at institutes, to journalists, business people, pensioners and others who made specific and sometimes vital contributions to my work.

This book has endured a long intellectual ferment, originating with concepts and ideas first encouraged and developed by a brilliant teacher at Queen's University Belfast, the late Frank Wright, when I was an undergraduate there in the late 1970s. My ideas have been nurtured by the work of scholars whose names are too numerous to mention. I hope it is sufficient to express my appreciation of this intellectual debt by the citations in footnotes. I am especially grateful to the series editors Bob Davies and Arfon Rees of the Centre for Russian and East European Studies at the University of Birmingham, who read the manuscript and offered invaluable suggestions for changes which have considerably enhanced the finished work.

I could not have written this book without the financial assistance of several sources to whom I am profoundly grateful. The British Council had the foresight to provide me with a small short-term visit grant to conduct a preliminary survey of Siberian archives in September 1990. The Nuffield Foundation awarded me a social science research grant in 1992, and the British Academy followed this with a small personal research grant in 1993–94, which enabled me to carry out without interruption the collection and investigation of the new archival materials on which the work is based. The efforts of Chai Lieven, Bob Davies and Bob Service in helping me to obtain these grants is deeply appreciated. I would also like to acknowledge the support for this research by Keele University, where I was employed as lecturer in Russian politics from 1989–94. Keele greatly assisted my work by the award of a special sabbatical leave in 1992: an award that freed me from teaching and administrative duties to concentrate on writing and also provided some financial assistance for my research.

Parts of Chapters 3 and 4 previously appeared in a somewhat different version in *Slavic Review*, to the editors of which I am obliged for their kind permission to draw from this piece. I warmly appreciate the efforts of all those at Macmillan involved in the publication of this book, with a special thanks to Anne Rafique who skilfully and efficiently prepared the typescript.

Finally, the greatest debt of all is due to my wife Julia, to whom the book is dedicated. For she has tolerated my long absences, whether in my study or in Siberia, and provided the companionship and partnership that sustains me and my work through good times and bad.

James Hughes
April 1995

List of Abbreviations

GAAK	State Archive of Altai Krai
GANO 1	State Archive of Novosibirsk Oblast (archive of former Siberian Krai)
GANO 2	State Archive of Novosibirsk Oblast, Corpus 2 (former regional party archive)
IS	*Izvestiia sibkraikoma vkp(b)* (Novosibirsk)
NLP	*Na leninskom puti* (Novosibirsk)
RTsKhIDNI	Russian Centre for the Preservation and Study of Documents of Modern History (former CPSU central archive, Moscow)
ZS	*Zhizn' sibiri* (Novosibirsk)

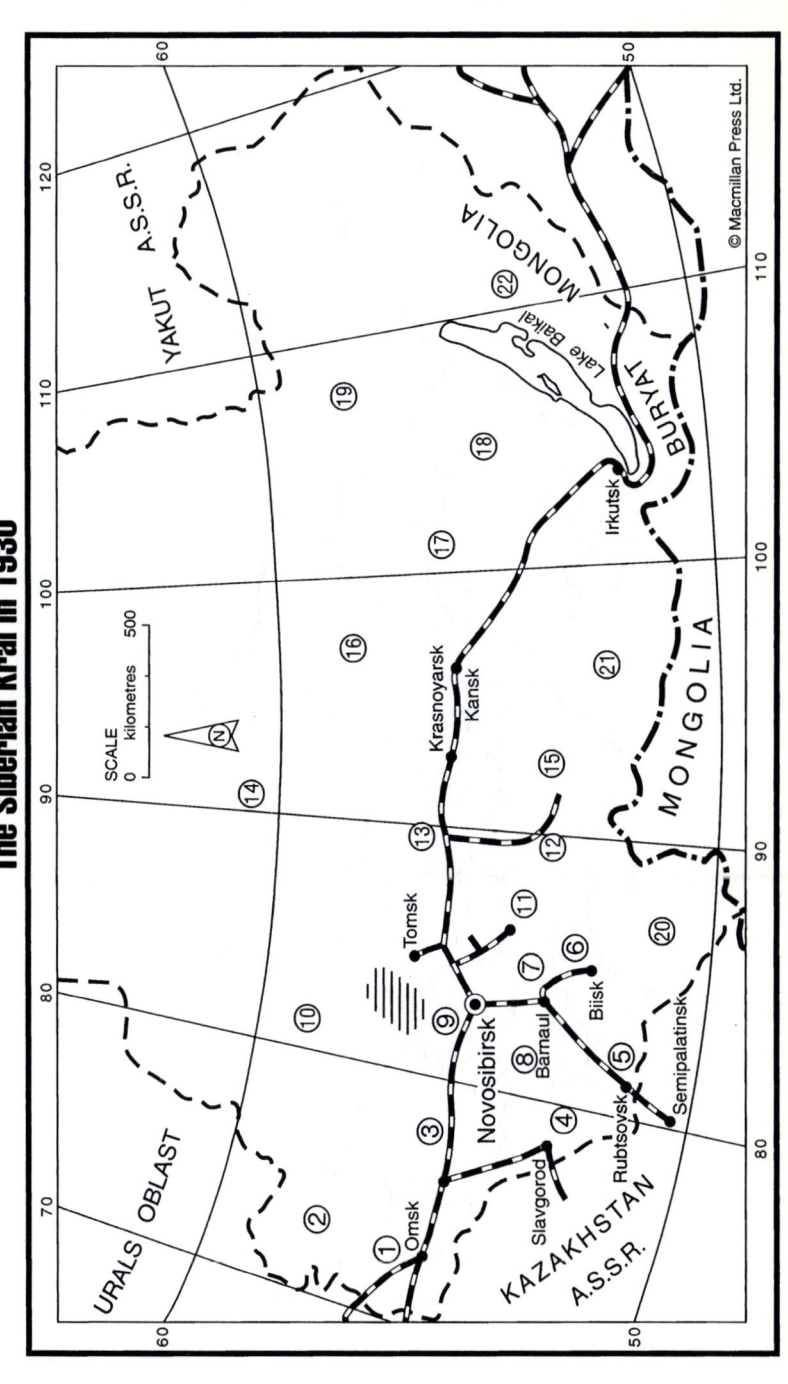

- ⊙ Krai Capital
- • Okrug Centre
- ━━━ Trans-Siberian Railroad and Branch Lines
- ┄┄┄ Okrug Boundaries
- ─ ─ ─ Krai Boundary
- ─ · ─ International Frontier
- ||||| Main zone of resettlement for category two kulaks

OKRUGS

West Siberia
① Omsk
② Tarsk
③ Barabinsk
④ Slavgorod
⑤ Rubtsovsk
⑥ Biisk
⑦ Barnaul
⑧ Kamensk
⑨ Novosibirsk

East Siberia
⑩ Tomsk
⑪ Kuznetsk
⑫ Khakassiya
⑬ Achinsk
⑭ Krasnoyarsk
⑮ Minusinsk
⑯ Kansk
⑰ Tulunovsk
⑱ Irkutsk
⑲ Kirensk

AUTONOMOUS OBLAST
⑳ Oirotiya

AUTONOMOUS REPUBLICS
㉑ Tannu-Tuva
㉒ Buryat-Mongolia

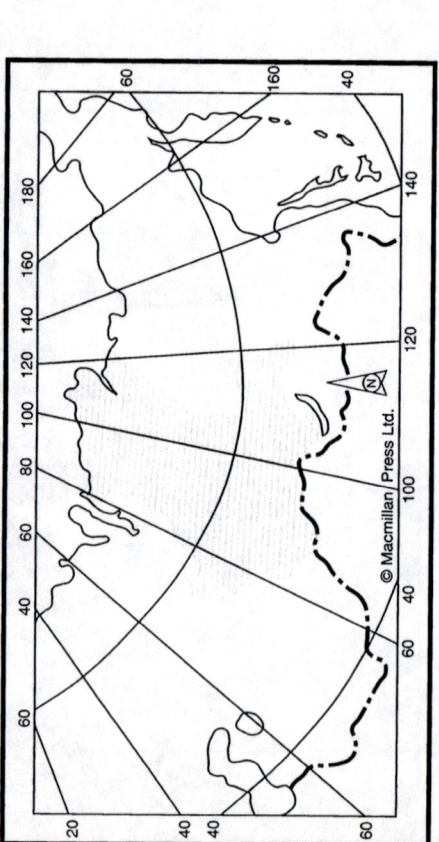

Location of the Sibkrai in the U.S.S.R.

The past year was the year of the great breakthrough on all the fronts of socialist construction.

Opening line of Stalin's article commemorating the twelfth anniversary of the October revolution, *Pravda*, 7 November 1929.

Eikhe (citing Lenin): *It might seem that this is a struggle for grain, but in fact, it is a struggle for socialism.*
Stalin: *Correct!*

From the stenogram of the November 1929 Central Committee plenum.

Who stole from his neighbours, set fire to property, and bore false witness at court for a bottle of vodka? The peasant. Who is the first to denounce peasants at village and other meetings? The peasant.

Chekhov, *Muzhiki*.

Introduction

The decision taken in late 1929 to go over to a policy of speedy, comprehensive collectivization (*sploshnaia kollektivizatsiia*) of agriculture, followed in January 1930 by the decision to dekulakize the countryside, was the culmination of an insidious Stalinist obsession with capturing the Russian peasantry for the state and harnessing the peasant economy to the demands of state-led industrialization. Interpretations of the reasons for these decisions vary widely; however, there is an orthodox scholarly consensus that the effect was to provoke a binary conflict between the state and peasants. There is a major difference of opinion over the significance of Bolshevik ideology in sealing off policy options and providing a conduit for certain courses of action. Perhaps the most enduring dispute of this era has centred on whether collectivization was a necessary precondition for crash industrialization and, more importantly, the extent to which a collectivized peasantry facilitated 'optimal' economic accumulation and enabled the state to exploit an agricultural surplus to finance industrial growth.[1] Those who believe that Stalin was indifferent to the economic illogicalities of his 'great leap forward' contend that his motives were base, derived from personal power ambitions and a distorted vision of Bolshevik ideological dogma.[2] The politics of the year of the 'great breakthrough' manifested itself in a consolidation of the Stalinist dictatorship. The shades of Stalin's paranoid psychopathology and power mania are addressed, however, only tangentially in this book, since this is a landscape that has been well furrowed by previous scholarship.

The standard analysis holds that the destruction of the free peasantry by collectivization and dekulakization had a sharply negative impact on industrialization. Indeed, with historical hindsight, it was such a disaster in economic terms that the state had to transfer resource allocations from town to countryside to compensate.[3] The questions of whether collectivization was an inevitable by-product of Soviet or Stalinist power, and of the real contribution of collectivization to industrial growth during the First Five Year Plan, should not cloud the assessment of the reasons for the launch of the policy and its practical implementation. Generally, those mystified by the speed of the transformation seek to explain the Stalinist transformational project as 'situation determined', inexorably driven by the tide of events in the late 1920s, particularly by the grain crisis. This interpretation began as a contemporary critique from the Trotskyite Left.[4] The slide of the Bolshevik regime from the New Economic Policy (NEP) to a revolutionary programme, it is suggested, developed as the spontaneous outcome of a haphazard and calamitous course of events set in motion by this crisis.[5] In this scenario the decision was unanticipated and impelled by a radical upsurge from the grassroots of the Bolshevik party, both within the regions and the industrial working class. During the late summer of 1929 this pressure from below catapulted the Stalinist leadership, in chaotic fashion, down the path of rapid collectivization.[6] Some advocates of the 'situation determined' approach have even exonerated Stalin of any personal responsibility for the policy decisions and outcomes.[7]

New interpretations of this period have been offered by social historians, who have attempted to shift the focal point of the debate from high politics to the social dimensions of the great breakthrough and its aftermath. This approach emphasizes the social destabilization and flux generated by the Stalin revolution, and concentrates its inquiry on such themes as social mobility and mobilization, the construction of identity, management, acculturation, and the nature of the command-administrative system.[8] The process of mobilization of workers, and the impact of generational conflict in the urban social classes and the peasantry has also provided a focus for social historians.[9] Arch Getty encapsulated the key Hobbesian strand of this approach when he summarized the Stalinist revolution as 'a war of all against all and the battle lines reflected social conflicts'.[10] Hobbes was wrong, of course, because when societies are plunged into turmoil what usually emerges is a war of group against group. Group conflict is the starting point for my investigations into collectivization and dekulakization.

Other scholars have identified collectivization as the antithesis of modernization, a reversion to a 'second serfdom' which enslaved the Russian peasantry to the Stalinist state in much the same way that it had been to the Tsarist state before 1861.[11] This linkage was uppermost in the minds of many peasants, for in wiping out the boundaries of peasant fields, comprehensive collectivization symbolically and literally erased the distinctiveness of peasant traditions and culture, drawing the peasantry into the orbit of state control and a captured status. The Bolsheviks regarded the peasantry as a behemoth that threatened to crush the nascent socialist regime and it was the year of the 'great breakthrough' that confirmed Stalin's reputation as the 'peasant-slayer'.[12]

There were historical precedents for state-led rapid modernization projects: the most obvious being those of the late nineteenth century and early twentieth century in Bismarck's Germany, Imperial Japan and Tsarist Russia. What set the Stalin revolution apart from the other attempts at rapid development were the nature, speed, scale and costs of the transformation imposed from 1929. Earlier cases of rapid industrialization occurred at a steady pace over a period of twenty to forty years based on interaction between the state and private business. The Stalin revolution was monopolized by the state and attempted a great leap forward in the space of five years, whatever the cost in terms of economic damage and loss of human life. In this sense the Stalinist regime had no precedents and no guidelines. Some scholars have tended to view the Stalinist project through the prism of contemporary concerns. Thus, the whole question of the universality of the Stalinist model of rapid development became of critical international importance, and a major academic issue, in the post-Second World War era, when the end of empires and decolonization created a swathe of newly independent 'developing' states in Africa and Asia that were anxious to achieve speedy modernization. Similarly, one recent analysis sought to explain the breakdown of NEP and the drive for collectivization as results of the Bolshevik regime's failure to pursue a tight monetarist policy![13]

The main previous studies of collectivization are by now rather dated, as they relied almost exclusively on central non-archival sources.[14] Nevertheless, the broad pattern of interpretations mentioned above continues to dominate analyses of the Stalin revolution. The starting point of my study does not differ from this pattern, for it is located within the paradigm that seeks to explain the Stalin revolution as primarily the product of historical context and structure. Thereafter my analysis diverges from the standard pattern, and aims to make a breakthrough in our understanding of this period by its focus on developments at the grassroots of Russian society: on Stalinism as a two-way driving force in centre–periphery relations, and on its impact in generating conflict with and within the peasantry in particular. My main hypothesis is that the Stalin revolution was as much a 'revolution from below' as it was a 'revolution from above'. In pursuit of modernization and the consolidation of an authoritarian regime, the Stalinist leadership designed and implemented a policy of mobilizing social influence and support in the countryside, specifically by stirring up social conflict between the broadly defined socioeconomic categories of poor, middle and kulak peasants.

In testing this hypothesis, I have drawn on the opposing methodologies of moral economy and political economy. These methodologies provide the context for the debate in other disciplines over the sources and conduct of peasant collective action, but hitherto they have not been utilized in studies of state–peasant relations in the Soviet Union.[15] The normative essence of the moral economy approach lies in a juxtaposition of contrasting economic structures: between the pre-modern subordinated 'embedded' economy and the autonomous 'disembedded' market economy. When E.P. Thompson revived the concept of the moral economy in the early 1970s as a challenge to the political economy notion of rational behaviour within capitalist market relations, he defined it as: 'a consistent traditional view of social norms and obligations of the proper economic functions of several parties within the community'.[16] Subsequently, the concept was developed by James Scott into an inclusive notion embracing 'peasant conceptions of social justice, of rights and obligations, of reciprocity'. Scott viewed the moral economy of the peasant as a communitarian 'subsistence ethic' based on the 'fear of dearth'. The political culture of the peasant had evolved, he argued, as a safety-first mechanism to prevent a recurrence of remembered scarcity and economic disaster, and to underpin peasant society with a kind of risk insurance against famine and social distress.[17]

Pre-modern non-market economies, it is argued, were regulated to ensure adequate provisioning by a broad framework of moral transactions conducted through social institutions, traditions and values. The commercialization of agriculture tears apart the social fabric of rural communities, shatters their moral universe, polarizes spheres of economic security, heightens levels of exploitation, and sharpens social conflict and 'moral outrage'. Structural factors, such as the impact of an intensification of market relations on the deterioration of the peasants' economic situation are presented as the classic precursors of peasant revolutionary outbreaks.[18] The triumph of the market defines a decline in peasant welfare that leads to an upsurge in peasant radicalism and rural protest in an attempt to defend or reconstitute the 'homemade' village order.[19] Evaluating peasant values and behaviour in the Soviet Union of 1929–30 is no easy task. Indeed, the whole notion of 'relative deprivation' (the peasant feel-good factor) is extremely difficult to validate and has been downplayed by Skocpol, who focuses instead on the impact of other structural factors, specifically the international position of a regime, on the capacity of the peasantry to enact 'internal leverage' against it and to organize collective action in defence of its interests.[20]

The moral economists, and theorists of modernization and peasant revolt generally, tend to have an over-simplistic view of the peasantry as a homogeneous social form which engages in a binary interaction with the state. They argue that the conservatism of the peasantry and the fragility of its social existence renders it reluctant to engage in acts of mass resistance. Rather, peasants resort to 'weapons of the weak' (go-slows, sit-down protests, sabotage, incendiarism, isolated acts of terrorism) to defend their interests.[21] When peasants do engage in collective action, the theory holds,

Introduction 5

it is usually in spontaneous, amorphous and unguided violent outbursts. The contours of this academic mindset were shaped by Marx's infamous denunciation of peasant conservatism: 'the class that represents barbarism within civilization'. Marx set the beat by which generations of scholars have danced, by his disparaging dismissals of the 'peasant chorus', whose insurrections he described as 'clumsily cunning, knavishly naive, doltishly sublime, a calculated superstition, a pathetic burlesque, a cleverly stupid anachronism, a world-historic piece of buffoonery and an undecipherable hieroglyphic for the understanding of the civilized'.[22] Peasant communities are perceived as culturally distinct 'part societies'.[23] Their protests are understood as 'defensive reactions' by 'natural anarchists', which are normally disorganized and 'expressive' of their 'homogeneity of interests' rather than 'instrumental' collective behaviour predicated on planned action by different groups and factions.[24] In the case of Russia, a Chayanovian belief in the distinctiveness and inviolability of the village commune and communal harmony is deployed in support of the view that peasant collective action was most frequently directed against 'outsiders'.[25] The task before us, then, is to demythologize the commune, to examine whether 'communal collectivism' and peasant norms of reciprocity were breaking down during NEP, and to evaluate whether socioeconomic differentiation created a social basis of support for collectivization and dekulakization among the village poor.

The moral economists' assumption that peasant collective action may be stimulated by commercialization and market forces has been criticized by political economy theorists who consider the peasant to be a rational actor whose decisions are grounded in an economic calculus of trade-offs between costs and benefits derived from investment logic.[26] This approach sees a fundamental flaw in the moral economy thesis in its presumption of a uniform impact on peasants when subsistence is threatened, for as Popkin observed there are 'differences in demand-making ability and the ways in which subsistence levels change' and, consequently, 'economic conflict over advancement to more secure positions is therefore inevitable within the village'.[27] The logic of peasant collective action is not, therefore, a kind of automated socialized community response, as the moral economists posit; rather its dynamic is one which is determined by individual and small groups of peasants weighing up the costs and benefits of participation. In this respect selective incentives and group size are critical factors.[28]

As Olson explained: 'Rational, self-interested individuals will not act to achieve their common or group interests.' Consequently, collective action is determined by the investment logic of rational self-interested *individuals* not *groups*, and individuals will only participate in collective action in pursuit of their interests when 'there is coercion or some other special device to make individuals act in their common interest'. By 'special device' Olson means incentives. Thus, participation in collective action is dependent on the inducement of benefits, particularly material benefits, that are excludable and selectively accessible through participation, that is to say that they are 'by-products' of participation over and above any collective good that may be achieved. Furthermore, the mobilization of latent, rational group-oriented action is a function not simply of material incentives but could also be organized on the basis of social interaction, particularly in small groups. The latter could be in the negative form of social sanctions, or in the positive form of social rewards and honours. Olson forecast that if selective benefits are not available then individuals will *free ride* in expectation of securing collective benefits. He also argued that small groups are more effective at mobilizing and acting in common interests because they optimize the provision of collective goods and selective benefits.[29] The rational choice approach contrasts 'moral propulsion and political competence' by shifting the focus of analysis from the elemental dichotomy of state versus peasantry, and from generic peasant collective action, to the role of individual peasants, their investment logic and decision calculus.[30]

Are the assumptions of the moral economy paradigm about the impact of commercialization on the social fabric of the countryside relevant to the conditions in the Soviet Union under NEP? To what extent did the Stalinist policy of mobilizing social support from poor peasants and targeting economic exactions on the well-off section of the peasantry appeal to notions of equity and reciprocity embedded in the custom law and traditional practices of Russian peasant society? Or did the policies of social influence, collectivization and dekulakization mobilize support from poor and middle peasants on the basis of a cost-benefit analysis, that is to say that the policies provided them with material rewards for support? What exactly was the nature of peasant collective action, support and resistance to Stalinist policies? Why and how were collectivization and dekulakization carried out? This book aims to address these and other questions. My goal is to break down the rigid paradigm of bipolarized state–peasant relations under Stalin, to deconstruct the orthodox image of peasant solidarity in the face of encroachment by the state. I aim to sketch out a more complicated, socially variegated tapestry for understanding the impact of the Stalin revolution on the Soviet countryside.

1 Capturing the Peasantry

By 1928 most of the Bolshevik party elite increasingly felt that the grand design for the building of socialism in the Soviet Union was being held to ransom by the peasantry's manipulation of NEP's relatively liberalized commerce. During the mid-1920s there was a 'green revolution' in parts of the Soviet Union, as peasants responded to the market economy by a rapid expansion in the production of cash crops, primarily grain. Nowhere is the commercialization of agriculture and the explosion of grain production more evident than in the Eastern producing regions, and in Siberia in particular, where peasants rushed into cultivation and rapidly turned the region into a major source of high quality wheat for domestic and export markets. The peasants' withholding of grain from the market during the grain crises of 1927/8 and 1928/9, was regarded by the Stalinist faction as politically motivated sabotage led by kulaks, whereas, in fact, the peasants were in the main simply responding in an economically rational and logical manner to changes in market conditions and prices.[1]

In the aftermath of the grain crisis of early 1928, the Bolshevik regime searched for an alternative to the *chrezvychaishchina*, the wave of excesses of repressive emergency measures that it had unleashed to override the market forces of the NEP and subordinate independent peasant agriculture to state control. The party leadership, under Stalin's direction, aimed to preempt any future difficulties in grain procurement by improving state organization and management of the countryside. Abandoning any pretence that NEP was a viable evolutionary strategy for building socialism, disillusioned by what they regarded as the structural constraints of its anti-socialist market principles, the Stalinists made a leap of faith from upholding the discretion of the free peasant to dispose of *his* produce as *he* saw fit, to divorcing the product of peasant labour from the jurisdiction of the peasant and locating it firmly within the realm of the state. Henceforth, the campaign against the peasantry on the 'grain front' assumed the proportions of an ideological crusade in defence of the existence of the socialist regime itself. The goal for the Stalinist wing of the party was to stabilize grain collection, subdue the countryside and secure a 'captured' peasantry for the state.[2] Molotov spoke of the crisis having 'plunged us into the deep end'.[3] He bluntly asserted the new formula for dealing with the peasantry at a gathering of regional party leaders in the Urals: 'We must strike the kulak such a blow that the seredniak will bow to us.'[4]

Far from being a 'year of drift' and a 'rudderless year', as Lewin described it, from the summer of 1928 the party leadership experimented with new mechanisms for tightening its control of the countryside.[5] The emergency measures had caused much peasant unrest and evoked political dissonance in the Politburo, its corporate decision-making being riven by the challenge of the nascent Right Opposition, headed by Bukharin, to Stalin's militancy. The spring and summer of 1928 saw some backtracking by Stalin to reach a new consensus with the Right on a united party strategy towards the countryside which included an emphasis on upholding 'revolutionary legality', pursuing the 'offensive against the kulak', promoting voluntary collectivization, the expansion of state contracts with peasant producers, and the creation of massive sovkhozes as 'grain factories' in the countryside.[6] The inherent weakness of the moderate consensus is illustrated by the diverging attitudes to the kulak question. The question of 'who is the kulak' dominated party debates on state–peasant relations in the late NEP period. The Right's conception of the kulak was strictly limited to a small, narrowly defined socioeconomic category. While I would not go so far as Lewin, and say that when Stalin and his supporters spoke of the 'kulak' they were thinking of the 'muzhik', certainly their construction of the term after the crisis of early 1928 increasingly emphasized political opposition to the Soviet regime. This is not to overlook the significant trend of socioeconomic differentiation among peasants as a result of the growth in the commercialization of agriculture during NEP – a trend that was particularly acute in Siberia, where rural change was marked by the emergence of an economically powerful petty-capitalist stratum of mechanized farms, and the growth of peonage.[7]

The moderate consensus of spring and summer 1928 accepted an instrumental shift in party policy by abandoning emergency methods of coercion against the peasantry and instituting a programme of organizational and fiscal measures of control. The new strategy involved five revisions of party policy in order to stabilize grain procurement and secure a captured peasantry for the state without resorting to a renewal of the *chrezvychaishchina*. First, there was a drive to tighten state control of the countryside by the development of the collective farm sector, including the creation of massive grain sovkhozes, and by the expansion of a binding state contract system (*kontraktatsiia*) with the peasantry. Second, there was a rationalization of the procurement agencies which, henceforth, were to be assisted by the permanent mobilization of waves of tens of thousands of party activists for rural duties. Third, Stalin embraced the notion of levying a 'tribute' on the peasantry to finance industrial investment. Fourth, in furtherance of the 'offensive against the kulak' a whole series of punitive measures were passed to restrict their economic growth. The fifth refinement of policy was that which opened the way for the emergence of the Ural-Siberian method, by moving the party formally away from the crude coercion of the peasantry as a whole to an increasing reliance on party-orchestrated 'social pressure' from poor and middle peasants against the well-off and kulaks.

COLLECTIVIZATION AND CONTRACTS

For much of the middle years of NEP, collectivization was held up as a long-term programmatic goal, but one which even the Stalinists viewed as somewhat illusory.[8] Following Stalin's lead, party rhetoric about collectivization and the fixing of contracts between state and peasant intensified in the course of 1928. The word rhetoric is appropriate because organizational inertia meant that very little by way of expanding the number of either was actually achieved in the country, and Siberia performed particularly badly. This was despite a whole series of orders and directives from the central and regional party authorities which followed in the wake of the report in late 1927 of a Politburo Commission on collectivization, headed by Molotov. The collectivization theme was reiterated in Molotov's report and the resolutions of the Fifteenth Congress which made voluntary collectivization the party's 'main task' (*osnovnaia zadacha*) in the countryside, in Stalin's speeches, in the resolutions of the March plenum of the Sibkraikom and of the July plenum of the Central Committee.[9] There was also a high profile media campaign in support of the new line, but to no avail. In theory, it was now a primary task of the whole party to accelerate collectivization not merely by political agitprop, but through preferential treatment in the matters of taxation, credit, machine sales, seed fund distribution and by example in the case of rural communists. Such instructions were given in the Kraiispolkom decree of 18 February and later by a Kraikom directive on 27 April, which set a target of a doubling of the number of collectivized households within one year.[10] A considerable obstacle to the realization of this plan was the drastic shortage of trained farm managers and technicians, a situation exacerbated by the decision of some regional party organizations to ensure a politically correct social profile in collective farm membership by excluding kulaks, who after all were the most advanced farmers.[11]

The contract system originated in April 1921, shortly after the introduction of NEP, and was initially geared to technical crops. Its evolution during the 1920s was stunted by peasant mistrust of state intentions and favourable market forces which rendered fixed prices at the outset of the season unattractive. The party hoped that *kontraktatsiia* would revitalize their relations with the peasantry as a 'new method of the *smychka*' but in 1928/9 there was again a poor take-up of contracts, with only 4.6 per cent of the sown area under such agreements. A Kraikombiuro decree of 21 August admonished the okruzhkoms for their failure in this area but the inertia continued for as late as November Eikhe was criticizing okrispolkom chairmen for not even bothering to reply to Kraiispolkom directives on securing contracts for grain.[12]

The new political line provoked rancour among a group of officials who had a pivotal role in the implementation of agrarian policy: the mostly non-party agricultural specialists in the regional economic departments, whose sympathies tended towards a neo-SR approach to dealing with the peasantry.[13] Discontent was also aroused in that significant section of the Siberian party organization which fervently supported the continuation of NEP as a strategy for developing the economic potential of private peasant agriculture. The statement of the communist Dobrygin to the Novosibirsk Okruzhkom plenum in early October was warmly applauded and must have been a fairly typical expression of the anxiety felt by this section of the party at the new emphasis on collectivization:

> Let's look at the individual peasant, he has three horses, three cows, three workers – what can he do in our Siberian vastness – he's just small fry. Some people fear his further growth; either he will become a kulak or a well-off peasant. It seems to me, that this is what we need in our Siberian conditions ... to change conditions for the peasantry ... I think that we should give free rein to our muzhik-seredniak, I'm not talking about the kulak, so that he increases his marketings – which we need.[14]

The extent of the Kraikom's concern at the obstructionist mood of rural officialdom is revealed in a secret letter from Kisis and Komarov to all okruzhkoms in late November which discussed the okrug and raion meetings held to work out ways of raising harvest yields. In the event, rather than discuss the implementation of party policy, the meetings had become a forum for general criticism of the party's approach to the countryside, particularly its tax policy and the emergency measures used in the previous year's grain procurement campaign. The Kraikom believed that the local party organizations were being used by 'elements hostile to us and against our policy in the countryside' and branded the participants as 'reactionary professors, agronomists and backward-looking peasants' who reflected 'kulak attitudes'. Instead of supporting collectivization, contracts and other forms of cooperation to improve productivity, the meetings often concluded by advocating large-scale capitalist farming. In future local party organizations were to ensure a compliant response from such meetings by selecting the participants from specialists who would not deviate from the party line and at least two-thirds of the total were to come from kolkhoz members and bedniak and seredniak activists.[15]

During his Siberian tour of January 1928 Stalin devised one solution to the grain crisis by setting a target of rapidly accelerating the construction of new collective farms so that this sector would be in a position to supply the state with about one-third of its grain needs within three or four years.[16] A Politburo decision to establish large-scale grain sovkhozes for the purpose outlined by Stalin was taken on 23 April and a special commission headed by Kalinin was created to work out the details. The commission met on 8 May and 12 May, and after consultations with Narkomzem it reported that the difficulties were such that Stalin's initial objectives were too ambitious. The resolution of the July plenum of the Central Committee on collectivization was modest: it proposed that new grain sovkhozes be established on unoccupied land in several regions, including Siberia, as a 'large-scale socialist economy' in the countryside to provide '100 million puds' of grain for the state 'within four or five years'. During the plenum debate Stalin himself had introduced a note of caution on the acceleration of collectivization, interrupting Sokol'nikov's speech at the point where he sketched out the resolution to suggest that perhaps this plan would be fulfilled 'even later', and Kalinin added 'within eight years'. The resolution emphasized that collective farms were to be formed on the basis of 'voluntary unions' of peasants. It was anticipated that these measures would stir up intensified opposition from capitalist elements of the peasantry.[17]

Given that the sowing season had passed, only nominal preliminary steps were taken in Siberia to prepare eleven new sovkhozes for construction in 1929. A Siberian department of Zernotrest was set up, under I. Ia Rettel', to coordinate the programme, the aims of which were much more radical than those set by the July plenum. Here the target was to provide half the annual marketable grain of Siberia within three to four years. It was not just the escalating demands of the central industrial regions for grain that had to be considered, but also the demands from Central Asia arising from the imminent completion of the Turk-Sib Railway. Eikhe told the Sixteenth Party Conference that while the overall number of kolkhozes trebled in Siberia between 1 October 1927 and 1 January 1929 (from 814 to 2,400) many were poorly organized and devoid of agronomists and equipment. This sector continued to play a miniscule role in the Siberian agricultural economy, with only 1.5 per cent of peasant households and little more than 6 per cent of the total sown area (192,000 hectares). The lack of enthusiasm for the concept meant that those peasants joining collectives were mainly bedniaks and even they preferred the tozi, the least socialized form of such farms.[18] Dominated by the poorest and least efficient peasants, and without adequate state support in terms of credit, machines and equipment, the collectives were doomed to failure. For these reasons, as the communist Bakstov told a conference of bedniak and seredniak peasants in mid-January 1929: 'Collectives grow like mushrooms, but no sooner do we gather them, baptise them, register them, then they die.'[19]

RATIONALIZATION AND MOBILIZATION

The party had learned some valuable organizational lessons from the grain crisis, and preparations were made well in advance for grain procurement in 1928/9. To eradicate the confusion, and indeed the often cut-throat competition, between rival procurement agencies the March 1928 plenum of the Kraikom implemented a rationalization by merging Sibmeltrest with Khleboprodukt and terminating the role of Sibtorg as an independent procurement organization. These reforms foreshadowed those enacted by the resolutions of the April plenum of the Central Committee, where Soiuzkhleb was made the primary procurement agency and Narkomtorg was given overall control of the whole grain procurement campaign. Furthermore, the plenum resolutions contributed to the general climate of increasing Stalinist militancy, calling for 'revolutionary discipline' and 'proletarian discipline' in the fulfilment of grain procurement tasks and economic plans.[20]

Concurrently, what had previously been emergency organizational forms for the party in the countryside were now institutionalized as permanent features of its operational structure on the 'grain front': the use of plenipotentiaries, the emergency committees of three (troiki), the drafting of worker communist brigades and the mobilization of peasant actifs. Under this new political line, the primary function of party and soviet officials in the countryside was to politicize village decision-making and to infiltrate and dominate the key local authority of the peasants, the village commune (mir) and its gathering (skhod) of male heads of households. This set in motion a process which would culminate in the participation of a worker contingent of twenty-five thousanders (dvadtstipiatitysiachniki) in the crusade for collectivization in late 1929.[21] For the sowing campaign in April–May, about 300 Siberian party officials were despatched by okruzhkoms to the localities, but the main mobilization for grain procurement was ordered by a Kraikombiuro decree on 3 July which required the recruitment of 24 communist workers' brigades in West Siberia for permanent organizational duties in the countryside. Each of the nine okrugs were to raise 2–3 brigades of 3–5 persons, selected from the most 'politically aware' worker-communist activists and Komsomol members. To ease the burden of such tours of duty and to maximize the number of communists with first-hand experience of dealing with the peasantry, this brigade system was organized on a rotational basis, with activists spending not less than two months in the countryside or in a particular area. In late August the Kraikombiuro added to the numbers already mobilized by sending another fifty okrug officials on attachment to raikoms while enlarging the number of rural organizers to 391 and handing out a 20 per cent pay rise to them. As in January 1928, the Central Committee mandated dozens of party officials and activists, including 100 from Moscow and Leningrad, to Siberia to assist with grain procurement. Prior to their being assigned, activists were given special induction courses on what to expect, including one on 'The Leninist approach to the peasantry' (sic).[22] Eikhe received a letter of recommendation from N.I. Kulikov, an official in the Secret Sector of the Central Committee, about just such a senior experienced outsider, a Ukrainian official, Torzhinsky, who had been mobilized to work for Narkomtorg. A former plenipotentiary of Narkomprod during the civil war, he had been Deputy Chairman of Stavropol Gubkom before being appointed as head of an Okrtorg department in the Ukraine.[23]

Consequently, by the autumn of 1928 a cohort of hardened urban worker-communists and regional party officials were in place to act as a leavening among rural party organizations to stiffen their resolve in dealing with peasant resistance in the grain procurement campaign. The overall number of these plenipotentiaries at any one time was small, and although assigned to roving duties in key grain raions or groups of villages where procurement had been problematic the previous year, the sheer scale of distances and poor communications infrastructure in Siberia had a disabling impact on their presence under normal conditions. After all, it was difficult for here-today-gone-tomorrow officials to act as a significant influence on remote peasant communities. At the end of 1928, however, there was a huge influx of around 13,000 Siberian urban communists, mobilized under the banner of the *shevtsvo* movement for the soviet election campaign in the countryside.[24] One of the main tasks of these election plenipotentiaries was to organize poor peasant meetings and actifs in order to mobilize the vote for communist and approved candidates.[25] Once the circumstances demanded, when the pressure from the party leadership for quick results intensified, the plenipotentiary system now had the manpower available to escalate violence and intimidation against the peasantry, actions that were magnified by the problems of distance and communications in the Siberian countryside.

TRIBUTE

At the July 1928 Central Committee plenum, Stalin devised two new concepts to encapsulate the essence of his changing approach to the peasant question and the grain problem. First, he used the archaic Russian word for the quota-based Mongol taxes on medieval Muscovy, *dan'* (tribute), to explain the new relationship between state and peasant. The historical outcome of such taxation practices had been the collective organization of agricultural production and a tied peasantry, ultimately leading to serfdom. Stalin employed the term reluctantly (perhaps feigned, as Stalin was reknowned as a consummate political actor): 'The matter of which I am speaking is an unpleasant one. But we would not be Bolsheviks if we glossed over this fact and closed our eyes to this, that without an additional tax on the peasantry, unfortunately, our industry and our country cannot make do in the meantime.' Stalin drew heavily, without attribution, from the work of the Leftist Bolshevik economist E.A. Preobrazhensky, who had devised the idea of 'primitive socialist accumulation' as an alternative form of economic development for the transition to socialism. Preobrazhensky proposed that, given Soviet Russia's international isolation, the backwardness of its economy and its lack of external colonies to exploit, the construction of socialism could be achieved by a policy of 'unequal exchange'. The idea was that rather than allow the relatively free market conditions of NEP to continue, the state should intervene to regulate industrial and agricultural prices in order to turn the terms of trade against the peasant. With the state acting as a kind of 'pump' (*perekachka*), these resources could be employed to purchase an industrial revolution.[26]

Bukharin regarded these ideas as an attack on the main pillars of the political settlement between state and peasant enshrined in NEP, and a strategy that would produce disproportions and dislocations in the economy. It was his alternative strategy of 'equilibrium' in NEP, or balanced growth that did not penalize the peasant, which held sway until 1926. Thereafter, Bukharin and the Right of the party increasingly accepted much of the economic logic of the Preobrazhensky thesis while adhering to a rather less cogently argued notion of social equilibrium. It was the latter that sustained their political opposition to the Stalinists' punitive policies against the peasantry from 1928.[27]

Adopting the Preobrazhensky thesis, Stalin specifically correlated the tribute with the state's pricing policy: the peasantry would pay more for the goods manufactured by state industries while receiving less for its grain. In this way the 'plundering' of the peasantry would secure the capital transfer from the countryside necessary to pay for industrialization, though, at this stage, Stalin envisaged that the transfer would take 'several years' to succeed. Secondly, Stalin formulated this fiscally punitive approach within a new ideological innovation, 'the intensification of the class struggle' in conditions of building socialism. Hereafter, the economic struggle against the kulaks assumed the form of all-out 'class war'.[28] The implications of the speech and policy were not lost on Bukharin, who denounced the new concepts as 'idiotic ignorance', branded Stalin as a 'Genghis Khan' incarnate, and later denounced the 'tribute theory' as 'military-feudal exploitation' of the peasantry.[29] A former Menshevik later described the tribute as 'primitive accumulation by the methods of Tamerlane'.[30]

OFFENSIVE AGAINST THE KULAK

Molotov's speech, 'On work in the countryside', at the Fifteenth Congress in December 1927 was a turning-point in the ideological approach of the party leadership to the peasant question. The resolutions of the congress indicated that henceforth the party's goal was to marginalize the kulak by improving its organizational control over the poor and middle peasantry, in particular by the establishment of party-controlled peasant actifs, an objective encapsulated in the new party slogan: 'Rely on the support of the bedniak-seredniak mass to develop further the offensive on the kulak.'[31] In April 1928 the Kraikom passed a series of decrees and directives instituting the central party leadership's demands for a renewed 'offensive against the kulak' based on economic measures. The most punitive measure was the reform of the agricultural tax system of 21 April, which introduced a more progressive sliding scale of payments to the detriment of the well-off peasantry. The objective was to soak up high peasant incomes which enabled the well-off to manoeuvre in the market and withhold grain from sale when they believed the price was not high enough – a major contributory factor in the grain crisis. The tax reform tightened up the income tax system that had been introduced by the Bolshevik government in March and April 1926 in place of the soul tax (*edok*), which had been levied mainly on a 'per-eater' basis.[32] The new tax assessments on agricultural income were sharply progressive, with a 5 to 25 per cent tax supplement levied on those farms with annual incomes in excess of 400 roubles. In addition, a top bracket composed of the 4 to 5 per cent kulak elite (*verkhushka*), as defined by a Kraikom commission established on 25 June, were subjected to a wealth tax to be set by raion tax commissions that toured the countryside from late June. Under this more punitive system tax avoidance by peasants was certain to be even more of a problem than it had been in the past, therefore heavy fines were fixed for non-compliance and the period for collection was reduced to three and a half months (1 October–15 February).[33] The latter stipulation institutionalized what had been an emergency measure adopted the previous January.

Alongside the tax reform, in late April, a Kraiispolkom decree severely curtailed the flexible arrangements for the hiring of labour under the Temporary Principles. Several categories of farms and entrepreneurs were excluded altogether (traders, owners of industrial enterprises, contractors, seasonal employers, tractor owners), as was the employment of labour for more than one full year, or 180 days of seasonal labour, or for more than 90 days by farms of taxable income of 400–600 roubles, or for more than 45 days by farms with 500–700 roubles.[34] If enforced rigorously this measure was potentially very damaging to kulaks in Siberia, given their wealth and propensity for hiring labour for long periods. In fact, however, the kulaks devised a clever ruse to circumvent these new restrictions, namely to legally subdivide their farms among sons while continuing to cultivate it as a single unit – a kind of informal self-dekulakization.[35]

SOCIAL INFLUENCE

The most significant of the new measures was a policy aimed at restructuring party and state organization in the countryside in a way which emphasized the mobilization of the social influence of poor and middle peasants within rural communities as an agency of support for the regime. The party proclaimed the social influence policy as an ideologically acceptable avenue for the progression of the doctrine of the party–peasant 'link' (*smychka*). Local officials and activists were to achieve this by enlisting the support of groups of poor and middle peasants, and organizing them into actifs which would form a caucus in the village gathering. In this way, the party leadership aimed to subvert the hegemony of the village gathering exercised by the kulak elite and, thereby, tighten its own management of the countryside.

The essential features of what Stalin later termed the 'Ural-Siberian method' (selective repression of kulak farms by organizing the *bednota* to use social pressure for the imposition of compulsory grain delivery quotas) were in evidence during the application of emergency measures against the peasantry at the height of the grain crisis in January 1928, but were widely condemned by party leaders as an excess to be eradicated. At this time, the party leadership, and the Stalinists in particular, were keen to promote the use of 'revolutionary legality' (namely Article 107) as the main weapon to combat 'kulak speculation' and refusal to market grain. In his telegram to all party organizations on 6 January, which put the grain procurement on an emergency footing and paved the way for the *chrezvychaishchina*, Stalin employed for the first time the phrase 'compulsory tasks' (*tverdiie zadaniia*) in relation to grain procurement, but at this time he applied it to regional authorities fulfilling their grain plans, not to peasant households (see Document 1). In fact, in a telegram to party organizations on 13 February 1928, Stalin complained that some peasant households had been subjected to requisitions of grain and to compulsory levying of the state loan. He used the term *razverstka* (requisition plan) to describe both these excesses, thereby equating them with the policy of planned exactions from the countryside enforced during the civil war. Similarly, in early 1928, the main Siberian party journal critically reported cases of grain deliveries being allocated by plenipotentiaries as binding duties or tasks (*zadaniia*) on whole villages or specific households.[36]

The problems involved in a return to *razverstka* methods of procurement were raised at the April 1928 joint plenum of the Central Committee, where Narkomtorg was criticized by A.K. Lepa for tacitly condoning the resumption of the practices. It had issued a regulation (*ustanovka*) ordering that regional grain procurement plans be redistributed downwards as far as rural soviets. Lepa challenged this policy, describing it as an 'excess', since it only encouraged soviet officials and plenipotentiaries to reallocate plans onto peasant households. He cited a directive of Belgorod district soviet executive committee, apparently acting on an initiative of a plenipotentiary for the region, Gordon, which had instructed that grain plans be distributed among households according to their ability (*moshchnost'*) to deliver and the size of their surplus, and that a 'state-social process' of explanation and pressure through village meetings be employed in the collection of the grain. Mikoyan and Chukhrit for Narkomtorg, Lepa claimed, had approved of the initiative in a telegram of 14 January 1928, expressing the hope that the experience could be applied in other regions. Their only recommendation was that the term 'quota distribution' (*razverstyvanie*) be replaced by 'plan tasks' (*plany zadaniia*). Mikoyan denied that he had approved of this method and asserted that Gordon's directive had been 'corrected' by Narkomtorg to exclude any repressive measures being taken against peasants who refused to cooperate with the procedure. If it was an 'excess', it was an excusable one in Mikoyan's view because 'we had to grope around for some means of getting at the peasantry.'[37]

As we shall see later, there are obvious parallels with the evolution of a renewed party emphasis on organizing the *bednota* from late 1927 through to the implementation of the methods of 'social influence' in early 1929 and earlier patterns of state–peasant relations in Russia. The key problem for the party, however, was one derived from Bolshevik ideology: how could the party lever itself into a position where its representatives and local agents would displace the dominant influence in village life, the kulak peasant elite (*verkhushka*)? For, as one observer put it: 'the man on the spot who has cattle and implements to lend, and money with which to pay wages, looms larger than the greater personage at a distance. The ordinary peasant admired, even if he hated, the successful neighbour and was inclined to follow his lead.'[38]

The return to a more activist and interventionist party policy towards managing the countryside was marked by Molotov's report to the Fifteenth Congress. His provisions for a new framework of grassroots party involvement in the political organization of the rural poor received a fresh stimulus from Stalin's assessment of the grain crisis.[39] The question of peasant social differentiation under NEP had been a hotly contested issue both within and outside the Bolshevik party in the late 1920s. Statistical surveys indicated that differentiation in the countryside had intensified during NEP, while confirming that the mass of peasants still fell within the seredniak category. The Bolshevik party, however, was increasingly convinced that there was an accelerating process of socioeconomic bipolarization between the strata of well-off kulak farmers at one end of the social spectrum and the impoverished poor at the other end. The Stalinists recognized the political potential of an increasingly impoverished and discontented poor peasantry, for here was a social force that could be harnessed for the achievement of the party's goals of controlling the countryside.

The poor peasant actifs organized by the party were to be a crucial element in its attempt to manage the countryside and it is important to remember what kind of peasants they were. A poor peasant's grain harvest might provide his family with a three or four months' supply. When these stocks were used up, the poor had to borrow or buy grain, usually from kulak or well-off neighbours. It was the misfortune of the poor peasant that in good harvest years the prices were low, and the richer peasants bought up their grain surpluses for storage, whereas in bad harvest years the prices were high, and the poor had to buy back the grain which they had previously sold to the rich. This inevitably led to a cycle of debt and impoverishment which is repeated in all peasant societies with an unequal distribution of land and capital, and that are orientated towards the market. For the poorest it meant peonage, while others were often forced into sharecropping, a phenomenon covered by the Russian peasant term *supriaga* (partnership (sic)), which supposedly originated in Siberia. Not surprisingly, these social realities begat deeply held, prolonged animosities in village life.

Stalin ordered the party to coordinate social pressure on kulaks by poor and middle peasants and suggested methods of inciting social conflict in the countryside which played to the rational self-interest of the vast majority of peasants. His measures concentrated on appeals to the investment logic of peasants and the provision of selective material incentives to the poorer strata to induce their support. He instructed that the *bednota* be rewarded with a 25 per cent bounty in the form of a long-term loan from grain confiscated from kulaks, and that privileges and relief of payments to the state (taxes, insurance, credit and so on) be stringently restricted to the poor and weak seredniak farms. Given the importance of payments campaigns in the countryside for absorbing peasant incomes and increasing the pressure to sell grain, Stalin urged the party to ensure a progressive levying of peasant self-taxation on kulak and well-off farms paralleling that of agricultural taxation, with a complete freeing of burdens on the poor and the commuting of taxes for the weak seredniak and families of soldiers. The campaign on self-taxation was to be conducted on the basis of 'stirring up social initiative (*podniat' obshchestvennuiu initsiativu*), with extensive involvement of the *bednota*, komsomol, plenipotentiaries and the rural intelligentsia', and with the *skhod* exercising 'general social control' of the matter. Stalin also directed the party to employ the 'influence and power of social organizations of the village' to allocate state loan bonds, again on the richest stratum.

The Right wing of the party was particularly irritated by the fact that the new emphasis on mobilizing the *bednota* reflected a distrust of the seredniak peasant, and that, moreover, this policy was enthusiastically embraced by regional leaders. One of the main complaints voiced by Frumkin's letter-critique of Stalin's new peasant policy in June 1928 was that: 'The party periphery concentrates its attention and concern only on the *bednota*.' Furthermore, he singled out Syrtsov and the Siberian party leadership as one of the keenest exponents of the new policy.[40] Admittedly, the party had made earlier attempts to secure the allegiance of poor peasants through the provision of financial incentives such as credits and freeing them of taxes. The new policy focus on mobilizing social influence from within the peasantry was a radical departure from the previous tactics because it combined the financial inducements with organizational pressure in a systematic manner. The new focus was significant in that it indicated that Stalin believed that a powerful social dynamic within the peasantry itself could be capitalized on, harnessed and channelled by the party in a way that would isolate, check and ultimately destroy the economic strength of the kulaks. Clearly, what began as social pressure in the area of payments could logically be extended, after suitable experience, to the problem of taking grain.

THE GRAIN CAMPAIGN OF 1928/9

That the Siberian peasantry had not been discouraged into abandoning production for the market by the emergency measures of early 1928 and the new tax increases on the well-off is clearly demonstrated by the 8.2 per cent expansion in the sown area in the 1928/9 season. Siberia now accounted for about one-sixth of the country's wheat sown area and a bumper harvest was expected because of this expansion and the fact that snowfall in the region had exceeded the winter norm by 25 to 40 per cent making soil humidity near perfect. The result was the largest gross grain harvest recorded in Siberia prior to collectivization, at just under 7.5 million tons, over one-third up on the previous year.[41] In August a Kraitorg report noted that a committee of experts had toured the countryside and estimated that there would be a substantial rise in the harvest yield. Consequently, an annual procurement plan of around 1.8 million tons was set, of which just over one-third was to be retained for Siberian needs and the rest shipped to the central industrial regions of Russia. This plan envisaged a 36.5 per cent increase in shipments to the centre compared with the previous year. Narkomtorg ordered substantial increases in the state purchase prices for grain (soft wheat by 16.3 per cent, hard wheat 15.4 per cent, rye 23.8 per cent and oats 22 per cent) in order to narrow the competitive margin with the higher free market prices and maximize the chances of a quick intake, but this was a losing battle.[42]

The party leadership looked forward to a trouble-free procurement campaign and anticipated a great success, especially since the emergency measures which had caused so much peasant discontent in early 1928 had been annulled by the July plenum of the Central Committee. At the beginning of August, Kisis informed okruzhkom leaders about the resolutions of the plenum, advising them to conduct propaganda work in the countryside in advance of the new grain campaign to notify peasants that emergency measures had been only temporary and that the party had reaffirmed its commitment to NEP. This did not mean that the 'offensive on the kulak' was to be weakened in any way. To ensure that party work in the countryside was conducted with the requisite sensitivity he suggested that the best okrug and raion activists be deployed in worker brigades that would be sent to villages where 'anti-seredniak distortions' had been perpetrated during the previous campaign.[43]

Even by early September there were signs that not all was well with the conduct of procurement at lower levels. A Kraikom decree of 10 August had established the parameters of how the campaign was to be organized but in late August Kisis sent another telegram to okruzhkoms complaining about their inactivity.[44] Similarly, in early September a letter from the Kraikom observed that its decrees had been largely ignored and stressed the need to prepare the apparatus for procurement work. The campaign had got off to an inauspicious start since just under 5,000 tons were collected in August compared with over 17,000 tons the previous year and the adverse consequences of this were borne mainly by Siberian consumers as large-scale shipments to the centre would not begin for some months. The letter blamed the 'extremely sluggish' work of party and soviet organs and the 'hold back attitude' of the peasants. Moreover, rather than provide accurate statistics of the harvest on which the krai grain plan could be established, raion and even okrug authorities attempted to build in an 'insurance' by underestimating their potential stocks and distorting the figures sent to the krai organs responsible for drawing up the plan. This subordination of state interests to 'narrow-minded local attitudes' was vehemently denounced and the local leaders were warned that they must provide a full accounting of the size of the grain market.

The main danger to the success of the grain campaign was seen as the 'passivity' and 'temporizing' of party officials. Given that the emergency measures of the last campaign had been revoked, this could only be countered by 'active leadership' and a more resolute approach from personnel, but without reinstating the plenipotentiary style of leadership to displace local organs used the previous year. Henceforth, there would be 'full responsibility' placed on officials for performance of duties to complete the grain plan, acting systematically and not from case to case or waiting for a repeat of directives from the Kraikom. In addition, this year a particular emphasis was to be placed on mobilizing rural party cells to carry out systematic mass explanatory work with the peasantry as opposed to raion 'shock workers' who did not really know the villages and whose interest did not extend beyond their tour of duty.[45]

The first indication that the grain campaign might not proceed smoothly across the whole country appeared by July when a severe drought hit the southern grain producing regions of the country (the Ukraine, Crimea, North Caucasus). The resulting poor harvest was gathered in late, and this was followed by early frosts in October which caused widespread winter-killing of grain crops in these same regions. This was the second consecutive harvest failure for these crucial grain regions, the previous year's having sparked the grain crisis of early 1928.[46] In November it was estimated that the gross grain harvest would be some three and a quarter million tons less than last year but by April 1929 the calculations had risen substantially, with the area affected measured at approximately five million hectares, and the losses put at a minimum of four million tons – an amount exceeding the total procured by the state in the Ukraine the previous year. Stalin later assessed the damage at '500–600 million puds' (from just over 8 to almost 10 million tons) compared with the gross harvest of 1927/8 (in the Ukraine, North Caucasus, Central Black-Earth Oblast and North-Western Oblast). In the Ukraine, for example, procurement of wheat and rye slumped to about 440,000 tons by 1 April 1929 – only about a tenth of the figure reached by the same period in 1928. In the Central Black-Earth Zone and North Caucasus procurement of wheat and rye fell respectively to about one-eighth and one-fourth of the previous year's levels.[47] Large tracts of the country were on the verge of famine. At the November plenum of the Central Committee, the party leadership admitted the grain procurement plan for the year had been drawn up 'with extreme tension' at the prospect of further difficulties. It was clear that the best harvests had been in the distant eastern parts of the country (the Volga regions, Kazakhstan, the Urals and Siberia).[48]

In the middle of September came the first evidence of increased pressure on the Kraikom from the central government for an acceleration of grain collection. A directive to okruzhkoms and okrispolkoms signed jointly by M. Zaitsev (acting for Syrtsov) and Eikhe advised local leaders of the threat posed by the harvest failure elsewhere and ordered them to eradicate a whole series of faults in the campaign. It appealed in a comradely fashion to them to stamp out the continuing practice whereby 'local interests' understated the size of the harvest (typically 'if the plan is less, we can work easier'). The recurrent deficiencies of the procurement agencies were highlighted (agiotage, lack of technical preparation for receipt of grain and personnel inertia). A worrying new feature of the scissors between state and market prices for grain was that peasants were even refusing to deliver grain due under the contract system finding it more profitable to return monetary advances with a forfeit. As usual 'kulak elements' were blamed for inciting this. Once again, it was emphasized that a centrepiece of this campaign would be to raise the awareness of rural communities of the importance of state procurement and, in particular, the organization and inclusion of the *bednota* and lower actifs in grain procurement operations. The directive ended by stressing that it was necessary to 'strongly adhere' to the party's decision to rescind emergency measures. If there was to be a motto for the campaign it was: 'Without emergency measures, without Article 107.'[49]

Syrtsov had confidently given a guarantee to Sovnarkom, the Central Committee and Narkomtorg that Siberia would complete a plan of up to 1.6 million tons of grain, and in the middle of October the annual plan for Siberia was set at 1.77 million puds (West Siberia would supply about three-quarters, and East Siberia the rest). The plan was over 40 per cent above the 1927/8 procurement level, and 90 per cent of the total was to be shipped to the centre. This was exceedingly ambitious in that it meant a severe constriction of Siberian demand in order to release extra grain for the centre. In late October, however, Syrtsov began to backtrack on these unrealistic figures and sent a strongly worded telegram to Stalin and Mikoyan, expressing his fears that things might go badly because there had been a failure to send large shipments of goods supplies to the countryside before the bad roads season and he described this as a 'repeat of last year's mistake'. In the light of this failure, he also referred to the increased procurement targets as an 'exaggeration'.[50]

In the event, the Siberian leader's initial optimism was borne out by the buyers' market for grain in the autumn and early winter of 1928, in contrast to 1927, as across most of the krai deliveries poured into the procurement points with virtually no pressure from the procurement agencies or the party. In contrast to Syrtsov's secret worries, the press reports of the Kraikom plenum held on 26 October–1 November reflected a picture of self-congratulation and confidence in the Siberian leadership at the initial high rate of procurement, attributed by some Kraikom members to the return to 'normal methods' and the end of emergency measures.[51] Indeed, by January 1929 over 65 per cent of the krai annual grain procurement target had been secured, compared with only about 37 per cent in the same period of the previous year but, as we shall see below, optimism had waned much earlier than this. This was due to poor results of the grain campaign in other areas which turned the withering gaze of the centre on to Siberia with demands for an even greater tempo of procurement.[52]

This propitious development allowed the Siberian party leadership to bask with a high degree of self-confidence in their relations with the centre, and it was during the second half of 1928 that Eikhe, in particular, consolidated his position as a vociferous supporter of Stalin at Central

Committee plenums. At the July plenum, where Stalin and Bukharin irrevocably split over policy on the peasantry, Eikhe supported Stalin's line on the use of emergency measures, attacked his critics Osinsky and Stetsky, and emphasized the positive attitude of the seredniak to the party's measures in the countryside (now beginning to focus on measures of social influence). Then, again, at the November plenum, where Stalin launched a blistering attack on the 'Right deviation' in the party, Eikhe strenuously defended the new radical line asserting that it 'must remain unchanged and there can be no vacillation'. In a devastating retort to Rykov's plea that the Trotskyitee were more of a danger than the Right, he declared: 'an enemy within the party is more dangerous than an enemy outside the party.'[53]

Grain procurement in the Ukraine in the second half of 1928 fell to only 32.8 per cent of the previous year, and by October–November the grain crisis began to have a destabilizing effect on large parts of the country west of the Urals. The peasant populations of a whole swathe of territory (Odessa, Kherson, Nikolaevsk, Melitopol', Zaporozhe, Krivorog) of what was normally the most productive agricultural zone of the Ukraine trekked north in search of food. An overall shortfall of approximately 20 per cent in the production of rye and wheat, the food staples, forced the state to curtail grain exports (as in 1927, thus scuppering plans for an accelerated tempo of industrialization) and reintroduce rationing. The shortages generated rampant inflation and speculation not only in grain deficit rural areas but also in towns, where consumer demand was growing rapidly. By the spring of 1929 soaring market prices for rye reached 333.2 per cent of the state procurement price in the Central Industrial Region, and 369.2 per cent in the southern Ukraine, while the price differential for wheat was 307.3 per cent in the North Caucasus and 429.5 per cent in the Ukraine. Gosplan produced figures which showed that the kulaks and well-off peasantry were taking advantage of the exorbitant free market prices and selling less grain to the state procurement agencies (indeed, Soiuzkhleb procured only 39 per cent of its annual rye target by the end of 1928 against 62.7 per cent in the same period of 1927). Whatever their accuracy, these figures seemed to confirm the perception in the Stalinist camp of the kulaks as a 'class enemy' and their suspicions of sabotage of state plans for accelerated industrialization.[54]

The spectre of famine hung over the Ukraine and the industrial heartland of the country. The only hope for the government, as it had been in early 1928, was to fall back on the East (Siberia and the Urals), where there had been a record harvest and a massive grain surplus. The problem was that this was precisely where the state procurement apparatus was weakest and communications least developed, and they were dreadfully slow in winter. Although by the end of the second quarter (October–December) the Siberian party leadership was basking in the glory of a great success in the grain procurement campaign, from early November it came under extreme pressure from the centre to complete the annual procurement plan in the shortest time possible in order to stave off the threat of famine in European parts of the country. Siberia was accursed by its very success in grain production and procurement, for the central authorities apparently felt that, as it was one of the few regions with a large surplus, a massive exertion of pressure here would bring maximum results.

Most of this pressure emanated from Narkomtorg, headed by Mikoyan, which had overall responsibility for the grain procurement campaign. It began rather innocuously with a Sovnarkom decree of 2 November 1928 revising upwards the milling tax in many regions. On 6 November a telegram from Mikoyan to his counterpart in Sibkraitorg, Zlobin, established a revised control figure for the milling tax in Siberia at 134,000 tons and ordered that, irrespective of the actual amount milled, no less than 98,000 tons of this taxed flour be delivered to a special central fund under Narkomtorg for the supply of consumer areas and an additional 10 per cent of the total to be set aside for the supply of the *bednota*. The Kraikombiuro implemented this order by amending its own okrug targets and recommending that the 10 per cent *bednota* fund be expended in the spring in order to give priority to deliveries to the centre.[55]

It was the high quality Siberian wheat that the centre needed and by the middle of November almost 40 per cent of the annual grain plan had been fulfilled, over 70 per cent of which was wheat. Confidence was high in the Krai leadership given that the procurement success constituted a rise over the previous year of 186 per cent, but the lack of concern was not shared by Zlobin who continued to reflect the pressure from the centre on to the localities by setting a new target of 80 per cent completion by 1 January.[56] The problem with such centrally determined plans was that they failed to take sufficient account of local circumstances. For example, already in Omsk Okrug the harvest was much lower than expected, at 15.5 per cent below average, because adverse local climatic conditions had brought problems of low yields, pests and mildew that had destroyed as much as 15 to 20 per cent of the crop. The Okruzhkom Secretary, Myshkin, asked Syrtsov to lower the area's procurement plan by about 10 per cent but to no avail. Yet Omsk was experiencing the kind of inflationary spiral and speculation (prices for flour and wheat on the free market had doubled) that gripped many European parts of the country.[57] Eikhe, however, in his report 'On conducting the grain procurement campaign' in late September, had already directed the Kraikombiuro not even to consider okrug appeals for a lowering of their plans or monthly targets. He confirmed this inflexible stance in a secret letter to all okrispolkom chairmen of 9 November, and warned that grain plans were to be fulfilled 'fully' given the 'great duty' of Siberia to supply workers' centres this year.[58]

In areas where grain procurement went badly, the spontaneous reflex of local authorities was to fall back on the tried and tested emergency methods that had proved successful the previous year. The Presidium of Rubtsovsk Okruzhkom ordered the reestablishment of its 'grain conference' (*khlebnoe soveshchanie*) in early October to intervene and take direct command of procurement away from the normal state channel for market forces, Okrtorg, and deal with difficulties reminiscent of 1927/8 (agiotage, goods shortages, disorganized transport, speculation). Although coercive measures were not to be condoned, it did reimpose 'personal responsibility' on officials for the success of the campaign, something which was bound to lead to excessive zeal. The order went on to vaguely stipulate that the cooperative network was to foster a 'social attitude' (*obshchestvennoe mnenie*) towards grain procurement – an early indication that the 'social influence' method was being taken on board at lower levels of the party. Yet, Eikhe's instructions on the conduct of the campaign had specifically stated that procurement this year was to be carried out by 'normal methods', without the use of coercion by plenipotentiaries or emergency measures. Consequently, in the middle of November the Kraiispolkom criticized the reversion to the 'character of last year's grain troikas' in Rubtsovsk and ordered that 'as yet' there was no need to conduct the campaign in this manner.[59] Nevertheless, the idea of reintroducing 'individual responsibility' continued to be urged on the Kraiispolkom by the highest levels of the cooperative apparatus.[60]

The Krai Procuracy saw itself as the institutional bulwark against repressive acts against the peasantry (who were after all the overwhelming majority of the Siberian population). Its leading officials adopted the position that it was their duty to prevent the reapplication of emergency measures, and in the latter half of 1928 they were busily engaged in ongoing investigations and prosecutions of both new cases of official abuses and cases from the previous year's grain campaign. The investigations of the procuracy into the sporadic use of emergency measures in various okrugs was regularly reported to Syrtsov and Eikhe to keep the issue politically alive and to the forefront. Such reports in October discussed numerous abuses in Kamensk, Biisk and Barabinsk Okrugs, often by the same plenipotentiaries as they were transferred around the area. For example, the plenipotentiary Razin operated in Pankrushikhinsk and Kulikovskii raions of Kamensk and apparently took the party injunction to apply social pressure to mean the conduct of show-trials of peasants in a 'social court' (*obshchestvennyi sud'*), in addition to enforcing military curfews, mass arrests and questioning of suspected grain speculators. The okrispolkom refused a procuracy request to institute proceedings against Razin, but did reimburse a bedniak peasant who had suffered loss at his hands. Other plenipotentiaries were similarly brutal, and there were regular shooting incidents and innumerable cases of sexual assaults. Only in a few cases, however, did the procuracy manage a successful prosecution and imprisonment of okrispolkom plenipotentiaries, whereas OGPU plenipotentiaries were untouchable and a law unto themselves. Evidently, it was difficult for the procuracy to counteract the tendency of certain lower level officials to resort to the use of emergency measures, for one raikom secretary in Barnaul declared that he was acting with the highest authority: 'Stalin gave us the slogan – keep on pressing and squeezing them' (*zhmi, davi i dal'she*) (probably delivered by Stalin during his visit to Barnaul in January 1928).[61]

Meanwhile in the countryside, although the peasants lived in fear of the reintroduction of emergency measures, the most widely hated reality of the grain campaign was the stringency of tax collection. It was the financial levers of the new progressive agricultural tax, and particularly individual 'wealth tax' supplements on the kulaks in both the agricultural tax and peasant self-taxation, that the krai leadership aimed to pull as one of the principal means of squeezing grain from the countryside. This is clear from directives issued on 22 September and 16 October which also aimed to protect well-off seredniaks from these levies. In addition, the sum of self-taxation was considerably increased from 7.77 million roubles in 1927/8 to almost 12.5 million in 1928/9, and if most of that could be levied on the kulaks, the thinking went, the loss of cash liquidity would force them to sell grain.[62]

In Biisk Okrug, despite the fact that only 1.2 per cent of farms had thus far been assessed for the supplementary wealth tax instead of the Kraikom recommended figure of about 9 per cent, the measure was cursed at peasant meetings and instead of the 'individual burden' the peasants called it the 'swindling burden' (*naduval'noe oblozhenie*). Khrishtal', the Biisk Okruzhkom Secretary, reported that even the rural tax commissions were unable to properly assess peasant wealth and, therefore, had to rely on 'class judgement' in using the tax as an instrument for 'reeducation' of 'hostile elements'. He revealed that the new tax system often worked contrary to the party's goals by hitting large families hardest as, for example, a seredniak farm with ten members paid 135 roubles the previous year but 242 roubles this year, while a bedniak farm of 12 members only paid

56 roubles the previous year and 155 now. In Slavgorod the Okrispolkom Chairman, Antipov, disclosed that over-assessment of tax was also a regular occurrence, but here there were many cases when it was used *ad extremum* as a device for 'outright dekulakization'. In Turukhansk, in the remote north, the rural soviet placed armed guards at the doors to prevent peasants from leaving the *skhod* until they had passed all the state measures. The authoritarian nature of the party and state apparatus, coupled with the weakness of central and regional leaders to control events in the localities, opened tremendous opportunities for abuses by local officials who were often motivated by personal gain and the desire to settle scores. Procuracy reports fed through from local to krai level detailing abundant cases of this type, for example the chairman of a *sel'sovet* in Biisk Okrug who took a thresher from peasants and threatened to levy individual taxes on them when they asked for it back.[63]

At the November 1928 Central Committee plenum Syrtsov conceded that the thresholds for the application of individual tax supplements were a cause of much discontent in the countryside because 'part of the kulaks fell outside' while 'very often' seredniak farms fell within the limits. The 'old Bolshevik' grandee, A.B. Lunacharsky, who travelled around Western Siberia in January 1929 and visited the large grain producing villages of Shipunovo and Aleisk in the Altai, typified the ignorance of party leaders of the impact of policies in the countryside. He was taken aback when confronted as a representative of the government by peasants vociferously complaining about the fine details of taxation.[64] Similarly, at the Sixteenth Party Conference, Kalinin disclosed that his office had been flooded with complaints, by letter and in person, from peasants who felt outraged at being landed with tax surcharges; indeed, he spoke of a 'lordly approach' (*barskii podkhod*) to the levying of individual obligations at certain levels of authority. Consequently, in December, a special commission was established by Stalin and Kalinin to examine ways of reducing the tax burden on seredniaks but it had only made a marginal reduction to overall tax revenues by the time of the party conference in April 1929.[65]

In his speech to the Central Committee plenum Stalin had breathed new life into Lenin's slogans of 1917 about modernizing the country and he coined a new slogan which would become the leitmotif of the 'year of the great breakthrough' in 1929: 'to catch up and to overtake (*dognat' i peregnat'*) the advanced technical development of the capitalist countries'. For Stalin, it was 'full steam ahead' as regards the industrialization of the country: 'Either we succeed in this, or we go under.'[66] The completion of ambitious industrialization plans for such a 'great leap forward' required high levels of grain procurement on a regular basis to fuel export-led growth. Difficulties in grain extraction from the peasantry were, therefore, regarded as an intolerable obstacle to the modernization of the country and the consolidation and further development of socialism.

Thus, on 29 November the pressure on the Siberian party leadership significantly escalated with the arrival of a telegram-directive from Stalin and Rykov, for the Central Committee and Sovnarkom.[67] They warned that the sharp fall-off in grain procurement in November was a danger signal and blamed not only the bad roads season but also the failure of local organs to learn from the mistakes of the previous year and take the requisite measures as outlined by the decisions of the July plenum of the Central Committee. November and December would be decisive months and it was 'absolutely necessary' to complete plans. The way forward lay in organizing a mass political campaign in the countryside among cooperative societies, by 'including the rural *bednota* in the business of grain procurement' and the rigorous implementation of 'all other measures' (collecting payments, goods supply, adhering to state prices and so on). They proposed several detailed measures on the basis of which the Siberians were to conduct the campaign.

First, the rural payments campaign was to be improved and fixed periods for completion were to be kept to, but within the constraints of 'revolutionary legality' and, they ordered, 'in no instance resort to methods of a coercive nature.' Peasant self-taxation was to be enforced, according to a Sovnarkom decree, no later than December. Second, state procurement prices were to be adhered to and speculation combated, but strictly by 'all means within the law and in no case should this assume a restraining character to the extent that there is no level of market exchange in grain and it obstructs the free sale of grain by the peasants'. In a move to impede the activities of roving speculators, they ordered that the sale of railway tickets be restricted for three months. Other measures included the priority delivery of goods to grain areas, no reductions in procurement plans, and paying special attention to the transport of grain from outlying areas and railway stations. Last, they advised that the political campaign in the countryside required the presence of senior regional officials on the ground. The telegram concluded with a veiled threat, by imposing as a duty on the Siberian leaders the fulfilment of the November and December grain procurement plans given to them by Narkomtorg and insisted on the speedy employment of 'normal methods' in the campaign.

The telegram was a typical piece of leadership duplicity and had a domino effect in passing the buck down through the authority hierarchy to lower level officials: on the one hand, it set abnormal targets for fulfilment in an extraordinarily brief period, yet on the other hand it demanded the use of normal methods of policy implementation which were impracticable if the former were to be realized. Syrtsov and Eikhe snapped to attention and over the next few days they transmitted the urgent tone of Stalin and Rykov to the secretaries of okruzhkoms and chairmen of okrispolkoms. On 2 December Eikhe sent a telegram blaming the decline in grain collections on lack of proper supervision by the local leadership and instructed them to reply within three days that they were executing the central directive. This was followed on 5 December by a joint order from Syrtsov and Eikhe which demanded that the grain plan be accomplished 'without emergency measures..., who forgets this wrecks socialist construction.' Some weeks later, on 20 December, to add further bite to the orders, Eikhe sent a telegram via the GPU chain of authority, commanding local leaders to take unelaborated 'immediate steps' to complete the monthly plan.

This flow of directives was without success for on 27 December the Kraikombiuro issued another, 'On the course of grain procurement', which blamed local officials for the failure to achieve a little over one million tons – a huge amount when set against the previous year's performance but insufficient to be on target for the completion of the massively increased plan. The directive also expressed dissatisfaction with the conduct of the rural payments campaign, and there was particular exasperation at the lack of a sustained application of individual tax supplements on kulaks, as previous decrees had ordered. This was highlighted as the decisive measure of 'economic influence' on grain procurement. The following day Syrtsov sent another telegram to okruzhkom secretaries admonishing them for the unsatisfactory level of procurement and blaming the failure on the 'absolutely inadequate leadership provided by raion party committees'. Clearly frustrated by the fact that local authorities were simply unwilling or unable to address the directives from above, Syrtsov threatened that 'sloppy idlers' would be brought to account and again stressed the need to collect rural taxes, specifically 'as regards levying individual supplements on kulaks'. Paradoxically, however, while striving to instil a sense of urgency, he again emphasized that they were not to 'in any way permit deviations towards emergency measures'.[68]

Given the experience of the grain crisis of 1927/8, local leaders must have been confused by the orders to go over to a virtual state of emergency in grain procurement but without utilizing emergency measures. This is evident from the response of the Biisk party leadership that it would deploy the OGPU and Procuracy against the 'most malicious' kulaks obstructing the campaign and charge them under Article 58 of the Criminal Code (against counter-revolutionary activities). Around the same time Krasnoyarsk Okruzhkom reported that some of its activists were resorting to 'more "real" measures' such as Article 107. Kuznetsk Okruzhkom ordered the registration of peasants with grain surpluses as a prelude to confiscation.[69] Meanwhile, in Barnaul, the okruzhkom secretary, I.S. Nusinov, invoked the new Stalinist radicalism, citing the ideological formula on the intensification of class struggle with the kulaks to a conference of the local party organization to justify the current militancy: 'You really would need to be extremely naive to claim that the kulak will be peacefully and impassively looking on as we restrict and displace him from the rural economy.'[70]

By December the Siberian leaders realized that a sharp decline in procurement was imminent due to manufactured goods shortages, for they received a communiqué from Narkomfin RSFSR advising of a disastrous drop in productivity in the central industrial regions. In the first quarter, only 41 per cent of Narkomfin orders for manufactured goods had been produced (45 per cent in Moscow) and, consequently, no more than 9 million roubles worth of the 21.5 million planned had been despatched.[71] The shortage of manufactured goods was one of the main reasons given by the okrug authorities for the stalling of procurement in November and December, along with price differentials between neighbouring areas and insufficient or unworkable rolling stock for shipment by rail (particularly in the key 'grain triangle' of south-west Siberia). All Narkomtorg could do was promise to request that the Central Committee consider increasing capital outlays on Siberian transport in the future.[72]

By the end of the year food supplies to towns were in a critical state and rationing was reintroduced as 'a lesser of two evils', as Rykov put it. In late December, given the uncertainty surrounding grain procurement and the need to maximize shipments to the centre, the Kraitorg was unable to give more than a monthly estimate of planned supplies to the workers of Novosibirsk. As workers were increasingly forced onto the private market for food, outrage at speculators became more vehement and rocketing food prices became the major political issue at factory meetings during the soviet elections.[73] The introduction of a rationing regime in early February 1929 was ideologically and politically motivated. The special ration books issued in towns, cities and rural areas divided the population into two categories. Peasants and other landholding persons were excluded. Category A included workers in factories and enterprises, railway and water transport, communications, civil service, construction, the armed forces and militia. Category B included families of workers and civil servants in towns, civil servants in rural areas (teachers, medical personnel, agronomists, etc.) and their families (if they did not have a landholding), pensioners, the unemployed and other workers. Rationing was prioritized to category A and to Moscow and Leningrad. For example, a category A worker in Moscow or Leningrad received almost double the daily ration of a person in category B or category A persons living outside these cities (900 grams against 500 grams), and three times the category B ration for those living outside (300 grams). Local authorities outside these cities could increase their category A ration to 800 grams for those engaged in 'heavy' work but only by reallocating local supplies and without diverting grain shipments to the centre.[74]

The everyday symptoms of the grain crisis – food shortages, speculation and ration books – were straining worker–peasant relations to breaking point and adding to the cumulative pressure on the party leadership to find a way out of the morass. By now, the prevailing mood among the Stalinists was that NEP had brought the party down a political cul-de-sac, where the ideological goal of a speedy planned socialist transformation through industrialization was blocked by the formidable barrier of market forces in the peasant economy. As the year 1929 progressed the minds of the radicals in the party, including many of those now roving the countryside on grain procurement duty, became obsessed with the question of how to break through this barrier, not how to manoeuvre around it. They had never forgiven the peasantry for humbling the Soviet government and making the party and towns kowtow before it for food in 1919–21. It was a humiliation that had been burnt into the collective memory of many Bolsheviks, workers and townspeople, and they were not prepared to tolerate a repetition.

2 Mobilizing Social Influence

THE TAX SQUEEZE

At the end of 1928 and the beginning of 1929 the party leadership, confronted by a *déjà vu* of the repeat of the previous year's grain crisis, was groping around in desperation for some new method to accelerate grain procurement other than falling back on outright emergency measures. The answer decided upon was to put the regional party organization on an emergency status and extend measures of 'social influence' on the peasantry, in particular by the levying of supplementary individual financial burdens for peasant self-taxation and the state loan, and the commencement of boycotts against non-sellers of grain. The method of social influence was normally enacted by the party under the cover of poor and middle peasant activism, whether or not it had successfully enlisted their collaboration. In late December and January a propaganda campaign was launched in the central press to this end which was gradually extended to grain collection.

The policy-making process in the party leadership under Stalin was shrouded in so much secrecy that it is often impossible to say how a particular policy originated or why it took a certain form. During this crisis the Kraikombiuro practised what can only be described as a 'decree mania', with telegrams of directives and decrees despatched almost weekly. However, this tells only part of the story. Many orders seem to have been given verbally in private meetings, whether it was Stalin dealing with Syrtsov and Eikhe, or the senior krai party leaders instructing their okruzhkom secretaries and so on down the chain of command, and one can even detect in the secret protocols of Kraikombiuro sessions an awareness that some politically sensitive instructions were best left unwritten and, indeed, the wording of some documents was doctored *post hoc* to keep up with changes in the party line. The evidence presented here, however, suggests that the Ural-Siberian method was not laid down in detail from above but rather emerged incrementally from an interactive policy process between central, regional and local authorities which demonstrated the complex and contradictory forces at work in the politics of this period. For not only was there an accelerating and swelling radical-militant dynamic from below in response to pressure for quick results from above, but also there was clearly reluctance among certain krai party leaders to extend the methods of social influence from the purely financial sphere (rural payments campaign) to the core concept of NEP – free trade in grain for the peasantry.

The organizational shift to an emergency footing by the Siberian party leadership came quickly on the heels of its series of fruitless directives in December and it began with a mobilization of the OGPU. During the grain crisis of 1927–28 the OGPU had played a pivotal role in the implementation of party orders for the use of Article 107 and outright coercion against grain-holding peasants. In late December 1928 the OGPU, Kraisud and Krai Procuracy reached a collective agreement that, henceforth, all cases of kulak terror, political hostility and anti-soviet activities were to be handled exclusively by the OGPU.[1] Shortly afterwards, on 14 January 1929, the administration of the western Siberian section of the Trans-Siberian railway system, the lifeline along which the grain would be channelled to the centre, was effectively transferred to the OGPU with orders that it immediately resolve delays that were holding up shipments of grain. The Kraikombiuro blamed railway disruptions on two main factors: lapses by workers and officials, and the shipping of grain by private individuals and businesses – termed 'speculative trade' by the OGPU. Zakovsky, Siberian Chief of OGPU, was ordered to supervise the railways, investigate delays and arrest and put on trial those responsible if necessary. This directive was issued despite reports from OGPU inspectors attributing some railway delays between Novosibirsk and Omsk to more immutable causes such as shortages of wagons and engines.[2]

The demands from the centre to step up procurement arrived in Siberia at a time when the regional party organization was distracted by the holding of okrug conferences and it was only after these had finished that local party bosses paid serious attention to the flood of directives emanating from the centre and the krai leadership. The attention of the Kraikom itself was also engrossed by a series of organizational battles, primarily preparations to combat alleged kulak authority in rural soviets in the forthcoming elections, but also in conducting a general purge of disenfranchised 'pro-kulak and estranged communists' from the party. There was even an attempt to dissolve organizations like the former partisans, now considered to be infiltrated by kulaks and hostile to the party's goals, who were no longer to be permitted to hold conferences.[3]

The soviet election campaign offered the party opportunities to enhance its organizational capacity in the countryside in two key directions. First, to harangue local party organizations into improving their coordinating work with groups of poor peasants. The importance of close party–*bednota* links had been stressed by the resolutions of the Fifteenth Party Congress in December 1927 but nothing much came of this until October 1928 when there was a renewed emphasis placed on this type of work by the Central Committee. Following the lead of the November plenum of the Central Committee, the Kraikom moved to mobilize and incorporate the rural poor into the party. Recruitment goals were set to enrol 3,000 batraks by the time of the Fourth Krai Party Conference in February 1929 and to improve their membership profile from 6.8 per cent of rural party organizations to 30 per cent by the end of 1929.[4] After all, if the implementation of party policy in the countryside was to rely on the mobilization of social support from the poor, then subjecting *bednota* activists to party discipline was essential.

Second, to enhance the party's control in the localities, thousands of worker-communists from the factories of Novosibirsk and the mines of Leninsk-Kuznetsk were mobilized for secondment to rural areas as part of the *shevtsvo* (sponsorship) movement: 'elder brothers to the peasantry', as the party literature hailed these workers. Party organizers in the factories were to set in place machinery which would allow a rolling mobilization of one to three workers for periods of five to seven days on duty in the countryside.[5] This gave the party a small army of reinforcements that could be called upon for grain procurement duties. Meanwhile, the preparatory propaganda battle was launched with *Sovetskaia sibir'* clamouring for the expulsion of 'kulaks and *podkulachniki*' from the party. Appeals from peasants were published, claiming: 'We are waiting for worker-brigades.'[6]

An organized registration of kulak farms had been in progress since July 1928 for the purposes of the new agricultural tax and it was these lists that were used to exclude peasants in the soviet elections and define the kulak category for punitive measures during the coming months. Upwards of 166,000 (4.4 per cent compared with 2.9 per cent in 1927/8) peasants were disenfranchised. In response, there was a sharp increase in what the party labelled 'terrorist acts' and 'banditry' by peasants, and attempts by 'kulaks' to preserve their leverage in the rural soviets by placing supporters on electoral committees and putting forward their own lists for election. They were particularly successful in Omsk, where supposedly 48 kulaks were elected chairmen of rural soviets, and the okrispolkom decided to dissolve the newly elected Tarsk raiispolkom and call fresh elections for all rural soviets in the raion. As a result of the campaign, only 2.3 per cent of the new rural soviet deputies were classed as from the well-off peasantry (those paying more than 25 roubles in agricultural tax).[7]

The turning point came in early January when a conference of Narkomtorg USSR officials decided that the annual grain procurement plan for the country should be raised by about 700,000 tons to cope with the crisis, the bulk of which was to come from Eastern grain producing regions.[8] The Kraikombiuro apparently concluded that the economic measures of pressure, such as collecting taxes and debts and targeting goods supplies, were not producing the kind of quick results demanded by the centre. Therefore, it was decided that Syrtsov should travel to Moscow to 'clarify all questions linked with the further conduct of grain procurement', namely how did the centre propose to fulfil the new grain plans without a reversion to coercion.[9] He clearly expected trouble from the peasants for shortly before he left he signed an order strengthening the liaison between party organizations and the Red Army in order to prevent disturbances by the sons of peasants subjected to arrests and confiscations during the grain campaign. Meanwhile the OGPU was to advise military units on the discharging of sons of disenfranchised peasants.[10]

In his absence, on the 17 January the krai leadership met and decided to pursue 'all measures of an economic character' in its directives on grain procurement consistent with the decision banning the use of emergency measures. A major plank of the renewed effort was the mobilization and inclusion of the *bednota* and seredniaks in the grain collections. A decree issued on 18 January demanding that okruzhkoms 'pay attention to the seriousness of the situation', and reminding them of 'your responsibility' for fulfilling the plan and securing a 'decisive turnaround', marked a significant new dimension to the grain campaign. The innovations in this decree constituted the genesis of a procedure for incorporating the poor and middle peasant masses in a sustained campaign of social pressure that would drive the kulaks into social isolation, where their economic strength could be more easily drained.

The decree ordered an escalation of the 'offensive against the kulak' by ordering a concentration on the acceleration of rural payments owed to the state and cooperatives. Okruzhkoms were instructed to make more use of tax supplements against kulak farms in those raions where there was speculation and a weak flow of grain, and specifically to single out two or three kulak farms per raion for these surcharges. In fact, this allocation of quotas of kulaks to be persecuted was a reversion to some of the repressive practices of the emergency measures of early 1928, when a small number of kulaks per raion were selected for trial under Article 107 as a method of intimidating the mass of well-off peasants. Other important elements of this decree struck at kulak economic power with the aim of pressurizing them to sell their grain. Firstly, it permitted the general meeting of peasants (enfranchised) to raise the proportion of self-taxation levied on certain individuals (i.e. kulaks) to 50 per cent of the total – this would dramatically increase the absorption of kulak finances. It was also a material inducement for support from the rest of the peasants. Secondly, village party cells were to organize a boycott of 'individual kulaks who are maliciously holding back their grain'. Each individual case was to be discussed, under party guidance, at bedniak meetings, the *skhod* and cooperative.

The party began to impose a social quarantine on kulaks. The social influence policy was now extended beyond the self-taxation process and outside the village unit as the raion authorities were to publish the names of 'malicious grain holders' in the local press so that everyone knew of the boycott of them. They were to be excluded from the cooperatives and refused the sale of deficit goods. The latter seemed to contradict an order to channel goods supplies directly to stimulate the sale of grain, which logically meant to the kulaks and well-off peasantry. Besides, the impact of this ban would be minimal given that the shelves of cooperative stores were frequently empty of goods. Finally, an extortionate 85 per cent tax was imposed on peasant milling and severe limits placed on the amounts milled for peasant consumption, thereby squeezing an additional source of kulak income and maximizing the amount of grain available for state procurement.[11]

The next day a bombshell arrived from Moscow in the form of a telegram from Syrtsov informing his colleagues that the centre now demanded an extra 164,000 tons from Siberia urgently, thereby increasing the annual plan for the krai to almost two million tons. Apparently, he had attended the Politburo session on 17 January and made a joint request with the Urals Party Secretary, I.D. Kabakov, for a reduction in the additional plan; however, this plea was rejected.[12] An abnormally small session of the senior Kraikombiuro leaders met immediately to consider the demand and it is interesting to compare their response with that of January 1928. On 8 January 1928 Mikoyan had sent a telegram proposing the exact same increase but the Kraikombiuro retorted that it was 'unreal and impossible' and an explanatory telegram was sent to the Central Committee. Subsequently, Stalin arrived in person in Siberia to ensure the necessary compliance and the course of NEP was irrevocably changed. Now, one year later, the Kraikombiuro complied immediately; indeed, they exercised great political deftness with the protocol of the meeting, even striking out the word 'order' and inserting 'proposal' when accepting the new target from the centre. This massive increase in the grain procurement target was not quite as 'unreal and impossible' as it had been in January 1928 given the bumper harvest but the speedy completion commanded by the Central Committee seemed preposterous in the absence of mass coercion of the peasantry. Nonetheless, the political survival of the krai leadership depended on success, and this necessitated that the krai party leadership infuse the regional party apparatus with an even greater sense of urgency than had been exhibited hitherto, completely reorganize the campaign in Siberia and, as the protocol put it, take 'other measures'.[13]

The crisis situation clearly required extraordinary solutions. At this point the conflicts which had riven Siberian officialdom during the 1927/8 emergency resumed between, on the one hand, those who advocated an assault on kulak farms with coercive measures and, on the other hand, those who counselled moderation. The reemerging tensions in the regional apparatus of power was illustrated by the *Molodoi rabochii* case in late January.[14] This Novosibirsk newspaper published an article on 20 January with a headline appealing: 'Who will correct the effrontery of the kulaks?' The article was a direct attack on the krai judicial organs, accusing them of ignoring kulak resistance to the state and of confusion in the jurisdiction of kulak cases which meant they often escaped retribution.

It cited the example of Novosibirsk Okrug Judicial Department which had processed only one case of 'kulak murder' in a year and bemoaned the fact that such trials rarely resulted in a sentence of execution. It also blamed the Krai Procuracy for opening only sixty investigations of kulaks in the year. The same day the chief editor of the newspaper and head of its rural correspondent department sent a request to the Kraiispolkom couched in unusually strong language which suggests that higher authorities were involved behind the scene: 'We ask you to inform us of what action you have taken with regard to the article . . . We expect your answer by 28 January 1929.' The Krai Procuracy responded with a detailed rebuttal in a report to the Kraiispolkom on 1 February, which revealed that the newspaper had deliberately distorted the picture. In fact, the Procuracy had opened sixty cases in December alone, and for the whole of 1928 the number of cases against kulaks had been 2,352, with a 'large number' of others dealt with by the OGPU in secret. There was a sense of foreboding and incomprehension at the article as the Procuracy asked: 'For what motives the leadership of the newspaper . . . published knowingly the incorrect information about the Krai Procuracy is not known.' This must have been confirmed by a *Sovetskaia sibir'* article of 22 February which was headlined 'The Krai Procurator defends the disenfranchised'. This claimed that the Krai Procurator Kunov had 'gladly protected' the senior assistant to the Krai Procurator, Verzhbovich, who had been purged as a 'former White officer and Kolchakist procurator' along with seven senior okrug procuracy officials in January.[15] Such manipulation of the press served both to raise heckles against the kulaks and to embarrass the leadership of the court system and procuracy whose defence of peasants against the use of Article 107 the previous year had made them anathema to the Stalinist radicals in the party.

Ironically, Syrtsov left for Moscow at a time when Mikoyan was due in the krai to address a conference of delegates of batraks and bedniaks, or perhaps he had foreknowledge that Mikoyan was to propose the 'social influence' method as a solution (see below) to grain procurement difficulties and thus decided to seek confirmation from Stalin personally as to what this exactly entailed. In his absence the Kraikom moved yet again to instil a sense of activism in local party organizations for work with *bednota* groups and bedniak-seredniak actifs as a means of marginalizing the kulaks, complaining that so far they had paid 'extremely weak' attention to this matter. At the Biuro session of 20 January Eikhe delivered a report on how the conference of *bednota* and seredniak actifs that would be held shortly was to be organized, and in the process he revealed just how such conferences were orchestrated by the party. The protocol of the session decided that: 'To demonstrate the link between seredniaks and bedniaks a delegation of 15 persons is to be selected from the participants at the meeting to attend the krai conference of batraks and *bednota*. Comrades Komarov and Reshchikov [Kraikom officials] are instructed to select the delegates.' Moreover, a commission consisting of Eikhe and other senior party officials was encharged with drawing up the resolutions of this second conference, before it had even been held.[16]

In his speech to the bedniak and seredniak conference Eikhe offered a simplistic and orthodox Stalinist explanation for the ongoing grain crisis. The problem derived from the growth of kulak farming, which was mainly based on exploitation of the bedniak and seredniak. Kulaks were holding the burgeoning towns and future industrialization of the country to ransom. Talk of the end of NEP was 'a lie'. Article 107 had been applied overwhelmingly against the kulak element, though of course there had been abuses and mistakes in places. This year's procurement campaign had gone well so far, as 1.23 million tons had been achieved by 15 January, almost double the amount collected in the same period of the previous year. But this year the demands of the state were greater and so, Eikhe declared, the struggle for kulak grain surpluses was to be escalated: 'Hound the kulaks for their withholding of grain surpluses, organize against them a social cooperative boycott.' If kulaks speculated on the free market in grain then they should look to the free market, not to the cooperatives, to provide them with goods. He did not elaborate any further but rather spoke in general terms about party policy, warning that the only long-term solution to guarantee high living standards and overcome the 'extreme backwardness' of agriculture was the promotion of industrialization, especially the expansion of heavy industry, and the construction of large-scale collective farms. Unlike the tsars, he claimed, party policy towards the peasantry was not one of 'eat less, export more',[17] although this was precisely the direction in which the Stalinists were moving.

Since this was a stage-managed rally, Eikhe attempted to sow discord in the peasantry, dismissing the notion of peasant solidarity and recalling to his audience how the kulaks had supported Kolchak, and how they had secured higher prices for their grain the previous summer, after the bedniaks and seredniaks had sold theirs to the state. If anyone thought that this was a sensible lesson for the future, he reminded them that Article 107 had 'rightly' been applied to kulaks. He publicly applauded the state policy of tilting the economic balance in favour of the peasantry by changes in the terms of trade between town and countryside, with decreasing prices for manufactured goods and increasing prices for most agricultural produce for this year's campaign (to the extent that whereas one pud of wheat bought 2.1 metres of cloth in 1926–27 now it bought 3.5 metres). Privately, however, he must have been horrified at such a policy, for it was bound to exacerbate the goods shortages, about which he frequently complained in secret exchanges with the centre, and thereby further complicate grain procurement.[18]

If the peasant activists were confused by Eikhe's vague reference to the role of the 'social cooperative boycott' in the grain campaign, they cannot have been any the wiser as to the meaning of 'social influence' when, on 25 January, the krai conference of 210 bedniak and batrak activists opened. Mikoyan addressed the gathering but his speech was also a paragon of imprecision when it came to detailing the proposed new methods. First, he restated the reason for the urgency of increased procurement from Siberia. Whereas the Ukraine had delivered almost four million tons of grain to the state last year, the harvest failure this year meant that eight of its most productive okrugs would be large-scale recipients of grain aid for food and seed. At this stage, he advised, since grain prices and goods supplies had already been increased, the only way to intensify procurement and fulfil the plan for Siberia on time was to 'use social influence, cooperative, soviet, bedniak, seredniak, on large-scale grain holders and those refusing to deliver grain'.[19] Evidence began to reach the party leadership that social influence was proving an effective and popular option in the countryside. If properly organized and coordinated by local party and soviet officials such measures of social influence could be made to work. In villages of Bol'she-Ulussk raion of Achinsk Okrug, for example, party activists, rural soviets and cooperative officials consulted bedniak and serediak peasants before drawing up a list of grain holders. A delegation was sent round these households to appeal to them to sell grain to the state. Later, a general meeting of the village, attended by 85 per cent of households, passed a resolution that all surpluses be sold by 20 February. The meeting even persuaded the listed grain holders to make it a 'compulsory duty' for themselves to sell grain.[20] Whether the forms of persuasion went beyond social pressure is not known.

SUPPLEMENTARY PEASANT SELF-TAXATION

Clarification that further measures to step up grain procurement would target, at this stage, the pockets of the kulaks had been given in the Kraikombiuro decree of 18 January and restated in a Kraiispolkom telegram-directive on 24 January. How these orders were transmitted on a 'shock work' status down through the party and state apparatus may be seen from the decree issued by a closed session of the Presidium of Novosibirsk Okrispolkom on 24 January embodying the directives of the krai leadership. Interestingly, on this day Syrtsov delivered a report to the Kraikombiuro on his trip to Moscow, but secrecy surrounded this session (the protocol merely states that Syrtsov's information was 'taken into account') and what new thinking he brought back from Moscow is unrecorded.[21]

Procurement had surged in Novosibirsk Okrug from 1,400 tons to over 2,300 tons in the third and fourth five-day periods of January, but the Presidium of the Okrispolkom considered this to be a 'weak' increase given the soaring demands of the state. The decree focused on the poor collection of rural payments by raiispolkoms as the main obstacle to the kind of storming tempo of procurement demanded by the Kraikom. Self-taxation collections had been trivial (only 76,200 roubles had been received, 14.3 per cent of the monthly plan) and, in particular, supplementary individual levies from kulak farms had been widely ignored. Accordingly, raiispolkoms were told to ensure a 100 per cent completion of the annual amount of peasant self-taxation by 15 February. In those villages where kulak influence had so far prevented the imposition of individual self-taxation supplements, okrispolkom plenipotentiaries were to be sent to conduct an agitprop campaign among the *bednota* for their immediate adoption. As instructed by the Kraikom, raiispolkoms were authorized to permit village general meetings to increase the amount raised by supplementary self-taxation to 50 per cent of the total, and to impose individual self-taxation burdens on limited numbers of 'malicious grain holders, kulaks and grain speculators' in each raion.

The self-taxation supplements were applied in much the same way that

Article 107 had been carefully targeted by the Kraikom in January 1928, with Stalin's assistance during his tour of the krai.[22] In Novosibirsk Okrug all but one of nineteen raions were allocated a quota for individual self-taxation levies of two to five farms on grounds of speculation (a total of 52), while eight raions had a similar quota for malicious holders of grain surpluses (22). Lists of candidates for the surcharge drawn from those peasants who had failed to deliver grain were to be decided upon in consultation with meetings of poor peasants, while a general boycott was to be imposed by peasant communities on other non-sellers. The small numbers involved suggest that the tax supplements and boycotts were intended very much as intimidatory measures to shift the procurement campaign into a higher gear. To ensure compliance and ward off the prevarication demonstrated at the local level with previous telegrams, lower officials were warned that they were now subject to 'personal responsibility' for the fulfilment of the January grain plan.

These orders did not have the desired effect for on 28 January the Kraikombiuro approved another decree, 'On further measures for improving grain procurement', which first and foremost blamed the poor performance of grain procurement agencies and okrug organizations for the failure to fulfil the January plan. In particular, the party leadership of Omsk, Slavgorod, Biisk and Kamensk were singled out as the most unsatisfactory. Consequently, the Kraikombiuro placed okruzhkombiuro members under 'personal responsibility' to guarantee the completion of the February and annual procurement plans. No doubt, in so doing Syrtsov and his colleagues were attempting to avert a repeat of Stalin's directive of 6 January 1928, during that year's grain crisis, when he had threatened to 'put to the Central Committee the necessity of changing the current leaders of party organizations' if they failed to secure a 'decisive breakthrough' in grain procurement. The months February and March would be decisive for a breakthrough since if grain targets were not completed by the end of this period the spring thaw would make road transport next to impossible for several weeks and scupper what was left of the annual plan for the centre. The Siberian leadership was determined to collect the bulk of the plan in February and the monthly target was set at almost 330,000 tons – an unprecedented monthly plan.[23]

To achieve the plan the Kraikom swung into action with a series of measures. Okrugs were instructed to intensify the collection of rural debts, not only from individual farms but also from the kolkhozes, especially where there were grain surpluses. To ensure the necessary compliance on the ground, 18 of the most senior Kraikom leaders (including Syrtsov, Eikhe, Kisis and Kavraisky) were mustered for attachment to okrugs, and the Kraikom Organizational-Distribution Department was instructed to draft from krai institutions the greatest possible number of workers for service at the lower levels of the grain procurement network. The persistence of obstacles to the speedy shipment of grain, particularly the problem of grain retention by local authorities in remote areas, was to be addressed urgently by the sending of special okrug officials to the larger railway stations where they were to have absolute authority and would exact personal responsibility from procurement officials for any delays. In accordance with a decree of Sovnarkom, compulsory requisition of animal drawn carts was introduced for the transport of grain in areas more than 75 kilometres from rail stations and wharves. The party fraction of the Krai Trades Union Organization was directed to allocate 2–3 officials to supervise the strengthening of labour discipline on the railways, with a supporting propaganda campaign in the regional press, and OGPU back-up lurking in the shadows.

Direct action against the peasantry followed the pattern of organizational measures laid down from the beginning of the year with some refinements. Contracts for grain were to be enforced, by lawsuits if necessary, milling taxes were to be stringently collected but the 10 per cent share for *bednota* supplies was not to be distributed until April at the earliest, and what goods supplies existed in the krai were to be allocated to raions on the basis of satisfactory levels of grain procurement. An attempt was also made to undercut grain speculators operating freely in Omsk and butter producing areas, as the Kraikom approved the decision of Omsk Okruzhkombiuro, taken with Mikoyan, to intervene on the grain market to drive prices down. By now the situation was so dire and deliveries to the centre were of such paramount importance that even when Rubtsovsk Okruzhkom proposed to release just one per cent of grain collected for *bednota* supplies the Kraikombiuro vetoed it.[24]

More decrees on the same themes were issued on 6 February and again on the 12th, when the Kraikombiuro considered a report from a special commission on the course of the grain campaign and concluded that procurement was so drastically sluggish that the monthly target was again threatened. The session adopted a decree, 'On measures for grain procurement', which again specifically highlighted the poor work of the party and cooperative apparatuses in the countryside and castigated their failure to apply Kraikombiuro directives, especially the decree of 18 January (emphasizing self-taxation and debt collection). That abuses against the peasantry were being perpetrated in the scramble for grain was recognized and the Kraikombiuro was frequently forced to condemn lower level officials who resorted to the use of emergency measures such as Article

107, Article 58 (10), and illegal acts such as land confiscation. The decree highlighted some of the measures that had produced good results. Henceforth, goods supplies, the bulk of which were being channelled into the countryside, would only be sold to consumer cooperatives in areas where grain delivery targets had been met and, in an unusual move tantamount to barter with the kulaks, the Kraiispolkom was instructed to release a certain amount of agricultural machinery to be sold directly to individual farms which supplied grain to an equivalent value (a decree followed on 6 February).[25]

Not for the first time in this crisis the Siberian party leadership was taking initiatives, though not without discontent in its own ranks, that precipitated like-minded measures from the central government. The move to ease the restrictions on the sale of agricultural inventory to private farms (including tractors) was encapsulated, with additions, by a Sovnarkom decree only on 9 February. This action to appease the well-off grain holders was subsequently described by one okruzhkom secretary as 'an emergency measure' and must have been a particularly bitter pill to swallow for those krai party leaders like Eikhe, who had consistently condemned kulak capital exploitation of the peasant masses through the renting out of machines.[26] Shortly afterwards, the Siberian party leadership complained to the Politburo about Sovnarkom's decision, describing it as a 'distortion of the party line' that would 'stimulate kulak industrialization' and enlarge their 'exploitatory capacity and accumulation'. In early March, the Politburo ordered Sovnarkom to amend its decrees to accord with the decisions of the Fifteenth Party Congress resolutions on restricting kulak growth.[27] It was also around this time that the central government, yielding to the flood of peasant complaints about excessive taxation, moved to ease the financial plight of seredniak and poor peasants and thwart the possibility of a grand peasant coalition forming against the party. Once again selective material incentives were the preferred option. A decree of 20 February restricted the imposition of individual wealth tax surcharges to the highest band and lowered the soul tax for large peasant households.[28]

The Siberian leaders were also very critical of the calibre of Central Committee plenipotentiaries sent to assist them with procurement. Lacking direction from the centre, and with no clear idea of their responsibilities, these officials proved a hindrance rather than a help to local authorities. On hindsight, however, this criticism was excised from the decree as the Kraikombiuro evidently reconsidered the wisdom of attacking the Central Committee. Significantly, the decree did not advocate extending the measures of social influence beyond commending the use of boycotts against those kulaks who refused to sell grain, something that had been proposed by Eikhe in mid-January. Where these had been carried out with the requisite explanatory work amongst the poor and middle peasants, the Kraikombiuro observed, positive results had followed. In practice, the attempt to raise the political consciousness of the peasants was not always reciprocated in the required manner, for in some areas boycotts were imposed not only on individual farms which refused to sell grain but as a collective punishment on whole villages.[29]

Some of the social influence measures employed by the party brought about a significant shift in the balance of financial outlays by the peasantry, and to that extent must have had some positive impact on pressurizing grain sales and winning over peasant hearts and minds. The balance of taxation, for example, was transformed. If in 1927/8 the proportions of the lowest and highest taxed groups was one rouble in every four roubles paid, in 1928/9 this had changed to one rouble for every ten, and if individual supplementary taxes were included then it was one for every 14. The Krai Financial Department estimated that kulaks lost about 28 per cent of their income in taxes, and 17.3 per cent of all farms in the krai paid almost 68 per cent of the total tax burden. Furthermore, the 3 per cent of farms subjected to individual supplements now accounted for one-sixth (about 2 million roubles) of all taxation. The other side of this coin was that taxes on poor and middle peasants had fallen sharply or been removed altogether and, consequently, they may have been more susceptible to party propaganda about the *smychka* being in their interests.[30]

Whereas in the crisis of 1927/8 the refusal of peasants to sell grain to the state was denounced as a 'kulak grain strike', in February–March 1929 it was branded a 'kulak boycott'. This was the justification for the 'social boycott' declared by the party against those who resisted the drive for grain. Such peasants were marked out mainly, but not always, for non-violent vindictive treatment and harassment, and worst of all their own communities often preferred self-preservation, either participating in or observing with subdued resignation the increasing injustices perpetrated by the party against kulaks. On the other hand, the party continued to rail against kulak infiltration of village party cells and rural soviets which, it claimed, led to a situation where in many villages kulak power kept their farms exempted from individual tax supplements.[31]

The boycott against kulaks involved a further institutionalization of party control over the countryside and was another incremental step towards the final liquidation of the kulaks as a socioeconomic category of peasants in late 1929. The protocols of the village soviet of Ust′-Insk, Novosibirsk Okrug, reveal that the inauguration of the boycott against 'kulaks' involved a whole series of measures that tightened party control and differentiated these peasants from the rest of the rural community. Measures included the drawing up of lists of kulaks regarded as 'malicious grain holders', exclusion from the cooperatives, attaching blackboards on their homes denouncing their refusal to sell grain, the publication of lists of those boycotted in local newspapers, the compilation of reports on the boycotted by the rural soviets.[32] On the other hand, in some areas kulaks retaliated against fellow villagers who collaborated with the state by staging boycotts of them – something which may have antagonized poor peasants normally dependent on the kulaks for work, hiring machines, milling, and the sale of grain and vodka.[33] That the social influence method was effective is demonstrated by the fact that the only area of the krai where there seems to have been any large-scale organized peasant resistance to the party was in an area of Rubtsovsk Okrug, and this was due to peculiar local circumstances.

PEASANT COLLECTIVE ACTION: THE POKROVSK AFFAIR

Rubtsovsk Okruzhkom had been one of the first to attempt to reapply the emergency measures of the previous year early in the campaign. As we noted earlier, when it reestablished its 'grain troiki' system in October 1928 it was severely reprimanded by the Kraikombiuro. This indicated a willingness to indulge in harsh measures against the peasantry; indeed such was the outrage at the behaviour of party plenipotentiaries in this area that mass peasant unrest was sparked off in Pokrovsk raion in early 1929. When the 'distortions' of party policy in this okrug were brought to the attention of the Kraikombiuro it sent a commission of investigation under Zakovsky, the OGPU chief, in February 1929, and his report was delivered and discussed on 14 March.[34]

Zakovsky himself described the events in Pokrovsk as a 'peasant revolt' (*vozmushchenie*) in response to actions by certain representatives of Soviet authority in the villages.[35] Immediately, he set out to focus on the tragic-comic 'abnormal' and 'unprecedented' methods practised there. In the village of Ust'-Kozlukh a form of 'carnival' (*karnaval*) was held. Forty-six grain-holding peasants, most of whom were seredniaks and only a few kulaks, were taken to the village school and 'worked over'. A voice asked if this had been 'behind closed doors', but no, Zakovsky responded, it had been in front of the whole village. The 46 were then ritually and publicly humiliated by being forced to march through the village carrying a black banner with the slogan: 'We are friends of Chamberlain.' The carnival was accompanied through the streets by rural activists and *bednota* with red banners accompanied by ululating women and children.

This was a case where the representatives of the state fell back on the Russian peasant custom of *samosud*, a kind of community policing that was normally peaceful and ritualized into forms of social censure and derision such as public humiliation, coventry and boycotting. In some cases *samosud* called for charivari, a kind of perverse carnival where offending peasants were publicly disgraced and paraded through the village on foot or towing a cart in a horse collar, often naked and tarred and feathered, carrying signs indicating the nature of the offence, surrounded and being beaten by neighbours with sticks, with the whole retinue accompanied by a babel of *paramusique*. When taken to an extreme this kind of self-regulation by peasant communities could lead to lynch-law. Students of this type of peasant behaviour would have us believe that it was those perceived as 'outsiders' who were at risk of death.[36] In fact, any peasant who seriously infringed peasant social norms was at risk. The author was told by an old Siberian peasant of two cases of *samosud*, both of which involved theft (grain and animals), where those judged guilty were chased or paraded through the village before being beaten to death (in one case a father and three sons).[37]

Something like the charivari occurred in Pokrovsk and elsewhere. The plenipotentiaries claimed that all this happened without any pressure from them and without opposition from the peasants. In reality, a teacher had beaten the legs of one of the kulaks with a flagpole and then the others joined the parade. At this point the secretary of the raikom, Fedotov, arrived from the nearby village of Nizhne-Kamyshensk, where the head of the rural department of the okrug (now plenipotentiary for grain procurement) was encouraging his subordinates to launch an anti-religion campaign. Following orders, Fedotov made an inflammatory speech calling for the church to be turned into a 'House of the People' and forced a vote in favour from those in the parade. Subsequently, the parade was broken up and those involved were allowed to return home, where they informed their families that the party was planning to do away with the church. As news circulated fast in such a small community, not long afterwards a huge crowd of peasants, mostly women, gathered at the church to prevent its desecration. A stand-off ensued until the okrug plenipotentiary ordered that a firehose be brought and the crowd of women was sprayed with cold water in a futile attempt to disperse them. This only strengthened the fanatic determination of the women and they responded by singing religious songs. By now the question of grain procurement had been overtaken by the symbolic power struggle between the party authorities and the mass of peasants over the church. Zakovsky described the whole affair as a 'colossal political blunder'.[38]

Rumours of the attack on the church quickly spread across the raion and the peasant mood assumed the character of a religious movement as similar events, accompanied by more brutal abuses such as the use of tar-collars against grain holders, were repeated in other villages. Zakovsky attributed a leading role in the organization of the abuses under the cover of 'social pressure' to the head of the propaganda group sent out by the Central Committee, Smirnov, who operated out of Rubtsovsk town as an okrispolkom plenipotentiary for grain procurement. He also blamed the Okruzhkombiuro for its decision of 27 January to apply Article 58 (10) (against counter-revolutionary activity) against five or six kulaks per raion to accelerate grain procurement which had led to the arrest of 65 to 70 persons so far. This was despite a recommendation from Mikoyan, who was in Rubtsovsk at that time, not to proceed with this measure. Zakovsky insisted that there was 'no need to use *razverstki*' by arresting grain holding peasants under Article 58, his point being that this would only complicate the OGPU's work in rounding up the real counter-revolutionary peasants and, he argued, this action had generated 'negative political consequences' in the countryside. It seems that more extreme measures were reverted to in Pokrovsk because social influence failed to break peasant solidarity. For example, in Ust'-Kozlukh a boycott of peasants refusing to sell grain was attempted by the Okruzhkombiuro plenipotentiary, Shishkov, but failed because other peasants bought whatever those boycotted needed from the cooperative store.[39]

One type of intimidatory social pressure aimed at wearing down resistance involved peasant non-sellers being brought before the rural soviet actif where they were made to stand on a bench while others tried to shame and humiliate them. Another method was to order non-sellers to choose between two boards, on one was written 'I am a friend of Chamberlain' and on the other 'Don't hand over grain, it is better to feed it to pigs'. Not knowing who Chamberlain was, the peasants would choose the second board and were then beaten. To assist plenipotentiaries with procurement a gang of thieves was released from prison and terrorized the countryside. They even called themselves a 'food detachment of Soviet power'. The gang of about thirty persons named itself '*trudguzh*' (labour cartage) and was drawn from the village of Pervoe Karpovo in Pokrovsk raion, whose inhabitants had a reputation as thieves. They went about the countryside stealing grain stored in the fields and selling it to procurement points; indeed, cooperative procurement agents supplied the gang with sacks and doled out advances of vodka. Their actions were condoned, if not openly supported, by inaction from local police officials and party plenipotentiaries as a means of intimidating peasants to sell grain quickly. In fact, the procuracy branded local party, soviet and police officials as outright accomplices for the gang. This was suggested by plenipotentiary Smirnov's comment to a general meeting of peasants in February that 'whoever finds grain in the fields can sell it', with the further warning that '*trudguzh*' might soon be extending its operations to include barns. After an armed clash with peasants in late February the gang was arrested by the police, ordered released by the raikom secretary, Fedotov, but the next day ordered rearrested by the raikom and put on trial.[40]

Abuses were not solely committed against kulaks. For example, in the village of Vtoraia Karpovka seredniaks were given individual supplementary tax burdens and disenfranchised in order to force them to sell grain. Such measures were not very successful since the procurement plan for Pokrovsk raion was only fulfilled by 42 per cent to March, and it is impossible to say whether this was because of or despite these extreme measures. In the case of Pokrovsk, the battle for grain was very much one fought out by outside party plenipotentiaries, with the support of poor peasants and criminal elements, against those grain holders designated as kulaks. The Rubtsovsk Procuracy even went so far as to talk of 'lynch law' by the *bednota*.[41] Rural communists and plenipotentiaries often found themselves in opposing camps and in Ust'-Kozlukh, for instance, 12 of 16 members of the party cell were expelled by the plenipotentiaries as 'rotten elements – grain holders and kulaks'.[42]

What is striking about the scale of peasant opposition in Pokrovsk is how isolated such incidents were. There were parallel episodes involving similar abuses in other areas of the krai. For example, a Procuracy report to Syrtsov on 19 March disclosed that 'smear teams' (*mazal'shchikov*) for putting on tar collars, demonstrations, black flags, blackboards, mock funerals of grain holders and other forms of social intimidation occurred in Kamensk and Novosibirsk Okrugs.[43] These practices did not generate, however, the kind of mass peasant opposition that was seen in Pokrovsk. It was so unusual, and taken so seriously by the Siberian leadership, that the krai OGPU chief was despatched to investigate the nature of the peasant protests. The protests erupted in response to a failure of local officials and plenipotentiaries to properly apply the social influence method. It was the local party's insensitive attacks on the village churches and the use of a non-discriminating criminal gang which sparked off mass unrest and not its assaults on kulak peasants *per se* – though kulaks were quick to exploit peasant fears. The problem for the okrug authorities was how, having antagonized the peasant masses, they could return to a more orderly grain procurement campaign which would isolate the large-scale grain holders. Plenipotentiaries guilty of abuses were removed and some were even arrested, and a request was made for Kraikom assistance, but this could not immediately transform the soured political atmosphere. Besides, as Zakovsky disclosed, okruzhkom and raikom officials had been aware of what was happening in Pokrovsk at the time; indeed some had toured the raion and indicated support for extreme measures by turning a blind eye to them.[44] As Fedotov put it to a plenipotentiary who asked if the 'carnivals' of grain non-sellers was legal: 'It's not our business – the *bednota* are doing it – we cannot intervene.'[45]

In the subsequent Kraikombiuro discussion of Zakovsky's report, some focused on the organizational lessons to be learned, regarding the 'slide into the course of applying administrative methods' as evidence of a 'lack of control' by the Rubtsovsk party leaders, many of whom had been away at conferences.[46] There were, however, others who were prepared to draw out more ominous political lessons, blaming the events on the degeneration of rural party organizations that were 'clogged up with elements alien to communism' and unable to work with the poor peasants. The Pokrovsk officials were 'nothing more than allies of the Right deviation' according to this view![47] Another blamed the propaganda group sent out by the Central Committee and recommended their removal: 'people who do not understand how to treat the peasantry and relate to the seredniak. In this group there are people who do not represent the good line of the Central Committee [sic].'[48]

The most senior Krai leaders endorsed the view that a general political lesson should be drawn about the state of local party organizations. Eikhe compared the events in Rubtsovsk with the 'Kuznetsk affair' of May 1928, when the Kuznetsk leadership had been purged for advocating the 'probing' of the seredniak for grain. He proposed that the okrug leadership should bear the greater responsibility for 'forgetting about NEP' and recommended that the Kraikom give more detailed instructions on acceptable methods of grain procurement. Kisis also called for the removal of some okrug leaders as a signal to the regional party, and was especially critical of D'iakov, the Okruzhkom Secretary, who only recently at the krai party conference had defended stepping up the pressure on seredniak grain holders. Finally, Syrtsov intervened strongly in support of the idea of 'individual responsibility' and moved that Shishkov and Smirnov, the two senior local officials most closely involved in the Pokrovsk events, be expelled from the party and brought to trial, while the Central Committee should be asked to withdraw the head of its propaganda group. After a brief debate, it was further decided to dissolve the Pokrovsk raion party organization.[49] The Kraikombiuro line was that the Pokrovsk affair was an isolated incident, and the officials involved should be scapegoats and pay the penalty for failure.

Meanwhile the central party leadership had reached the conclusion that only the most resolute action based on measures of 'social influence' against kulaks would overcome the crisis. On 16 February a *Pravda* editorial publicized the new line and urged the wholesale application of the 'social method' and 'mass pressure' in grain collections. *Pravda*, however, did not specify any new mechanisms for applying social pressure. One week later a report on the tours of inspection by Narkomtorg officials of eastern parts of the country (Siberia, the Urals, Kazakhstan) to check on the course of the grain campaign stated that the correct implementation of 'social influence' was having positive results.[50]

It is with the notion of 'social influence' (and, as we have seen, this actually meant cooperative boycotts, pressurized debt collection, punitive supplementary self-taxation and other forms of harassment) which was vaguely propagated in the press in December–February (and earlier) that the Ural-Siberian method has been confused.[51] Individual supplements of self-taxation, party inspired boycotts of 'malicious grain holders' and other forms of 'social influence' were incremental steps in the application of systematic social pressure against kulaks, and as such were part of the first stage of dekulakization. The Ural-Siberian method involved a radically new initiative and a new stage in this process: it meant the extension of the peasant self-taxation procedure to grain collections. The latter method was first considered as a solution to the grain problem, among other proposals, at the Fourth Siberian Party Conference held in late February and early March 1929.

3 The Search for a New Method

THE SIBERIAN INITIATIVE

For several months the Siberian party had been struggling in the grain collections under an official slogan of 'social pressure' which had not been elaborated in much detail and had not produced the massive procurement level needed to complete the plan. Two months had passed without a breakthrough. The party leadership was haunted by the prospect of a repeat of the events of the previous year when the import of 200,000 tons of grain during the spring and summer in a manoeuvre to alleviate shortages had stunned the Stalinist wing of the party by depleting hard currency reserves intended to finance industrialization. This year capital construction plans were even more ambitious and the party leadership was determined that they should not be obstructed.[1] By early March 1929, the inevitable advance of time, the looming danger of failure to achieve the remainder of the grain plan and the real possibility of removal from their posts served to concentrate the minds of central and Siberian party leaders on the problem of how to secure a breakthrough in the crisis. It was not a Stalinist blueprint that determined the march of events in this crisis; rather the contingency in Siberia, and in the country, at this crucial juncture generated a peculiar dynamic in policy-making. Time was a critical factor, as the pressure intensified to find a solution to the grain shortage before the spring thaw turned hard sleigh roads into impassable mud that would bring transport to a standstill in the countryside for several weeks. By the middle of March, the bad roads season had already gripped the grain areas of the south of the country (in the Ukraine and Kuban steppe), focusing attention on Siberia and the Eastern grain producing areas, where the spring thaw would not arrive until April.

There had been a massive surge in grain procurement in Siberia over the 1927/8 level and by the beginning of March about 1.4 million tons had been collected without serious effort representing an increase of about 40 per cent on the same period of 1927/8 (when Article 107 had been enforced). This tremendous achievement did not, however, satisfy the voracious appetite of the centre as it left a huge procurement hurdle of well over half a million tons to be surmounted before the end of June but, effectively, most of the remaining plan would have to be fulfilled in two months (March–April) because of the bad roads and the sowing season in May.² This target was obviously discharged down to local level in some cases doubling the amount collected the previous year. For example, in Kamensk Okrug almost 69,000 tons had been collected in 1927/8 but, after the plan hikes early in 1929, a revised target was set at almost double this figure, and by the end of February over 98,000 tons had been collected.³

It was against the background of tension and apprehension at the course of the procurement campaign that the Fourth Krai Party Conference convened in Novosibirsk from 25 February to 4 March with the 'grain question', and especially the problem of 'how to take grain', top of the agenda. In his opening address Syrtsov emphasized that the kulak's share of marketable grain had increased significantly from the estimated 22 per cent in early January, and thus the main blow in the campaign should fall on them, particularly as a 'significant part of the kulaks were sabotaging grain procurement'. It would, however, be 'absolutely incorrect' and 'the politics of adventurism' to follow those who sought a return to the 'easy' method of Article 107. There had been divisions in the party leadership over its use last year and, though it had proved effective then, the decision had been taken not to revert to it in the current campaign.

Syrtsov considered the basic problem to be one of organizational failure: 'If last year grain procurement was carried out by us under the sign of taking grain surpluses by Article 107, then this year grain procurement must be carried out under the sign of taking away party cards from certain rural communists, who clearly have a surplus of these same party cards.' He recommended the example of the Rubtsovsk party organization which had purged 15 to 17 per cent of its rural members as 'kulakized communists', as the way to deal with such 'kulak agents' and break the perverse '*smychka*' between rural communists and kulaks.⁴ Lauding the success of the measures of social influence pursued by the party, he observed how when individual supplementary self-taxation had been levied with the assistance of bedniaks and seredniaks not at 10 per cent but to levels of 30 to 40 to 50 per cent then procurement had been best. Goods boycotts of kulak non-sellers of grain had also produced 'positive results'. Consequently, further pressure on the peasantry in the grain campaign was to be based on these measures with the carrying out of 'social work' among the bedniaks and seredniaks to mobilize their support in applying them.⁵

Later in the conference, foreshadowing his speech to the Sixteenth Party Conference in April, he outlined and lent his support to the fundamental principles of Stalin's 'general line'. He explained the need for expropriating a 'tribute' (*dan'*) from the peasantry to finance industrialization, and criticized Bukharin's labelling of this as 'military-feudal exploitation' of the peasantry at the recent Politburo meeting.[6] In agriculture, there was now a 'wager on the large-scale collective farm' and, reflecting the views of Kavraisky and Nusinov's work on peasant differentiation, he stated that in Siberia 'kulak accumulation in a whole series of cases has now reached its limits' with the result that any further development of their farms would see them 'raise the issue of political power'. He added: 'We must remember that kulak grain tomorrow will pose the question of kulak power, of a return to capitalist construction. Those who put a wager on the kulak farm inevitably must put a wager on a bourgeois-democratic refashioning of the USSR.'[7] One speaker was prepared to take this line openly to its logical conclusion by demanding of Syrtsov that 'counter-revolutionary kulaks', those who consistently obstruct party measures, be shot rather than imprisoned.[8]

On 27 February a secret conclave of the combined leadership echelons of the Kraikom, Kraiispolkom, okruzhkom secretaries and okrispolkom chairmen met during the conference to discuss a new initiative – what it euphemistically termed a 'compulsory grain loan' (*prinuditel'nyi khlebnyi zaem*) from the peasant *verkhushka*. That day the Kraikombiuro sent a telegram to Stalin formally requesting that they be immediately given permission to raise such a loan in Siberia (see Document 2). The hope was that the telegram would elucidate a positive response from the Central Committee while the inner core of the Siberian party organization was gathered in conference and this would facilitate a speedy mobilization of officials for implementation of the new method.

The Siberian party leadership had been driven inexorably into a corner by the pressure for grain from the centre and it now concluded that only a return to some form of *razverstka* would secure the additional plan. Emergency measures were needed to realize such an extraordinary plan. The problem was how to reconcile different versions of the loan mechanism and deciding how it should be cloaked ideologically and legally, given that the Central Committee had repudiated the use of emergency measures at the July 1928 plenum. The proposal for a loan articulated a mood among the Siberian officials that while the previous measures of social influence had been exhausted the principle of the policy was sound and alternative means of squeezing grain from the peasantry had to be found quickly. It was also recognized that there were lessons to be learnt from the successful implementation of the social influence policy. A shotgun approach of generalized pressure and sweeping actions to free grain from the peasantry as a whole was ruled out as politically counter-productive. Instead the spirit of the social influence policy was to be carried forward by a rifle approach of selective targeting of repression on kulaks and key grain holders in the villages, and appeals to the investment logic of the mass of peasants by the provision of material incentives for the poor and middle peasants for their collaboration.

The Siberians warned Stalin that under the existing methods the decline in procurement was accelerating so fast that only an estimated 1.64 million tons would be collected by the end of the year (about a third of a million tons short of the plan). They proposed that a 'compulsory alienation' (*otchuzdenie*) of grain surpluses in the form of a loan to the state be implemented in the territory of Siberia, whereby a quota of 6 to 8 per cent of farms who were 'sabotaging' procurement would be separated out and a total of '15–18 million puds' (the amount of the shortfall in the plan) would be distributed among them. Theoretically the loan was to be repaid, in money after one year or, if preferred, in grain after two or three years. If a peasant household refused to cooperate a fine of five times the amount of its grain loan would be exacted and, if this was not paid, confiscation of all property with internal exile for three years. Under this scheme, the middle peasant would not be directly targeted for further exactions. Furthermore, in a move designed to enlist poor peasant support for the campaign, and reminiscent of Stalin's 25 per cent grain bounty of January 1928, the Siberians suggested that 10 per cent of grain collected by this method be left in the villages and used for food and seed supply for the *bednota*. This proposal was the prototype for the 'Ural-Siberian method'.

FORCED LOAN OR 'DEMOCRATIC RAZVERSTKA'

Thereafter the idea of the compulsory grain loan dominated the conference proceedings. At that day's conference session the crux of the grain question was confronted by the Biisk Okruzhkom Secretary, Spirov, who frankly stated that the 'existing forms and methods of grain procurement will not guarantee for us ... a 100 per cent fulfilment of the grain procurement plan'. He set out to demonstrate how the different forms of party pressure worked in the Biisk countryside; the individual self-taxation surcharges up to 50 per cent of the total with collection fixed to 1–15 March, goods boycotts, *difpai* (progressive cooperative membership dues), debt collection and so on. None of these methods, he asserted, would guarantee the completion of the additional grain target set by the centre and therefore the major problem facing the Siberian party was how to fulfil the March and April grain plans. In Spirov's opinion the plans could only be achieved if radical 'new methods' were introduced, namely a compulsory loan from the kulaks and upper strata of the peasantry which would also pressurize seredniak grain holders to sell. This method would be supported by poor peasants, organized by rural party organizations, if a grain fund for food and seed supplies was created from a portion of the loan.[9]

This kind of militancy was lambasted by Strikovsky, Head of Sibkraisouiz, in a speech which was subjected to considerable heckling. Before abandoning social methods for others of a more coercive nature, he noted, it was essential to bear in mind that 'all strata of the countryside' (except the *bednota*) had grain and most was held by the seredniaks. Measures of 'administrative influence' (i.e. force) would, in his opinion, unnerve the peasantry and destabilize the imminent sowing campaign. The answer was to persevere with the measures of social influence which according to the evidence from his own experiences on visits to Rubtsovsk Okrug had hardly been tried. He suggested that the party should brace itself for the possibility of a large under-fulfilment ('15–20 million puds').[10]

Strikovsky was clearly out of touch with the prevailing atmosphere and was the butt of much criticism; indeed, ironically, he was later accused of proposing a 'cooperative *razverstka*' on a visit to Barnaul.[11] He was immediately attacked, to loud applause by Nusinov, Barnaul Okruzhkom Secretary, who couched his speech in Stalinist rhetoric. To even consider the possibility of non-fulfilment of the annual plan was an abrogation of duty, he retorted. At the same time, it was clear to him that on the basis of existing methods a 100 per cent completion of the plan was uncertain. The well-off-kulak *verkhushka* had a 'significant part' of the grain and their refusal to sell made the grain question an issue of 'class struggle', a weapon aimed at the 'dictatorship of the proletariat'. Nusinov reminded those who argued against extraordinary measures, such as Article 107, that the methods of social influence currently applied were not 'normal' and were far from a commercial means of procuring grain, and moreover, force had not led to a reduction in sown area last year. He advised the conference to focus its attention on the question of undertaking forced seizures of a limited quantity of grain from the well-off and kulaks.[12]

Eikhe agreed partially with Strikovsky and those who stood against the adoption of 'new measures' in the campaign in so far as he agreed that the social influence methods had not been exhausted. Fulfilment of the remaining half million tons or so (32–3 million puds) in the plan, however, seemed a terrifyingly ambitious prospect when Eikhe broke it down, and the plan itself created an irrefutable logic in favour of some new initiative other than more of the same. The bulk of the remaining plan would have to be completed in two months (March–April), or twelve five-day periods of procurement. Successful completion required a rate of procurement of about 2,700 puds per five-day period, compared with the preceding average of 1,400–1,500 – a huge increase on what was already a record procurement level. There was to be no room for doubters (like Strikovskii) as action had to be taken immediately and decisively before it was too late. Therefore, to speed up procurement, Eikhe supported the idea of a compulsory grain loan from the kulaks but only in the same carefully selected manner as Article 107 had been applied the previous year as this would have the intimidatory effect of pressing more grain from the seredniak.[13]

Following Eikhe's lead, several okruzhkom secretaries spoke in favour of 'additional measures' of procurement and the compulsory grain loan. Those who did so tended to link the stalling procurement campaign (in the sense that it was not matching the exorbitant demands of the centre) with obfuscation by 'petty-bourgeois' 'counter-revolutionary' 'right opportunistic elements' in the party. Buzov, Achinsk Okruzhkom Secretary, described the relaxation of controls on the sale of advanced machinery to kulaks as an 'emergency measure, only from the other end', something which only the Right could live with.[14] Krylov, Kamensk Okruzhkom Secretary, was particularly forceful and imaginative in respect of the implementation of new methods and the 'planning' of state procurement of peasant grain. He believed that the political dynamics of the countryside were such that the party could easily organize the poor and middle peasants to intensify the pressure on the kulaks in a form of 'class struggle'. As evidence of the political mobilization of the peasant masses, he pointed to the success of the rural soviet elections which had seen average turnouts of over 62 per cent and up to 76 per cent. Like Strikovsky, he rejected the notion that the party had exhausted existing methods but advocated a very different political perspective:

> Comrades, what have we basically done up to now? We have tried to persuade the peasant very strongly, but everything, that should have been done, we have not done. I think that it would be far better and more politically advantageous if we now tighten all the screws of our rural social organizations and pose the question in this way – that the basic mass of the peasantry by itself take the grain from the kulak, from the grain holder, and not by the issuing of a state decree. By this method, we shall rely on the authority of lower soviet (rural) power.

Krylov then gave an outline of the procedure he had in mind: 'The village gathering [*sel'skii skhod*] will meet, grain holders will be exposed – kulaks and other holders of grain surpluses – and the *skhod* will decide on the question of the sale of grain, breaking down the plan by peasant farms and compelling holders of grain surpluses to sell a defined amount immediately to the state.' This method he termed 'a democratic *razverstka*' (sic). He believed that it would yield much more than the loan and was the only way to guarantee a 100 per cent completion of the plan. It was much better to 'conduct this matter from below than from above', he concluded.[15]

Kuznetsov, a Kraikombiuro member, offered the following logic in support of the loan in his speech on 28 February. Statistics provided by Kavraisky and Nusinov revealed that the kulaks held about 22 per cent of the marketable grain surplus in January. The grain plan for Siberia stood at almost two million tons and 22 per cent of that figure (the kulaks' share) amounted to over 400,000 tons. Research had shown, however, that the kulaks had not sold much grain, at most only around 164,000 tons, leaving a huge amount that came to about half the amount the Siberian authorities had to procure to fulfil the plan. That even the statistical analysis as to who held most grain in the countryside was disputed in the krai party leadership was demonstrated by the interjection of another Kraikom official, Komarov, who declared that Kuznetsov's figures ignored free market sales and were 'just made up' (see below).

Kuznetsov agreed with those speakers who had argued for 'additional measures' to intensify procurement, but whereas *razverstka* was an emergency measure, how could a grain loan, he asked, be described as such when the law already provided for a peasant financial loan (*krest'ianskii zaem*)? Kuznetsov reasonably suggested that the proposed grain loan should not be taken for nothing; rather it should be repaid to the peasant *verkhushka* with interest, as was the case with the financial loan. This provoked uproar in the hall with calls that it should be a forced loan and cries of disbelief. Immediately, he backtracked somewhat and admitted that the details of the loan were still to be confirmed but the key to improving procurement lay in strengthening existing methods. A heckle from the floor, 'and then?', went unanswered.[16]

Clearly, not all officials were fully convinced of the efficacy of the forced loan and preferred an alternative. Given the prevailing climate of militancy, opponents of the loan were very circumspect in their criticism. Behind the scenes, away from the platform, the loan was described as 'basically Trotskyism'.[17] Astute critics took cover under the notion of a returnable forced grain loan. In contrast to Kuznetsov *et al.*, Komarov, who was a Kraikombiuro member, controversially argued that the kulaks had already disposed of much of their marketable surplus on the free market and to the bedniaks, and frankly stated that most of the remaining marketable grain surplus was held by the seredniaks, thus explaining why the problem of taking the grain was so politically sensitive. He warned that the scale of the additional procurement plan was so high that fulfilment would entail the party eating into peasant insurance stocks, something that would stiffen peasant resistance. Komarov's form of the grain loan may have been more acceptable to the hardliners in so far as it was interest-free for the state, but he cannot have endeared himself to them by suggesting that the state guarantee repayment from next year's harvest to the extent that grain be imported if necessary to make good any shortfall – a view that smacked of Rightism. The idea of more grain imports was anathema to the many industrializers in the audience who were amazed at the thought given that the countryside was awash with grain.

In any event, as Komarov pointed out, the proposed grain loan was doomed to failure in the absence of a wholesale propaganda campaign to dispel the peasant's belief that this measure was as objectionable as 'a contract without an advance'. Furthermore, he attempted to assuage the fears of those who reckoned that a forced loan would have negative consequences for the spring sowing campaign by depressing peasant incentive to grow more marketable grain. He disclosed astonishing figures from the Krai Financial Department which proved that the application of Article 107 in 1927/8 had not resulted in any detrimental impact on the sowing of the farms with a large sown area (16 or more desiatins), indeed, as farms sowing more than 24 desiatins (without question in the kulak category) had actually increased their sown area by an average of 11 per cent, he was able to declare that, 'the bigger the sown area, the less they decreased'.[18]

Some senior krai leaders had qualms about the introduction of a grain loan but accepted that it was an 'extreme measure' to deal with the 'extreme situation' confronting the Siberian party. Kisis, Syrtsov's deputy, stressed that even if the high February rate of procurement continued into April, although there were indications that the rate had fallen towards the end of the month, it would still leave a gap of '15–20 million puds'. The amount outstanding in the annual plan had to be realized 'to the last pud' if the country was to emerge from this political and economic crisis. Refusing to be drawn on the question of who had the grain, and correctly pointing out that at that point in time there were no accurate statistics to resolve the issue one way or the other, he chose to focus on the advantages arising from the bumper Siberian harvest that had not existed last year; firstly, the *bednota* was adequately supplied with grain and would therefore be less dependent on the kulak and more amenable to party activism; secondly, the kulaks had more than enough surplus to meet the demands of the loan without being ruined. The key to success, according to Kisis, lay in properly applying the loan with exactitude on the kulaks and without touching the seredniak. Unfortunately, the telegram of 27 February vaguely referred to those 'sabotaging' procurement as being liable for the loan, something which was unlikely to clarify precisely how candidates for the loan were to be identified on the ground.[19]

The problem of identifying the kulaks was one of the most politically contentious issues which obsessed the Bolsheviks in the latter 1920s, and was the rationale underlying the numerous statistical surveys and analyses of peasant social differentiation carried out in this period. In 1927–29 the official Kraikom investigations of peasant differentiation in Siberia were supervised by Kavraisky and Nusinov, close political supporters of Syrtsov. In early 1929 they published a study, based on sample spring cluster censuses for the period 1927/8, employing a sophisticated 'sliding scale' methodology of assessment of different peasant social groups. Their indices were those of particular significance in Siberian agricultural conditions (hiring of labour, renting out of machines, size of sown area) which were then combined with the value of property owned. By this method they assessed kulak strength in the region at 7 per cent of the peasantry.[20] This was the median figure around which the Kraikombiuro based its estimate of the number of farms to be imposed with a loan.

Anxious that the proposed forced grain loan should be selectively applied and not confused with supplementary individual self-taxation levies, tax surcharges or disenfranchized peasants, some conference speakers attempted to ensure that the Kavraisky and Nusinov figure was confirmed as the definitive measure of the size of the kulak group. Zakovsky, however, suggested that it would be a good idea to include the top 1 to 2 per cent of the well-off seredniak grain holders in the loan as a way of intimidating the seredniaks as a whole and dislodging them from kulak influence not to sell. Kavraisky himself recommended that the 'forced seizure of grain', as he bluntly put it, be applied not only to the '5 per cent–6 per cent *verkhushka* farms' but also to 'a number' of the wealthiest seredniak farms.[21]

In his closing speech Syrtsov bemoaned the fact that only the dire circumstances of harvest failure in the Ukraine and North Caucasus had placed the Siberians in this difficult situation, as otherwise they had been on target for a triumphant procurement campaign. Choosing his words with care, he was distinctly unenthusiastic about the idea of the forced loan; nevertheless, he had evidently reconciled himself to its inevitability and saw it as a far more preferable alternative to the reintroduction of Article 107 and the use of coercion (*prinudilovka*). What the campaign lacked above all else, he considered, was a sense of activism in the use of existing methods, and he railed against the 'passivity' of party, soviet and cooperative officials, comparing their psychology with 'that of the hussar, who wants to wear a nice uniform but does not want to go into battle'. Strikovskii, in particular, was denounced for his complacency and declared a 'prisoner of his own system', something which was to cost him his post.

Syrtsov attempted to distinguish the forced loan under discussion from the Left Opposition's similar proposal in late 1927: 'Their's had been for 150–200 million puds compared with only the 10–12–15 million' envisaged in Siberia. That provoked a cry from the hall 'in Siberia' which jolted Syrtsov to insist: 'I did not hear, comrades, a proposal to implement a grain loan in the whole of the Soviet Union. The issue refers only to Siberia. Here we are talking about limited areas, it is a question of 10–15 million puds of grain.' He proceeded to sharply rebuke Krylov whose 'lighthearted' use of the terms '*razverstka*' and 'democratic *razverstka*' indicated a 'muddled head', as this was a breach with NEP and a direct road to a confrontation with the seredniak peasant.

The speech offered some detailed instructions as to how the loan would be implemented. He observed that 'the essence of the loan lies not so much in the loan itself, as in creating a powerful stimulus for quickening the sale of grain', because for every kulak farm burdened with the loan ten others would be intimidated. The loan also obviated the need to conduct search and seizure operations in the countryside which aroused so much peasant hostility. Statistics were available in the villages recording how much surplus each peasant had and the quantity sold to procurement agencies. These records could be used to assess the loan in the following manner: limited numbers of peasant grain holders would be asked to deliver the loan to the state, and if they refused they would then be liable to a substantial monetary fine, many times the value of the grain loan, if apprehended selling grain on the free market. He emphasized repeatedly that the final decision on the matter could not be made by the Siberian party alone but must be settled by the Soviet government and the Central Committee, and from the content this suggests that he was raising the possibility that the proposal would be thrown out as too extreme: 'The Central Committee may not go along with this measure and will try to find other measures. I do not know whether they have it in their arsenal.'[22]

In the meantime the Siberian party conference witnessed a radical turnover in the local elite as the Kraikombiuro, no doubt with the approval of Stalin, used this opportunity to rejuvenate its leading ranks with militants and remove precisely those key officials who had opposed and obstructed the use of emergency measures against the peasantry during the crisis of 1927/8 and in the current grain campaign. Of the 68 members and 32 candidates elected to the Kraikom in March 1927, 36 (53 per cent) and 25 (80 per cent) were deselected. In the Kraikombiuro itself, four out of ten full members and all seven candidates were new. Notable departures included the heads of the Krai Procuracy (Kunov), Kraisoiuz (Strikovsky), and Kraisud (Kozhevnikov) (the latter two were also dismissed from candidate membership of the Kraikombiuro). At the same time, Syrtsov consolidated his own position by elevating Kavraisky, his counsellor on peasant affairs, from Head of the Statistical Department of the Kraikom to candidate membership of the Kraikombiuro, a seat on the Secretariat and Head of the Krai Agriculture Department.[23]

That Stalin was initially reluctant to include the concept of a compulsory grain loan or some variant thereof in the party's armoury of political weapons for controlling and managing the countryside was evidenced by the Politburo decision on 4 March to 'flatly reject' the Siberian initiative (see Document 2). The refusal of the centre to countenance even a modified and more sophisticated emergency method must have been a devastating blow to the morale of the Siberian leadership as it struggled against impossible odds to fulfil the plan. On 9 March a *Pravda* editorial again urged the use of social pressure against peasant grain holders but it did not go beyond previous orders from the centre linking social pressure to agricultural tax surcharges, supplementary peasant self-taxation and cooperative boycotts, as vaguely outlined by Mikoyan to the Siberians in late January.[24]

The Kraikombiuro had few options left to it other than further tightening its organizational control at local level. That same day it fell back on mobilizing another 21 of its most senior officials to be seconded to okruzhkoms for work on grain procurement and the spring sowing campaign.[25] The regional party apparatus was prepared for a final assault on the countryside before the spring thaw. The resolutions of the conference ensured that all party organizations were fully cognizant of the new directive from the centre which had imposed 'supplementary duties' on Siberia to supply grain to the Central Industrial Region and peasant grain deficit areas 'in the shortest possible time'. This grain was to be found in the hands of the 'well-off kulak stratum' and 'all necessary measures' were to be taken against them in order to fulfil the plan.[26]

THE 'NEW METHOD' AND STALINIST POLICY-MAKING

The transformation in the thinking of the Stalinist leadership at the centre seems to have occurred during the middle weeks of March. Stalin's interest in the possibility of a return to some form of the *razverstka* method of War Communism had obviously been stirred by the Siberian telegram, but at this stage he was reluctant to accede to the idea of a grain loan. We can be certain of this because of a telegram that he sent to Syrtsov and Eikhe on 11 March.[27] In the telegram Stalin exonerated the Siberian leaders while venting his usual rage against the 'less committed' lower level officials, blaming them for the decline in the procurement level. Nevertheless, he threatened the Siberian leaders and put their posts on the line by warning that if they did not 'do everything' to turn the situation around soon then things would be 'in a mess'. He was adamant that the crisis should not be solved by the import of grain, claiming that there was no hard currency to do that, and even if there was he believed that it was unacceptable to divert funds from industrialization and weaken the international position of the country. Stalin was exasperated by the worsening crisis: 'There is grain in the country, it is only necessary to know how to take it.' He believed that the idea of a forced loan was inappropiate because it amounted to outright confiscation and stressed twice that the krai leaders must take 'all legal paths' to repress the kulaks and secure a breakthrough.

After some hesitation, the central leadership embraced the Siberian proposals for a compulsory grain levy from the peasant *verkhushka*, for it gave a sense of immediacy to the plans of the Stalinist majority in the party for strict control of the countryside. Later, Stalin praised the new policy and coined the term 'Ural-Siberian method' to describe it at the April joint plenum of the Central Committee and Central Control Commission.[28] Possibly a Politburo commission, headed by Kaganovich, was established to review policy in the light of the Siberian proposal. In his telegram Stalin informed Syrtsov and Eikhe that he would shortly be sending Kaganovich to advise them on the measures to be taken to resolve the problem. In fact, Stalin's intentions were overtaken by events and the actual Politburo decision to adopt crisis measures and employ a new method of grain procurement was taken on 20 March, at Kaganovich's suggestion (see Document 3), and approved for immediate application in Kazakhstan, the Urals and Siberia at the Politburo session held the next day. This sequence of events was later confirmed by Tomsky at the April 1929 Central Committee plenum, where he noted that he, Bukharin and Rykov had been surprised by the Politburo's decision to endorse Kaganovich's proposal, coming so shortly after its rejection of Syrtsov's initiative.[29]

The new policy marked a new stage in the 'offensive against the kulak'. It was a radical departure from the emergency measures applied in early 1928 and transcended the programme of measures approved by the Central Committee in July 1928. Previous scholarship does not sufficiently disentangle the qualitatively new design of the Ural-Siberian method from the measures of 'social influence' (boycotts, tax supplements and so on) pursued after December 1928, and are particularly dismissive of the party's claim to have effected an upsurge of intra-communal strife in the villages.[30] The confusion arises because previous accounts are based on secondary, metropolitan Russian sources, the most important of which are central newspapers, journals and the stenogram of the Sixteenth Party Conference (23–29 April 1929): all of which are very ambivalent and muddled in distinguishing the new method of grain procurement from previous measures. As Tanuichi admitted, the historical literature on the 'Ural-Siberian method' has been profoundly incomplete because studies have been based on 'scattered information' in party publications and periodicals, rather than archival sources.[31]

Russian historians have been as equally confused as their Western counterparts on this subject. Moshkov claimed that two joint sessions of the Politburo and the Central Control Commission, meeting on 30 January and 9 February, took the decision to apply the 'Ural-Siberian method' in Eastern regions of the country. It was approved by a Central Committee plenum in February, and on 10 March a formal telegram-directive for the implementation of the method of 'social influence' in the grain campaign was sent to all republic and regional party organizations.[32] Vaganov more reliably reported that it was a motion (*predlozhenie*) from the party committees of the Urals and Siberia that first proposed to the Central Committee that the method of social pressure on kulaks used in the peasant self-taxation process be extended to grain procurement (although he does not give a date). This would tie in with the recommendations of the Kraikombiuro telegram of 27 February and the discussions at the Fourth Siberian Party Conference. The Siberian initiative at that point was not, however, as precise as Vaganov relates, focusing instead on the idea of a grain loan.[33]

The procedure of the new method was laid out in some detail and was clearly inspired by the Siberian telegram and *razverstka* method. Grain delivery plans were to be allocated to villages as compulsory duties (*tverdiie zadanii*) to the state, not by grain procurement representatives or organs of power but on the initiative of social organizations, *bednota* groups and actifs and, subsequently, promulgated by the general meeting of citizens. It was emphasized that the 'kulak *verkhushka*' should be separated out from the other peasants in order that most of the village plan be redistributed on to it. The assignment of grain delivery quotas to peasants in different social categories was a job to be left to either the general meeting (*obshee sobraniia*) or special commissions acting on its authority. No limit was established for the share of the plan to be distributed among kulaks, but whatever was left over was to be divided among the rest of the peasantry in accordance with self-taxation rates. The whole process was to be conducted in tandem with mass agitational-propaganda work by the party and the mobilization of what it termed 'proletarian social influence on the peasant masses', presumably a reference to the worker-brigades then roaming the countryside.

As is usual with executive meetings, no stenogram was kept of Politburo sessions and therefore we shall never know the exact details of leadership conflicts over the introduction of the new agrarian policy. The protocols of the Politburo record that on 25 March there was an unusually long debate on an agenda item relating to a commission headed by Mikoyan, where 23 senior figures spoke, including the 'Rightist' leaders Bukharin, Rykov and Tomsky. Whatever passed at this session, it was so sensitive that the subsequent decision was consigned to the 'special folder' (*osobaia papka* – files holding the Politburo's most secret deliberations). It may be that this was the session when the new policy towards the peasantry was debated.[34]

Vaganov recounts that Rykov was bitterly opposed to the new method, labelling it 'the worst type' of emergency measure. Apparently, Rykov and Bukharin countered by suggesting to the Politburo that grain imports be resumed, as they had during the 1927/8 crisis when about 200,000 tons had been purchased, and consumer grain supply norms be lowered temporarily as a cost-cutting measure. At the April plenum Stalin stated that Rykov had first proposed 'the import of 80–100 million puds' (approximately 1.3–1.6 million tons) at a cost of about 200 million roubles in hard currency. Later, the demand was decreased to half the amount. The idea of raising prices was raised and eventually Rykov was reduced to advocating the acceptance of foreign credits to pay for grain imports. The majority of the Politburo were unwilling to countenance such imports, regarding them as a squandering of precious hard currency reserves set aside to finance imports of capital equipment needed for the acceleration of industrialization as outlined in the Five Year Plan. The second proposition was rejected as too much of a belt-tightening emergency measure against grain consumers, while Stalin viewed the offer of credits as an international conspiracy against the Soviet Union by the capitalist powers. As far as Stalin was concerned it was 'better to pressurize the kulak and squeeze grain surpluses out of him, of which he has quite a bit, than to waste hard currency'.[35]

The conflict over peasant policy was a central component of the wider political dispute between the Right and Stalinist factions of the party leadership over the tempo of industrialization in variants of the Five Year Plan. It was precisely at this moment in time that Rykov's proposal for a diluted two-year industrialization plan was finally rejected as too moderate. In March–April 1929, the majority of the party leadership decided in favour of the Stalinist 'optimum' variant for rapid industrialization. The Stalinist variant was approved by the Central Committee plenum held on 16–23 April and ratified by the Sixteenth Party Conference which followed it.[36] What is indisputable is that the decision was taken against the stark background of a plummeting rate of grain procurement in Siberia – the region on which the regime depended for salvaging the annual grain plan. Despite repeated exhortations the rate of grain procurement fell sharply in each successive five-day working period of March, with an 8 per cent drop in the second, 9 per cent in the third and a startling 35 per cent registered in the fourth (16–20 March).[37] Undoubtedly, this decline, coupled with the pressure of time, jolted the Politburo into adopting the new method when it did.

The Politburo directive on grain procurement was relayed to the appropiate provinces and on 21 March the Kraikombiuro approved its own Directive No. 43 sanctioning the use of 'self-taxation methods' in the grain campaign and issued it to the okruzhkoms the following day. The protocol of the Kraikombiuro session noted that the Central Committee was to be informed about the 'measures of influence' taken against those peasants who did not comply with the 'self-taxation' in grain procurement.[38] The decree which formed the basis of Directive No. 43 was set out in the supplement to the protocol. The key section is in the first paragraph, where the Kraikombiuro instructed the okruzhkoms 'to impose compulsory tasks of procurement on individual villages by a voluntary procedure (at the initiative of the *bednota* actif)' (sic).[39]

The Siberian party leadership must have felt a mixture of disgust and relief at the change of tack in Moscow, for Kavraisky later implicitly attacked the hesitation at the centre when he spoke of the 'grandiose delay' in applying new methods, and claimed that the full Siberian grain plan would have been met if they had implemented the method sooner.[40] The decision was also not without opposition from within the Siberian apparatus. As late as 19 March the Krai Procurator, Lisin, had sent a report to Syrtsov detailing abuses of the 'basic principles of revolutionary legality' perpetrated by party officials against peasants. In particular, he highlighted three forms of abuse in grain procurement which contravened the Kraikom directive of 12 February banning any reversion to emergency measures.

First, in Chulymsk raion of Novosibirsk Okrug plenipotentiaries drew up lists of grain holders, carried out searches and on discovery of grain gave peasants three days to deliver it to a procurement point or face arrest.

Second, in Omsk Okrug there were cases of the application of Article 107 against peasants. Third, in the same okrug, in late February Omsk Okruzhkom and Okrispolkom had issued a joint directive on the new procedure for peasant self-taxation which declared: 'Above all else, in all those villages where self-taxation has not reached 50 per cent and at the same time there are grain surpluses, a decision of the rural soviet with the participation of the bedniak-seredniak actif may apply self-taxation of 50 per cent on kulaks and other well-off farms withholding grain surpluses.' Lisin regarded the latter as a blatant infringement of the law on self-taxation which stipulated that it be conducted through the general meeting of peasants, not through the state structure, and he reported that there had been innumerable complaints from well-off and seredniak peasants about this 'second tax'.[41]

Coming in the wake of directives prohibiting the application of emergency measures, the new policy must have initially added to the confusion in the localities where the distribution of compulsory grain delivery quotas to farms was often regarded as an illegal return to the civil war policy of *razverstka*. Slavgorod Okruzhkom, for example, had as recently as 16 March issued an order stating: 'It is absolutely forbidden to allocate control figures for procurement to different farms (reminiscent of *razverstka*).'[42] In contrast, a *bednota* meeting in the village of Ust'-Insk, Novosibirsk Okrug, was pressurized by a raiispolkom plenipotentiary to approve compulsory grain delivery quotas from 'malicious grain holders' as early as March 13.[43]

MORAL ECONOMY AND POLITICAL ECONOMY

The 'new method', the 'self-taxation method' or, more commonly, the 'measure of social influence' as the new policy was referred to in party documents (only Stalin called it the 'Ural-Siberian method') was much more sophisticated and ideologically more sound than the proposals for a 'forced grain loan' so vociferously advocated at the krai party conference. Significantly, it was very similar in concept to Krylov's proposal for a 'democratic *razverstka*' made at the conference and sharply criticized as too radical by Syrtsov. Now this upward current of radicalism 'from below' for a return to the methods of War Communism was given the approval of the Politburo. The responses of the Soviet government to the grain crisis of 1927–29 had powerful resonances with previous patterns of state–peasant relations in Russia. The key features of this peasant policy were composed in part of traces of the 'political folkways' or state traditions of medieval Muscovy, partly a direct continuation of the practices of the late Tsarist era and of Bolshevik policies in the civil war, and partly the resumption of experimental actions applied briefly during the grain emergency of 1927/8.

The move to a policy of social influence in the late 1920s has much in common with the debate over state grain procurement policies in 1914–21. The institutionalization of state coercion in grain procurement began in the late Imperial period, in 1914 with the onset of the First World War, with the establishment by the Minister of Agriculture, Aleksandr Krivoshein, of an apparatus of plenipotentiaries (*upolnomochennyie*) to act as commissioners for compulsory purchasing of agricultural products for the armed forces. Krivoshein appointed over 2,000 plenipotentiary agents, mainly from provincial *zemstvo* chairmen, and endowed them with extraordinary powers to regulate the rural market, set prices, requisition produce, and even to impose embargoes by cordoning off areas and coercing sales. Lih characterized this as the 'gubernatorial solution' to the problem of agricultural supplies, and contrasts it with the 'enlistment solution', an attempt from March 1917 by the Provisional Government to incorporate the peasants themselves into the process of procurement. The latter involved the creation of food supply committees and the mobilization of what Aleksandr Chayanov called a peasant 'army of ants' to assist the state procurement apparatus. This method was a more statist approach to controlling the countryside and involved the imposition of a state grain monopoly (*monopol'ka*), a countrywide grain register (*uchet*) and the setting of peasant consumer norms above which produce was to be sold to the state at fixed prices. The problem for the Provisional Government, however, was that in the conditions of revolutionary breakdown and chaos of 1917, there was not much of a Russian state operational that could enforce this method.[44]

The Bolshevik regime that came to power in October 1917 rested on an ideology that was statist by nature and praxis, and demanded intervention in every sector of economy and society. Moreover, given that the failure to guarantee a stable and cheap supply of bread to the cities had been a primary factor in the collapse of both its predecessor regimes, the new Bolshevik government considered it a priority task to make its writ effective in the countryside. The 'food supply dictatorship' established by a series of measures in the first half of 1918 aimed to enforce the state grain monopoly and it relied on a mixture of outright coercion and 'enlistment' of support from peasant communities. In fairly short order the initial promises of the October Revolution to liberate the peasants and give them land were betrayed in the course of 1918 by land nationalization (February), the establishment of the Kombedy (June) and the use of worker militias for requisitioning. The concept of engendering 'class war' and exploiting social divisions within the peasantry to achieve state goals and facilitate party control of the countryside was intrinsic to Bolshevik ideology in its civil war version. The *Kombedy* were created as part of the War Communism strategy, when the Bolsheviks made their first attempt to construct socialism rapidly.

Based on the experiences of grain collection in West Siberia in the spring of 1918, the Bolsheviks launched a two-pronged offensive against the countryside as part of a bloody 'class war' to get grain. Organizational wedges for infiltrating Soviet power into the countryside were created. A massive state procurement apparatus was formed under the auspices of Narkomprod, headed by Tsiurupa, and its militarized coercive arm, the food army (*prodarmiia*), utilized worker-militia blockade detachments (*zagraditel'nye otriady*), usually on railways but also on cordons on rural roads, to confiscate grain from 'speculators', whether urban 'sackmen' (*meshochniki*) or 'malicious kulaks' (loosely defined as any peasant with a surplus of grain). The ideological-political arm of the offensive sought to mobilize the village poor in committees (Kombedy) as a 'bulwark' (*opora*) of the state's tax-collecting apparatus and a lever that would split the peasant community. Both the decrees on commodity exchange (March) and the establishment of the Kombedy aimed to stir up social divisions in the peasantry by appealing to the rational self-interest of the poor by empowering them to inform on and root out kulaks, and giving them a material stake in the new order through nominal control of the distribution of manufactured goods and grain.[45]

By the summer of 1918 these measures had failed to yield the state adequate grain supplies and a more refined method emerged after experiments during a procurement campaign in Viatka Province. The new method entailed the levying of compulsory delivery quota assessments on particular areas (*prodovol'stvennaia razverstka* or *prodrazverstka*). Approximate delivery targets were set by procurement officials which were then redistributed to areas and villages. Local officials were issued quotas as compulsory duties or tasks (failure meant removal and punishment) and they dealt through the village commune leadership, imposing collective responsibility on villages for the fulfilment of delivery quotas. The Kombedy were also awarded material incentives for their collaboration as agents of the state in the collection process. Accurate quota assessments would have required a thorough registration of grain stocks household by household (*podvorny*), but as this was too cumbersome and would prolong the campaign, rough assessments were levied village by village (*posel'nyi*). Inevitably, the absence of a targeting mechanism in this method meant that the mass of peasants were affected. The peasants regarded this method with great hostility and recognized it as an arbitrary state tax-in-kind of the worst kind. It was wholly differentiated from the indirect sales taxes imposed by the Tsarist regime by its visibility, and unlike the Provisional Government the Bolsheviks had made the state operational in the countryside once more. Bolshevik faith in 'class war' among the Russian peasantry did not last beyond November 1918 when the Kombedy, seen more as a hindrance than a help, were dissolved in Russia (in fact, they were never introduced in Siberia). Eventually, peasant revolts forced the Soviet government to abandon *razverstka* for a less punitive food tax in February 1921, as part of the introduction of NEP and the resurrection of market relations.[46]

The *razverstka* procedure has been stigmatized as a reversion to the 'Chinese–Mongol system' of state–peasant relations. Historically, the Great Moscow Prince collected a tribute (*vykhod*, later *dan'*) for the Golden Horde which was a poll tax exacted, through other princes, from the peasantry in the form of compulsory delivery levies of agricultural produce. Contrary to popular belief, the Mongol empire was interested in the long-term management of the extraction of wealth and services from its subject peoples, including those of Rus'. As the Mongol empire expanded this tax system was attuned to Russian conditions of imperialism by proxy. This required precise plans based on census returns (*chislo*), and 'inquisitions', registering people and property (*pistsovye knigi*), which were broken down and distributed among districts, villages, communes and households. Mongol taxes, like those of most nomadic steppe peoples, were progressive (proportional to the wealth of the payee) and levied on the basis of collective responsibility (*krugovaia poruka*) of the whole community – a logical response to their environment. When the Moscow princes threw off the 'Tatar yoke' in the fourteenth century emancipation for the peasantry did not follow, as many Mongol institutions and practices were retained. For administrative convenience, continuity and fiscal efficiency, the Muscovy *samoderzhets* kept the peasantry shackled to the principle of collective responsibility for the payment of state taxes, and to this can be traced the origins of restrictions on peasant movement, the tied peasant commune and serfdom. Moreover, Russian peasant common law (*obychnoe pravo*) continued to adhere to the practice of distributing outside material burdens imposed on the whole community on the basis of the principle of proportionality, that is to say progressively, according to ability to pay (*po sile*). This fundamental principle was the core element of the moral economy of the Russian peasant. From it evolved the levelling redistributional land commune, and a mesh of peasant social norms constructed around equity and reciprocity. Even though Stolypin's reforms ended the legal *poruka* of the commune for state taxes the custom continued. These fiscal factors largely explain the close bonds of interdependency embodied in the Russian peasant commune, its ubiquitous peasant institutionalized jealousy, and the obsession with *raventsvo* (social equality).[47]

It was this inheritance of state traditions and an ancient peasant moral economy that Stalin invoked and reasserted when he used the word 'tribute' at the July 1928 plenum of the Central Committee to encapsulate the essence of his new approach to the peasantry and grain collection. The social influence method fully accorded with the traditions of state–peasant relations in Russia. The registration of property and people is a vital instrument of state control and resource mobilization and distribution in any society but the new method drew on the ancient Russian customary law which made the commune (and via it the peasant community) legally responsibile for state taxation, peasant self-taxation and self-government. For centuries the Russian state had relied on the moral authority of the commune over the peasantry and the new Bolshevik policy merely locked into the traditional function of the commune for collecting material burdens and extended it to the collection of a progressive state duty on the peasantry to supply grain. It had long been a slogan of the Bolsheviks that the kulak was a *miroed*, a devourer of the commune – a viewpoint strongly determined by the hegemony exercised by the wealthy peasant elite over the commune. By acknowledging the persistence of peasant tradition in order to implement the social influence method the party implicitly recognized that its policy of supplanting the authority of the commune by rural soviets, pursued since the revolution, had failed.[48]

In this situation it made sense to exploit the enduring cultural hold of the commune on the peasant psyche, particularly since the periodic redistribution and levelling practices in land tenure that characterized the traditional commune were increasingly abandoned during NEP. The status quo in land tenure in the countryside coupled with the impact of commercialization was an affront to the moral economy that left a large stratum of peasants disaffected. Now the party was trying to wrest control of the commune away from local peasant elites and subvert it from within by mobilizing support from peasants, in particular poor peasants, for ancient moral economy notions of equality and communitarianism.

The social influence policy was a refinement of the War Communism *razverstka* model, but as the symbolism of its name suggested, it evoked an ideological emphasis on mobilization and incorporation of the poor peasant commmunity as an arm of the state. Both policies were introduced at a time of crisis to secure food supplies for the central industrial regions, cities and armed forces. When the concession of NEP guaranteeing free trade to the peasants was finally undone in March 1929, it was by returning to a policy of *razverstka* but this time targeting it against the kulaks. Like the Kombedy, the *bednota* actifs of early 1929 were formed under the guidance of local soviets and party plenipotentiaries. Both were established to act as agents of the state in grain collection. In the same way that during *prodrazverstka* 'ill-will was created in the countryside and neighbour began to fear neighbour' so did the 'social influence' method of grain procurement exacerbate social tensions. The description provided by the early Soviet historian, A.M. Bol'shakov, of the conduct of *prodrazverstka* in 1918–19 could just as easily apply to grain collection in March–April 1929 in Siberia:

> The central authorities calculated how much of various exactions in their opinion could be collected from the entire country ... this total was broken down or allocated by guberniyas; the guberniyas made uezd allocations taking into account their economic situation; the latter made allocations for each volost', and these for settlements. In the settlements a gathering of the heads of households determined who had to pay and how much. Since all were bound by a collective responsibility, by mutual surety, and there was no possibility of reducing the amount of the requisition, these gatherings were exceedingly noisy and sometimes even ended in blows: everyone wanted to pay as little as possible, but then his neighbour would have to pay more.[49]

This comment indicates that not only moral economy notions were at work, but also that peasant responses were rational and risk minimizing. In such circumstances, it was the village elite who had most to lose, and who were naturally most distressed by the new policy. They had benefited most from state directed attempts to modernize agriculture through marketizing rural society in the generation after Stolypin's reforms, and their economic power had surged ahead under NEP. The primary purpose of the mobilization of the rural poor was to assist the state in extracting grain surpluses from kulaks and the well-off in return for a share of the grain at cheap prices. On the other hand, although the militarization of grain procurement organization assumed a higher status after March 1929, the scale of operation of armed requisition detachments did not reach the levels of August–September 1918. Nevertheless, the notion of compulsory allocation of village plans and household compulsory delivery quotas was, whatever the party chose to call it, a direct reversion to the *razverstka* crisis measures of the civil war and to Russia's feudal past.

4 The Ural-Siberian Method

THE 'ZAV'IALOVO EXPERIMENT'

By itself the decision in Kraikom Directive No. 43 to borrow the peasant self-taxation process for grain procurement was still only semi-precise, though the okruzhkoms no doubt were jolted into action by the decision given that it had the stamp of authority of the Politburo. As a consciousness-raising exercise for the party as to the rationale for the new method and the procedural practicality of its implementation, on 22 March *Sovetskaia sibir'* carried a leading story about the use of the method of 'social influence' in the village of Zav'ialovo, Novosibirsk Okrug, under the headline: 'Bedniaks and seredniaks make the kulak well-off element in the countryside sell grain surpluses to the state.' The time had come, it went on, to 'stop nannying the kulak' and 'begging him to sell grain'. That this story was dreamt up as a propaganda exercise is suggested not just by the fact that its content was a tissue of lies but also that OGPU and Novosibirsk Okruzhkom reports on the implementation of the 'new method' nowhere discuss the events in this supposedly prototypical village.[1]

The newspaper article emphasized that the process was a spontaneous 'local initiative' by the peasants themselves without the involvement of either the state authorities or procurement agencies. It was claimed that the village community (*sel'skaia obshchestvennost'*) of Zav'ialovo decided to force kulaks to deliver grain immediately by 'applying self-taxation at a five times rate against malicious grain holders'. A village commission to assist with grain procurement, composed of poor and middle peasants, was elected by the *skhod*. It drew up lists of kulaks and large-scale grain holders and then divided up the bulk of the grain procurement plan for the village amongst them. The commission allocated compulsory grain delivery tasks (*tverdiie zadaniia*) for individual households to provide at state prices, with a quota of 65 to 70 per cent of the total plan levied on kulaks and well-off households and 30 to 35 per cent on the poor and middle peasants. Refusal to comply incurred a fine of five times the original amount (the guilty being branded *piatikratniki*), and failure to settle accounts could lead to the seizure of all or part of a farm's property or arrest.

The new method was presented as a 'brilliant' alternative form of 'direct action' to emergency measures. The attitude of the kulaks in Zav'ialovo had been: 'Emergency measures have been revoked, if I want to – I will sell, if I want to – I will let it rot.' Indeed, at first they had not taken the

Table 4.1 The *piatikratniki*: registrations and compulsory auctions of peasant property in Siberia (March–May 1929)

Okrug sample	Households registered	Number of auctions	Amount raised (roubles)
Biisk	1,047	750	218,100
Irkutsk	566	168	130,856
Kamen'[1]	1,264	581	130,376
Omsk[2]	1,419	435	184,198
Slavgorod[3]	153	70	47,091

1. 11/13 raions.
2. 21/22 raions.
3. 6/13 raions.

Source: GANO 2, f. 2, op. 2, d. 386, l. 273–6.

new method seriously at all, thinking it '*ocherednoe puzhanie*' (loosely translated as 'the last thing to worry about it'). Once the fines began to be applied, however, they took notice. Indeed, often they had to buy back grain they had sold on the private market to meet their delivery obligations. The directive received a mixed response in the localities. A Kamensk raikom (Novosibirsk Okrug) plenum on 22–23 March warmly applauded the new method, seeing in it the only way to achieve their plan. Other lower level party bodies remained unsure, however, as to exactly how they were to proceed. This confusion is illustrated by a 'service note' sent to Syrtsov on 25 March by one raikom plenipotentiary in charge of grain procurement and the 'operational *troika*'.[2] It included a copy of the raikom directive on procurement issued the previous day and asked Syrtsov to clarify whether 'any paragraphs of this instruction are incompatible with the directive "No Application of Emergency Measures"'. This confusion on the ground may have been one of the factors in the lack of consistency with which the new policy was applied. The key grain areas of Omsk, Biisk, Kamen' and Slavgorod, for example, had wide discrepancies in both the registration of kulak property for non-fulfilment and the auctioning of the property. The stringency of application was also not clearly related to the significance of grain production in an area as Irkutsk (a minor grain area) far exceeded Slavgorod in its application of the policy (See Table 4.1).

The raikom directive evidently took the Zav'ialovo method as its model and ordered that the grain plan was to be adopted 'on the initiative of the population itself, without any official participation of grain procurement

The Ural-Siberian Method

agencies and official government bodies'. This was to be achieved by the following procedure. Party and Komsomol cells would hold joint meetings to establish an 'initiative group' from seredniak and bedniak activists. This actif would then call a meeting of poor peasants and seredniaks who had sold their whole grain surplus, together with members of the soviet, village party cell and other activists, presumably to organize a caucus. Finally, a general meeting of enfranchised peasants was to convene and select a commission consisting of three, five or seven persons whose duty it was to allocate fixed grain delivery quotas on kulak and well-off grain holders who were to be given the greatest part of the village plan, the remainder being distributed among other peasants with grain surpluses. A ten-day period for completion was set (in any case no later than 10 April) and in the absence of a quorum for the general meeting 'any quantity of persons present will do'.

The latter stipulation indicated a singular lack of confidence by this raikom in the party's capacity to mobilize peasant support for this method of procurement, for after all the law of 10 January 1928 amending self-taxation procedures had accepted as a legal quorum for meetings of enfranchised peasants an attendance of only one-third of those eligible, if an earlier meeting had failed to produce a quorum of one half.[3] In other words, the raikom anticipated that activists might fail to secure the minimum quorum of supportive peasants and empowered *any* group of voting peasants, however small, to impose the new method on their entire community. In the event of non-fulfilment of the fixed quotas the commission or soviet was to impose a fine, within five days and without any right of appeal, of up to five times the value of the grain and no less than twice the value. If peasants failed to pay the fine the soviet was to seize property in lieu. Throughout the process, the raikom emphasized, work should be accompanied by intensive agitation and propaganda, 'proletarian social influence' and a 'careful and deliberate class attitude' with no distortions or excesses tolerated.

In Ust'-Insk, Novosibirsk Okrug, an extended meeting of the rural soviet with plenipotentiaries, activists and representatives of social organizations heard complaints from grain procurement workers that it was impossible for them to go to every peasant farm in search of grain. A list of those with the largest surpluses was essential to expedite collection of the village plan, and this could only be drawn up by those with local knowledge and in consultation with the *bednota*. A *bednota* meeting was convened to assist with the list and later a general meeting was called to discuss and formally sanction the new method. This meeting fulfilled its quorum as more than half the enfranchised peasants attended (197 out of

384) and a *troika* was elected from the poor peasants to distribute the village grain delivery plan on a 'class basis', primarily on the *verkhushka*. In all 33 peasants were to be issued with a warrant (*putievka*) obliging them to deliver a total of about 19 tons grain (well above the village plan) by 5 April or face five times fines.[4]

The Siberian historian, Gushchin, relates how the new method was conducted without the preliminary distribution of grain quotas in the village of Golumet', Cheremkhovsk raion, Irkutsk Okrug. It began with a bedniak meeting, probably under the supervision of party plenipotentiaries and activists, which 'unmasked' a 'kulak group' of seven farms which had not sold grain and were supposedly fomenting resistance to state procurement operations. The matter was taken before the *skhod* which passed a resolution that seems to reflect more the thinking and wording of a party plenipotentiary than the peasants, declaring: 'The aforementioned group consists of the most malicious non-sellers of grain, who are affected neither by boycott or other measures of pressure. They are wrecking not only the procurement plan, but also the *smychka* between town and country.' The *skhod* ordered that they be penalized with a five times fine.[5]

MOSCOW INTERVENES

Once the central party leadership had decided to act on the Siberian initiative it forcefully intervened to directly supervise the implementation of the new grain procurement process. On 25 March a telegram giving general endorsement of the Kraikombiuro directive arrived from Mikoyan (see Document 4). Mikoyan approved the decision to allocate the remainder of the plan as compulsory duties on whole villages, with the general meetings of peasant voters or special committees dominated by the bedniak-seredniak actifs distributing the bulk of the grain plan on to the kulaks and well-off. He recognized this was perhaps the only way left to complete the increased Siberian grain plan (estimated at 540,000 tons at the krai party conference), plus a special task of an additional 57,000 tons in July.[6]

Stalin now despatched Kaganovich to consult with the Siberian leaders, with the clear intention of refining the new technique, and on 27 March he attended a session of the Kraikombiuro where the main agenda was taken up by a discussion of the new policy. Kaganovich suggested significant amendments to the Kraikombiuro decree of 22 March, emphasizing the need to continue with economic measures of influence (debt collection, self-taxation and so on), recommending that the commissions elected by village meetings operate on a regular basis (henceforth, they were to be the formal organizational lever of party control in the countryside), proposing the establishment of 'shock villages' that would serve as a model for others in grain collection, and highlighting the need to focus on class differentiation in the villages when the grain plan was being distributed so that the kulaks would bear the brunt of the burdens. His most shocking addition, however, was that trials be organized in the countryside on the basis of Article 61 of the RSFSR Criminal Code. This article covered the rather dubious offence of 'non-fulfilment of compulsory state duties', but much as Article 107 had been prior to the crisis of early 1928, it had not been designed for use against the peasantry. Article 61 was eventually formally amended on 28 June by the addition of a new clause 3 which specifically cited 'refusal to deliver grain' as a criminal offence (see Chapter 6), but Kaganovich had preempted this move by three months.[7]

To see for himself how things were going on the ground, Kaganovich then went on a tour of two key grain areas, Rubtsovsk and Barnaul okrugs, where he visited Chistiun raion with Nusinov, Barnaul Okruzhkom Secretary. Here, he made further adjustments in a resolution of Barnaul Okruzhkombiuro on 31 March, with the aim of reconciling the main goal of taking grain with the party's stated ideological commitment to the peasant masses and the requirement of avoiding general peasant unrest. In a letter to Syrtsov on 1 April he disclosed how it had become clear to him during his rural inspection that insufficient attention had been paid to the accuracy of the actual plan distribution process in the villages. 'If we allocate formally 300–400 puds to each farm', he noted, 'which it cannot meet, we fool ourselves and the grain will not turn up – we need a realistic accounting.' There had to be a tightening up of the whole process by the keeping of accurate lists of who held grain and how much. He also suggested that it would be better to 'separate out the kulaks' from the well-off peasantry in order to sharpen the focus of the attack by subjecting them to additional burdens. To minimize general protests he appealed to the self-interest of the mass of peasants by making it a requirement that the kulak and well-off share of the whole village grain task amount to no less than 50 per cent of the total.

Kaganovich observed that the *piatikratniki* were greatly antagonizing the countryside, mainly because they were levied in an arbitrary manner extra-judicially by village commissions and rural soviets. A decision through the courts on the basis of Article 61, he believed, would be much more acceptable to the peasants and would also enable the party to exercise more control over the whole matter to prevent it from taking on a mass character. As for the inclusion of bedniak activists in the special commissions, he advised that they should be induced to participate not just in the allocation of the grain plan but also in the collection and completion of tasks. This would ensure a confrontation between different social strata within the villages. All of these additional refinements proposed by Kaganovich in Barnaul were included verbatim in a Kraikom instruction-letter sent by Kavraisky to the okruzhkoms on 2 April.[8]

The Chairman of the Krai Judicial Department, Branetsky, was reluctant to embrace Kaganovich's cavalier approach to the law and in late March he sent a memorandum to the Kraikom complaining about the method of stimulating grain procurement by 'judicial repressions' and other 'exceptional measures', often under the cover of a struggle against 'counter-revolution'.[9] Despite this opposition the new line was imposed on the judicial officials, and a new emphasis on the use of Article 61 was reflected in a directive from the Krai Judicial Department and Krai Procuracy to their okrug departments on 5 April. This advised that while the 'main repressive blow must be made on social grounds', by self-obligation and non-fulfilment of social duties incurring a five times fine of grain withheld, Article 61 should be reserved for cases of the 'most severe' kind where a demonstration of the 'correctness' of party policy was required for the local population. A final clarification from the Kraikom followed on 9 April which specified that the auctioning off of sequestered goods in lieu of grain was to be conducted on the basis of Article 271 of the Criminal Code.[10]

The problem of defining who the kulak households were was addressed by a special 'instruction' from the Krai Financial Department, which attempted to draw together various definitions and exclusions in party and government decrees in order to delineate those kulak farms that could be subjected to supplementary taxes (and by definition grain quotas). The instruction provided specific examples of types of farm and rural economic activities to illustrate its categories.[11] A TsIK USSR decree of 8 February 1929 had categorically prohibited the levying of supplementary taxes on seredniak households, thus the primary defining feature of the 'clear kulak' farms was established as 'unearned [*netrudovoi*] income' from exploitatory activities. This ruled out peasants who had very high incomes, as long as the income was derived from their own labour or non-exploitatory activities. It also supposedly offered some protection to peasants who had previously been labelled 'kulak' by arbitrary decisions of officials: because they had decreased their sowings, hired batraks in the past, had a 'kulak setup', and so forth. A Kraiispolkom decree of 27 March had designated the 'clear-kulak' household as one which, although outwardly a peasant farm, was engaged in, or individuals who were members of the household were involved in, the buying and selling of products, trade and usury; or, if the farm engaged in the 'systematic exploitation' of the *bednota* and seredniaks, through use of grain, money and agricultural machines, and industrial enterprises. Special conditions were applied to the production of handicrafts; for example, such farms were exempt from the kulak category if they worked solely with family labour.[12] Such detailed categorization was part of the carefully drafted attempt by the party's policymakers to surgically isolate the kulak element in the countryside, but in practice, such complicated instructions were unlikely to be adhered to by officials on the ground whose function was to implement policies in the villages, like grain and tax collection, as quickly as possible.

STALIN AND BUKHARIN ON THE 'URAL-SIBERIAN METHOD'

When the joint plenum of the Central Committee and Central Control Commission convened on 16–23 April 1929, immediately prior to the Sixteenth Party conference, it was the forum for the final recriminations between Stalin and Bukharin over the abandonment of NEP in everything but name. Despite the outward consensus, from the summer of 1928 Bukharin viewed Stalin's peasant policy as extremely dangerous, telling the disgraced Kamenev in secret conversations that Stalin was pushing policies which were 'leading to civil war' and 'War Communism and death'.[13] Bukharin's speech to the April 1929 plenum was a last gasp impassioned defence of NEP and denunciation of the use of emergency measures as a way of squaring the circle between the competing demands of industrial growth and grain prices. He castigated the Stalinist faction for their state of seige mentality in 'closing off all our exits and entrances'. Bukharin reserved his most sarcastic and ascerbic remarks for Stalin's clients in the inner circle of the party leadership (Molotov, Ordzhonikidze, Mikoyan, Kaganovich, *et al.*), picking them off one by one like targets in a shooting gallery. Unrealistically, he expected Stalin to accept that his use of the 'illiterate and harmful' theoretical construct of 'tribute' was a 'slip of the tongue'. Drawing a line between Leninism and Stalinism, he observed: 'Lenin had nothing comparable to the Stalinist tribute from the peasants'. As for the new social influence policy, Bukharin bluntly termed this 'a new application of extraordinary measures, including *razverstka* from the middle peasant'. For Bukharin the answer to the dilemma of economic development of whether to prioritize 'metal or grain' was to do both in proportion. This provoked cries of 'eclecticism' and 'dualism' from the Stalinists.[14]

In his speech, 'On the Right Deviation in the VKP(b)', Stalin countered by an all-out attack on the Right's misplaced faith in kulak economic power and proclaimed his enthusiasm for the new peasant policy before a wide party audience. It was then that Stalin coined the term the 'Ural-Siberian method', and he seized upon it as the mechanism to give reality to his promise at the July 1928 plenum of the Central Committee to levy a grain 'tribute' on the peasantry.[15] Stalin's speech was a typical display of demagogic brilliance from the *vozhd*, in its simplistically concise explanation of the politics of the continuing grain procurement difficulties, and its vaudevillian derision of Bukharin and Rykov and their supporters. Stalin noted that the development of a new approach to the grain problem had two causes. First, the serious harvest failure in the Ukrainian steppe and parts of the North Caucasus, the Central Black-Earth Zone and the North-Western Oblast meant a 500–600 million pud shortfall in the gross grain harvest compared with the previous year (itself a bad year). Inevitably, the party leadership looked to the East, to the Urals, Siberia and Kazakhstan, as they had done during the crisis of 1927/8 to make good the deficit.

The second problem was the persistence of opposition by kulak elements to the state procurement policy, a factor that the Right, according to Stalin, were prone to pass over in their analyses but which was central to understanding the political situation in the country. The state required approximately 8.2 million tons of grain to feed the towns, factories, Red Army and technical crop areas but at best only 5.7 million tons had been raised by regulated market methods using fixed state prices. The experience of the past two years had demonstrated that the shortfall could only be taken by what he called 'organized pressure' on the kulaks and the well-off peasants. The 'psychology of spontaneous flow' (*samotek*), which for Stalin was synonymous with market forces, had to be eliminated as a 'harmful and dangerous thing', especially since the kulaks regarded their grain as 'the currency of all currencies' and would only part with it for high prices which the state could not afford.

Stalin evidently had decided that there was no other option but to return to a more militant policy towards the peasantry. At the same time, he wanted to avoid openly supporting a resurrection of the *chrezvychaishchina* that had characterized party actions in the countryside following his Siberian tour of January 1928, a position from which he had been compelled to retreat by political weakness in the face of opposition from Bukharin and Rykov during the summer of 1928.[16] He wanted the assortment of *ad hoc* coercive measures which had been applied then to extract grain to be refined, regularized and systematized. The advantage of the 'Ural-Siberian method' was that it provided a political cover for ongoing state repression in the countryside to maximize grain procurement, while allowing Stalin to claim that it was an ideologically sound policy centred, with some justification, on the mobilization of the 'social support' of the bedniak-seredniak mass of peasants for state measures against the kulak. The organization by the party of the power of this political reservoir, a 'multi-million political army' was how Stalin referred to it, constituted 'one of the most important, if not the most important result of the Ural-Siberian Method'. The message was clear: if this political army of poor and middle peasants could be successfully orchestrated into squeezing the kulaks in order to intensify grain procurement by the state, then they could be directed along similar lines to realize other goals set by the party in its attempt to manage and control the countryside, namely collectivization and dekulakization.[17]

Bukharin dismissed this view as 'monstrously one-sided' and a 'clear overestimation of the possibility of influencing the basic mass of peasants' – something which could only be achieved, he argued, by 'market relations'.[18] The utter scorn with which Stalin addressed his erstwhile opponents Bukharin and Rykov in this speech reveals just how far the political balance in the party leadership had tilted in his favour over the previous year. When at the July 1928 Central Committee plenum Bukharin warned: 'if this proletarian government forces the muzhik into the commune . . . then you will get this result, you will get a muzhik revolt that will be harnessed by the kulak', Stalin's response was restrained to a sarcastic jibe, citing the old Russian proverb: 'Terrible is the dream, but merciful is God.'[19] At the November 1928 plenum his impatience was wearing thin and a proposal from Rykov to increase state grain prices produced the following outburst: 'The point is not to cuddle up to the peasant and see in that the establishment of improved relations with him, for you won't go far on a cuddle.'[20]

Now, he openly mocked the 'comical howling' from Bukharin and Rykov about the effects of party policy in the countryside. During the political showdown in the Politburo in February, Bukharin and Rykov had gloomily described the party's 'overburdening' of the peasantry with taxes as tantamount to 'military-feudal exploitation'.[21] Stalin now seized the opportunity to hit back at their 'most popular line' – constant nagging about 'excesses' and emergency measures. 'But what is bad about that? Why is it forbidden to sometimes, in certain conditions, apply emergency measures against our class enemy, against the kulaks?' he asked. It seemed to him quite illogical that the Right should accept the arrest and deportation to the remote Turukhansk Krai of Siberia of hundreds of urban speculators, yet defend the kulaks and believe the 'horrors' told in peasant letters of complaint about the grain campaign. Stalin was outraged by their attitude: 'but from the kulaks, speculating in grain and trying to seize the Soviet government by the throat and enslave the *bednota*, is it forbidden to take grain surpluses by the process of social pressure at state prices at which the bedniaks and seredniaks had already sold grain to our procurement organisations?' He was irritated by the complete rejection of his new policies and refusal on principle of Bukharin and his associates to countenance the use of emergency measures. The Rightist position was set out by Tomsky, who rejected the Stalinists' talk of a '"new" *smychka*', declaring: 'there is nothing new here, but there are emergency measures and ration books.'[22]

Exactly one year before, at the April 1928 plenum of the Central Committee, Stalin had spoken in a similar tone and raised many of the same issues; the difference now was that he named names and was unrestrained in his attacks on the Right. In April 1928 he had generated a burst of derisory laughter and applause by denouncing an unnamed party member (by innuendo Bukharin) as 'not a Marxist but a fool' for thinking that 'we can conduct a policy in the countryside that will please everyone, both the rich and the poor'. Now he felt that his leadership was secure enough to publicly brand Bukharin's position as a 'bourgeois-liberal policy, and not a Marxist policy'.[23] Moreover, the attempt by the Right to compare the 'social influence' method with the Kombedy of the civil war (a policy which Lenin had abandoned as anarchic and unworkable) was an exaggeration, for as far as Stalin was concerned it was 'not even a drop in the ocean in comparison with the policy of the Kombedy'. The suggestion was that the new approach was a rather soft way of dealing with the peasantry.

The ideological breach between Stalinists and the Right had been personalized since the summer of 1928, but this was the first plenum of the wider party leadership where the bitter and irreparable nature of the schism was openly broadcast.[24] Stalin repeatedly stressed the theme of the Right's political naiveté in hoping that the kulaks would sell grain voluntarily at state prices. 'Have they gone mad?' he goaded, for as far as he was concerned they did not 'understand the mechanics of class struggle' and had lost all sense of political reasoning and insight into the peasant question. In recounting a parable about a party procurement worker who was asked to dance for a few pud of grain by a kulak in Kazakhstan, Stalin was delivering the ideological message in his inimitable folksy and pseudo-biblical style that this was a class war and the kulaks could not be negotiated with: 'Yes, comrades, class is class. You cannot get away from this truth.' The time had come to put an end to the Bukharin group's 'chattering about excesses' in grain procurement once and for all, argued Stalin, because this masked their real political intent which was an 'opportunistic line', a 'deviation', designed to use the cases of excesses to reverse the new policy and return to the concept of peaceful 'growing together' (*srastanie*) of state and peasant. A current of radicalism flowed throughout Stalin's speech as he desensitized the party leaders to the need for harsh measures and he brusquely declared: 'Name even one political measure of the party which was not accompanied by some or other excess.' The repeat of the grain crisis, the response of the Siberians and other party organizations, and the success of the new policy of 'social influence' in securing grain, supported Stalin's analysis of a radical dynamic from below supportive of a more militant anti-kulak drive. This must have been confirmed in his mind by the speeches of regional party leaders at the plenum and, later, by delegates at the Sixteenth Conference.

BREADWINNERS

At the April 1929 plenum, Syrtsov delivered a highly critical speech against the Right, focusing in particular on its failure to recognize that kulak economic growth now posed a real threat to Soviet power which required a reevaluation of NEP. While dismissing the rumours of peasant uprisings in Siberia which circulated in Moscow, he accepted that there had been 'massive excesses' in the campaign in Siberia, but he put these down to the 'low quality' of lower levels of the party apparatus and to delays in Moscow over the introduction of the new policy. He even suggested that Bukharin was simply misinformed about the countryside and might reassess his views if he was sent into the countryside on party work for two or three months.[25]

The annotated commentary to the 1962 edition of the Sixteenth Conference stenogram confusingly implies a synonymity between the 'Ural-Siberian method' and the emergency measures of 1927/28, such as Article 107, locating both in the 1928/9 campaign. Furthermore, some speakers with inside knowledge, including Syrtsov and Eikhe (see below), consistently referred to the new policy as 'the measure of social influence', but others were unable to distinguish anything new at all. Kuibyshev disclosed that a Central Committee decision had ordered the application of the new 'manoeuvre' against kulaks in certain areas only – Urals, Kazakhstan, Siberia – to 'soften the difficulties' in grain procurement. Khloplyankin, Lower Volga Kraikom Second Secretary, could not discern anything new in what had transpired and disputed the Siberian's claim to an important initiative. He attempted to stake out a share of the credit for overcoming the crisis, asserting that 'this method of social influence was applied by us as well', to which Eikhe responded: 'later, later'. Khloplyankin clearly did not understand that the new method was an extension of the other measures of social influence (boycotts, tax supplements) which his region had been applying since February.[26]

Khloplyankin's party chief, Sheboldaev, described how the application of Article 107 had been abandoned for the use of 'financial levers' against kulaks, and these had developed into the method of social influence. In this way, he declared, 'from month to month we "grew into" emergency measures' (a pun on Bukharin's phrase about the kulaks 'growing into' socialism which provoked laughter in the hall). He differentiated the emergency measures applied last year 'by the state' with the emergency measures conducted this year 'by a social process' – the only common feature was that both applied 'extreme pressure on the kulak'. Namelessly denigrating the opposition of moderates, like Bukharin and Rykov, he observed how some comrades 'propose therefore that last year we had law and order, but now tyranny [*proizvol*, a term associated with the arbitrary justice despatched by the pre-revolutionary gentry] and licence [*samoupravstvo*]'. Sheboldaev recognized that many party members were baffled and proceeded to explain how the core concept of the new approach was the controlled devolution of power to rural communities to act as agents for the state in the war against the kulaks: 'Comrades do not understand this, that the community [*obshchestvennost'*] is the main guarantee for the correctness of measures applied. In this the state only exerts an influence on the carrying out of those community decisions which are adopted.'[27]

In their conference speeches Syrtsov and Eikhe strove to justify the 'new method' and demolish the argument of the Right to the effect that they had 'achieved practically nothing'. Eikhe provided statistical evidence to demonstrate the correlation between the surge in grain procurement and the decision to change policy (though he used the Kraikom estimates in a rather confused manner). Whereas almost 10,000 tons were procured after the third five-day period of March, at a time when sleigh roads still operated, the first five-day period of April saw the amount rise to over 26,000 tons. For the period 1–20 April over 75,000 tons came in (with an estimated additional amount of upwards of 50,000 tons stockpiled in remote procurement points). It was an unprecedented amount for this time of year, and this was during an unusually early spring thaw which turned rural roads to mud and hindered shipment (see Table 4.2). Eikhe proudly boasted: 'Never in the past did we procure as much grain in April' and 'We got the grain, although certain comrades allege that we only got bad results.' As for the criticism that the new policy amounted to nothing more

Table 4.2 A comparison of procurement levels in Siberia in March–April 1928 and 1929 (in tons)

Five-day period	1928 March	1928 April	1928 May	1929 March	1929 April	1929 May
1–5	41,236	18,509	721	18,346	27,273	7,879
6–10	31,728	8,092	2,408	16,921	19,672	9,550
11–15	29,287	3,685	2,195	15,332	14,742	7,895
16–20	28,632	2,162	2,309	10,057	14,742	5,340
21–25	23,604	1,671	4,947	13,202	15,594	—
26–31	30,647	1,212	7,322	18,903	11,581	—

Source: GANO 2, f. 2, op. 2, d. 386, l. 292–3, Supplement No. 1 of Kraikom Information-Statistical Department Report, 30 May 1930.

than the party 'acquiring citizen's methods of *chrezvychaishchina*', Eikhe retorted that this was a 'panic' response for the experience of Siberia demonstrated that the main blow fell on the kulak and the increase in the sown area of seredniaks and bedniaks proved that they were satisfied with the party's conduct of grain campaigns.[28]

For someone outside the top ranks of the party leadership, Syrtsov's speech was quite long and imbued with unusual *gravitas* and self-confidence in addressing the key issues of the day – a sign that he was about to be coopted into the top leadership.[29] It was also littered with the kind of anti-kulak militancy that went down well with Stalin, but which was inconsistent with Syrtsov's erstwhile moderation in his Siberian speeches on the peasant question. Indeed, just a few weeks previous to this, at the Fourth Siberian Party Conference, he had robustly condemned sentiments similar to those he now expressed. The kulaks, he declared, could not be overcome by agreement. They raised political issues and demanded machines, civil rights and an end to the new methods which left them 'politically isolated' in the villages. Some resorted to violence. Their share of marketed grain had risen from about 22 per cent at the outset of the campaign to extend to the 'basic mass of marketable grain' by March. They owned approximately 36 per cent of local industries and some government decrees easing their access to machines were a 'lifejacket' to them. Whereas some stood on the platform 'to increase production do not hinder the kulaks', Syrtsov argued that their economic power would be translated into a political threat: 'Every free pud of their grain will become a weapon against Soviet power.' At the Siberian party conference Syrtsov had denounced Krylov's call for a 'democratic *razverstka*' as out of step, wild and muddled; now he himself grasped the the kulak nettle stating that the 'edge of the boundary' where kulak accumulation could be tolerated had been reached – an allusion to their ultimate destruction as a social group.

It was fortunate for the party, Syrtsov explained, that the kulak lacked a countrywide organization, and the political slogans and authoritative leaders to create a mass movement because in Siberia there was evidence that he was developing a 'class awareness', putting forward 'class demands' and considering himself to be part of 'a specific class stratum with its own special interests and tasks'. Counterbalancing this was the evolution of 'social pressure' on the kulaks which was generated from within the 'bedniak-seredniak mass' and not 'from above'. With some irony he viewed the very success of the new method of procurement as indicative of the power of kulak farms, for they had easily paid the multiple fines for non-sale of their grain and bought back their property sequestered and sold off in lieu of debts. He supported the concept of a reformulated NEP as the means 'to advance to socialism', a 'new form of *smychka*', based on mass collectivization excluding the kulaks, for allowing them into collective farms would be like 'letting a goat into a vegetable garden'. As to the fate of the kulaks – Syrtsov ended his speech by quoting the 'Leninist' line on the peasantry. The policy goal was to 'destroy classes' and not to depend on 'small-scale producers'.[30]

The accomplishments of the Siberians in overcoming the grain crisis saw their political influence in Moscow on the ascendant. At the Sixteenth Party Conference there was some good natured jibing to the effect that they were now the regime's 'breadwinners' (*'nashi kormil'tsy'*).[31] Given the harvest failure in the southern grain surplus regions, this year the weight of state grain procurement shifted markedly to the Eastern regions of the country (Siberia, the Urals, Kazakhstan), with a planned share of 41 per cent (of which Siberia accounted for just over 20 per cent) of the USSR total of 8.1 million tons (Siberia accounted for about one-quarter of the RSFSR figure).[32] More importantly, it was Siberian grain which saw the regime through the precarious winter and spring months. In April 1929, immediately following the introduction of the new methods of procurement, more than 205,300 tons of grain were collected in the Eastern regions, a 273 per cent increase on the amount gathered in the same month of 1928. In Siberia alone there was an increase of over 77,000 tons in April compared with the same period of 1927, while over the whole year just under 1.8 million tons were procured, a one-third increase over the previous year. Consequently, the actual share of Siberia in state grain procurement rose from 12.2 per cent in 1927/8 to 19.8 per cent in 1928/9.[33] In fact, this year Siberia was the largest single region for all types of grain collection, even overtaking the Ukraine, the traditional bread basket of the country.[34] Once again, as in 1920/1 and 1927/8, the ransacking of the Siberian peasantry had staved off famine in the Central Industrial Region and possibly secured the survival of the Soviet regime itself. Siberian grain also helped to salvage the party's plans for industrialization by securing domestic supplies and allowing the accumulation of hard currency from the resumption of grain exports. It was a significant political triumph for the Siberian party leadership and must have erased from Stalin's memory the image of recalcitrance and vacillation that he had carried away after his tour of January 1928.

Stalin crowned the success of the Siberian leaders by two political gestures of late May. In the guise of a hardliner, by borrowing the idiom of the Stalinist militants at the centre and in his own regional organization, as well as tailoring his own views to suit the new Stalinist *Weltanschauung*, Syrtsov secured his promotion to the highest echelon of the central party leadership. As Siberian Kraikom Secretary, Syrtsov had been part of the outer circle of Stalin's patron–client network. They had worked closely together in 1921–23, when Syrtsov had been head of the Accounting and Distribution Department of the Central Committee and his office was next door to Stalin's. At that time Syrtsov was Stalin's chief administrative assistant in the construction of the party *nomenklatura* across the country, cataloguing its membership, and, as one leader termed it, building up a record of the party's 'physiognomy'. There were rumours that political disagreements in 1924 put some distance into their relationship and Syrtsov was moved out of his post in the central apparatus to less administratively powerful but more politically significant posts in the party organization, first in Leningrad, and then to Siberia in early 1925. After the grain procurement successes of 1928 and 1929, Syrtsov's political ties with Stalin appear to have been reforged. He took most of the credit and was rewarded with a promotion to the inner core of Stalin's circle to the post of Chairman of Sovnarkom RSFSR, displacing the Rightist Rykov. This was followed in the middle of June by his cooption as a candidate member of the Politburo. Eikhe, who would prove to be a more durable Stalin loyalist, had to settle for a personal article in *Pravda* lauding the success in Siberia and taking Syrtsov's seat as Kraikom Secretary.[35]

MORE GRAIN – MORE UNREST

The brief, relatively peaceful interlude of late April–early May in Siberia, when the krai leaders were still basking in the afterglow of their success as 'breadwinners', was shattered almost as soon as the sowing season had been completed by renewed pressure from Moscow for more grain. At an enlarged Politburo session on 3 May 1929, attended by Syrtsov and Eikhe, it was decided to extend the application of the new methods of procurement from beyond the Urals to the rest of the country (with the exception of the areas of harvest failure in the south) as the key component of the continuing mobilization of party and state forces to complete the grain plan. At the end of May, key regional soviet leaders (including Eikhe), gathered in Moscow for the Fifth Congress of Soviets, were called to another enlarged Politburo session and sent homeward with the instruction for a 'maximum increase in grain procurements'.[36] A Kraikom directive of 17 May ordered the cancellation of all leave and a new wave of party, Komsomol and soviet officials and worker activists were sent on procurement duty in the countryside. By early June over 1,300 plenipotentiaries had been sent from urban areas, including a handful of the hundreds mobilized in Moscow, who were assigned to Slavgorod (six) and Rubtsovsk (seven) – key grain areas where procurement was slow.[37]

When Zlobin made his report on the grain campaign to the joint plenum of the Kraikom and Kraiispolkom held on 1–3 June, he informed his colleagues that the Central Committee had recently imposed a new task, demanding just under 200,000 tons for the quarter May–July, and with any shortfall in May carried forward into June. Since deliveries in May amounted to a little over 40,000 tons, that left a huge gap to be filled in June–July. By 1 June a massive 1.65 million tons of grain had been collected in Siberia (86 per cent of the annual plan and about 40 per cent more than the previous year's total), proof if any were needed, observed Zlobin, that the centre had no reason to be dissatisfied with the rate of procurement in Siberia. The fact was that the national deficit in grain meant that, despite the previous successes, the grain stocks in consumer areas of the central industrial regions of Russia would be reduced to two or three days' supply if the Siberians failed to ship more until mid-summer when grain from the southern Ukraine and Kuban steppe would arrive.[38]

It was clear to krai militia chiefs and the Political Commissariat of the Red Army in the region that renewed pressure on the countryside for grain, following immediately in the wake of the events of March–April, would inflame peasant 'unrest' (*volnenie*).[39] In fact, party leaders seem to have resigned themselves to more disturbances given that additional procurement meant that a wider spectrum of peasants would be affected and that peasant insurance stocks would be threatened.[40] If Zlobin's speech to the Kraikom plenum held in June is a gauge then the krai political leadership recognized no alternative other than the renewal of 'social influence' procurement methods. The success of the strategy now depended on correcting mistakes that had occurred and Zlobin listed a catalogue of errors committed in applying the new method. He referred to the problem of *podmena* (supplanting) in the villages, cases when 'commissions were replaced by plenipotentiaries', who then applied *razverstka*, especially when the plan was rejected by a village. Commissions were also frequently supplanted by rural soviets.

These were factors which indicated that the system of mobilizing officials at higher levels for local duties required reexamination. As one official put it, their ignorance of the peasantry rendered plenipotentiaries 'harmful for work'. The main problem in the conduct of the new method in some areas, according to Zlobin, was that plans were often 'unrealistic' and 'exaggerated', and there was no 'class approach' in allocating quotas; rather, mass repressions affected the mass of middle peasants as well as the kulaks. Certain organizational failures must have been particularly galling to the peasants, as for example in Biisk Okrug where procurement officials did not use scales in measuring grain and presumably their rough estimates erred on the side of the state. Yet Zlobin himself seems to have been operating a double standard, for he was sharply heckled from the floor for personally having forbidden an accurate assessment and breakdown of grain stocks by okrug, raion and village – something that was essential for a fair distribution of grain quotas.[41]

Krylov, the Kamensk Okruzhkom Secretary, who had coined the controversial phrase 'democratic *razverstka*' to describe the new methods of grain procurement, was irked by Zlobin's refusal to discuss the details of *how* the additional grain plan was to be fulfilled. He was adamant that there was only one method open to the Siberian party: 'administrative-social pressure from below'. Whereas Zlobin expressed concern at the blundering actions of ill-trained plenipotentiaries, Krylov urged the Kraikom to throw all available activists into the countryside, and especially into those key grain areas, like Rubtsovsk, where procurement had been difficult. To ensure the requisite zeal he suggested that the threat of a party purge be related to the fulfilment of a fixed grain plan. There was also cheating by lower levels of the apparatus who deceived the Kraikom by understating the size of their grain reserves, according to Krylov, because if in calculations they said six the Kraikom invariably imposed a collection task of seven. Krylov, however, was unhappy with the working of the new policy and, already looking ahead to the next harvest and beyond, he was searching for a final solution to the grain problem and the kulak by a further strengthening of state control. Now that the free market had been 'strongly paralysed' there could be no return to this route and he asked the Kraikom to raise with Moscow the issue of a more 'organized sale' of grain in next year's campaign. A more effective and 'organized way' had to be found that would 'knock the kulak off his feet' without the effort and costs of constantly mobilizing party activists for rural duties.[42]

The technical necessity of finding a permanent solution to the grain problem was taken up by another speaker, Gromov, who advised the Kraikom that a 'more realistic method' had to be found – one which did not constantly disrupt the work of party and state institutions for half the year. Planning was the key and the peasant, he argued, must be told how much to sow, harvest, eat and sell. When challenged that he was only interested in 'fleecing' the peasant, he retorted: 'Do you think that he isn't being fleeced now?' Planning would allow this to be carried out in a 'more discerning fashion'.[43] The mood in the Siberian party elite was increasingly shaped by an anti-peasant tendency. Many now wanted the party's field of fire in the countryside widened to include, not just the kulaks, but also the strong seredniak. Zlobin had recently written of the urgency of applying 'social *moral* influence' against the seredniaks to get them to accept grain delivery quotas, and in the event of their refusal to accept them, to exact multiple fines from a small number to intimidate others.[44] Kavraisky wanted to 'put the *verkhushka* of the countryside in the firing line' in the autumn campaign but affirmed that the Kraikom was against Krylov's version of *razverstka* since there was no 'class line' involved in applying it to whole villages. Voronin, wanted the '65,000' kulak farms in Siberia allocated with compulsory delivery quotas to make up the supplementary plan from Moscow. Eikhe, whose appointment as Kraikom Secretary was confirmed at the plenum, represented a much more hardline approach to dealing with the peasants compared with Syrtsov. He referred to 'kulaks' and 'sub-kulaks' (*podkulachniki*) who must all be levied with compulsory grain tasks and henceforth there was to be no more 'going cap in hand' to the kulak. Such was how Eikhe regarded Syrtsov's handling of the peasantry. Spirov, Biisk Okruzhkom Secretary, wanted the 'ideological leaders' and 'initiators' of protests against grain procurement shot and grain tasks allocated not just to kulaks and strong seredniaks but to 'seredniaks in general'.[45]

For the moment such radical solutions to the grain problem were rejected as too extreme. Nevertheless, the views of the krai leadership had evidently been hardened by the experiences of the previous months and, in the Stalinist party oligarchy in general, there was a new consensus emerging around rapid, forced collectivization and dekulakization as a final solution to the problem of state–peasant relations. The 'Ural-Siberian Method' had been embraced by the Stalinist leadership as a temporary panacea for the perennial problems of party–peasant relations. Here was a process which could be considered as ideologically correct, relying on class antagonisms and the mobilization of the 'rural proletariat' composed of poor and middle peasants against the kulaks. The formal incorporation by the party of the rural crowd (*bednota* actifs and the *skhod*) in the application of the new method gave it a pseudo-democratic gloss. Economic penalties by way of boycotts from consumer cooperatives, tax surcharges, additional compulsory grain delivery quotas, multiple fines and the sequestration and auctioning of property created an environment of fear and intimidation in the villages where 'guilt by association' was the likely fate of those who had a friendly relationship with 'kulaks'. In this way the method of 'social influence' as applied from late March proved an effective mechanism for marginalizing the kulaks in their own communities. It created a 'little community' of marginalized kulaks within what Redfield termed the 'little community' that was peasant society, and prepared the way for a surgical strike against the peasant *verkhushka*.[46] Most importantly, it proved to be a highly successful mechanism for grain procurement.

5 *Volynki*: The Russian *Jacquerie*

THE CONCEPT OF PEASANT COLLECTIVE ACTION

Peasant collective action against the new state policy assumed some of the traditional forms and expressions of rural protest: the *jacquerie*, a generic term for peasant protests and revolt covered by the Russian term *volynka*. The experience of peasant collective protest in the pre-industrial age interacted with new types of action, channels of expression and technologies of communication, and was not dissimilar to the concept of a 'forwards-backwards' dialectic in peasant protest postulated by George Rudé for revolutionary France.[1] Peasant collective action often exhibits its own peculiar protocol of, what one historian termed, the 'disorderly order' of the crowd.[2] By definition *volynki* were a type of non-violent direct action, characterized by phased acts of mass obstruction and non-compliance leading into sudden explosions of violent protests and riots. Such protests were an indicator of the, as yet, uncaptured status of the Russian peasantry, despite the modernizing goals of the Russian revolution, and a symptom of increasing peasant opposition to party policies. Whether or not they can be classified as 'amorphous' or 'guided' political actions, where they occurred it demonstrated either widespread peasant frustration with state policy, or efforts to reestablish the traditional social order of *verkhushka* domination in the village against the incursions of the state.[3] In examining peasant protest in Siberia we need to determine not only the nature of the actions, but also their geographic spread. What prevented a mass peasant uprising was the targeting of the tax burden and grain quotas by a *within-village* process supervised by the commune, under party direction, on the kulaks and well-off households that had sufficient surpluses and could afford to pay – something which inevitably released the social tensions that were never far below the surface veneer of social harmony in the countryside.

As we discussed earlier, for centuries Russian peasant custom law sustained pre-industrial practices and values which held that outside material burdens imposed on peasant comunities be distributed proportionally, according to principles of ability to pay and collective responsibility. The slow dissolution of the Russian village commune in the half century after the emancipation of the serfs, the development of an industrial society, culminating in Stolypin's reforms, and the 'wager on the strong' peasantry in 1906–9, forced changes in the social structure of the countryside. The mutating social structure of the peasantry was reflected in the erosion of communal solidarity. By the late 1920s there emerged a divergence of conflicting popular cultures in the countryside: on the one hand, the modern capitalist values of an emergent kulak farmer stratum, which found little common ground with the levelling, collectivist traditions of the peasant commune; and on the other hand, the swelling ranks of the demoralized and pauperized *bednota*, who looked for a bulwark of social protectionism in the preservation of traditional values. In its own perverse 'forwards-backwards' paradox, the Bolshevik regime embraced these traditional peasant values as an instrument of modernity, to assist in the process of destroying the kulaks and capturing the peasantry for the state.

When as part of the social influence policy the Bolsheviks encouraged a return to the traditional communal values of proportionality and collective responsibility, in practice, it meant a disproportionate allocation of economic obligations to the state on the kulaks. This effect in turn appealed to peasant rationality as the cost-benefit analysis of the mass of peasants favoured the policy of targeting kulaks. In this way, the policy stirred up social conflict *within* the peasant community. That is not to say that the party activists always got it right for the central and regional leaderships frequently complained about 'excesses' and 'distortions' that sparked off more general peasant protests. We should note, however, that there was a pattern to the riots. Geography and the nature of the local agricultural economy were obviously key factors given that the state's policy was directed at 'taking grain'. Consequently, the *volynki* were concentrated in the grain producing villages of south-west Siberia, where there was also the highest number of kulaks. The resurgence of socioeconomic differentiation within the peasantry during the 1920s was particularly acute in the main grain belt of the south-west.[4] Although the author found no evidence in the archives to suggest this, one also wonders whether one of the dynamic social factors in the conflicts between peasants was status as 'old' and 'new' settlers. Between 1924 and 1929 some 550,000 migrants came to Siberia (only one-third of whom were 'planned' by the authorities). Many of the migrants were *bednota* from areas west of the Urals in search of land and a better life. The problem for them was that the most fertile agricultural area, the Altai steppe, had been closed to new settlement in 1924. Nevertheless official estimates were that more than 60 per cent of new migrants made their way into the Altai. In the absence of unsettled land, and given the prevalent obsoleteness of the redivisional land commune, these peasants were consigned to peonage and poverty.[5] As the party's 'offensive on the kulak' was targeted against the 'old' settlers who were the largest landholders, the new migrants may well have formed an important base of support for the party in the countryside.

As two renowned historians of the peasant *jacquerie* have observed – and this is just as applicable to Siberia a century later – the uneven local distribution of protest, the reason why riots erupt in one village and not in others, is an intractable problem:

> A village is a subtle complex of past and present, of the permanent and the changing, of nature, technique, social and economic organisation, men and communications. What happens in it depends on the landscape and the soil which condition the nature of its agriculture at the given levels of knowledge and skill; on its geographical situation which determines its place in the larger social division of labour; on the size and structure of its human settlement, the pattern of its landownership and occupation and the social relations of production of its agriculture. It depends on the nature and interests of its ruling groups, or those who create the framework of administration and politics in which it functions, on the nature and dispositions of its own leaders and activists, and on the pattern of its communications with neighbouring villages and the wider world. And it depends not only on what these things are *now*, but on their changes: on whether population is rising or falling and at what rate; whether poverty has increased, is diminishing, and by how much; on whether labourers are in the process of losing their land, their status and security, and how suddenly or dramatically; on whether a new road is opened or an old one by-passed. What happens in a village depends on all these factors simultaneously, and on various others also.[6]

Bolshevik leaders claimed that in the implementation of the new methods of grain collection there was 'minimal participation by organs of power, especially from above'.[7] Under the guise of social influence and 'moral' pressure from the 'bedniak-seredniak mass' the party imposed arbitrarily determined grain quotas on villages which bore no semblance to the peasants' actual ability to deliver. This policy skirted the edge of social catastrophe and was in danger of provoking what one historian termed 'the two traditional replies of the peasant: the short-term reply of concealment of stocks and the long-term reply of refusal to sow more land than was necessary to feed his own family'.[8]

During this campaign the opt-out culture of peasant society that prefers life without the state emerged in peasant manoeuvres to avoid compulsory state duties and liabilities. Most peasants tolerated the Communist Party and embraced NEP so long as there were cheap manufactured goods for sale and high prices for agricultural produce. Once the Soviet regime began to make demands and economically squeeze the well-off peasants, however, they responded with resistance, violent and non-violent, and failing that by the ultimate recourse of flight to remote areas. Turned upon as scapegoats by their neighbours in the rush to satiate the demand of the state for grain, the only realistic option of non-compliance open to kulaks, other than ruination through multiple fines, was to sell up their property and flee before the state sequestered it. In Loktevsk raion, Rubtsovsk Okrug, kulaks argued for a mass flight into the Altai Mountains and Oirotiya, while in Kansk they slipped off into the taiga. Indeed, Slavgorod Okruzhkom regarded as an abuse the practice of giving 'malicious grain holders' an 'ultimatum' to sell their grain rather than immediately allocating fixed duties, registering property and selling it off precisely because it gave time for concealment or flight. It had no qualms about describing the new method as 'the severest measure of administrative pressure'. Syrtsov also spoke of kulaks destroying grain rather than sell it to the state, their frame of mind being: 'If I can't have it, the government shall not have it.'[9]

Given that the new method was much more discriminatory against the kulaks as a social group it was very difficult for them to rouse mass peasant resistance to it. Official reports reflected the current party line that peasants who protested against the regime were kulaks or *podkulachniki*. Consequently, it is impossible to assess with any certainty the extent to which protests were confined or dominated by real kulaks. It would be reasonable to assume that opposition from the predominantly wealthier peasant households who were subjected to the enforcement of individual grain tasks, fines, forced seizures and arrests stiffened as time passed. In Krasnoyarsk mass meetings of peasants complained of 'state fleecing' and although the *bednota* were willing to take grain from kulaks this was more from a self-interested fear about famine than a desire to send it to the towns. In Barnaul and Biisk there were mass attempts to hide property and grain in the fields to protect them from commissions, while in Kansk peasants derided party plenipotentiaries as 'gentry' (*pomeshchiki*).[10] There were acts of terror and reprisals against the village authorities and outside plenipotentiaries, peasant members of *skhod* grain commissions and poor peasants (or their families), most commonly assaults, shootings, murders, animal-maiming and, perhaps the most traditional form of peasant retaliation, incendiarism. In the summer this would normally have meant arson attacks on crops in the field and rick-burning, but in late winter and early spring of 1929 it involved fire bombings of cooperative barns and official buildings, and attacks on the homes of peasants who collaborated with the new method.[11]

When peasants responded with violence it brought them into a head-on conflict with local officials, and gave party plenipotentiaries an excuse to retaliate in kind with arrests, imprisonment or, increasingly, execution. A safer and more shrewd tactic for disgruntled peasants was for women to take the leading role in direct opposition as past experience had shown that the local authorities were reluctant or incapable of handling crowds of protesting women. The structure and *mentalité* of peasant society was, after all, patriarchical and either resigned itself to mass women's protests, for as proverbial peasant wisdom had it 'there is no law for women or for cattle', or viewed mass female hysteria (*klikushestvo*) superstitiously as the manifestation of an evil spirit (*kikimora*) and something not to be tampered with. The advantage of the 'social influence' method, however, was that usually violence was easily isolated and suppressed. The Siberian OGPU and Procuracy, whose function it was to inform and warn the party of the impact of its policies, reported that only in a few areas did the new policy kindle outbursts of peasant riots, that is to say, violent opposition.

VOLYNKI

The *volynki* were spontaneous localized acts of mass resistance, often passive civil disobedience and non-cooperation with the authorities, notably refusal to deliver grain or pay fines, but sometimes they turned into violent outbursts. Frequently, women were in the forefront, to such an extent that the riots were often termed 'women's riots' (*babii bunti*). They were an attempt to reestablish the traditional social order of village solidarity against the incursions of the party and state. Usually, they began with protective human cordons around households targeted for sequestration of property to prevent officials supported by the militia from carrying out their duties, and escalated into ritualistic charivari and sporadic demonstrations (*skopom*). Occasionally, the pent up anger and frustration of peasants exploded into *volynki*, with the destruction of the rural soviet office, looting of state and cooperative property, attempts to make villages no-go areas for party and state officials and the application of *samosud* against peasants who collaborated with the party, or any officials unlucky enough to be caught.

The occurrence of *volynki* was clustered in certain areas of Biisk and Barnaul Okrugs. In Biisk there were over twenty such incidents, spread across 14 raions and 36 villages with upwards of six thousand peasants involved. Most demonstrations were several hundred strong and women played a key part in the disturbances.[12] Local party accounts of 'women's riots' give us an insight into the mood of seething anger of peasants in these areas, but of course they are far from objective reports of events.[13] In the village of Kytmanovo, Verkh-Chumysh raion, Barnaul Okrug, almost three hundred peasants attended the general meeting on the grain plan, fifty of whom were women. After the plan was adopted and the meeting closed, some women began to shout 'the decision isn't right', 'we must vote again' and 'they have robbed us, the bastards, we will not hand over grain'. With that the crowd went off down the street and beat up a demonstration of cooperative members and schoolchildren supporting the new grain plan. In the same raion at the end of March, in the village of Osochno, a crowd of one hundred and fifty men and fifty women gathered to defend the home of the 'kulak' Pshenichnikov, who had been imposed with a five times fine by the soviet and was now to have property seized because of non-payment. The peasants formed a commission of their own and presented a list of demands to the visiting plenipotentiary, including the return of grain taken earlier and the end of boycotts. When he refused the peasants turned on him and he had to flee on horseback with a posse of peasants chasing him off their land.

Another typical incident occurred in the village of Novo-Baraba, Verkh-Chumysh raion, in late March. When the village commission, rural soviet officials and militiamen went to the home of a kulak to seize property for non-payment of a multiple fine for non-delivery of grain, they were chased away by a crowd of stick wielding women. The next day when the officials returned to the 'well-off sector' (an indication that socioeconomic differentiation was territorialized within the village: author) of the village to seize property from other kulaks, the church bell was sounded as a tocsin to call the peasants to the defence of their neighbours. The officials retreated when confronted by a huge crowd of about three hundred peasants armed with axes, sticks, and farm implements. The peasants proceeded to burn down the soviet building and beat up the village teacher, who was probably regarded as the nearest representative of 'outside' state power that they could get their hands on. A few days later an experienced worker brigade of plenipotentiaries arrived in the village and quelled disturbances by making the bedniaks and seredniaks 'realize their mistake'.

In Kamyshenka, Sychevsk raion, Biisk Okrug, the general meeting of peasants to adopt fixed quotas was disrupted by a crowd of about a hundred women headed by the daughter of a kulak, screaming that their menfolk had no surpluses to sell and that everything had been taken already. The meeting had to be abandoned and reconvened at a later time. The *verkhushka* of the village attempted to reaffirm its dominance of village life by subjecting peasants who collaborated with state representatives to informal forms of control. Since the *verkhushka* had been expelled from the main institutions (the *skhod*, soviet and cooperatives) that regulated village life, it had to rely on social censure to exert its influence. The bedniak activist who had taken a leading role in the adoption of the plan was refused service in the privately owned village store. The wives and daughters of those who assisted the plenipotentiaries – bedniaks, soviet and cooperative officials – were subjected to abuse and put into coventry. On 8 April a crowd of women came to the plenipotentiary and bedniaks pleading again that they had no grain surplus and if more grain was taken then they would starve. The bedniaks were in no mood for compassion, however, after one bedniak woman told of how she had been threatened by the wives of kulaks: 'You have a devil for a husband . . . we must drive you out of the village . . . you are speaking out against us, bitch.' Others were warned: 'You are cowards . . . you go through with the collections and we will show you.' That evening the plenipotentiary held a meeting with the kulaks and well-off peasants to discuss the grain plan, while large numbers of women crowded round the door shouting that only 'cowards' attended.

The next morning cooperative officials, accompanied by a militiaman went to the home of the kulak Davydov to take grain in accordance with the compulsory allocations. Davydov and his son stood in front of their barn, threatening: 'You may kill me here but we will not give you grain.' Soon a huge crowd of one hundred and fifty to two hundred old men, women and children gathered, surrounded the barn and forcibly prevented the removal of the grain by beating off the officials with sticks. Eventually the militiaman pulled out his revolver and ordered the crowd to disperse but a woman threatened to chop his head off with an axe. Again the officials retreated and reported to the plenipotentiary and party secretary, who decided to seek assistance from the raikom. Meanwhile, a demonstration marched around part of the village crying: 'if the grain is taken – we will chop them all to pieces.' According to the official party report the *volynka* was pacified only after a bedniak meeting was held on the evening of 9 April, at which 69 peasants attended, though how order was restored is not stated. It may be that once it was fully understood that the bulk of the plan was to be distributed on to the *verkhushka*, and that a proportion of grain collected would be retained within the village for supplying the *bednota*, the peasant community divided against itself. One also wonders what kind of back-up the raikom provided to secure procurement in the village.[14]

In the villages of Stol'nikovo and Tula in Berdsk raion, Novosibirsk Okrug, the *volynki* occurred at two separate social levels, rich and poor, but each displaying a common rational self-interest in local retention of grain stocks. On the one hand, after a new grain plan was rejected by both *bednota* and general meetings in April, the harassment and intimidation organized by the raiispolkom plenipotentiary, including the hanging of blackboards on the gates of non-deliverers and the holding of torchlight parades outside their houses, was ignored by the grain holding peasants. In early June, however, a *volynka* was sparked off by hungry *bednota* who, refused help by their grain holding neighbours, prevented grain procured by the state from being transported out of the area and ground it up for food.[15] A Biisk Okruzhkom report stated that there were 36 'mass protests' involving approximately 5,300 peasants, in addition to other unrecorded incidents. The report claimed that a 'link' (*smychka*) had been formed between the kulaks, the well-off peasants and priests to organize the protests.[16] Spirov, the hardline Biisk Okruzhkom Secretary, denounced the 'blatant counter-revolutionary demands' of 'kulaks' in certain villages and singled out Mikhailovka and B. Sliudyanka as areas of the greatest resistance.[17] Here, overtly political demands were linked with traditional moral economy norms of reciprocity. In Mikhailovka a meeting of about two hundred men and seven hundred women constituted an attempt by the peasant community to reach a social consensus without state interference. The meeting elected a presidium, in which women were strongly represented, and decided to return all confiscated and auctioned property, with the exception of grain surpluses, to end the boycott and restore voting rights to those disenfranchised, supply the poor with seed and food, regulate and lower cooperative dues, and investigate the activities of the village commission which had assisted officials in the uncovering of grain surpluses (see Document 5). The party regarded such spontaneous outbursts of organized peasant opposition as extremely dangerous. Peasant meetings held outside of party control were likely to be denounced, as in this instance, as a 'counter-revolutionary' act and the committee was arrested as a 'kulak-bandit presidium'. According to the above-mentioned party report, the Mikhailovka protest lasted 12 days and involved an attempt to spread resistance further afield. Apparently, the peasants drew up a proclamation 'to all rural soviets from the Caucasus to the Altai', calling for the overthrow of the regime of 'communist fools', and sent representatives to neighbouring villages and raions.[18]

Overwhelming armed force and arrests must have been major factors in the ability of the state to control such village disturbances. In the village of Krasnoyarsk, Chistiun raion, the community refused to cooperate with the authorities and organized its own carnival crying: 'The river has burst its banks, here armed force will not help, what we want we will do.' Peasants imposed with grain quotas prophetically appealed to their neighbours:

'Today they rob us, but tomorrow it will be you; help us.' When the plenipotentiary and militiamen were attacked with sticks and stones, several arrests were made and later two kulaks were executed.

The Kraikom recognized the above mentioned Verkh-Chumysh and Chistiun raions of Barnaul Okrug as the two worst areas for *volynki* and it was in the latter district that Kaganovich toured with Nusinov in late April. Verkh-Chumysh raion had been singled out at the beginning of 1929 as an area where kulak influence was such that they had supposedly 'captured the commanding heights of the countryside'.[19] Certain common factors were put forward to account for these clusters of disorders. First, both areas lay at the heart of the Siberian 'grain triangle' (Biisk–Barnaul–Rubtsovsk) and were obviously in the front-line of the procurement campaign. Second, these areas had been identified in surveys as having a large kulak element. Third, many of the peasants had been partisans or served in the regular forces of both sides in the civil war. Not surprisingly, not only did these experienced peasant fighters have a lot to lose from the new method but also they were not easily intimidated and many certainly harboured hatred of communists from the civil war. Peasants such as these had notoriously buried Red Army soldiers alive, upside down, in pits during the civil war in Siberia: a memory that the Bolsheviks were not likely to forget or forgive.[20] The problem was not, however, limited to these two okrugs. Indeed, the above cases may have served as models for peasants in other districts to follow. For instance, the Kamensk Okruzhkom Secretary, Kovalev, informed Eikhe that women played a major role in organizing peasant resistance and told him of a not untypical incident in the village of Novinka, Baevsk raion, when a group of seventy peasants, led by an ex-Red Army company commander, marched to the soviet office and declared that they were seizing power to reduce the grain plan and prevent grain from leaving the area.[21]

Syrtsov referred to *volynki* in his speech to the Sixteenth Party Conference but dismissed them as marginal events. Linking them with minor cases of repression of kulaks and the absence of village party cells, he observed: 'In those places where we broke kulak resistance, after a *volynka*, we noticed how there immediately began a mass inflow of grain, as if a kind of cork had been removed.'[22] The lesson for the party, as Syrtsov noted, was that the *volynki* were localized phenomena and, although there was some evidence of 'kulak' class action and organization, they did not assume the form of a mass movement by peasants seeking wider political goals. Therefore, it would be fair to characterize the incidents of peasant resistance in Siberia as small-scale 'expressive' collective behaviour as opposed to widespread 'instrumental' action to achieve general political demands.[23]

TARGETING THE KULAKS

The attempts to win over the poor and middle peasants to the side of the party were sometimes exploited by these same constituencies, and there were many cases when such peasants came before party plenipotentiaries with the spurious demand: 'Give me grain so that I will not fall under the influence of the kulaks.'[24] The example set by the party's licence in extorting grain from the kulaks was taken even further in Shelabolikhinsk raion, Barnaul Okrug, where gangs of poor peasants hijacked grain delivered to the cooperative procurement agents and distributed it among themselves. The mood of poor peasants in Barnaul seems to have been characterized by profound mistrust of the Soviet authorities: 'Soviet power helps the bedniak only with words, not actions; it swindled us last year.' Even village communists in this area refused to serve on commissions.[25]

To say that the state disrupted communal harmony in the countryside is an idealistic and distorted vision of village realities. For all the close ties of kinship, neighbourliness and friendship which promoted social peace and equilibrium were matched by intra-village jealousies, long-standing feuds and rivalries. Peasant attitudes had not changed much since Chekhov's observation: 'Who stole from his neighbours, set fire to property, and bore false witness at court for a bottle of vodka? The peasant. Who is the first to denounce peasants at village and other meetings? A peasant.'[26] Social disharmony and conflict was the common currency of village life and it was such pent up tensions that were frequently released by the social influence method. While peasants of the village of Sakharovo, Barnaul Okrug, responded to plenipotentiaries that 'we have no seredniaks and kulaks here, all are peasants', in the villages of Barabinsk Okrug many seredniaks were only too willing to collaborate with the authorities in exposing grain surpluses of wealthy neighbours and eagerly helped register property for sales. It is important to note that neighbours were among the principal beneficiaries of auctions of sequestered kulak property at knock-down prices. In Tulun, however, seredniaks were afraid to expose kulaks, fearing that their own surpluses might be seized. Meanwhile, in the village of Khlopunova, Rubtsovsk Okrug, bedniaks surrounded the plenipotentiary crying 'hurrah' when he announced the new measures, and in Kuznetsk bedniaks 'liquidated' kulak farms.[27]

The conflict between risk-minimizing self-interest and loyalty to the community must have been quite confusing for peasants. The dilemma is well illustrated by the bedniak woman and Red Army veteran, Mikheeva, who told a meeting of *bednota* and batraks in the village of Ust'-Insk, Novosibirsk Okrug, called to discuss a list of farms to be allocated compulsory delivery quotas: 'Why should we reveal the rich, when the rich help us? If the state helps us, then let us bring them the rich.' Despite such pragmatic doubts the peasants had more to gain from going along with the consultation process with party activists and influencing the composition of the list, since the raiispolkom plenipotentiary threatened to impose it unilaterally if they refused to comply.[28] Mobilization of poor peasant support was often achieved with special material inducements in addition to a share of the collected grain issued by the rural soviet from special kiosks in the village.[29] When a Cooperative Union plenipotentiary arrived in the village of Tes', Minusinsk Okrug, he selected a group 20 to 30 strong from a joint meeting of the soviet and the bedniak actifs to go and terrorize households with grain surpluses. Free tobacco and goods from the consumer cooperative store were issued to those who participated. The use of tar collars and the organization of carnivals against grain holders was a regular occurrence in this area.[30] Although the Siberian party leadership attempted to avoid the obvious recurrence of emergency measures, by early April it had publicly reverted to the slogans used during the grain crisis of the previous year and the procurement problem was described as a 'grain strike by kulaks'.[31] Some local officials welcomed the new measures with great enthusiasm and relief: 'At last what we have been waiting for, now we can take the grain,' reported Tarsk Okruzhkom.[32]

As head of the Siberian delegation to the Sixteenth Party Conference, Syrtsov required detailed information on the results of the application of the new method and no doubt wanted to be well briefed for his report to Stalin. Consequently, the okruzhkoms were instructed to provide by 20 April in-depth assessments covering such factors as the number of households listed, the number of compulsory sales and amounts raised, the social characteristics of households involved, the amount of grain taken, cases of distortions, the number of cases involving seredniaks, the social profile of complainants, the mood of the different social groups of peasants and the sowing campaign.[33] Reports to the Kraikom from okrugs revealed just how successful the new method was. Occasions when peasants refused to adopt the new method through the *skhod* were rare. The majority of villages adopted the grain plan and by mid-April only five villages in Barnaul, 48 in Slavgorod and six in Biisk had refused, although these were key grain areas. At the end of May a Kraikom report on the mood of the peasantry confirmed that the number of refusals to adopt plans were small (the above mentioned figures, plus nine villages in Kuznetsk, 11 in Irkutsk, 15 in Achinsk, 15 in Kansk).[34] In contrast, the use of multiple fines, property registration and the compulsory auctioning of farm property were very common, suggesting widespread resistance to the new method from those peasants who had been given quota obligations.

Okruzhkom reports to the Kraikom in April indicated that the number of farms listed for compulsory grain deliveries in Kansk was 794, of which 378 had property auctioned; in Irkutsk the corresponding figures were 566 and 168, in Biisk 1,047 and 750, in Omsk 1,419 and 435, in Rubtsovsk 589 and 411, in Slavgorod 61 and 43, in Kamensk 1,264 and 581, in Tomsk 478 and 170, and in Barnaul 1,110 and 697.[35]

Okruzhkom reports on the application of the new method claimed to have successfully targeted it on the kulaks. For example, in Kamensk by mid-April 1,264 peasant households had been listed for compulsory grain deliveries, of which 581 had refused to comply and had property to a value of 130,376 roubles sold, and of these 380 were classed as kulaks, 162 well-off and 39 seredniaks. The farms that had property seized and sold off were declared to be 'malicious grain holders', but this was a catch-all label for anyone who resisted delivering the compulsory grain quotas. While seredniak and, more rarely, even poor households were sometimes included on lists, the okruzhkom had placed a check on such abuses by ordering that raikom troiki sanction all sell-offs. A problem for the authorities was that seredniaks had a large amount of grain, were often the most determined grain holders and yet the party was immunizing them from the kind of pressures to sell applied against kulaks. Peasant resistance seems to have been limited to the burning down of one cooperative building, the destruction of some machines and kulak agitation for a decrease in sowings: 'It isn't necessary to sow a lot, it will be taken away all the same.' The Okruzhkom felt safe in declaring that: '*Bednota* and batraks have come over to the party en masse and are actually helping with the implementation of measures, especially where cells have worked well with them.'[36] A rather more clouded picture of events in Kamensk was presented by a student from Sverdlovsk who had been mobilized and sent there for the grain campaign. In a letter of complaint to Syrtsov, he described how the party deputy secretary for Baevsk raion had arbitrarily divided up the grain delivery plan between villages, refusing to match the plan targets with estimations of grain stocks or previous deliveries. Thus, some villages were given targets well below their previous deliveries, and others had targets foisted on them which were unrealistic. Krylov, the Okruzhkom Secretary, was apparently unmoved by the student's complaints.[37]

In Biisk Okrug, the arbitrary distribution of grain quotas, indiscriminate listing of 'kulaks', and auctions of property were common practices, even seed grain and household goods 'down to the doorhandles' (*do ruchki*).[38] Here peasants vigorously resisted the new method with widespread protests, and party plenipotentiaries countered with arrests and coercion. One practice of the Biisk authorities was to refuse to accept monetary payments to the value of the grain delivery quotas; rather when there was a refusal to sell they auctioned off peasant property at cheap prices as an exemplary punishment.[39] Although such actions produced a flood of complaints to higher state authorities and the procuracy the official response, as we shall see later, was minimal. Later in the year, in the autumn when the grain had been collected safely, party reports on the campaign became more circumspect and critical of abuses. The Rubtsovsk Procuracy condemned numerous 'illegal acts' in grain collection when plenipotentiaries enforced '*razverstka*'. Villages were sealed off by foot and horse patrols preventing peasants from leaving. Meetings were then called and the peasants were held until they had adopted grain delivery plans. In the words of the plenipotentiaries, their tactics were 'to reduce by starvation'.[40] A report by a Kraikom instructor into the performance of the party organization of Mikhailovsk raion, Biisk Okrug, revealed that grain delivery quotas had even been levied on collective farmers.[41]

Thousands of arrests, trials and property seizures under Articles 61, 58, 107 and others spread across the krai in late March–July 1929 as the party ruthlessly stamped out peasant refusals to comply with the grain plans. The overall number of farms involved was small, reflecting the generally careful manner in which the new method was targeted. Official figures state that there were 3,030 arrests, the vast majority (2,078) being kulaks and the rest made up from town speculators (108), rural speculators (51), seredniaks (78), bedniaks (12), cooperative employees (477), kolkhoz officials (49) and others (177). Some 3,172 peasant households were subjected to five times fines, with 601 cases in Biisk Okrug alone – a further indication that this area was the fulcrum of peasant resistance. During the year the party also claimed to have destroyed 91 'kulak and anti-Soviet bands' with 682 members.[42]

By the end of April approximately only half of one per cent of farms in the okrugs of Barnaul, Biisk and Rubtsovsk, and even less in Slavgorod, had property sold for failure to pay a multiple fine. Figures for 13 okrugs (mostly in West Siberia) reveal that by May about 8,000 farms had property sequestered, of which 4,200 were auctioned off in their entirety. This figure should be put into the context of an estimated 65,000–75,000 kulaks in the krai. Most of the owners were, official sources claimed, 'kulak and well-off' peasants, already disenfranchised and subjected to individual supplementary agricultural tax levies, and many had previously been tried under Article 107 for withholding grain from sale. There were cases, as we have seen, when seredniaks and bedniaks were caught in the net, subjected to fines and had property sold off.[43] At the Sixteenth Conference one regional party secretary blamed a 'right deviation' in local party organizations for this excess, claiming that because 'they do not know where the kulak is' organizations and village communities go for a 'levelling' of the grain plan on households and in this way seredniaks were affected.[44]

DEALING WITH EXCESSES

In mid-April a sudden panic seems to have taken hold in the Siberian leadership. The reasons for this appear to have been related to worries about peasant complaints to Moscow which it was ordered to look into and fears that the sowing season would be disrupted, with catastrophic implications for the following year's harvest. Consequently, the Biuro instructed the localities and plenipotentiaries to throw their full weight behind organizing sowing before 20 April, to cease applying *piatikratki* and proceed with 'normal methods' of grain procurement. Excesses in the application of *piatikratki* as regards seredniak and poor farms were to be rectified urgently by drawing on a special fund for compensation that was to be established in each okrug.[45] Telegrams from Eikhe to local party leaderships voicing concern at abuses illustrate the mounting pressures on those involved in the campaign at all levels of the hierarchy. On 17 April he told Gusev, the Irkutsk Okruzhkom Secretary: 'We have a complaint of mass seizure of seed in Zalarinsk raion. This complaint is causing unease among certain Muscovites. Go to the place immediately, investigate and telegraph by 10 a.m. on the 20th. Give detailed information of the results of the investigation and measures taken.' The certain Muscovites in question could only have been Stalin and Kalinin.[46]

Investigations of peasant complaints do not appear to have significantly altered the outcome or the application of the new method. For example, on 27 March 1929 the bedniak commission of Kubitet, Itatsk raion, Achinsk Okrug, a village of about 1,000 inhabitants, sent a telegram to Kalinin and the Central Committee complaining about a 'misunderstanding' in the size of the grain delivery plan demanded by the raiispolkom plenipotentiary, Mukhin. According to the peasants, in 1928 the village had a sown area of 1,200 desiatins with an average gross harvest of 45 puds per desiatin. The total amount of grain collected was 54,000 puds, of which some 20,000 was sold to the state before the new methods were introduced. The food demands of the local population required 22,000 puds and a further 12,000 puds had to be reserved for seed (about 1,000 desiatins worth). The peasants claimed that these figures demonstrated that there was no marketable grain surplus left in the village. They did not convince Mukhin who, following orders, demanded that the *bednota* commission immediately allocate delivery quotas amounting to 15,000 puds on individual households. The peasants now feared that their seed grain for next year's harvest would be appropriated, for while Mukhin accepted that seed grain should not be included he was adamant that a plan of 15,000 puds would be completed at all costs.[47]

Within a few days the central authorities responded by copying the complaint to Eikhe and Syrtsov instructing them to investigate, and they passed it down to the okrug authorities. The report of Achinsk Okrispolkom Presidium into the matter drew from agricultural tax returns to brand the village as 'rich' with a 'significant element of kulak-exploitatory farms'. Moreover, it revealed that the trouble was rooted in conflicting assessments of the village harvest. Whereas the local peasantry asserted that only 54,000 puds had been collected, local land organs estimated the harvest at an average of over 60 puds per desiatin and arrived at a total of over 73,000 puds. Of this figure just over 34,000 puds was for intra-village demands, leaving approximately 39,000 puds of marketable grain. There was also a wide divergence of opinion over the amount sold to the state as the receipts of local procurement agencies registered that only 6,860 puds of the village grain had been sold to them.[48] Clearly, either the peasants or local authorities were massaging the figures to justify their case; in any event the okrispolkom's version seems to have been accepted for there is further mention of the affair. Tax returns were not only at the disposal of the party but were used by peasants to support claims of excessive demands for grain. One peasant delegate from the village of Kozhevnikov, Bogorodsk raion, Tomsk Okrug, travelled several hundred kilometres to Novosibirsk and appealed in person to the Kraiispolkom about the imposition of '*razverstki*' of 50 to 450 puds on each household. To prove that these quotas were beyond the means of the peasants he presented a list of their agricultural tax assessments.[49]

Having encouraged local authorities to exert extreme pressure on the countryside via the new methods, the Siberian leadership moved to extricate itself from any blame for excesses perpetrated in the course of the campaign, especially now that the grain crisis seemed to have passed and Moscow was focusing on peasant complaints. Lisin, the new Krai Procurator, proved to be as vehement in his condemnation of abuses of legal norms as was his recently purged predecessor, Kunov. In late April he sent a circular to okrug procurators denouncing 'crude distortions' in grain collecting at local level, particularly as regards lumping together the seredniak and kulak farms for self-taxation, property sequestration and sales, and boycotts. Practices in the use of the 'social influence' method had bordered on 'outright crimes', assumed the 'characteristics of hooliganism' and involved 'gross breaches of revolutionary law'. He instructed procuracy officials to make it a priority to ensure the return of property to seredniaks or fully compensate them if this was not possible. In the few cases which involved 'strong seredniaks' property sales were to stand. Kulak opposition, on the other hand, was to be crushed by legal methods, trials and, when necessary, executions. Lisin set in motion a rigorous review of all cases of *piatikratniki* and sale of property, demanding to know how many there were, the social origin of the accused, the amount of grain plans, and the number of farms that had property returned.[50]

Legal reviews of peasant complaints fell on deaf ears in the party. In early April several peasants from the village of Chisto-Ozersk, Zav'ialovsk raion, Kamensk Okrug, complained to the Kraiispolkom, Kamensk Okrug Procuracy and then, when they did not receive any satisfaction, sent a telegram to Kalinin about the 'chaotic, illegal acts' and 'loutish methods' of the 'robbers' raid' perpetrated by lower organs during grain procurement. The peasants were outraged that property, including livestock and equipment and not just grain, had been seized without a judicial process. The peasant Filippov complained that he had been ordered by the rural soviet to sell 300 puds which he did not have. Consequently, 85 puds of grain were taken from him leaving his family of seven without a single pud for food or seed, as well as his animals (two horses, four cows, 37 sheep), two carts and an imported harvester. When told to investigate by Kalinin's office the local party organization denied that any abuses had occurred. The village commission for grain procurement not the soviet had ordered the sale of property belonging to those who refused to fulfil their delivery quotas in order to pay for their multiple fines. Fillipov and the others were described by the okrispolkom as 'kulaks' and 'malicious grain concealers' who had been previously disenfranchised and subjected to individual surcharges of taxes.[51]

Okrug plenipotentiaries could have a decisive influence in the conduct of the grain campaign at local level. In the Petropavlovsk raion of Kamensk Okrug the entire local leadership was removed, with some expulsions from the party, for illegal acts perpetrated at the direction of the okrug plenipotentiary, Kytmanov, in mid-July. His methods involved dividing village populations into two groups: the first was composed of an actif of members of the rural soviet, *bednota* and 'honest deliverers of grain surpluses to the state'; the second was formed by those who refused to accept the grain plan distribution who were branded 'evil non-sellers'. In this context the method of 'social influence' was implemented by Kytmanov as follows. Peasants in the group of non-sellers were brought one by one to a table and presented with a demand to deliver their grain quota. If they refused the actif surrounded them and pushed them around, tied boards on their necks, all the time subjecting them to verbal abuse, shouting 'give grain', 'kulak', 'skunk', 'bastard'. Over a hundred peasants had this 'circle' method of influence inflicted on them, ten or 15 times day and night, for the meetings continued round the clock in order to torture victims by sleep deprivation until they submitted.[52]

Local party organizations were slow to correct such 'distortions' and 'excesses'. As late as the middle of August Kisis continued berating them for failing to free bedniaks and seredniaks arrested for refusal to sell grain and compensate them for sequestered property from the special fund.[53] In fact, the actions of local leaders were guided less by the possibility of sanctions against excesses and more by the threat of removal from their posts if they failed to complete grain procurement targets. Biisk Okruzhkombiuro even removed the party secretary of Srotinsk raikom simply for being in last place for procurement, though he was also used as a scapegoat for 'distortions' against seredniaks.[54] Leadership echelons were simply unsure how to act when confronted by clear cases of abuses against peasants. The Rubtsovsk Okruzhkom Secretary took until late October before he submitted a report to Eikhe on the notorious case of the '48-hour shock workers' for grain procurement in Shipunovo raion, brought to his attention by the Krai Procuracy in mid-July. The case illustrates how the pressure for taking grain flowing down the party apparatus resulted in an explosion of militant extremism at the interface between party and peasantry in the villages.[55]

As a solution to falling procurement levels in several villages the secretary of Shipunovsk raikom, Danilov, and the chairman of the raiispolkom, Bakholdin, decided on 20 July to organize an extraordinary 'accord' among the peasants to complete the grain delivery plans by 'shock work'. A special 'military command' headed by Danilov was established to coordinate the units of activists in the countryside. In the villages the 'shock work' under the slogan of 'give grain' was launched by the pealing of bells. Komsomol activists requisitioned peasant carts to transport the hoped for deliveries and specially recruited partisan veterans strode around bedecked in military medals and ribbons to invoke a wartime atmosphere. Meetings were called in the village quarters and the edict of the 'military command' was read out. The peasants were instructed to pass a resolution for 'voluntary self-obligation' on the basis of '48-hour shock work' to deliver grain.

All peasants of 18 years and over were taken away to a nearby spot and divided into groups according to their social status and sex: bedniaks and seredniaks together in one place, kulaks in another and women elsewhere.

Each group was told to elect a presidium to uncover the size of the grain surpluses held by each and every peasant. The meetings went on all day and night and no one was allowed to sleep, but whereas the bedniaks and seredniaks were permitted one or two hours' break to eat, the kulaks were guarded by special commissars and not even allowed to eat the food brought by relatives. After all this the plan had still not been completed so the 'shock work' was prolonged for another 48 hours. From the party leadership's point of view the most criminal aspect of this episode was not so much the treatment of the peasants but the fact that the orders to deliver grain took no account of social position. Moreover, seredniaks who delayed in handing over the grain were branded as part of the 'kulak group', the 'kulak troika' or 'kulak command' and such peasants were to be sent off for 'reeducation'. Refusal to obey incurred denunciation as an 'enemy of Soviet power' or a 'fat-headed Chamberlain' and threats and beatings followed. As a result of this kind of brutality one seredniak peasant died, probably from a terror-induced heart attack according to the testimony of his daughter.

The Krai Procurator, Burmistrov, described the activities initiated by the raion leaders as 'outrages'. Not only had they perpetrated abuses but they had attempted to conceal them by falsifying their reports to the okrug and krai authorities. For example, the raion report claimed that 106 households had their property sold off in April and May whereas the true figure was 178. Similarly, 77 persons had been tried under Article 61 instead of the 11 claimed in the report. The raion leaders had even overstated their grain procurement, claiming almost 1,200 tons instead of the actual 861 tons achieved. As a consequence of this 'shock work' method there was a sharp decline in peasant sowings in the villages subjected to it. The procuracy recommended that 13 party officials who had been key participants in the affair (nearly all raion officials but including several secretaries and an okrug-level judge) be removed from their posts and charged under Article 110 of the Criminal Code (for abuse of office). Previously, in early September, the Kraikombiuro had sanctioned the decision of the Rubtsovsk Okruzhkom to apply only a party penalty against the activists involved but later, when Burmistrov had been in Moscow, he had been informed that the Central Committee wanted to know the results of the case from the RSFSR Procurator's office. Now he was unsure whether to send the activists for trial. Eikhe's decision on the matter is not known.

The party leadership routinely preferred to punish one or a few scapegoats rather than a large contingent of perpetrators since this would indicate a general official malaise and cast a shadow over the new methods themselves. This response is evident from the outcome of another infamous case. Extraordinary excesses occurred in the Blagoveshchensk raion of Slavgorod Okrug where the introduction of the new methods of procurement in March was taken by local officials as an excuse for what can only be descibed as the organized looting of peasants. An OGPU investigation of the case in late 1929 disclosed that the raikom and raiispolkom had ignored the fundamental principle of selective targeting of pressure on the kulaks. On 30 June a raikom directive gave plenipotentiaries on the ground a virtual *carte blanche* in deciding which peasants could be listed for individual delivery quotas and have property compulsorily sold. Mass abuses and illegal acts inevitably flowed from the enormous power exercised without check by officials in the villages.

Plenipotentiaries ordered that individuals be listed and subjected to forced sales of property not only for not obeying the compulsory grain delivery quotas but also for not paying self-taxation surcharges. Often these peasants were not registered as kulaks for tax purposes or disenfranchised but were seredniaks that had rented out equipment or hired labour for a short period or even bedniaks. There were mass arrests and while many peasants were held in barns or taken to the villages from where the plenipotentiaries operated, 178 were sent to the raion centre for trial. Once again the social profile of these prisoners demonstrates the arbitrary nature of this kind of repression: 29 were kulaks, 90 seredniaks and 66 bedniaks and of these only 40 were released by the court. Some peasants had seven times, ten times and even fifteen times fines imposed on them and, astonishingly, 1,055 out of 5,718 peasant households in the raion (18.6 per cent) were sold off in their entirety. Although the official report branded this as 'dekulakization and the liquidation of farms' it was not a systematically accurate process since many of the victims were seredniaks and bedniaks. In most cases everything was sold off, including the boots and overcoats of the unfortunate victims.

The plenipotentiaries were accompanied around the countryside by traders and bargain hunters who, together with peasants, snapped up the property and household goods sold for a pittance at auction. Of course, the officials conducting the campaign were among the greatest beneficiaries of the sales. For example, one village party cell secretary who acted as a plenipotentiary bought a four-roomed house worth 700 roubles for 25 roubles. Furthermore, monies raised from the sales frequently went astray and the plenipotentiaries set a poor example for the conduct of the campaign by their general drunken and dissolute behaviour. For this litany of abuses only one person was punished, removed from office and expelled from the party – the okrug plenipotentiary responsible for the area, who happened to be the Okrug Deputy-Procurator.[56]

6 A Prologue of Repression

ARTICLE 61: JUSTICE BY DECREE

Following the success of the 'social influence' procedure in grain procurement in Siberia and Kaganovich's recommendations for greater use of Article 61 against kulaks, the party leadership decided to widen its catchment and entrench its use against the peasantry. On 3 June a Sovnarkom RSFSR circular ordered its application in all areas except those in the south where again there had been a harvest failure. The aim was to collect as much grain as quickly as possible in the early stages of the coming campaign.[1] In the middle of June the Politburo directed Narkomiust to devise a series of legal measures for curbing the kulaks. Its recommendations were incorporated into the report of a Politburo commission composed of Yanson, Syrtsov and Mikoyan which proposed amendments to Article 61 to extend the power of local soviets over grain procurement. Keen to establish a legal mechanism for allocating grain procurement plans to each individual village, the Politburo approved the commission's draft decree on 27 June (see Document 6).[2]

The following day, in what must have been one of his first acts as the new Chairman of Sovnarkom RSFSR, Syrtsov signed two new decrees formally giving legal effect to the Politburo's decision. The first, entitled 'On Extending the rights of Local Soviets in Relation to Achieving the Fulfilment of General State Tasks and Plans', was supposedly in response to numerous petitions from the mass of peasants in grain producing areas for government action to 'curb kulak speculative elements'. This decree provided a two-tiered formal administrative-legal entrenchment for the procedures of the social influence method of grain procurement. On one level rural soviets were now empowered to levy five times fines by administrative action in cases of non-compliance with the grain delivery quotas determined and allocated by the *skhod*. In addition Article 61 of the RSFSR Criminal Code was amended to give the state a choice of instruments with which to punish the grain-holding peasantry. This made it a criminal offence either to refuse to comply with orders to sell grain under the new method or to oppose the collection of village grain plans. The revisions to Article 61 gave it a draconian scope, for Clause 1 now criminalized virtually any act designated as civil disobedience by the authorities by making it an offence to refuse 'to fulfil responsibilities, general state tasks or productive work, having a general state significance'. A first offence of non-compliance with the decision of the *skhod* was to be dealt with administratively by the rural soviets by the infamous five times fine, seizure and forced sale of property and arrest for non-payment. A repeat offender was to be dealt with judicially with heavier sentences of imprisonment or forced labour for one year, while conspiracy to oppose or active resistance to any official carrying out his duties brought imprisonment for two years with confiscation of all or part of one's property and possibly exile. In essence, although well-off and kulak peasants were not specifically mentioned in the revisions to Article 61, the intention behind the widening of its scope was to make it legally binding for them, and any others nominated by village commissions, to sell grain surpluses to the state at fixed prices.[3]

Once again selective material incentives to induce peasant support were built into the process. Local authorities were to set aside 25 per cent of the sums raised by fines and forced sales of property to be used as a fund for cooperation and collectivization of the *bednota*. This was a tactic clearly borrowed from Stalin's recommendation during his Siberian tour of early 1928 that a 25 per cent grain bounty be distributed to the *bednota* from grain seized under Article 107.[4] As with the 'Zav'ialova method', once again the local press was a key channel of communication between the regional leadership and the lower network of party and state officials as detailed instructions on the use of Article 61 were published in *Sovetskaia sibir'*.[5]

A conference of Krai Judicial Department officials on 8 July highlighted the confused manner of enforcement of Article 61 by the local authorities. There were a 'massive number' of excesses according to a report by the Krai Procuracy, with peasants who had been administratively fined for a first offence being brought before the courts without sufficient time to fulfil their grain delivery plan, or being subjected to a double jeopardy of both types of punishment simultaneously. The krai leadership moved to tighten up the use of Article 61, and on 17 August a Kraiispolkom decree ordered that administrative fines only should be applied in the case of a first refusal by a peasant to fulfil the grain delivery quota he had been allocated by the *skhod* within the prescribed period. In cases where there was a repeated refusal to fulfil the allotted grain tasks, not just in the current campaign but over two or more, then peasants should be prosecuted through the courts.[6] Local officials were also reminded not to rely on Article 61 as a catch-all device but to continue to use Article 107 for cases involving the hoarding of large grain stocks, but only for one or two cases per raion where a significant quantity of grain was involved (300–400 puds or more).[7]

On the ground this administrative figure was not consistently adhered to and the local authorities drew on the variety of punitive resources at their disposal, as is illustrated by the following case from Biisk Okrug. In late March 1929 the peasant Kozlov from the village of Bystriansk was allocated a compulsory grain delivery quota of 119 puds. Kozlov was an ex-partisan, had been imprisoned twice (once for 'counter-revolutionary activities' and once for 'hooliganism') and was disenfranchised. When he refused to comply Kozlov was penalized with a twice times fine amounting to a monetary value of 238 roubles and on 2 April a trader was appointed to sell property sequestered from him. The authorities found only about half the grain quota on his farm so the rest of the fine was made up by the sale of a horse, cow and other goods. In late June the militia conducted a search of Kozlov's farm in connection with a robbery and discovered a pit and underground store containing in approximately 100 puds of wheat, 25 puds of flour and 5 puds of seed grain. On 26 June Kozlov was sentenced under Article 107.[8]

The Siberian Krai Procuror, Burmistrov, tendered a detailed report to the Kraiispolkom assessing the grain procurement campaign in 1928–29 and the first half (August–December) of that of 1929. There had been 6,850 prosecutions under Article 61 in the latter stages of the 1928/9 grain campaign and he concluded that the Krai Procuracy had failed to uphold 'revolutionary legality' by defending peasants from arbitrary abuses perpetrated by plenipotentiaries. He advised against the drafting of procuracy and judicial officials as plenipotentiaries for grain procurement work; rather their expertise should be deployed in the supervision of legal measures of repression, particularly given the increasing reliance of the party on legal forms of repressing kulaks.[9] Such a leavening of legal officials among the cohort of grain procurement plenipotentiaries might well have avoided the embarassing situation, revealed in an official survey, where 60 per cent of all cases of repeated refusals to complete grain tasks involved serednyaks. This was not only politically troubling for the party but conflicted with previous directives on the need for a class line in the application of Article 61. Consequently, to ensure a more politically correct social profile in the cases brought to court raiispolkoms and rural soviets were instructed to provide the courts with extensive documentation detailing the nature of fines against first offenders, the distribution of the village plans on households by the *skhod*, inventory lists of the property of those fined and the size of their families, protocols of rural soviet decisions on each case, and full information explaining the socioeconomic character of the peasant households in question.[10] This widening of the functions of local officials promoted greater bureaucratization and state regulation of peasant society and laid an institutional foundation for dekulakization.

In the summer of 1929 the Soviet state geared itself for the general application of Article 61 in the forthcoming grain procurement campaign, though in Siberia there was some uncertainty about this in the Kraikombiuro. On 31 July Eikhe sent a telegram to Zlobin, who was visiting Moscow, asking him to consult with Mikoyan and clarify the methods to be used in the coming grain campaign. Specifically, he wanted urgent confirmation of whether 'the method of directing the plan to each farm' was to be reapplied or whether a suggestion by Kuznetsov, now Kraiispolkom Chairman, that contractual agreements for grain sales be reached in advance with farms was acceptable.[11] That the state aimed to rely heavily on the use of Article 61 in the forthcoming campaign was confirmed by Mikoyan in an article published in *Bol'shevik* in the middle of August.[12] The Russian historian, Danilov, rightly interpreted the revision of Article 61 as the first act of legal dekulakization and the immediate 'prologue to collectivization'.[13] Certainly, if NEP was terminated *de facto* in January 1928, the amendment of Article 61 in June 1929 signalled its *de jure coup de grâce*, for the authorities now had the legal net to capture the peasantry by suppressing the free market and compelling them to sell grain at low state prices.

THE ROAD TO FORCED COLLECTIVIZATION

In the aftermath of the June plenum of the Kraikom the ideological war against the kulaks was intensified in order to justify the normalization of the compulsory grain levy and the social influence method. Party pronouncements warned that Siberia offered the 'widest base for petty bourgeois pressure against the ramparts of the party'.[14] In the forthcoming grain campaign the Kraikom leadership was determined to stamp out abuses and ensure the effective targeting of kulak farms in the first months. The decree on grain procurement issued following the plenum aimed to focus the minds of the party apparatus in the countryside on reserving the social influence procedure for application against kulaks exclusively. It banned the allocation of 'unreal' high or low delivery plans on villages, the redistribution of plans within the villages on an 'even' or 'fair' basis and the mass use of multiple fines and sequestration of property. Instead, it demanded a step-by-step surgical operation to isolate the kulaks and marginalize them.[15]

Meanwhile, the Kraikombiuro was following the resolutions of the plenum which instructed it to work out a 'control process' to put the grain stocks of the *verkhushka* at the disposal of the state in the first months of the procurement campaign. Zlobin summed up the two priorities of the new party line when he stressed the need to mobilize rural communities (for only it could organize the 'control process') and ensure that accurate plans were levied. Unlike the procedure as applied in the spring, this year area and village plans would be drawn up *after* consultation with village party cells and bedniak-seredniak meetings so that the okrug authorities could take account of local conditions (not only the size of the village harvest, but also the breakdown of the harvest among different social strata) when distributing plans. In addition, once again goods supply by the state to the countryside was to be related to the sale of grain.[16]

At the same time as Article 61 was amended the experience of mobilizing the *bednota* and institutionalizing party control in the villages gained from applying the social influence method in March–June was codified. A rather vacuous Central Committee decree of 15 June set out the guidelines for general party work among workers and peasants to mobilize them for the 'tasks of socialist reconstruction'. It placed a particular emphasis on the need for lower party organizations, soviets and state bodies in the countryside to raise the level of their work with the *bednota*, peasant women and peasant delegate groups. The latter were to serve as the 'pioneers ... for the reconstruction of agriculture on a socialist basis'.[17] The need for tighter party control in the villages had been hotly debated at the June plenum of the Kraikom. There was concern that the actions of party activists 'ordering the peasants about' were driving a wedge between the regime and the countryside: 'Peasants attend meetings and do not speak because they are afraid,' observed one official, or 'When communists and wives of communists have been driven out of meetings only then have peasants opened their mouths.' It was noted how when communist activists arrived in an area the word spread 'like an electric current from village to village and house to house'.[18]

A much clearer benchmark for the activities of the rural party apparatus was provided by a Kraikom decree of 27 June: 'On the Position of *Bednota* Groups'. In fact, four months later, in mid-October, the Central Committee decree on organizing the *bednota* for mass collectivization (see below) adopted many similar provisions to this Siberian decree. Dispelling any misconceptions that may have existed in the localities that the *bednota* groups were autonomous, the decree made it clear that, whatever the name of the groups suggested, they were not to be spontaneously elected by the *bednota* but must be stringently organized at village and raion levels by the party.

The groups were to be formed within the full range of party and state bodies in the countryside: party cells, rural soviets, raiispolkom plenums, the boards of Peasant Committees of Mutual Aid and cooperatives. Activists elected from the *bednota* would form a leavening of peasants in the combined force of party and state representatives engaged in controlling the villages and implementing policy. One imagines that their presence was probably largely symbolic. Party cells even had the power to coopt additional *bednota* activists, and while unelected seredniak and bedniak peasants could attend meetings, they had no vote.[19]

The goal of extracting the 'lion's share' of the annual grain plan in the first months, and certainly by the spring, was restated in a Narkomtorg directive of 3 July 1929. Mikoyan observed how the state had been forced by poor grain procurement in the previous two years to take emergency measures towards the end of the agricultural year. This year things would be different. The use of the social influence method by the 'soviet rural communities' to allocate grain delivery plans for areas and villages was to begin at 'the very outset' of the campaign. The plans were to be 'realistic' and to avoid antagonizing the peasantry they were not to be increased in the course of the campaign. Mikoyan advised that the plans include an 'insurance' and be set at a higher level at the beginning. He promised further directives later in the month after consultation with the local party authorities.[20] A Kraiispolkom directive ordering the reapplication of the social influence method and Article 61 followed on 14 August.[21] Similarly, in late August, a conference of the heads of okrug militias drew up an instruction for their units engaged in grain collection which set out operational guidelines; the new method of social influence was to be applied in the first instance, followed by Article 61, while the OGPU and armed intervention was to be a last resort. Seizing arms from peasants, especially those designated as kulaks, was declared to be a top priority for the beginnning of the campaign.[22]

For the sowing campaign of 1929 the agenda of the Stalinist leadership had remained fixed on the expansion of state contracts with peasants and the establishment of large-scale grain-producing collective farms on a voluntary basis. Theoretically, the former was reasonably successful in Siberia as about one-third of the total sown area and just under 2.4 million hectares sown to grain were under contract and Zlobin estimated that, given current yields, they would generate around 860,000 tons of grain.[23] The peasantry, however, were notoriously unreliable and often reneged on state contracts after the harvest, when market prices tempted them with higher profits. Meanwhile, the gradualist and voluntary approach to collectivization had brought few converts from the peasantry. While the overall number of collective farms had risen from 2,179 to 3,421 in the period January to June 1929 (a 57 per cent increase), most (1,844) were of the least socialized *toz* type. The collective farm sector was still largely irrelevant to Siberian agriculture as it accounted for a miniscule proportion of the Siberian peasant population, some 308,000 peasants (about 6 per cent of peasant households), and only 600,000 hectares (from a total of around 9 million). Lack of mechanized equipment was a major stumbling block to the formation of collectives. For example, tractors were supposedly the power horses dragging in the new Soviet dawn in the countryside, yet when the first three tractor columns in Machine Tractor Stations were organized in West Siberia in the spring of 1929 they operated with a paltry number of machines (15 in Novosibirsk, ten each in Slavgorod and Rubtsovsk).[24]

Given that the socialized sector had no appreciable impact on grain marketings in the krai, producing a negligible 6 to 7 per cent of the total for 1928/9, the Kraikombiuro approved a decision on 11 June to construct an unspecified number of additional large-scale grain collective farms (20,000 hectares or more). Even as late as September 1929, however, the Siberian leadership anticipated that the contribution of the socialized sector to grain marketings would rise to no more than 17 to 18 per cent of the total.[25] In Moscow, the Stalinist leadership simply ignored poor results from regions like Siberia, and focused instead on those regions which activated high levels of collectivization. An article in *Pravda* in mid-September, entitled 'On the road to comprehensive collectivization', pointed the direction in which the regime was heading.[26] Over the next two months, in the build up to the November 1929 Central Committee plenum, the Stalinist leadership orchestrated a concerted political campaign which promoted the idea that comprehensive collectivization was developing momentum spontaneously at the grassroots, with the Lower and Middle Volga regions held up as models of the new order in the countryside.[27] The Stalinist leadership was already looking beyond the immediate battles of this year's grain procurement campaign, and envisaging a final solution to the problem of reconciling private small-scale peasant agriculture with 'building socialism'. The political goal was how to impose rapid collectivization through the use of the 'Ural-Siberian method' and 'socialist emulation'.

THE HARVEST OF 1929

The party leadership assumed that an early application of the social influence method would pressurize grain-holding peasants into quick sales at the outset of the 1929/30 campaign. There were optimistic forecasts from Mikoyan and Syrtsov that the size of the harvest would exceed those of

1927 and 1928, given the estimated increase of 5 to 6 per cent in the sown area and 2.5 per cent in yields. A wildly over-ambitious collection plan was drawn up with a target of 12.5 million tons – a 30 per cent increase over the previous year. By the early autumn it was clear that the initial optimism was misplaced as the harvest, at 71.7 million tons, was substantially lower than previous years, with the output of grains 2 to 5 per cent down on 1928 figures.[28] Whereas in 1927 and 1928 the harvest had been poor in the grain producing regions that were geographically convenient to the central industrial heartland of the country (the Ukraine, North Caucasus) and excellent in the remote Urals and Siberian regions, this year the positions were reversed. A good harvest in the Ukraine was countered by harvest failure in Siberia. Despite an almost 11 per cent increase in the sown area of Siberia in 1929 a harvest failure in the grain belt of the south-west brought an abrupt halt to the unbroken run of three golden years of rising grain production. There was a 24 per cent drop in grain production in the krai as a whole, while in south-west Siberia production plummeted by 38 per cent.[29] Grain collection was not expected to exceed 1.3 million tons, an amount well below the levels of 1927 and 1928, and Narkomtorg initially set the krai grain collection plan at this level.

In an escalation of pressure on regional party leaderships, the Politburo now demanded that Narkomtorg provide reports at each of its weekly sessions, based on information from the regions and OGPU, on the progress of the grain procurement campaign and the fulfilment of its directives. These weekly reports supplied a steady flow of bad news to the party leadership and, henceforth, discussion of ways of improving grain procurement became a regular feature of Politburo deliberations. The Politburo's strategy had been to force the pace of procurement in the early months of the campaign by means of the speedy collection of agricultural taxes and debts and the imposition of village plans with high compulsory grain delivery quotas on kulaks, and the use of Article 61 against the recalcitrant grain holders. By the middle of September this strategy did not appear to be working and the central leadership's concern at the 'unsatisfactory' progress of the campaign turned into anxiety and anger. To force the tempo, the Politburo defined time limits for key grain regions to implement a plan of compulsory quotas not 'in a broad sense' but exclusively on the kulak and well-off peasants (Siberia was given to 1 October to complete its plan).[30]

The reduced size of the harvest caught the Kraikom by surprise and, given that the dependence of the centre on Siberian grain had steadily accumulated in the latter years of NEP, it created an urgency bordering on panic in the Siberian party organization. The political reputation of the

Siberians as the regime's 'breadwinners' was at stake and for a hardliner like Eikhe, who was eager to please Stalin, the looming prospect of a political failure by dashing Stalin's expectations must have been bitterly disappointing. A mass implementation of the social influence method was enacted immediately to salvage state grain procurement in the krai. In early September a joint letter-directive of the Kraikombiuro and Kraiispolkom ordered the allocation of compulsory grain delivery quotas on kulak farms calculated on the basis of estimates of their marketable surplus. Any pretence of a free market in grain was abandoned as the quotas were to include 'all grain surpluses of any kulak farm'.[31] It was akin to a 100 per cent profit tax and eliminated any residual incentive left to the well-off peasantry to produce a marketable surplus.

Raion plenipotentiaries were sent into the villages on grain procurement duty from 14 September and the order-instruction (*nakaz-instruktsiia*) which provided the framework for their operations demonstrates how the party attempted to enlarge its control and achieve the further *étatisation* of the countryside by an increasing bureaucratization of party and state relations with the peasantry at the village level.[32] The plenipotentiaries were instructed to divide the peasantry into a basic tripartite social categorization dependent on grain-holding status: kulaks (who were to bear the brunt of exactions), bedniaks (those with no grain surplus) and a third group (those seredniaks and bedniaks who had grain surpluses). In distributing the bulk of the village delivery plan on the kulak group plenipotentiaries were to take into account the general presumptions that the yields of kulak plots were larger and that kulaks normally worked hidden plots and engaged in sharecropping to augment their total grain harvest. Both factors were, of course, almost impossible to assess with any degree of accuracy and this gave the plenipotentiaries virtual arbitrary power in fixing the amounts a given kulak household had to sell to the state.

The party even went so far as to attempt to define annual norms of grain yields (138 kg per desiatin), family consumption (196 to 230 kg per individual) and livestock feed (82 to 163 kg per head) in order to maximize the surplus product of households. Such generalized figures did not take into consideration local variations of yields and usage and added to the potential for abuse and overburdening of those defined as kulaks. Kulak households were given fixed periods to comply with their grain delivery task (50 per cent by 1 October and the other 50 per cent by 15 October) or face multiple fines. While the remainder of the village plan was to be distributed by general meetings the plenipotentiaries were to try and get the allocations approved on the basis of self-obligation (*samoobiazatel'stvo*) as opposed to the compulsory task imposed on the kulaks. In practice, the semantic difference between the terms may have been blurred and the distinction between both groups ignored in order to facilitate the compulsory extraction of grain surpluses, irrespective of the social status of the household.

A Western traveller to Russia was told by German peasants fleeing from Siberia that officials inspected their harvests in the field before reaping and estimates of the potential yields were made and delivery quotas allocated on this basis. The peasants reported that the first official inspector set low quotas, but he was arrested. A second inspector then doubled the original quotas. The peasants claimed that the only way they could fulfil their quotas was to buy extra grain on the private market at many times the state procurement price.[33] This method of estimating the harvest was later regularized as the 'biological yield' method of procurement from collective farms.

Once plans were drawn up members of the village grain procurement commission and plenipotentiaries had to sign them and, in so doing, accept personal responsibility for their fulfilment. A significant widening in the construction of a bureaucratized state under Stalin can be dated to this period, for the keeping of lists and records (registers of kulaks, village plans, grain quota lists, protocols of meetings of cells, *bednota* groups, the *skhod*, the grain commission, the rural soviet) was to be one of the most important functions of plenipotentiaries and officials in the villages and this plethora of documentation was forwarded to the raion authorities and up the administrative hierarchy.[34]

Shortly afterwards the krai leadership sent a report to Molotov at the Central Committee advising that, given the harvest failure in the region, the maximum procurement plan had been lowered to 1.03 million tons and warning that any attempt to increase it would be 'unrealistic'.[35] While this may have been a device to forestall the kind of exorbitant demands that had emanated from the centre for Siberian grain over the previous two years, the regional leadership was sufficiently realistic to know that local agricultural difficulties were unlikely to generate much sympathy from Stalin and were not a mitigating circumstance for non-fulfilment of orders from the centre. Nevertheless, the annual plan for Siberia was sharply reduced from the record of almost 2 million tons achieved the previous year and fixed by Narkomtorg at just under 1.23 million tons. This was still a figure that would have been a good target in any normal year. Moreover, the plan called for a shift in the main burden of grain procurement from western to eastern okrugs of Siberia, where the government and procurement apparatus and transport infrastructure were even less developed. Whereas western okrugs had collected almost 1.4 million tons in

1928/9, this year their target figure was reduced by almost one half, to just over 720,000 tons. The target for eastern okrugs, on the other hand, was slightly increased to compensate, from just over 586,000 collected last year to just over 670,000.[36] Grain procurement slumped in Siberia, with only 64,000 tons (52 per cent of the monthly plan) collected in September.[37] It was against this background of plummeting procurement that Stalinist radicalism for immediate collectivization and dekulakization intensified.

PREPARING FOR DEKULAKIZATION

In late September, a stern reprimand was issued in a new Politburo decree to the party leaderships of the main grain regions for 'a lack of preparedness and a weak tempo of grain procurement'. From this time on direct physical repression of 'kulaks', as opposed to economic exactions, began to assume a greater significance in Politburo directives and, indeed, a special commission composed of Kaganovich, Syrtsov and Chernov was established to draw up guidelines for allocating grain plans and 'measures of influence against kulaks'. Kulaks who failed to complete compulsory quotas were not only to be punished with the array of repressive legal measures under Article 61, but 'especially malicious kulaks and speculators' were now also to be increasingly subjected to forced exile and 'show-trials' with severe punishments. Kulaks who organized 'acts of terrorism' and 'other counter-revolutionary demonstrations' were to be punished as a rule through the courts, but in especially urgent cases through the OGPU with the sanction of higher party authorities.[38]

A Kraiispolkom decree of 22–23 September established okrug collection targets, with the target date for completion of the annual plan as 1 February 1930. In view of the Politburo's intensifying pressure, the Kraikombiuro decided on 1 October to minimize the political damage of a shortfall in the plan by collecting as much grain in the shortest possible time. A procurement target of just under half a million tons of grain (about 43 per cent of the annual plan) was established for the month. The Kraikom designated 7 to 9 per cent of farms in the krai as 'kulak and well-off' and set compulsory grain delivery quotas amounting to a minimum of 246,000 tons (about 24 per cent of the Siberian plan for 1929/30) to be completed by 15 October 1929, that is to say within two weeks. The decree instructed raion level authorities to distribute the compulsory grain delivery quotas to kulak farms by no later than 5 October.[39] As the Kraikombiuro decree put it: 'The most severe repression must fall on the heads of the kulak counter-revolutionaries.' In accordance with the ominous new Politburo guidelines, refusal to comply with grain quotas no longer just incurred five times fines and arraignment under Article 61 but also dispossession and exile. An explanation of the operation of Article 61, prepared by the Krai Procuracy, was published in *Sovetskaia sibir'* and other local newspapers over the following days. To ensure the requisite speed in the processing of cases relating to grain procurement, special two-man judicial teams were established in each raion, composed of one judge and one procurator. These teams were to act as emergency circuit courts trying 'malicious grain holders'.[40]

These decrees and orders systematically intensified the pressure on local authorities to escalate the level of repression against the peasantry. To further ensure that this harsh response was adhered to, the Politburo ordered, on 5 October, the sending of another 150 communists from the centre to Siberia.[41] At the same session, the Politburo approved the harshest measures of repression, including extra-judicial summary execution by shooting by the OGPU of those kulaks accused of engaging in acts of terrorism against party and soviet officials and of other 'counter-revolutionary' actions.

Concurrent with the pressure for grain procurement from kulaks, the Kraikombiuro included instructions in several of its decrees for 'clear kulak households' to be targeted systematically for individual tax supplements, and the Krai Financial Department drew up a scheme for this purpose based on its instruction of April 1929 on what households fell into this category.[42] Each okrug was allocated a plan for kulak individual supplementary taxes based on estimates of the numbers of 'clear kulak households' in their jurisdiction. The norm for Siberia was established at 3.5 to 4 per cent of households, with regional variations: for example, the grain okrugs of the south-west had norms of 5 to 6 per cent. Work on the collection of these taxes was supposed to be completed by 1 December, but the Financial Department reported that many okrugs had fallen behind. By the deadline 64,446 households had been identified as 'clear kulak', and 48,688 had been levied with individual tax supplements.[43]

The Siberian Krai Procuror, Burmistrov, tendered a detailed report to the Kraiispolkom assessing the grain procurement campaign in 1928/9 and the first half (August–December) of 1929/30.[44] It contained statistical breakdowns of the use of social influence measures and Article 61 in connection with grain procurement in the region which provide a unique insight into the campaign and its impact on the peasantry. One has to keep in mind, of course, that the peasant social categories employed are nowhere defined, other than that they were derived from taxation lists, and

Table 6.1 Compulsory grain quotas on peasants in Siberia in 1928/9 and 1929/30

Okrug	Number of farms in 1928/9	Number of farms in 1929/30
Omsk	13,026	16,677
Slavgorod	7,512	8,500
Barabinsk	2,407	3,772
Novosibirsk	10,112	10,302
Kamen'	5,416	5,416
Barnaul	10,749	9,980
Biisk	6,761	12,045
Rubtsovsk	4,957	5,000
Tomsk	5,603	5,667
Kuznetsk	4,000	3,801
Achinsk	5,832	5,832
Krasnoiarsk	4,500	6,000
Minusinsk	4,649	5,094
Kansk	5,000	6,000
Irkutsk	6,290	5,290
Total	95,420	108,228
Grain quotas (in tons)	299,017	328,992
Share of annual plan	17%	25%

Sources: For 1928/9: *GANO* 1, f. r-47, op. 4a, d. 260 'a', l. 5, report of the Siberian Krai Procuracy on the grain procurement campaign, 3 February 1930; for 1929/30: *Zhizn' sibiri*, No. 11–12, November–December 1929, p. 24.

that we are presented with a series of snapshots from the official viewpoint. Frequently, there was only a partial association between those farms allocated quotas and those assessed as kulaks for the purposes of taxation, since in many okrugs there was often double the number of the former compared with the latter. A comparison of two sets of statistics on grain quota distribution, one provided by Burmistrov for 1928/9, the other drawn up by Kraitorg for 1929/30, reveals that the number of kulak households designated for grain quotas was sharply increased for the grain campaign of 1929/30 (see Table 6.1). The first round of policy implementation involved 95,420 kulak farms imposed with grain quotas amounting to a total of almost 300,000 tons (about 17 per cent of the 1.8 million tons collected that year). For the second round in 1929/30, the head of Kraitorg, Zlobin, set a plan of 108,228 farms to be allocated compulsory quotas amounting to 329,000 tons (about 25 per cent of the annual plan of almost 1.3 million tons). This further tightening of the screws on the kulaks marked the beginning of the dekulakization process that reached a crescendo in early 1930.

There was a lack of correlation between the concentration of kulak households allocated compulsory grain delivery quotas, which were weighted towards the eastern okrugs of the krai, and previous Kraikom studies conducted by Kavraisky and Nusinov, which found the bulk of kulak farms to be in the south-western okrugs of the Siberian grain producing triangle. For example, in the 1928/9 campaign the largest number of households allocated quotas was in Omsk (13,026 or 8.2 per cent of all peasant households) and the largest proportion was in Barnàul (10,749 and 8.4 per cent); other key areas of the south-west had comparatively low figures: Biisk (6,761 and 4.6 per cent) and Rubtsovsk (4,957 and 5.9 per cent). The figure for Biisk almost doubled for the 1929/30 campaign, a factor which may help to explain the surge in peasant protests in this area. In contrast, the proportion in certain okrugs of East Siberia was relatively high: Irkutsk (7.5 per cent), Achinsk (7.8 per cent) and Minusinsk (8.2 per cent). Similarly, the average grain quota levied per farm in many eastern okrugs ranged from two to four times that allocated in many western okrugs. Such differentials may be explained by the need to extract more grain from the eastern okrugs in late 1929 given the harvest failure in the south-western grain areas and the higher than normal annual plan for eastern okrugs.[45]

The weak adherence of local officials and plenipotentiaries to Kraikom targets is a reflection both of their lack of understanding of the process of defining kulak farms, and of the pressure they were under to extract grain from a wider range of grain-holding peasants. This is clear from the fact that only six okrugs managed to keep within the Kraikom recommended figure of 7 to 9 per cent for the number of kulak households to be allocated grain quotas, while most were substantially below. This did not mean, however, that the grain quotas were reduced; on the contrary, they were often distributed wrongly onto seredniaks and poor peasant farms. This lack of control is also evident in the wide disparities between okrugs in the share of kulak quotas as a proportion of the total plan. The kulak share ranged from 20 to 33 per cent with the highest in Novosibirsk (40.4 per cent), Omsk (33.6 per cent) and Barabinsk (33.7 per cent), and the lowest in Rubtsovsk (12 per cent). Burmistrov suggested that it was no coincidence that the first three ranked highest in fulfilment of the annual plan, while the latter was in last place, for, he observed: 'The use of repression [against kulaks] had a positive impact on the intake of grain from other sources: kolkhozes, seredniaks and weak farms.'[46] This was an open admission that measures ostensibly targeted on kulaks also had the desirable effect for the authorities of intimidating the mass of peasants into parting with their grain. Despite Kraikom instructions that the allocation of grain delivery quotas be stringently guided by the 'class line' and targeted on kulak farms, in some villages officials practised 'levelling' by distributing the village plans 'fairly' across the social spectrum. This meant that middle and poor peasants were imposed with quotas which they could hardly afford, thus infringing the moral economy norm of proportionality and negating the political economy material incentives.

The report revealed that there had been a doubling of the number of 'repressions' (under Articles 61 and 107) by the beginning of December compared with the whole of the 1928/9 campaign. The concerted intensification began with the declaration of the grain campaign as a 'military task' in September. A joint Krai Judicial Department and OGPU 'order no. 1' on 24 September 1929 ordered greater use of Articles 107 and 61 and, in effect, according to Burmistrov: 'put a stop to free market sales' of grain. Burmistrov disclosed that 150–200 trials were held under Article 107 in late September and early October in order to thwart attempts by kulaks to sell on the free market the grain which they would have had to deliver to the state as a compulsory quota. It was only after 20 October, when about half the complement of the staff of the Krai Procuracy and Krai Judicial Department were sent into the countryside on grain procurement duty, that Article 61 began to be put into effect, with some 1,000 cases being held within a matter of days. By early December 1929, while there were only 373 cases heard under Article 107, 14,673 farms had been prosecuted under Article 61, most (10,390) under the catch-all Clause 1. Almost one-third of all cases were conducted in the grain triangle of Biisk–Barnaul–Rubtsovsk, and almost one-third of the 4.7 million roubles raised in fines under Article 61 were levied in these okrugs, despite the harvest failure and peasant distress in that part of the krai.[47]

'The repression was severe', noted the Krai Procuror. Some three thousand peasants were sentenced to periods of imprisonment under Article 61, and about half of these exceeded the legally stipulated maximum of up to one year (see Table 6.2). Concurrently, harsh exemplary punishments, such as exile and forced labour, were frequently imposed. For example, 59 per cent of those sentenced to prison terms were also sent into exile, and about one-third were assigned to hard labour. Burmistrov was indignant that insufficient use had been made of fines and confiscation of grain stocks, as these were punishments that had been emphasized in the framing of the article and also in the revisions made to it in late June 1929. A major problem in the use of fines, however, was their collection, as

Table 6.2 Punishment policy under Article 61 in Siberia in 1929/30

Okrug	Imprisoned			Forced labour	Exiled	Fined				Amount of fine			Number of cases	Confiscation				
	Up to 1 year	Over 1 year	Total			Administrative	Court	Court second offence	Total	Administrative	Judicial	Total		Grain (in puds)	Cattle	Machines	Mills & enterprises	Unknown
Achinsk	59	177	236	61	57	875	48	—	48	149,981	36,795	186,776	—	33,412	257	67	—	—
Biisk	117	153	270	70	170	1,058	13	50	1,119	—	21,450	21,450	166	34,040	—	—	—	—
Barabinsk	18	9	27	66	48	329	41	18	388	118,389	26,709	145,188	41	3,613	32	18	7	23
Barnaul	279	324	603	83	247	961	2	137	1,100	—	56,573	56,573	380	—	—	—	215	485
Irkutsk	103	66	169	62	71	—	97	—	97	—	34,748	34,748	71	2,028	58	19	—	89
Kansk	152	21	173	113	31	615	24	180	819	680,985	102,775	873,760	35	16,050	109	16	—	—
Kamensk	135	93	228	14	132	825	1	79	144	195,748	23,255	219,003	104	5,872	158	86	2	6
Kuznetsk	94	159	253	282	207	1,800	85	75	166	—	32,763	32,763	182	13,900	75	16	6	—
Minusinsk	20	112	132	51	95	148	7	17	24	109,770	20,923	139,693	134	2,350	28	18	—	36
Novosibirsk	207	52	259	24	147	—	12	84	295	95,099	14,248	109,347	187	9,269	258	65	—	—
Omsk	18	198	216	115	178	782	24	11	815	194,483	19,100	213,583	199	11,207	147	72	—	23
Rubtsovsk	125	49	174	44	119	1,227	7	142	1,234	622,420	36,650	659,070	72	2,160	43	27	2	—
Tomsk	111	86	97	24	211	363	221	306	527	—	—	—	200	33,100	20	3	—	—
Khakassiya	—	2	2	3	2	109	—	1	110	50,000	500	50,500	2	—	—	—	—	—
Total	1,438	1,501	2,939	1,013	1,715	9,090	584	1,100	6,886	2,216,875	426,579	2,643,454	1,773	167,801	1,185	334	232	662

Source: GANO 1, f. r-47, op. 4 'a', d. 260 2 'a', l. 70b.

illustrated by the situation in Rubtsovsk Okrug. Although over 600,000 roubles in fines had been handed out by 20 November, only 9.5 per cent of this sum had been collected. This was partly because the rural soviets and raiispolkom authorities had failed to take into account the propertied status of those fined, and partly because the traders appointed to sequester property and goods sold them off very cheaply. Local corruption must have been a factor, and there were reported cases when sequestered property was kept by local officials.[48]

As if in confirmation of the old Russian proverb that 'the law is a rudder' which you move according to where your destination lies, the krai legal authorities proved to be highly flexible in their interpretations of the criminal code when it came to the tightening up of the procedures for repressing kulaks and increasing grain procurement. The requirement in Article 61 that peasants who refused to comply with compulsory delivery quotas be first subjected to fines (the notorious *piatikratniki*) before being brought to trial for repeated refusal was regarded on the ground as an invitation to kulaks to hide their property or transfer it to friends and neighbours. After some argument and pressure from the Krai Procuracy on the Krai Judicial Department in early November, eventually in early December this legal requirement was amended in practice to allow for immediate prosecutions and prison sentences. There was a similar dispute between the two legal agencies over the interpretation of Article 271, which was designed to punish kulaks who sold off their property in order to avoid tax and other agricultural payments, as to whether it could be part of the armoury of legal weapons wielded by the state in grain procurement from the kulaks. Once again, the Krai Procuracy's more flexible and hardline – approach won and on 19 November it issued a directive ordering the application of Article 169 which laid down a stiff five-year sentence and confiscation of property for fraud, and included penalties for accomplices.[49] Alongside these legal forms of repression the authorities activated a series of measures to crack down on sluggish grain procurement, including punishment for delays in kolkhoz grain deliveries to the state, limitations on the operation of private mills, and further increasing the tax and self-taxation burden on kulak farms.[50]

The repression was doubly severe on the peasants of Western Siberia because of the grain harvest failure. Peasants who produced certificates from rural soviets proving that their crops had failed had them ignored at best and were punished for deception at worst. To evade the compulsory quotas, peasants resorted to the practices and ruses they had used during the previous spring, but with even less success: dispersing and hiding their grain and property among relatives and poorer neighbours or traders in the towns ('to become bedniaks'), hiding it in pits (and even in one case in graves), disrupting *skhod* meetings to prevent adoption of compulsory plans, bribing officials for false receipts, intimidating and attacking peasants who collaborated with the procurement process, organizing *volynki* to resist seizures. Often, the ultimate recourse taken by named defaulters was 'to go on the run'. The repression was not restricted to grain collection. Kulaks who refused to allow their milling machines to operate were dragooned into 'forced milling' by the committees of social influence.

The corollary of the tightening of repression was the simplification of the judicial process. Peasants who disrupted or resisted the grain campaign were now more likely to be charged under Article 58 of the Criminal Code, which covered the ambiguous offence of 'counter-revolutionary act'. For this year's campaign the government had simplified the court procedures and whereas in the spring a case under this article could take two or three months to process, now it took only one or two weeks. By late December 1929, 193 cases had been tried under Article 58 in Siberia, with 46 peasants shot and 113 sentenced to periods of imprisonment ranging from 2–10 years. Yet in the month of December alone, there were 827 acts of violence against rural soviet officials and peasants involved in village commissions for procurement, while for the period October–December there were 525 incidents of a 'counter-revolutionary' type. The divergence in these figures indicates that the use of Article 58 (the harshest in the state armoury against its enemies) was controlled and reserved for a small number of targeted cases in order to generate a wider intimidatory effect.[51]

Despite the successful tempo of procurement, officials and activists involved in the campaign were heavily criticized. The central party journal *Bol'shevik* cited a comment by an unnamed party leader recently returned from Siberia which claimed that the peasants of the region had been given the 'impression of a full amnesty' in grain procurement by local party organizations.[52] Some of these local officials were regarded as being too sensitive to the 'well-being' of their area to extract the maximum amounts stipulated in grain plans. Altruism was not the only motive here, for some local officials in Novosibirsk Okrug had learned from experience not to fulfil their plans too zealously, noting: 'If we fulfil the plan quickly, the okrug will just give us a second plan.' The other side of this coin was the tyrannical behaviour of plenipotentiaries, who subordinated rural soviets and other local agencies to their diktats. Often no distinction was made between kulaks and seredniaks in the allocation of plans, or the threat of this was used to force seredniaks to vote for the plan at the *skhod*. Methods of terrorizing the peasantry favoured by plenipotentiaries included the imprisonment of recalcitrant grain holders in freezing barns or out-buildings, followed by beatings and forced sleeplessness, and mock executions with the ubiquitous revolver carried by the plenipotentiaries, until the peasants told where their grain was hidden. In Kamensk, the Okrug Procurer gave his officials the following injunction when dealing with the sequestration of property: 'Do not be in a hurry to sell, first add more, then sell.'[53]

The perceived 'softness' of local officials led to a hardening of the orders for repression. By early December, raiispolkoms were categorically forbidden the practice of allowing rural soviets and 'committees of influence' in grain procurement to decide the pace of fulfilment of compulsory quotas by kulaks. Kulaks were to be given three days to complete their plans, and if they failed to do so their property was to be immediately sequestrated and sold to pay for multiple fines, with the 'particularly malicious' sent for trial.[54] This kind of licence to pillage the peasantry was restrained at its worst extremes by the procuracy and the courts, as all cases connected with grain procurement were to be reviewed at the okrug level. Appeal courts moderated sentences, threw out cases that clearly involved seredniaks and poor peasants, and plenipotentiaries responsible for the worst abuses against these peasants were occasionally arrested and convicted.[55] The attempt by the party leadership to instil a 'class line' in the application of the law seems to have been borne out by the punishment policy of the courts in the implementation of Article 61: those designated as kulaks were more than twice as likely as seredniaks to be imprisoned, and about twice as likely to be sent into exile, whereas seredniaks tended to be punished with hard labour and fines.[56]

MILITARIZATION OF THE CAMPAIGN

In late October 1929 the central party leadership formally institutionalized in the country the approach that the Siberians had taken towards the organization of the *bednota*. Party control was to be infiltrated into the villages under the cover of *bednota* activism and the well orchestrated *bednota* groups were to serve as the instrumental force for enlarging collectivization and destroying the kulaks. A Central Committee decree of 20 October 1929, 'On the Organization of the *Bednota*', ostensibly in national areas but directed at the party as a whole, conceded that the questions of 'widening mass collectivization and the severe intensification of the class struggle against the kulaks' demanded an 'urgent decision'. The weakness of this kind of work hitherto was blamed on the 'harmful influence' of the Right, elements 'alien' to the party and Komsomol, and the preference for administrative paper-pushing in the apparatus.

Stepping up the militarization of the campaign in the villages, the decree referred to the unification of batrak-bedniak 'fighting units' (*iadra*). Spontaneity and autonomy of action by the *bednota* in the form of 'unions' outside of party control was completely ruled out as dangerously reminiscent of the kulak call for a 'peasant union' to resist the Soviet government. The goal was to exploit the batrak-bedniak unit as a spearhead for collectivization and counterpoint to kulak attempts to 'explode them [kolkhozes] from within'. The groups would also serve as a recruiting agency for the party to infuse itself with new blood from the poor peasantry. Following the Siberian example, the Central Committee ordered that the groups be formed in elected village organs, including members of rural soviets and boards of cooperatives, and especially in newly established kolkhozes. If a village had no party, cell groups could be formed elsewhere by communists and Komsomol members, or even non-party batrak and bedniak activists, to act vicariously on behalf of the *bednota*. The practice of calling regular meetings of all the *bednota* groups of a village, area conferences of groups and conferences of group leaders to discuss economic and political tasks with special party instructors was used to coordinate and control their activities. This mobilization of mass-induced participation by poor peasants laid a foundation of organizational levers for the conduct of forced collectivization and dekulakization, and readied them to be engaged at a command from Stalin.[57] Mikoyan referred to such groups in a telegram to Zlobin of 28 October, when he ordered the Siberians to complete their annual procurement plan by 1 January and advised them to achieve this by mobilizing 'special brigades' of bedniaks and activists from areas where the grain plans had been completed and sending them into areas lagging behind.[58]

As far as grain procurement was concerned the adopted measures were remarkably successful in an even shorter space of time than had been the case the previous year. Concurrent with heightened political pressure from Moscow for the completion by the target date of 1 January 1930, the massive intake of grain after late October was such that the krai leadership declared, in mid-November, that 100 per cent of the annual plan should be completed by 15 December. This was achieved, as grain stocks collected in major procurement points, excluding those held in remote points, reached 101 per cent of the annual plan by this date, with some okrugs far exceeding their annual plans (Barabinsk achieved almost 168 per cent, Novosibirsk 118 per cent, Omsk 108 per cent, and Krasnoyarsk 108 per cent) in a manner which suggests that local procurement officials did not regard the plan as a constraint on procurement. Despite the grain harvest failure in the most productive western parts of the krai, the level of procurement was as successful as it had been during the same period of the previous year as 1.06 million tons had been collected by the middle of December 1929, compared with 1.13 million by 1 January 1929.[59]

In January 1930 work on the collection of the compulsory quotas was still continuing in some areas due to peasant resistance but by then events had moved on. The political target was to finish with grain procurement as quickly as possible and then in a massive pivoting manoeuvre to throw the thousands of party activists operating in the countryside into the campaign to impose Stalin's 'revolution from above' of all-out collectivization and the 'liquidation of the kulaks as a class'. For in the last months of 1929, Stalin decided that the social influence method had created a basis for a final solution to the grain problem in Soviet Russia through collectivization and dekulakization.

THE MOVE TO COMPREHENSIVE COLLECTIVIZATION

From late 1928, Stalin elaborated a doctrine of Bolshevik millenarianism, professing that the country was on the eve of a new socialist order which would transcend the 'age-old' legacy of Russian backwardness. Since the November 1928 plenum the leitmotif of the Stalinist regime had been 'to catch up and to overtake' (*'dognat' i peregnat'*). The goal was to outperform the advanced capitalist countries, and create a bulwark against their hostile 'encirclement' of Soviet Russia, by a modernizing crash programme of industrialization and the collectivization of agriculture.[60] By late 1929 the struggle for grain had assumed in the minds of the Stalinists the proportions of a struggle for the existence of the Soviet regime itself. In his article, 'The Year of the Great Breakthrough', published in *Pravda* on 7 November 1929, the twelfth anniversary of the October Revolution, Stalin invoked Lenin's authority in support of the new radicalism, citing his statement on the introduction of NEP in 1921: 'We are retreating now, why are we retreating backwards, well we are doing this so that at first we retreat and then we make a run and strongly leap forward.' This year, declared Stalin, the party was fulfilling Lenin's 'instruction' for a great leap forward.[61] Some months later, he specifically dated the breakthrough in the party's agrarian policy to the summer of 1929 – following the launch of the 'Ural-Siberian method' and the use of Article 61 against kulaks.[62]

The political 'breakthrough' was three-pronged, according to Stalin, each of which paved the way for a new advance in the building of socialism: a surge in labour productivity arising from 'socialist competition', the party's choice of a maximalist variant for industrial construction in the

First Five Year Plan, and the growth of collectivization in the countryside. As regards the peasant question, Stalin portrayed the party's role as one of facilitator: 'We have successfully organized this profound change in the hearts of the peasants themselves.' Assisted by workers' brigades and 'armed' with tractors and machines, the kolkhoz movement had become a 'mass movement' among the peasants, encompassing 'whole villages, districts, areas and even regions'. This scale of collectivization was what was *new*, and moreover, claimed Stalin, 'the seredniak has joined the kolkhozes'. He confidently asserted that grain crises were a thing of the past and forecast that within three years Russia would become 'one of the richest grain producing countries, if not the richest grain producing country in the world'. There was no suggestion at this stage of dekulakization; however, Stalin aggressively pointed out that there were 'dark forces' opposing progress and pronounced that the private property of the peasantry was the 'last hope for the restoration of capitalism', and as such it had to be eliminated as a threat to the existence of the socialist regime. He summoned up the ghost of Russia's 'age-old "dissipating" backwardness' to justify the party's forced march down the 'highway' to socialism via rapid industrialization and collectivization. Alluding to his 'catch up and overtake' slogan, he appealed to Russian's ancient fear and loathing of the West, exhorting the country to join in the modernization crusade: 'For when we seat the USSR in a motor car and the muzhik on a tractor – let the respectable capitalists try to catch us up, as they strut around their "civilization". We shall see then which country is "determined" the backward and which the advanced.'[63]

The Central Committee plenum held from 10–17 November 1929 was a crucial turning point in the drive for comprehensive collectivization. Stalin reiterated his main theses on the potential for a 'great breakthrough', declaring that the grain campaign had been transformed into a 'mass offensive by the bednota and seredniaks against the kulak'. Many speakers followed the lead provided by Stalin and Molotov to endorse the view that collectivization was developing rapidly and spontaneously 'from below' and with the active participation of the seredniaks.[64] Molotov warned the regional party leaders that developments on the ground now meant that comprehensive collectivization of the main agricultural areas was a task that must be completed not during the Five Year Plan, but 'in the coming year'.[65] The resolutions of the plenum declared that the country was on the eve of 'a new historical stage of the socialist transformation of agriculture by means of strengthening the productive linkages between the proletarian state and the basic bedniak-seredniak masses'. The issue was now formulated for regional party organizations in this way: 'The kolkhoz movement is already placing the task of comprehensive collectivization before individual regions.' This was a Stalinist code for a demand that the regions outperform each other in encouraging comprehensive collectivization as a corollary of building socialism in a 'historically minimum period'.[66] The plenum also witnessed the final capitulation of the Bukharinist Right wing of the party, with a joint declaration from Bukharin, Rykov and Tomsky, recognizing their 'political mistakes' and considering it their 'duty' to support the party leadership and 'all of its decisions'.[67]

Eikhe caught the mood of the moment when he aptly recalled Lenin's observation on the grain campaign of 1918: 'It might seem that this is a struggle for grain, but in actual fact, it is a struggle for socialism.' Stalin approvingly interjected: 'Correct!' Eikhe also drew the following lesson: 'Where we hit the kulak with a strong blow, the grain came in much easier.'[68] As keen advocates of the rapid industrialization of Siberia, Eikhe and Syrtsov frequently linked the solution of the 'grain problem' to the growth of collectivization, which in turn depended on an improved railway system, a developed industrial manufacturing and processing base, and an ever increasing supply of tractors and agricultural equipment. These were factors that could only be realized by capital investment in heavy industry, and the 'metal' industries in particular.

As far back as their speeches to the November 1928 plenum the Siberian leaders began a concerted attempt to impose a strategic linkage in the minds of the central party leaders between the consolidation of Siberia as an agricultural base for the country and its development as a new industrial region. During 1928–29, however, the Siberians adhered to the Stalinist line that the socialist transformation of agricultural would be 'a prolonged one' and that individual peasant farms would play the main role in agricultural production 'for a long time yet', while recognizing the inevitability of an intensification of the 'class struggle' in the countryside.[69] These issues were subtly linked with budgetary policy, specifically the delays in investment funds being released for the construction of the Kuznetsk industrial complex in Siberia. Rykov, who had overall charge of the preparation of the First Five Year Plan, dismissed such complaints from the 'victims of nightschool'. Eikhe and Syrtsov objected to the 'bureaucratic red-tape' and 'vacillation' surrounding the Kuznetsk project and Siberian railway construction, arguing that the Siberian grain on which the centre depended required an enlarged railway network for its efficient and speedy transportation. Syrtsov even reminded Stalin of his own recent experience of the chaos on the overloaded railways in the region when the General Secretary had visited Western Siberia during the grain crisis in January 1928.[70]

At the November 1929 plenum Eikhe rebuked Mikoyan's 'golden words' about a balanced programme of investment for collectivization and expressed fears that the focus on grain was creating a crisis in the livestock industry of Western Siberia. He cited figures for Barabinsk Okrug (the main dairy and livestock area) which showed that the price scissors between butter and grain had widened threefold within the space of one year, so that whereas last year a pud of butter purchased the equivalent of 20 puds of grain, this year it earned only seven puds. The tempo of growth of the collectivized sector had been colossal in Siberia and had soared during the previous year from 150,000 to 689,000 hectares, with a plan for over 1.6 million hectares in the coming year. It was at this gathering that Eikhe firmly committed himself to favouring the commune as the most preferable form of kolkhoz. Once again he linked collectivization to industrialization: 'Kolkhozes cannot be organized as large-scale farms without tractors. It is just like building a factory without mechanical equipment. Without tractors large-scale communes cannot exist.' The centre meanwhile distributed tractors without regard to the number of kolkhozes in a given region, or their size, or the tempo of their growth. In 1928/9 Siberia received only 400 tractors for the kolkhoz sector. Consequently, if in 1926/7 there were seven tractors for every 1,000 hectares of kolkhoz sown area, in 1927/8 this fell to five, and in 1928/9 to two and a half. Most of the new Siberian kolkhozes had sown areas of not less than 2,000 hectares and tractors were indispensable for efficient production, particularly given the short Siberian sowing and harvesting season. Stalin's only concern was whether the Siberians would provide export products, to which Eikhe responded that they would 'strain every nerve' to provide exports if it meant that Siberia wouild receive more tractors.[71]

In his speech to the plenum Syrtsov described the current situation in terms of the 'class struggle' and viewed it as a 'decisive, most important economic turning-point' for the countryside. Collectivization offered an opportunity for the isolation of the kulak and well-off section of the peasantry, as the mass of peasants, supported by the working class, were abandoning the kulaks to 'their personal fate, their personal lot'. As Stalinist policy had swung further leftwards in the latter half of 1929, towards a policy of all-out collectivization in the short term, Syrtsov almost immediately began to use his new authoritative position in the central leadership to advise caution. As early as 3 July 1929, at an all-Russian conference of kolkhozniks, he warned against 'uncoordinated actions' in implementing collectivization, the need for thorough preparations and a linkage between tempos and regional peculiarities.[72] At the November plenum Syrtsov's speech was laced with similar notes of caution which were noticeably out of tune with the Stalinist euphoria and exhortation for over-fulfilment of plans. Undoubtedly, mass collectivization would be a success and the state would be able to build a large reserve of grain and other agricultural products; however, 'perhaps a significant share' of these reserves would turn out to be 'dubious, fictitious' and would necessitate further changes in policy. There were 'warning signs' that food supply difficulties were straining the political mood of the working class.

The main problem for Syrtsov was that the government's control figures for kolkhoz construction had not taken sufficient account of 'quality' and he feared that many would not be good value for the money invested. In most cases over 50 per cent of the kolkhoz funds were made up of state property and often the kolkhozes were set up as covers for the continued operation of private farms which exploited poor peasants. The aim was to keep the number of unworkable kolkhozes to a minimum; after all, observed Syrtsov, when the government orders the construction of 100 new factories it does not accept in advance that '25 will be useless, but 75 will be good'. As a matter of urgency, lower organizations had to be informed of methods of organizing kolkhoz labour, socializing property and creating capital funds and of principles of leadership. For at this time, they were confused and simply lumped together the different types of kolkhoz.[73]

Syrtsov proceeded to quote at length from a critical report from an official of Khoper Okrug, Lower Volga region, an area held up by the hardline Stalinists as a model for the implementation of comprehensive collectivization.[74] The tempo of collectivization was out of control. Having gone from 1.5 to 2 per cent on 1 June 1928 to 6 to 7 per cent by 1 June 1929, thereafter the pace was breathtaking: 12 per cent by 1 August, more than 50 per cent by 15 October, and complete collectivization targeted for 1 January 1930. Given such a breakneck pace the local authorities could only organize huge kolkhozes, but without any advance plans, by using methods of 'shock work' and campaigning under the slogan 'who is biggest'. Peasants who resisted were branded 'enemies of soviet power'. As a result, peasants had lost all incentive to work, did not plough for the spring sowing and started to sell off their livestock. Clearly irritated by this daring and jarring point of realism, Stalin made it clear which side he stood on by interjecting: 'Do you think everything can be "organized in advance" by us?' Syrtsov's reply was couched in terms which he would repeat consistently in the coming months: that the party's aim should be to avoid 'Potemkin villages and Potemkin kolkhozes' and look to the *quality* of collectivization, not indulge in a mad rush for rates. It was the beginning of Syrtsov's breach with Stalin, which would culminate, following further critical outbursts, in his sacking in December 1930.[75]

7 Stalin's Final Solution

THE DRIVE FOR MASS COLLECTIVIZATION

On 5 December, a Politburo commission on collectivization was established under Yakovlev, the head of Narkomzem USSR, and included regional representatives. Two main subcommissions were formed within it: one on rates of collectivization, headed by Kaminsky, and another on the kulak question, headed by Bauman.[1] Ostensibly, the key function of the commission was to draw up workable plans of collectivization for the regions but, in reality, its work was framed within a background of wholly inadequate preparations for the success of comprehensive collectivization. Perhaps the most striking indication of the failure of the Politburo's forward planning was that a decision to sharply increase tractor production in the country came as late as 5 November 1929, on the eve of comprehensive collectivization. The Supreme Council of the National Economy (USSR) was ordered to increase projected production targets from 15,000 to 20,000 units in Leningrad's Putilov Works in 1930–31, from 40,000 to 50,000 in the Stalingrad tractor plant, while the output of the Chelyabinsk tractor plant was to soar from 1,500 units in 1930–31 to 30,000 in 1931–32. The crucial point about these projected production targets is that the kolkhoz sector would not receive large-scale tractor deliveries for at least another year – after the 1930 season. Even a subsequent decision to import an additional 6,000–8,000 tractors from abroad for the spring sowing season of 1930 could not bridge this massive gap in productive capacity.[2] Whereas party policy had traditionally linked the collectivization of the countryside with the large-scale mechanization of agriculture, in October–December 1929 party organizations were told that the supply of tractors should not dictate the pace of collectivization. The party leadership now exhorted the localities to raise productivity in the short term by the large-scale deployment of collectivized peasant implements and livestock in 'horse columns' and ploughing brigades.[3] Consequently, it became the main task of the Politburo commission to pressurize regional party leaderships into adopting unrealistic tempos of collectivization. This signalled a move into the third and final stage in the evolution of the policy of social influence: its employment as a mechanism for mass collectivization and dekulakization.

A member of the commission, deputy chairman of Sovnarkom RSFSR, Ryskulov, who in recent months had proved to be one of the most ardent

Stalinist advocates of a drive for rapid and comprehensive collectivization, informed the Siberians that their existing planned tempo of collectivization was 'unsatisfactory', did not accord with the demand of the commission for the total collectivization of 'all main grain areas within a two-year period', and advised them to submit new figures.[4] The regional party leaderships struggled to make sense of the work of the Politburo commission and the centre's rapidly evolving policy on collectivization. The Kraikombiuro strove to keep pace with the ever increasing tempos dictated by the political situation in Moscow by adopting a decision to accelerate mass collectivization on 3 December 1929, followed by a detailed decree on 15 December.

The latter posed a task for the regional party organization of the comprehensive collectivization of 28 per cent of the rural population and 31.2 per cent of the sown area during 1929/30 (36 per cent in south-west Siberia), with 100 per cent collectivization in the krai by the end of the Five Year Plan, which would encompass no less than 85 per cent of peasant households. The decree divided Siberia into three areas of collectivization. Not surprisingly, the key grain producing area of south-west Siberia was to be more speedily collectivized as a top priority: in 1930 Rubtsovsk, Novosibirsk and Slavgorod Okrugs were to be 50 per cent collectivized, with completion by 1 October 1931; Omsk, Barabinsk, Barnaul, Kamensk, Biisk, Kuznetsk and Kansk Okrugs were to be 30 per cent collectivized this year, with completion by 1 October 1932; all remaining okrugs were to be collectivized by 1 October 1933.[5]

Contemporary Siberian historians have described this target as 'realistic' and appropriate to conditions in the krai at the time; however, as with grain procurement campaigns, the decrees on tempos of collectivization created a hysteria for fulfilment and over-fulfilment of plans among lower party organizations and predisposed them to the commission of excesses in attaining targets.[6] They were caught in the middle, for on the one hand the Kraikombiuro, and above it the Central Committee and Politburo, systematically demanded impossible tempos of collectivization, while on the other hand periodically dispensing reprimands for 'excesses' and 'distortions' in the localities. The use of 'administrative methods' in forcing peasants into collectives appears to have been widespread from late 1929 and, in a letter to okruzhkoms on 30 December 1929, Kisis warned against the local practice of declaring: 'Anyone who does not join the kolkhoz is a counter-revolutionary.'[7] A Kraikombiuro decree on 5 January, however, sent out ambivalent signals to the Siberian party organization by favouring large-scale kolkhozes and ordering that collectivization be applied to 'whole villages', with small villages combined into one large-scale kolkhoz, while at the same time 'not permitting measures of compulsion or administrative influence'.[8] It was in the critical weeks of late December 1929 and early January 1930 that the campaign for collectivization spiralled out of control and degenerated into an orgy of plan over-fulfilment at the grassroots. The atmosphere was captured by a headline in the main Siberian journal for collective farmers: 'Our marching orders have been given – everyone to the front.'[9]

At its session on 5 January 1930 the Politburo basked in the extraordinary fact that by now the collectivized area for the coming spring sowing stood at more than 30 million hectares (almost one-third more than the whole area intended for completion during the First Five Year Plan). The final report of the commission on collectivization instilled a euphoric atmosphere and a mood of revolutionary transformation in the party leadership. The Politburo session resulted in a new decree, 'On the Tempo of Collectivization and Measures of State Assistance for Kolkhoz Construction', which claimed that the rate and speed of mass collectivization enveloping the countryside was such that it was now possible to immediately move forward and 'replace large-scale kulak production with *large-scale* production by kolkhozes'. The Politburo session took the momentous decision to embark on a final solution to the problem of 'taking grain' by 'liquidating the kulaks as a class' (see below). Kulaks were to be isolated by being denied entry to kolkhozes, in preparation for their social and economic destruction through mass physical displacement and by execution and exile to remote regions of the country, primarily in the Siberian taiga. Speed was the defining characteristic of the implementation of the new policy. Instead of the 20 per cent collectivization planned for the whole period of the Five Year Plan, 'the great majority' of peasant households were to be drawn into collectives within a much shorter timespan.[10]

The country was divided up into sectors of collectivization with staggered tempos of completion. A primary sector composed of the traditionally largest grain producing regions (the Ukraine, Lower Volga, Middle Volga, North Caucasus) was to be totally collectivized by autumn 1930 or spring 1931 at the latest. Siberia was placed in the second sector which was to complete collectivization by autumn 1931 and spring 1932. In addition, the Politburo instructed Narkomzem as a matter of urgency to draft model rules for the agricultural artel, hitherto proved to be the most popular form of kolkhoz organization for peasants because it involved the collective ownership only of the major means of production, so that they could be transformed into communes, where all property and labour was collective – a form more in step with the new maximalist Stalinist ideological approach. Credit was to be made available for the creation of 'machine-tractor stations' (MTS) in the countryside which would provide the mechanized arm of the kolkhoz movement, but the peasantry were to repay the costs of the establishment of the MTS within three years. It was implicitly recognized that it would be some time before industry would generate the quantities of machines required, thus the Politburo ordered that rates of collectivization were on no account to be held back on the grounds of the lack of mechanized equipment. On the contrary, the pace of collectivization was to be forced by 'socialist competition' at the grass-roots of the party rather than by 'decree mania' from above, from the leadership.

Beginning with collectivization, and then quickly extending to dekulakization, a dynamic of *over-fulfilment* of plan targets was unleashed by the Politburo. This kind of dynamic was to be the most prominent hallmark of the 'Stalin revolution' and a defining feature of the First Five Year Plan. Syrtsov ploughed a lone furrow with his calls for an emphasis on quality rather than quantity of collectivization and his constant repetition of the critical formula: 'Potemkhin kolkhozes are not necessary for us.' He warned against allowing collectivization to degenerate into 'a sporting contest' between regions over tempos.[11] Nevertheless, the dynamic of a radical upsurge 'from below' was evident in Siberia. When Kraikom leaders questioned the excessive over-fulfilment of plans by some raion officials, the response was: 'Why didn't you make the plans like this [i.e. excessive]?' As Eikhe explained to a Kraikom conference on collectivization held on 30–31 January, the targets fixed for collectivization in November–December were now an 'anachronism' and the current position was 'to demand from all officials in all okrugs the maximum forcing of the tempo of collectivization'.[12]

A mass mobilization of the party apparatus was enacted with the appointment of plenipotentiary officials to spearhead the collectivization drive. In the coming months more than 10,000 regional party and soviet officials were sent into the countryside. At the same time, the Central Committee mobilized the so-called twenty-five thousanders, the hardened cohort of urban activists and worker communists sent to the agricultural regions to assist with the collectivization campaign. As its allocation from this group, the Central Committee sent 1,730 experienced communist factory workers from Leningrad to Siberia (over one-third of all twenty-five thousanders sent out from the city). An additional 170 officials were mobilized for the campaign locally. This group formed the core of the brigades that roamed the countryside enforcing collectivization. Most of the Leningraders were sent to the grain areas of south-west Siberia: Slavgorod (300), Rubtsovsk (300), Novosibirsk (200), Barnaul (175), Biisk (100), Omsk (100).[13] If the party report on their deployment in Barnaul Okrug was typical, the Leningraders were met in the localities by organized welcomes involving hundreds of people, bands and much flag waving. The vast majority (87 per cent) of the Leningraders were appointed to key controlling positions as chairmen, deputy chairmen and members of the boards of administration in kolkhozes.[14] As they were agriculturally inexperienced city types, this was hardly likely to imbue peasants with confidence in the kolkhozes.

Party officials and activists sent into the countryside infused with an idealistic spirit of revolutionary change were soon confronted by peasant conservatism and obstructionism. The sense of frustration was caught by Chayanov, writing of earlier party attempts to transform the life of the peasantry:

> It is no wonder, therefore, that many of our comrades, especially our younger comrades, whose minds are still full of images of the goals and achievements of the present-day industrial economy, and who are impatient to achieve something similar in their own provinces, are often reduced to utter despondency after a few months' work. They come close to desperation as they get jolted in a peasant cart on a rainy November evening along impassable roads from somewhere like Znamensk via Buzayevo to somewhere like Uspensk.[15]

Such frustration created a mood among officials, plenipotentiaries, twenty-five thousanders and activists that favoured coercion, particularly when they were under pressure to over-fulfil targets quickly. As the chairman of the organization of Novosibirsk grain cooperatives explained: 'Collectivization will not move forward by the use of explanatory work alone, the only real measure is repression. We must intimidate the muzhik; only then will he join the collectives.'[16] Around this time a member of Novosibirsk Okruzhkom, Anan'in, told a meeting of rural officials in Ordin raion: 'Kolkhozes which do not socialize goods and all livestock down to chickens, are not kolkhozes but pseudo-kolkhozes.'[17]

The organization of collectivization was achieved by dividing the rural soviets of a raion into sectors (*kusti*). For example, the 42 rural soviets of Novosibirsk raion were organized into six sectors, into each of which was sent one brigade composed of five persons. To obtain an idea of the scale of the task confronting these brigades, it is worth noting that the first sector contained six rural soviets with some 3,205 households. Given the numbers involved, the brigades could not possibly hope to complete the task on their own, but required the active support of rural officials and at least part of the local peasantry.[18] Kharlamov, a senior Kraikom official, spoke of collectivization being conducted by '2–3 day raids, where we rush into a village and knock together some kind of kolkhoz, and then we leave'. He also described the overstretch in conducting the campaigns, for despite the assistance of a cohort of twenty-five thousanders from the centre, on average two plenipotentiaries were allocated to each rural soviet, which meant they covered two or three villages, and perhaps many hundreds of peasant households.[19]

The accelerated pace of collectivization was the focus of intense discussion at a Kraikom conference held on 23 January 1930. Bazovsky, a senior Kraikom official who had visited two villages in Shipunov raion of Barnaul Okrug, complained that local officials were so obsessed with the new political drive that they were pursuing 'collectivization for the sake of collectivization, i.e. to combine x number of households and that's it'. Meanwhile other campaigns, such as the sowing campaign, were ignored. Eikhe, on the other hand, left the senior Siberian party officials in no doubt as to his stance when he interrupted one speaker, who reported how he had told the peasants that collectivization was voluntary, with the rebuke: 'You rode around as a reducer of collectivization.'[20] In fact, it was precisely by 'decree mania' and pressure 'from above' that the Kraikom intensified the tempo of collectivization in the krai. On the basis of his knowledge of the thinking of the Stalinists at the centre derived from his participation as a member of the Politburo commissions, Eikhe sharply increased the pressure on his Siberian subordinates. On 27 January he told a gathering of Novosibirsk Okruzhkom leaders that the pace of collectivization had to be intensified: 'We must put pressure on our apparatus now, when the *bednota* and serednyak masses are going into the kolkhozes, so that we can reduce to a minimum the period for the completion of comprehensive collectivization in Siberia.'[21]

The key turning point was a Kraikom conference with the secretaries of okruzhkoms on 30–31 January 1930 which passed an absurd resolution favouring the comprehensive collectivization of the whole Siberian peasantry by the end of spring 1930. The requisite Kraikom decree followed on 2 February which stated that the 'most important' task of the Siberian party organization was to collectivize the 'main mass of batraks, bedniaks and serednyaks' during the spring of 1930. As if to sidestep dubious okrug leaderships and reach out directly to lower level officials and plenipotentiaries, shortly afterwards an 'appeal' to all Siberian communists from the Kraikom was published in *Sovetskaia sibir'* calling for the completion of collectivization as soon as possible.[22]

By the middle of January 1930, the first signs that collectivization was degenerating into a disaster became apparent. Whereas the social influence policy of targeting kulaks and the provision of material incentives had successfully mobilized or neutralized the mass of peasants, collectivization involved a substantial negative material impact on the mass of peasants. For this fundamental reason, the cost-benefit calculus of the mass of peasants turned against the party policy. Rather than have their property 'seized' by collective farms, peasants of all strata took a line of least direct opposition to the authorities, and one which most reflected their rational self-interest. Evidence of peasant economic sabotage prior to entry to collectives began to flood into the party hierarchy. Mass sales of equipment and livestock, the slaughter of livestock, reluctance to pay off debts and other acts threatened to make the kolkhozes unworkable. The shortage of seed grain and the peasants' refusal to bring their seed into the kolkhozes was a major issue at the conference of okruzhkom secretaries organized by the Kraikom on 30–31 January. When, in the middle of February, the collection of seed for kolkhozes still only hovered around 25 per cent of the required amount to equal the previous year's sowings, solving the problem was declared a 'military duty' by the Kraikom.[23] Even prior to collectivization and dekulakization, peasants were resorting to mass slaughtering of their animals as a form of economic sabotage in reaction to the new procurement quotas introduced in late September. This is evident from the fact that in September and October 1929 66,700 head of cattle (an increase of 47.9 per cent on the same period of 1928), 60,300 sheep (8 per cent) and 5,400 pigs (125 per cent) were slaughtered, and these figures were for official selling points only. At the same time, the number of horse hides procured increased from just over 1,000 in October–November 1928 to over 5,100 (a 410 per cent increase) in the same months of 1929.[24]

The party blamed 'kulak agitation' and the Politburo ordered that guilty peasants be stripped of their property and charged under Article 61 for 'non-fulfilment of state tasks'. In Siberia, the Kraikom denounced rural communists for 'petty bourgeois ownership tendencies', because rather than combating these acts of resistance, they often participated in them. Later, Eikhe branded this 'inability or unwillingness to fight' as 'direct aid for the class enemy', and paved the way for a political purge of rural organizations.[25] B. Kavraisky, an official in the Kraikom Secretariat, told a Kraikom conference on collectivization on 23 January: 'Without decisive dekulakization a quick and successful implementation of collectivization will not happen, and we can see evidence of this in the villages.'[26]

The special judicial brigades organized in the okrugs in late 1929 as roving courts provided the quick conveyor-belt justice necessary for the processing of the huge number of cases arising from collectivization. By 2 February over 800 cases involving 'kulak opposition' to collectivization had been heard, rising to 2,382 by 11 February and reaching 9,757 by 20 March.[27] Most of these cases dealt with the mass slaughtering of livestock, which the state perceived as economic sabotage. A Kraikom decree of 25 January ordered that 'self-imposed duties' for the sale of meat be applied to seredniak farms and that meat be confiscated from kulak farms. These supplies were to be drawn from frozen stocks, not from new slaughterings.[28]

The sheer scale and suddenness in the growth of collectivization is difficult to imagine. In bare statistics the growth in Siberia was as follows: on 1 October 1929, in the 15 main okrugs, there were 776 communes, 855 artels, and 776 tozi; on 1 April 1930, there were 2,741 communes, 3,352 artels, and 1,457 tozi. The peak level of collectivization was reached in the middle of March 1930, when approximately 781,800 peasant farms (almost 53 per cent of the total in Siberia) had been collectivized in 8,548 kolkhozes.[29] Novosibirsk Okrug, an area designated for 50 per cent collectivization in 1930, had the highest rates of kolkhoz growth: by 15 January the level of collectivization reached 18 per cent, with some raions completing over 30 per cent, and by the beginning of February 46 per cent of households were collectivized, with Maslyanin raion achieving a level of 68.8 per cent. By 20 March a peak of just over 57 per cent was reached in this okrug.[30]

The role of collectivization in the process of capturing the peasantry and its property for the state entailed not merely the destruction of autonomous peasant village culture and society, and the supplanting of relatively autonomous peasant institutions such as the *skhod* by local state officials, but also the imposition of specific forms of state controls over the peasantry. The experience of the collectivization drive in late 1929 and early 1930 demonstrated that the most widespread form of kolkhoz organized by party activists was the commune, where the main property, means of production and labour was collectively organized. The form most favoured by the peasants themselves, was the artel or toz, where labour was socialized but property remained largely privately owned: a form which was more in tune with traditional peasant culture. Under the ideological cloak of 'socializing' agriculture and ensuring 'real collective production', the state was actually structuring its relations with the peasantry so that it could exercise the maximum control and extract the maximum resources.[31] The kolkhozes were intended to facilitate state mobilization of the countryside, whether in the extraction of economic resources, for the advancement of political campaigns or for the attainment of social goals. The Politburo decided, however, that the soviets would continue to be the main organizational lever of political control of the countryside, as a state authority outside the kolkhozes but with supervisory functions.[32]

THE FINAL SOLUTION TO THE KULAK QUESTION

The commission of the Politburo created in early December 1929 to examine the question of accelerated collectivization was also inevitably drawn into analysing what to do with the kulaks. Not surprisingly, it was Stalin who first publicly revealed the direction in which the regime's policy was headed when he electrified a Conference of Agrarian Marxists on 27 December by announcing that the time was now ripe for the immediate and irrevocable transition from 'a policy of *limiting* the exploitative tendencies of the kulak to a policy of *liquidating* the kulaks as a class'. He admitted that this was a 'U-turn' (*povorot*) in party policy but, coming in the wake of the success of the social influence policy, he asserted that this situation had been spontaneously created by 'millions of the basic mass of the peasantry' who were flooding into the kolkhozes: a movement that constituted a 'powerful and growing anti-kulak avalanche ... smashing the kulaks and clearing the way for widespread socialist construction in the countryside'. Moreover, dekulakization was being carried out 'by the bedniak-seredniak mass itself during total collectivization ... not by simple administrative methods'. Whereas the aim of the Stalinists in the summer of 1928 had been to strike a blow against the kulaks and 'make them bow' to state power, now the goal was to hit this group in such a way that 'it can never rise to its feet again'. Echoing statements which he had first made almost two years before, during his tour of Siberia in January 1928, Stalin asserted that the path of building socialism followed by the Bolsheviks could no longer tolerate the contradiction of small-scale private peasant farming. The task now was to build up the kolkhozes and sovkhozes as 'strong points' for the party in the countryside. While repeatedly emphasizing that the role of the kulaks had to be 'substituted' by socialist forms of production, he posed the issue in uncompromising zero-sum terms: 'either *back* – to capitalism, or *forward* – to socialism'.[33]

Stalin's speech did not address the complicated issue of the actual process for exterminating the kulaks as a social entity (dekulakization). A general programme for dekulakization was drawn up by the commission on collectivization, but there was serious disagreement over what was to be done with this human mass amounting to many millions of people. The Politburo decree of 5 January on collectivization affirmed Stalin's plan for the 'liquidation' of the kulaks without specifying a detailed process. Consequently, a new Politburo commission, chaired by the Stalinist hardliner Molotov, was established on 15 January 1930. It had the foreboding, self-explanatory title: 'The Commission to Work Out Measures Towards the Kulaks'. Not surprisingly, given the nature of its work, this commission was exceptionally large and authoritative, and was initially composed of 21 members, but expanded to 26 by the time it reported in late January. It consisted of representatives from the main party organizations, ministries and state agencies that would be involved in the implementation of any recommendations, including Eikhe and Syrtsov.

While Stalin set an increasingly militaristic beat for the conduct of the campaigns in the countryside, encapsulated by an article in *Krasnaia zvezda* on 21 January which called for the opposition of the kulaks to be 'smashed in open battle', a press campaign was launched which employed vocabulary designed to dehumanize and demonize the kulaks in a manner comparable to that used later in the 1930s by the Nazi regime in Germany against the Jews.[34] In this environment the Molotov commission reported to the Politburo on 30 January 1930: 'On Measures for the Liquidation of Kulak Households in Areas of Complete Collectivization'. Its recommendations on the procedures for dekulakization were so sensitive that they were assigned to the top secret 'special folder' of the Politburo. The sensitivity of the party leadership on this issue was clearly evidenced by a Politburo decision to reprimand the North Caucasus and Lower Volga Kraiispolkoms for publishing this 'especially secret' decree on dekulakization in the local press. This secret party decision was not a matter for 'newspaper blabbering' declared the Politburo.[35]

A distilled version of the decree was formally ratified by the Central Executive Committee and Sovnarkom USSR on 1 February 1930 and published in *Izvestiia* the next day.[36] The version for public consumption was short and rather vague. It declared that existing laws on the leasing of land and the employment of hired labour by peasants were now revoked in areas designated for comprehensive collectivization, with certain exemptions for seredniaks requiring the approval of raiispolkoms and okrispolkoms. In these areas 'all necessary measures' were to be taken against kulaks, including total confiscation of their property and their exile from these areas. Confiscated property of kulaks was, after the deduction of the value of debts to the state and cooperatives, to be channelled into the indivisible funds of kolkhozes as a contribution towards the joining payments of bedniaks and seredniaks.

A more detailed 'top secret' instruction on the implementation of dekulakization was sent by the Central Executive Committee and Sovnarkom to the soviet authorities in the country on 4 February 1930.[37] This ordered the 'immediate' deportation and resettlement of kulaks in order to nullify their influence in dissuading other peasants from joining the kolkhozes. The first priority was for the OGPU to organize the deportation of kulak 'activists' drawn from the richest and 'quasi-landlord' strata to the far regions of the USSR or to distant areas within the borders of a given region. Other kulaks were to be resettled by local authorities on uninhabited land within the region but outside of the kolkhozes. The numbers of kulaks involved was to be strictly related to statistical assessments of the number of kulak households in the region and was not to exceed averages of 3 to 5 per cent of total households (approximately 750,000 to 1.25 million households: author). Lists of kulaks for deportation were to be drawn up by raiispolkoms on the basis of decisions taken at meetings of kolkhozniks, bedniaks and batraks, and then confirmed by okrispolkoms. This was clearly a device to infuse the process with a democratic sanction, as if the peasant community was 'dekulakizing' itself. The family members of exiled kulaks could with the permission of raiispolkoms remain in the area, but they were to be resettled in special small villages under the management of troikas or plenipotentiaries. They were to work under a regime of specific production tasks and had to deliver the whole of their marketable surplus to the state and cooperatives.

The above mentioned decree and instruction had been preempted by an even more detailed top secret instruction on dekulakization approved by the Politburo on 30 January and sent to all regional party organizations.[38] Eikhe, who had been a member of the Molotov commission, had already told a meeting of the Novosibirsk city party actif on 27 January, before Molotov's report was formally deliberated by the Politburo, that the 'most hostile reactionary part of the kulaks' were to be immediately resettled in remote areas of the far north, in Narym and Turukhansk (traditional locations for exiled political prisoners and criminals) as a preliminary measure to wholesale dekulakization. Eikhe stressed that the enlistment of the collaboration of the poor peasants was crucial to ensure that the kulaks were accurately targeted and the seredniaks not harmed.[39] On 31 January he informed a conference of Siberian party leaders, including okruzhkom secretaries, that the decision had been taken to seize 'all means of production' from the kulaks 'within a matter of days'. He estimated that the process would involve the liquidation of 5 per cent of households in the country, which meant 'about one hundred thousand households' in Siberia, and 'about eight million persons' in the country. When he told the gathering that a certain number of the 'most hardened' kulaks, those who took part in 'counter-revolutionary' acts, the 'kulak activists', were to be rounded up by the OGPU and incarcerated in concentration camps, a voice from the floor asked: 'Why can't we shoot them?' Eikhe responded that mass shootings were not presently on the agenda, but if it was deemed necessary then 'here in the Kraikom there are no vegetarians, and we will not feel too shy about shooting them'.[40] The number of this 'kulak *verkhushka*' in Siberia was estimated at 5,000 persons by the OGPU, and they were to be arrested by OGPU-led armed groups organized at raion centres. The remainder (in fact the bulk) were to be dispersed in forced labour colonies across the Siberian taiga.[41]

A special Kraikom commission grappled with the problem of complying with the new political line by interpreting the rather vague orders and exhortations coming from the Central Committee and contained in the provocative speeches of Stalin and Molotov published in the press. The commission drew up resolutions on collectivization and dekulakization; however, its work was largely overtaken by the secret Politburo instruction of 30 January.[42] The Politburo instruction provided the framework for a corresponding eight-page long Kraikombiuro 'top secret' decree issued on 2 February 1930: 'On Measures to Fulfil the Decision of the Central Committee VKP(b) on the Tempo of Collectivization and the Liquidation of the Kulaks as a Class' (see Document 7).[43] Another week or more passed before complying decrees were issued by okruzhkoms, and a Kraiispolkom decree to formally legalize the whole process was issued only on 12 February.[44] The Kraikom decree clearly stated that the goal was to accelerate collectivization before the spring sowing campaign, and that this was to be achieved concurrently with dekulakization. It ordered the mobilization 'within twenty-four hours' of an additional 6,000 town communists and workers from enterprises, institutions, factories and plants with large party organizations. They were to be organized into 'worker brigades' and their members were supposedly drawn from the 'best and most class conscious', that is to say, they would be the most disciplined in the execution of the unpleasant business of eliminating the kulaks and enforcing collectivization. A massive agitational campaign in towns and industrial plants would ensure that the party's message that collectivization and dekulakization was essential for industrialization was propagated. In addition, 800 bookkeepers were to be recruited for work in the organization of kolkhozes. Collectivization as a process of accounting was a phenomenon later reflected upon by Stalin in a report to the Politburo on 25 February, when he ordered the mobilization of 20,000 komsomol members for sending to kolkhozes as bookkeepers, after short courses in accounting. This was perhaps a reflection of Lenin's primitive thinking in *The Next Tasks of Soviet Power*: that 'socialism is unthinkable without the organization of accounting and control'.[45]

Collectivization and dekulakization were inextricably tied together by the party. The expropriation of kulaks had to be conducted in parallel with an accelerated tempo of kolkhoz formation. The Kraikom decree strongly warned against '"Leftist" anti-seredniak deviations': attempts to construct kolkhozes by coercive administrative measures. It banned the practice of 'naked dekulakization', that is to say confiscating kulak property and not then using it as an inducement to 'persuade' the mass of peasants into joining the kolkhozes. While *all* kulak households in areas of comprehensive collectivization were to be subject to expropriation, this was to be conducted only by an 'organized process'. Previously, as Maynard explained: 'It had been an insult to call a man poor. It was now a welcome compliment.'[46] For the lists of kulaks who had been subjected to an individual tax supplement, or otherwise defined as the wealthiest peasants, were the starting point for the OGPU and local authorities when they prepared the scheme of dekulakization. According to the Krai Finance Department, just under 1.55 million peasant households were assessed for agricultural taxation in 1929/30. Eikhe's estimate of 100,000 Siberian households to be dekulakized amounted to 6.5 per cent of this total.[47] In fact, approximately 70,000 were declared to be kulak households for tax purposes, and only 63,280 were subjected to individual tax supplements: a considerable shortfall on Eikhe's dekulakization target. Consequently, there was pressure to increase the number of kulaks defined by taxation, but even so by April only 75,586 (4.9 per cent) households were placed in the kulak category.[48] In order to avoid seredniaks being caught in the net of dekulakization, the decree adhered fairly rigidly to the tax assessment figure for kulaks by setting strict limits of 4 to 5 per cent of all households in Siberia to be dekulakized, though the average number in each raion would vary in accordance with figures previously established for the tax campaign of 1929/30.

To further minimize the risk to seredniaks, the accuracy of the tax lists were to be verified again before being used for dekulakization, with the lists of kulaks being extracted in the first instance from those households subjected to individual supplements in the tax campaign of 1929–30. According to one OGPU official, 54,989 households, consisting of 346,430 family members, fell into this category. It was initially proposed that in each of the 68 raions designated for comprehensive collectivization in the krai, 205 kulak households would be dekulakized, making a total of 13,940. The OGPU, having been advised by economic organs, envisaged that upwards of 240,000 households (including those from outside Siberia) could be resettled in remote areas of Tomsk Okrug which could sustain grain farming, while others would be sent to Kiren and the Angara basin as forced labour in forestry and railway construction.[49] These limits were more than sufficient to cope with the 100,000 dekulakized households envisaged by Eikhe.

To make the whole process more manageable for local authorities and party activists, the Kraikom decree, following the Politburo instruction, subdivided the kulaks into three categories. Category One kulaks were those classed as 'counter-revolutionary'. They were to be 'immediately liquidated' by incarceration in concentration camps, while any of them guilty of 'organizing acts of terrorism, counter-revolutionary uprisings and insurgency' were to be shot 'without hesitation'. Category Two included the remaining 'activist element' composed of the 'richest kulaks and quasi-landlords'. Lists of these were to be composed by raiispolkoms, and confirmed by okrispolkoms, in theory, on the basis of decisions taken by meetings of kolkhozniks, and gatherings of batraks and bedniaks. This category was to be exiled to the most remote parts of the USSR and to remote parts of the krai. Finally, the Category Three kulaks were those regarded as 'least dangerous', though criteria for membership of this category only emerged in the course of the campaign: they were allowed to remain within the boundaries of raions but settled in new land outside the kolkhozes. The order of this resettlement was left to okrispolkoms.[50] In this decree and other party documents a major definitional distinction was drawn by the use of the following synonyms: 'exiled' (*vyslannye*) and 'removed' (*vyseliaemye*) kulaks refered to those of Category Two; 'settled apart' (*rasseliaemye*) kulaks refered to those of Category Three; 'resettled' (*pereseliaemye*) kulaks refered to both categories.[51]

That the policy of dekulakization was regarded by the party as a continuation of the 'social influence' process, is clear from the fact that the party designated the rural soviet as the formal organizational mechanism for the implementation of the policy. The procedure was laid down in a stylized form: first, the rural soviet was to conduct a meeting with batrak and bedniak peasants, seredniak actifs, and representatives of 'village community organizations' (meaning local party cells, komsomol, peasant committees of mutual aid, kolkhozes, cooperatives). These meetings were to confirm the tax lists of kulak farms, and make any necessary corrections, though the possibility of their vetoing the process was not entertained. Indeed, as we shall see in the following chapter, plenipotentiaries frequently regarded this process of consultation with the village community as ideologically decorative, and even fictional. The next stage involved a vote of approval by the general meeting of enfranchised peasants. Its decision was then formally ratified by the rural soviet with the participation of representatives of raiispolkoms and the OGPU. Only then could the dekulakization process begin. Once the lists of kulaks were confirmed by the raiispolkom, the OGPU was to conduct the registration and confiscation of property, and its transfer to kolkhozes. Moreover, the party was keenly aware that dekulakization of particular groups required a cautious approach. The confiscation of property and exile were not to be perpetrated against the families of Red Army soldiers and officers.[52] Similarly, the Soviet Foreign Minister, Litvinov, ensured that kulaks of foreign extraction (from countries with which the USSR had official ties) were exempted, though they were to be targeted for multiple fines and tax supplements.[53] A 'special care' was to be exercised when it came to the dekulakization of ex-partisans and families of kulaks who worked in factories and enterprises.

The Kraikom decree gave a comprehensive guide on the kinds of goods to be confiscated: working and productive livestock, domestic and farm buildings, all agricultural, industrial and transport equipment, grain products, forage, seeds, hemp, industrial materials, livestock products, trade shops, warehouses and their contents, money, shares and valuables. The property was to be secured 'under the protection of the state'. Exiled and resettled kulaks were to be left with only the most basic household articles and some means of production 'according to the character of their work in the new places'. Since many were destined for forced labour colonies this provision was largely redundant. The kulaks were also supposed to be left with an 'initial minimum of food' and a small sum of money (up to 500 roubles per family) to pay for their travel to areas of resettlement and construction in these areas. Confiscated household articles were to be used for 'social needs' by rural soviets and kolkhozes. Whereas money, shares and other valuables taken from kulaks were to be handed over to the financial departments of raiispolkoms, other property and means of production in particular were to be handed over to kolkhozes as the joining payments for bedniaks and batraks to the indivisible fund, once debts to the state and cooperatives had been deducted. All weapons were to be delivered to the OGPU.

Those kulaks who were permitted to remain in the locality but outside the kolkhozes were to be dispersed in small settlements controlled by troikas and plenipotentiaries nominated by the soviet authorities. These kulaks were to be left with the minimum agricultural equipment necessary to sustain agricultural production and, as noted above, were to be given specific production targets and were compelled to deliver their surpluses to the state and cooperatives. The okrispolkoms were ordered to devise plans for the use of these kulaks as 'special labour detachments and colonies' in forestry, road construction, land reclamation and so on. The party recognized that the deportation of large numbers of kulaks would be traumatic and was bound to give rise to resistance. As regards kulak families exiled beyond their raions, it was recommended that attempts be made to stir up generational conflict within these groups by recruiting, when possible, groups of young kulaks for voluntary work on behalf of local soviets or for poor peasants, or their organization into 'special artels' for agricultural and other work. It was deemed essential to keep the exiled kulak families socially fragmented and disorientated by reserving the basics of community life for young collaborators. Only they were to be allowed subscriptions to newspapers, access to libraries, common dining halls, and 'other features of cultural life'.

The party leadership was concerned that dekulakization did not degenerate into a 'mechanical' pillaging of the peasantry as a whole across the country and had drawn up a detailed instruction for the precise purpose of targeting the kulak elite in the most developed rural areas. Indeed, this concern was in evidence almost as soon as the decree had been issued, when the Politburo ordered Moscow Obkombiuro to revoke its decision of 31 January to send into exile 9,000–11,000 kulak families who fell into Category Two, because it had not followed the stipulations laid down by the Politburo instruction of 30 January.[54] A Politburo decision of 30 January established a target number of 63,000 Category One kulak households to be sent into exile in Siberia. The Siberian authorities, however, protested that they were simply unprepared at such short notice to cope with this influx. Consequently, at its session on 5 February the Politburo set new, marginally lower, targets for the OGPU. The exile of dekulakized peasants to Siberia was to be carried out in three waves: the first wave was to consist of no more than 60,000 families from Category One and Category Two, and was to be completed by the end of April; the second and third waves were to be considered for a special decision at a later time. The OGPU was instructed to break down the number of exiles by area, determine fixed periods for their removal and assign destinations, while regional party leaderships were to ensure their plans conformed with those of the OGPU.[55] The best estimates are that the Politburo's schedule involved the dekulakization of just over one million peasant families (including Category Three kulaks), and some five or six million people.[56] The initial estimate for the number of kulaks that were to be sent into exile at this stage (i.e. the total for Categories One and Two) came to about 213,000 persons.[57]

THE ORGANIZATION OF DEKULAKIZATION

Dekulakization was a massive organizational task that necessitated two Kraiispolkom decrees, the first on 12 February, and a second on 1 March which elaborated, and in some ways moderated, the dekulakization procedure.⁵⁸ The first decree allocated to each okrug a control figure of the minimum number of households to be dekulakized. The first step, before kulak families could be arrested and sent into exile, was to register their property – a process that began almost immediately after the issuing of the dekulakization decrees.⁵⁹ Following the arrest of Category One kulaks and the confiscation of property, Category Two and Three kulaks (overwhelmingly families) were to be resettled in special zones (*uchastki*), once lists of kulaks were checked by raiispolkoms to exclude seredniak and other peasants wrongly included by rural soviets, and to ensure that the requisite number of kulaks had been dekulakized. In practice, the authorities established a special 'collection point' (*sbornyi punkt*) in each raion where the raion troika on dekulakization checked the lists. From there kulaks were directed to a 'control-holding point' (*kontrol'no-propusknoi punkt*) in each okrug, where all Category Two and Three kulaks were organized for resettlement. A major consideration in this operation was to prevent the concentration of large numbers of kulak households at any location at any given time. The Novosibirsk authorities designated the village of Pikhtovka, in Baksin raion in the remote north of the okrug, as the 'control-holding point'. During the period 27 February–7 March 1930, in the middle of the Siberian winter, staggered convoys of dispossessed kulaks were escorted there along special routes and according to a strict timetable.⁶⁰

Perhaps the logistical difficulties of the operation led to the Kraiispolkom decree of 1 March which blurred the distinctions between kulak categories by instructing that all Category Two kulak families that had not yet been designated for exile to the far north were to be settled apart from other peasants, *within* the okrug, on land outside the kolkhozes. It is not clear from the decree whether those falling within this redefined Category Two were to be settled with or apart from Category Three kulaks. Moreover, within this new Category Two were included many Category One households who were not now to be sent to the north as follows: if they did not have the food and equipment norms established by the Kraiispolkom; those who voluntarily fled their villages and were detained on railways if they did not constitute a 'special social danger'; families due to be sent to the north if the raiispolkom did not regard them as a 'special social danger'; families who had sick members that could not work, particularly if there were pregnant women. It was emphasized that confiscation and exile of both Category One and Two kulaks was not to be carried out if: they were families with serving members of the military; they were foreigners from countries with 'normal diplomatic relations' with the USSR; they were former Red Partisans and active participants in the civil war who had been wounded or had service distinctions, except when such kulaks opposed collectivization and were involved in group opposition. The following ethnic groups were also exempted from confiscation and resettlement: Tatars, Germans, Lithuanians, Estonians and Latvians.

Moscow had given the Siberian leadership a target of 25,000 Category Two kulak households to be sent into exile. The Kraikom increased this figure and established a new target of 30,000 households, which constituted just 2 per cent of the 1.55 million peasant households in the krai. The plan of resettlement was drawn up by the Siberian OGPU on 24 February. The militarized nature of the operation is clear from the OGPU's use of the military term 'distribution' (*dislokatsiia*) as the heading for the table which allocated to each okrug a plan of the number of kulaks to be resettled and which specified the holding centres, the railway stations and the wharves for the onward transportation of kulaks, and their zones of destination (see Table 7.1).[61] The Kraiispolkom decree of 1 March projected an intra-okrug resettlement plan of 50,000 kulak households of all categories (3.2 per cent of the total number of peasant households), excluding those already being sent into exile in the north. Furthermore, as the OGPU estimated that each resettled kulak household had on average five to six members, the number in this category approached 300,000 persons.[62] The combined total, excluding Category One kulaks, of those going into exile in the north under the OGPU's command (30,000) and those to be resettled apart locally (50,000) amounted to around 80,000 households – a figure that was much closer to that of the krai tax authorities than to the 100,000 proposed by Eikhe in late January. As with economic plans, control figures for dekulakization were allocated to the okrugs and raions which could only be exceeded with the express permission of the Kraiispolkom (the idea of under-fulfilment was not entertained). The territory of the special zones of resettlement, the specific nature of the work of the new settlements and their organization and control were all matters for the okrug authorities, though they were to select sites from where kulaks would find it difficult to flee (surrounded by bogs, rivers, the absence of roads). Okrugs such as Tomsk, Kansk, Krasnoyarsk, Irkutsk and Achinsk, whose territories extended into the far north of the krai, were prohibited from resettling Category Two kulak families in zones in northern areas which were designated for the exile of Category One kulaks. Okrugs which did not have large uninhabited areas (Omsk, Barabinsk, Kamen', Novosibirsk, Kuznetsk) but were located in the north sent their kulaks to resettlement zones in the taiga of Tomsk and Krasnoyarsk by cart. Other okrugs (Oirot, Biisk, Barnaul, Slavgorod, Khakassiya, Minusinsk) were to transport kulaks to the northern holding centres by railway, and some 65 special trains came from these areas in this period.[63]

Table 7.1 Siberian OGPU statistics on dekulakization, to 24 February 1930

Okrug	Number of kulak farms	Dekulakized						Fled	
		Total	Piatikratniki	Courts	Latest methods	Self-liquidate	Other	With families	Without families
					By method				
Omsk	12,170	8,430	1,893	2,316	2,747	942	532	635	929
Slavgorod	4,876	4,731	897	1,232	1,236	1,206	160	801	515
Barabinsk	4,732	3,584	1,103	672	1,529	280	—	41	202
Novosibirsk	5,691	4,768	545	364	2,587	169	1,103	365	415
Kamensk	4,433	3,357	697	299	1,212	270	879	357	452
Barnaul	7,507	6,370	1,105	1,364	2,908	368	625	591	745
Biisk	8,300	5,594	1,978	395	3,085	85	51	39	63
Rubtsovsk	5,204	5,017	2,645	185	2,102	85	—	117	243
Tomsk	2,961	984	172	408	310	72	22	79	300
Kuznetsk	2,097	2,357	1,483	197	569	108	—	196	360
Achinsk	3,082	2,804	974	524	905	88	313	183	29
Minusinsk	3,675	2,889	796	797	1,168	128	—	71	162
Khakassiya	854	848	—	459	389	—	—	1	11
Krasnoyarsk	2,053	1,507	99	100	1,274	29	5	29	69
Kansk	3,175	2,573	172	173	2,156	72	—	55	150
Irkutsk	4,739	2,279	59	976	1,138	106	—	56	244
Oirotiya	785	1,146	88	167	886	—	5	13	34
Total	76,334	59,238	14,706	10,628	26,191	4,008	3,695	3,629	4,923

Source: GANO 1, f. 47, op. 5, d. 103, l. 65, Table no. 2.

Lists of Category Two kulaks drawn up by raiispolkoms were to be checked by okrispolkom plenipotentiaries, whose job it was also to ensure that the kulaks were supplied with essential household goods, food, basic equipment necessary for the work they were to do at the new locations, and at least 500 roubles per family to build a new home. At the behest of the Siberian OGPU command, a secret kraiispolkom decree specified that the okrug authorities must give each kulak family 25 roubles to buy food supplies for their journey, and additionally provide them with a 'fund in kind' (*naturfund*) to enable them to function as farmers in the resettlement zones; 7 puds of flour, a little over 13 puds of seed grain, 2 puds of potatoes, 27 puds of oat feed, 70 puds of hay, a horse, various items of agricultural equipment and two months of food stocks.[64] If they were not adequately supplied, the okrispolkom plenipotentiaries had the power to order the raiispolkoms to furnish the kulaks with the necessary supplies. The point was that the state required the new kulak zones to perform productive agricultural work and complete plans; therefore, it was self-defeating to deprive them of the equipment to enable them to function as farmers. At the same time not all the kulaks were to be sent to the new zones; some were to be conscripted into special labour squads and colonies for forestry, road construction, land improvement, mining and other types of work. The collection points and holding centres established by okrispolkoms could only move kulaks to the zones of permanent resettlement when small settlement areas had been marked out and special officials assigned to organize the new settlements. The exile of Category Two kulaks to the north was to begin on 25 February and be completed by 15 March, and it was envisaged that the operation would be finished by 1 April.

In theory, the whole process of exiling and resettlement of Category Two and Category Three kulaks was to be carefully detailed by the okrug authorities to correspond with the above mentioned Kraiispolkom decrees and OGPU blueprint. Reverting to the *modus operandi* of emergency rule by the Bolshevik regime, special troikas were established at each territorial level of the krai to implement dekulakization. These normally consisted of a leading party official, the chairman of the ispolkom, and the relevant OGPU officer.[65] At the village interface, however, where local officials acted against those households segregated for dekulakization, organizational and administrative formalities revolved around decisions adopted at general meetings, however automatically, and discussions of the fate of kulaks were kept to a bare minimum. Unique records of a village dekulakization held in the Novosibirsk Regional Museum are an illustration of this process. Three handwritten notes in pencil on faded pieces of paper document the decision of Mochishe rural soviet to deprive the family Syzov of their civil rights and exile them to unpopulated areas of the Siberian Krai, the reason in this case being the use of hired labour, and despite a significant reduction in the household's wealth between 1928 and 1931. The first is an extract from the protocol of the general meeting which decided their fate (see Document 8). The second is a three lines long Act (*akt*) ordering their expropriation and exile. The last, in illiterate Russian, lists the property confiscated from the family. Such scraps of paper sealed the fate of millions of peasants across the country.[66]

To illustrate the huge task involved in dekulakization, let us examine the process as implemented by Novosibirsk Okrispolkom. It was given a plan by the OGPU to resettle 2,964 Category Two kulak households (perhaps as many as 20,000 persons) to a zone in the taiga on the basin of the Kengi river in Tomsk Okrug. Subsequently, the okrug authorities decided to transport its kulaks to a 'colony' of 70,000 hectares along the river Galka in Kargat raion *within* the okrug. This location lay in the remotest northern part of Novosibirsk Okrug, not as far north as the Siberian OGPU command had planned, but still in the inhospitable taiga. Due to insufficient supplies for these families, the party and soviet organs in the okrug had to reduce the number involved to 1,864 (62.8 per cent of the control figure for dekulakization, and about one-third of the estimated number of kulak households in the okrug). When the Kraiispolkom decree of 1 March set new control figures for dekulakization, an okrispolkom decree was issued on 6 March which set a target of 2,500 Category Two households to be resettled, with again the number designated for the taiga reduced to 1,680. A further 20 kulak households from Baksin raion were to be placed in a settlement on the river Shegarka (also in the taiga). The remaining 800 households were allocated to hard labour projects; 600 for forestry work in Kargat raion, the lower Ob' river and Talitska, and 200 for quarrying work in Novosibirsk city. To prevent them mixing with the other workers, the latter were housed in barracks guarded by the OGPU and militia. In the event, the supply situation was so bad that the number exiled to the Galka river area amounted to only 500 households and the rest remained in Novosibirsk Okrug and were resettled along with Category Three households in the Shegarka river settlement.[67]

Dispersal was the key to the control of the resettled kulaks, so their villages were not allowed to number more than 100–125 households, with each household given a parcel of land according to a norm of $1\frac{1}{2}$ to 2 hectares per family member. Control in the resettlement zones was to be effected mainly by special troikas of party and soviet officials selected and given their instructions at the okrug level, backed up by OGPU and militia units. In each settlement a plenipotentiary was appointed to answer to the troika. The Siberian decrees also incorporated the Politburo's suggestion that young kulaks be weaned away from the influence of their elders so that they could act as trusted assistants in controlling the settlements, but only under the 'most strict supervision'.

In practice, the evidence from OGPU reports demonstrates that the process of dekulakization was disrupted by the reluctance of local officials to ensure the availability of food, seed, agricultural equipment and transport for the kulak households. For example, the Novosibirsk kulaks were to be given a food supply for two months, and a horse (except for those sent to the city), and if resettled for agricultural work, they were to be supplied with a plough, harrow, a wheeled cart and agricultural equipment, 1–2 tsentners of seed per household, and 500 roubles. Even if they did provide these goods, the rural soviets tended to short-change the kulaks, most importantly by giving them old or sick horses. That only served to slow down the rate at which the convoys could move to the place of resettlement, and made productive work in the new settlements almost impossible. Without fit horses the kulaks simply could not be moved on to the resettlement zones quickly, and large numbers of them began to concentrate at collection points: a factor which caused some concern in the okrug leadership about the possibility of an uprising.[68] Some okrugs hardly made any effort to move their kulaks to the resettlement zones; for example, by 22 March, Slavgorod had forwarded only 129 Category Two households provided with 'funds in kind' instead of the 2,916 planned; Kamen' Okrug had shipped out only 137 households from a target figure of 1,938.[69]

Similarly the krai OGPU command complained that resettlement sites in the taiga had few kulaks because of lack of transportation. The idea of the initial plan of dekulakization for Categories One and Two kulaks was to resettle them in areas which were completely cut off from the outside world, in remote northern parts of the krai where the taiga would act as a *cordon sanitaire* from the inhabited agricultural belt and make the return to their native villages almost impossible. The failure of the raions and okrugs to guarantee the supplies to kulaks had thrown this plan into chaos. For example, the Karabul' zone in Kansk Okrug, a location some 280–320 kilometres from the nearest railway, had received only just over 1,000 kulak families instead of a planned 12,000, largely because of the lack of carts to transport them. The OGPU was also anxious to transport kulaks to resettlement zones on the basins of the Chertala and Kengi rivers in the northern taiga area of Tomsk Okrug, before the onset of the spring thaw turned the area into an impassable terrain of boglands 10 to 40 kilometres wide and up to seven metres deep, though how the kulak families were to survive in such conditions did not seem to be a matter for consideration. The revision of resettlement plans meant that the aim of isolating the kulaks in such areas was put on hold, for, as the OGPU complained, they were now being placed in zones along the rivers Lagyl'iakh and Galka in Tomsk Okrug, from which in the summer months it was possible to reach other inhabited areas. In early April the OGPU advised the krai party leadership that kulaks were not only being poorly provided with the goods they needed for resettlement by raiispolkoms, but there were even cases when kulaks who had managed to retain some of their own good quality horses, carts and so on had them seized from them by officials at points of departure and at loading and unloading points and collection centres, to be replaced with poor quality substitutes. Kulaks were also frequently robbed of articles and money en route to holding centres. Consequently, the OGPU warned: 'The future success of the whole operation depends exclusively on the finding of "funds in kind" at the uttermost initiative of each okrug.'[70] In accordance with the Kraiispolkom decree of 1 March, old people, the sick, invalids, pregnant women and women with babies and very young children were sent back to their villages from the collection centres, a sorting process which obstructed the task of moving kulaks to the resettlement zones. The returnees were forced to hand back their 'fund in kind' to local soviet officials, thus reducing them to impoverishment.

There was also the problem of the large-scale flight of kulaks, as they sold up and moved out of the areas designated for complete collectivization in advance of dekulakization. The OGPU reported that kulaks were moving into work in the new industrial projects starting up in Siberia, such as Kuznetskstroi, or were moving to other areas and pretending that they were seredniaks, or fleeing into the taiga. The problem also extended to kulaks from other regions, such as the Urals, and even as far away as the Ukraine, who sought refuge in Siberia.[71] Coincidentally, the author interviewed a Siberian kulak who fled and took refuge with his mother's family in the Ukraine. In Novosibirsk Okrug, according to OGPU reports, 461 kulak families in 12 raions moved to other areas in the three months to the end of December 1929. By February, the OGPU estimated that 200–300 kulak wagons daily headed into the Narym taiga, and from Baksin raion alone some 2,000 wagons departed in January. Ironically, the kulaks sought to escape dekulakization by fleeing into precisely the remote taiga areas which the party had designated for their resettlement. Some Siberian kulaks even made the journey to the American embassy in Moscow to inquire about emigrating to America, and while they were arrested by the OGPU, their villages awaited news.[72] In Achinsk Okrug, kulaks attempted to escape confiscation and exile by moving from rural areas to worker settlements.

In Novo-Omsk raion, Omsk Okrug (an area designated for complete collectivization by spring 1930), of 853 kulak families listed for dekulakization 123 (14 per cent) escaped with their whereabouts unknown.[73] By the middle of March this 'mass flight' affected the seredniaks and bedniaks, who fled to remote areas of the countryside to avoid the intimidation and arrests which characterized forcible collectivization, fearing that their property would be confiscated and that they would be sent into exile like the kulaks.[74]

The disorientation of those families that had been uprooted from their native villages must have been compounded beyond our imagination by their despair on arrival at the resettlement zones. As OGPU reports starkly reveal, there they found themselves and their horses confronted by the prospect of starvation due to lack of provisions, having to sleep in the open or under what cover they could construct to protect them from the harsh Siberian winter, without any medical assistance for the many who were ill or weakened by the journey.[75] Many must have considered that those of their number that had already been shot or died on the way were the fortunate ones.

8 *Barshchina* and *Maroderstvo*

PEASANT *MENTALITÉ*

Ascertaining the views of peasants is extremely difficult given that the only interpretation of peasant attitudes is that which was reflected through party, soviet and OGPU officials, and other urban visitors to the countryside (journalists, writers, foreign travellers and so on). The opportunity for a direct rendering of the *mentalité* of some peasants in their own words, in the midst of forced collectivization and on the eve of dekulakization, is offered by a series of five letters written by Siberian peasants, one of which was from three soldiers home on leave, to the editor of the Novosibirsk Okruzhkom newspaper *Sel'skaia pravda*. The letters were written in response to a letter published in the newspaper from a French peasant, who was curious about the condition of the Russian peasantry under communism. The editor, branding the peasants as 'kulaks', passed copies of the letters to the Kraikom and the OGPU, which have survived in the Siberian party archive as a rare testimony of peasant distress.[1]

The longest (over three pages) was, sensibly given the circumstances, an unsigned letter from a self-professed 'bedniak' from the village of Kliuchik, Suzun raion, Kamen' Okrug. In response to the question of whether the Russian peasantry was better off living under communism than it had been under Nicholas II, the peasant bluntly stated that 'life is difficult'. He remarked how the communists had promised that 'he that does not work, will not eat', but now 'how they rip apart any peasant who works a little bit more land, even if without hired labour'. 'The state', the letter claimed, 'cleans out the muzhik's grain at cheap fixed prices, but there is no state grain for sale to the bedniak, the bedniak becomes hungry and has to enter the collectives under perpetual discipline.' In retrospect, the peasant asserted that 'before the October revolution ... horses did not plough the fields on empty stomachs, but were full of grain, there was plenty for all, but now you would never think of feeding a horse grain.' Collectivization was despised: 'How can this be regarded as free labour, if every day the peasant must go out and do work set by somebody else, under orders from the administration? If that is not exploitation of labour, it is hired labour [*batrachestvo*] in perpetuity.' As for party officials coming into the countryside and telling the peasants how to run their affairs, he retorted: 'Let each do what they do best.' The tragic consequences of forced collectivization, such as the mass sale of livestock, was a product of the refusal of peasants to participate in an economic levelling on joining the kolkhozes: 'We ask you, if in any factory or plant there is such a common pot as in the collective? We think not.'[2]

The party's 'soldierly discipline' was simply inappropriate for the peasants' way of thinking, affirmed this peasant. The notion of planning envisaged by the Bolsheviks was an alien concept to the peasant mind:

> As much as the peasant worked the land, so much was his profit ... when the state did not buy up his grain, he sold it in the bazaar and the price depended on the harvest, a bad harvest – high; if it was a good harvest year – cheap. But now the peasant does not try to plough so much, so that his grain procurement plan is not unbearable, machines are only sold to organizations, they make conditions for five years ahead then change them after two.[3]

Stalin's Russia was one of 'troubles' (*boliachki*), where peasants who bought machines and did not make the repayments due to harvest failure had their property confiscated, where the state was rich 'only in its propaganda', villages that did not have a cooperative had no kerosene, while paper, soap and tobacco was in short supply. The peasants had been terrorized by party officials to such an extent that he warned his French brother: 'You could never expect such a letter from the majority of villages.' 'The government has lost our trust,' concluded the peasant. 'It made many promises, but kept few, and it fleeces the muzhik.'[4]

Another 'bedniak' letter of early January 1930 lamented that 'in our Russia flourishes coercion, executions, exile ... especially from the beginning of 1928'. This peasant gave the example of grain procurement to illustrate the harsh treatment by the state: 'They give a control figure to each village, which is impossible to fulfil; the peasants say – this is unbearable, all the same, we shall press the kulaks. The commission looks for kulaks, and here is Ivanov, he has two horses, a wooden house, let us allocate 200 puds to him.' This 35 year old peasant had served during the First World war, had been captured and imprisoned in Germany, but, he asserted, he had never seen hunger on the scale that it was now afflicting the Siberian countryside, all because of the Soviet state's insatiable demand for grain. There were no legal norms or redress for the peasants, he complained, for the only 'law' recognized by the state was during the grain procurement campaign when the plenipotentiary came to the villages and said 'here is your figure' and 'give us your surpluses'.[5] Likewise, the letter of the three soldiers, written in late December 1929, remarked on the shock of returning home to find 'the peasants oppressed'. They spoke of 'a return to serfdom' and blamed state procurement for 'leaving the peasants half-starved, and expecting famine in the spring'. They insisted that the peasants lived '90 per cent worse' than they had before the October Revolution. In Russia, they advised the French peasant, what existed was 'not socialism, but really oppressive capitalism by another regime'.[6]

FORCED COLLECTIVIZATION AS *BARSHCHINA* (CORVÉE)

Confusion among peasants over what collectivization involved was as rife as it was among the party activists conducting the campaign, but what is clear is that the carrying out of collectivization left no time for winning over peasant hearts and minds. Lenin had inculcated into party cadres the notion that the seredniak was possessed of 'two souls': the would-be kulak, and the non-exploiting, exploited labourer. The sympathy of the seredniak peasants was crucial to the success of the whole collectivization project, but in the rush to over-fulfil targets and tempos, party officials had little time to indulge in propaganda to energize the seredniak's anti-kulak side. Moreover, the success of collectivization rested on the party's ability to reconcile the essential dual nature of the peasant, for as one observer commented: 'The peasant has an inborn sense of the communal meadow, the communal wood, the communal shepherd. He is of a collectivist disposition; but he insists upon his own house, his own furniture, his own horse, his own cow. He surrounds his garden with a stout hedge. He locks his door. He has just as much sense of property as anybody else.'[7] It was precisely because of infringements by party activists and state officials of the mass of peasants' jealously guarded proprietorial rights that collectivization quickly ran into difficulties.

Details of implementation and official excesses in the campaign were furnished to the krai leadership in regular procuracy and OGPU reports.[8] A report from the procurator of Novosibirsk Okrug explained just what 'forced collectivization' (*prinuditel'naia kollektivizatsiia*) involved. The campaign was conducted almost bereft of explanatory work among the peasantry. Peasants were simply ordered to join the kolkhozes, and if they refused, local officials applied a variety of intimidatory threats and punishments until they agreed: tax supplements, grain quotas, disenfranchisement, confiscation of property and administrative exile. In this okrug alone, by 4 January 1930 some 400 verbal and 30 written complaints had been made by peasants to procuracy officials.[9] That the practice of 'twenty-four hour' collectivization in effect meant 'either the kolkhoz or exile' for peasants may be illustrated by some cases.

The following excerpt from an official complaint from a peasant from the village of Temnaia, Novosibirsk Okrug, reveals that no time was allowed for reflection on the critical decision of whether to enrol in the collectives or not, and changes of mind were ignored:

> When I registered in the commune and told my wife, she protested. I went back to the brigade for more explanation, but they did not give me an explanation, in fact, they threw me out of the meeting saying 'we have struck you from the list, we don't need your sort'. Three days later they came to me to conduct a stocktake of my property and against my wishes they did this ... They say that once registered in the commune your farm is already communal and you cannot get out for a year.

Meanwhile, many party activists reported that peasant meetings adopted decisions to collectivize and exclude kulak farms with 'stormy applause by the bedniak-seredniak mass'.[10]

OGPU reports from Novosibirsk Okrug revealed that authoritative figures in village communities, usually middle-aged seredniaks who were ex-partisans, often spoke out against collectivization at general meetings. It was no doubt precisely because of their influence over village communities that the Kraikom had banned congresses or any meetings of partisan organizations in late November 1929 until such time that 'massive explanatory work' created a more positive attitude towards the party in areas with large numbers of partisans.[11] A common theme in the peasant opposition was the idea that collectivization represented a new form of serfdom: 'collectives are just like the old landlord estates,' objected peasants in Inderskoe raion; 'they will work everyone to death in the communes and there will be *barshchina*,' claimed peasants in the village of Tatar, Cherepanovo raion; 'we used to work for the landlords as batraks, but now the communists want us to return to being batraks through collectivization,' was the agreed view of peasants in the village of Iurt Akbalyk, Kolyvansk raion.

There was also a deeply ingrained suspicion of the party's motivation in launching collectivization: 'the communists themselves do not want to work in the collectives, but they like to order us to do so'; 'let all the communists sign up first, and then let's see.' Whereas the party activists had an uphill task in persuading the seredniaks to join the kolkhozes, and their presence was crucial to the economic viability of the whole enterprise, the 'great majority' of the bedniaks had, according to the OGPU, 'a positive attitude to the question of mass collectivization', and were 'leading actors and assistants'. Though even among the bedniaks of Novosibirsk there was anti-kolkhoz sentiment, expressed in terms of a contrast between free peasant labour and the discipline of 'hourly work' on the collectives:

'it is better to be a bedniak than a slave', concluded some. In many villages most peasants followed the lead of kulaks in an orgy of slaughtering their livestock in advance of being forced into kolkhozes. One should not overlook the element of peasant rational self-interest and envy underlying much of the destruction of property prior to collectivization, for as peasants in villages of Kolyvansk raion, explained: 'sooner to see everything destroyed than to regard it as belonging to someone else,' and: 'We will join the kolkhoz only when ... everyone is equal.'[12]

In a typical case, a raiispolkom plenipotentiary, Kiselev, who was a 25 year old member of the komsomol mobilized from a Kazan VUZ, came to the village of Verkh-Kamyshenka, Chumysh raion, Barnaul Okrug, to carry out collectivization. Following his arrival the general meeting passed a resolution declaring that anyone who did not abide by its decisions was 'an opponent of Soviet power' and would be sent into exile 'to Turukhansk Krai and the polar bears'. Kiselev demanded that the village form itself into a commune, but when many bedniaks and seredniaks attempted to dissuade him from this course of action and protested that they would prefer a *toz*, the plenipotentiary arrested 25 peasants, beat them with rifle butts, threw them into a dark room and interrogated them one by one. He warned each: 'anyone who votes against the commune will be exiled to the north or even shot,' and 'you have two paths, one leads to being shot, the other to the collective'. One peasant, Shatilov, who refused to join the collective was brought before an 'emergency tribunal' headed by Kiselev, who pronounced the sentence 'execution by shooting'. Kiselev freed Shatilov on condition that he immediately went around the village recruiting peasants into the kolkhoz: a method which worked because the peasant begged his neighbours: 'If you do not enter, they will shoot me.' Kiselev and his brigade were accused of being 'systematically drunk' and riding around the countryside like victors striking fear into the peasantry. When Kiselev was brought to trial for these abuses many of the peasant witnesses were intimidated and the okrug court dismissed his accusers as 'kulaks'.[13]

In some areas plenipotentiaries called peasants to meetings to discuss collectivization and simply put the question in this way: 'whoever is against Soviet power raise your arm'. In the absence of raised arms, the decision to collectivize was taken as passed.[14] In the village of Staryi Koiak, Chulym raion, Novosibirsk Okrug, the plenipotentiary arrived on 12 January and immediately called a peasant meeting where he threatened that if they did not vote for collectivization: 'One tenth will be sent to Narym and one tenth will be shot.' When the peasants protested, the plenipotentiary moderated his stance and promised to shoot only the kulaks.[15]

The peasants of the village of Vyatsk, Achinsk raion, Kansk Okrug, recorded the events in their village in a letter of complaint signed by 17 peasants and investigated by the Kraiispolkom in April 1930. Collectivization had been carried out in the village while a large number of the men were away on a wood-cutting expedition. In their absence the brigade came to their households and, without any kind of agitational work, registered their property for inclusion in the kolkhoz. When the men returned and protested against their forcible collectivization, they were warned: 'You have two roads: to the kolkhoz, or with the kulaks; the latter road you know well . . . to Turukhansk.' The peasants felt helpless. The kolkhoz had been established a year previously with 15 households, but the 'old kolkhozniks' now treated the newcomers as their subordinates to be ordered about: 'We are the bosses, not you.' Without any consultation, all the livestock was rounded up and enclosed in a 'socialized' stockyard. The kolkhoz did not have sufficient or adequate forage for the huge influx of animals and they began to starve. When next the kolkhoz administration decided to 'socialize' all the pigs in the village, it provoked the mass slaughtering of almost all the pigs in one night. In the Siberian winter of 40 degrees of frost, the peasants had to obtain the permission of the 'old kolkhoznik' administration before they could use their animals to draw wood and water. Anyone who attempted to use their animals without permission was beaten up by the old kolkhozniks or the brigade. When the village party secretary eventually gave permission for peasants to leave the kolkhoz, the old kolkhozniks refused to return the peasants' property. Without horses or seed many familes now faced the prospect of starvation the following year, and 48 villagers had already left the countryside for towns. The peasants appealed to the Kraiispolkom to intervene and force the local authorities to return their property: 'so that we can return to the honest, peaceful labour which is the nature of us peasants, to again rebuild our large families, and also to help the Soviet state to solve the grain and produce problems in more satisfactory conditions. Then it would be possible to examine collective labour.' The consequences of a failure to get their property back would be a 'descent into apathy'. The outcome of this case is not known.[16]

In Novosibirsk Okrug, a brigade led by a party member from the commune 'True Path', Bannikova, posed the question of collectivization as follows: 'Anyone who is against the commune, is against Soviet power.' In this area the party relied heavily on existing commune members as activists in the campaign, a fact which exacerbated social conflicts among the peasantry. For example, under the leadership of a raiispolkom plenipotentiary, a crowd of some 450 commune members from four local communes marched through the village of Tikhonovo with red flags, banners and harmonicas. The communards lined up on one side and the villagers on the other and a meeting was held to persuade the villagers to join the communes. When the villagers refused, the communards denounced them: 'You are all kulaks, kulak lackeys, bastards against the kolkhoz.' According to the OGPU, the hostility of the communards to the peasants was such that the meeting threatened to degenerate into a 'pogrom'.[17] The dubious example of the 'True Path' commune was raised by the bedniak Fedotov, in the village of Kazakovo, Kochenevo raion. At a village meeting to discuss collectivization attended by 175 peasants, he declared:

> I have been a communist since 1905, then we Bolsheviks fought not for the collective, not for serfdom, but for the freedom of the masses from any type of bondage. Whether collective or commune its the same as the old *barshchina*. I personally do not see anything good in the collective. The leaders are coopted, for example, as the chairman of the commune 'True Path' they sent some guy with gold teeth, who doesn't do anything at all, yet he receives high wages.[18]

Threats and arrests, not discussion, were the usual response of local officials to peasant reluctance to join the collectives. The raiispolkom plenipotentiary in Baksin raion, Rabot'ko, told peasants who wanted to establish an artel or *toz*: 'Anyone who does not join the commune will be thrown into the cooler.' The bedniak, Kitenko, told a general meeting of peasants of Petropavlovo rural soviet in Maslyanin raion: 'They cannot drive us into the commune by force, we can join quietly by ourselves if we want to. I read the newspapers and I know the law.' He was arrested on the orders of the raiispolkom plenipotentiary.[19] It was not just the intimidation and coercion practised by officials that turned peasants against collectivization. For example, in Shipunov raion of Barnaul Okrug plenipotentiaries went around peasant homes registering all their personal possessions for the kolkhoz indivisible fund, including their clothes. In these villages a major social cleavage over the issue of collectivization was that between men and women. The men tended to vote for the kolkhoz, but three-quarters of the women, who were more numerous at the meetings, voted against, apparently in protest at the registration of personal property. Such divisions within households often caused divorces.[20]

Intra-village divisions over collectivization sometimes reflected territorial splits within the community. For example, Sergei Timofeevich Rudakov, a former chairman of the kolkhoz 'Red Star' in the village of Toropovo, Novosibirsk Okrug, remembers how collectivization polarized the village by kinship ties and territory. One part of the village originated from Kursk province in central Russia, the other part were Ukrainians. The households of the 'Kursk territory' (*kurskii krai*) decided to join the commune while the Ukrainians refused.[21]

The crafty Russian peasants devised many ruses to protect their property from the kolkhozes. One form that assumed a 'mass phenomenon' was for peasants, particularly the wealthy, to subdivide their farm and property and 'share' it with other members of the household who did not join the collective. In this way the household had a foot in both camps – it could legitimately claim to have joined the kolkhoz, but at the same time it retained a base for continuing private farming. Moreover, the peasants frequently left their best land, livestock and equipment with the family members who stayed outside the kolkhoz, or sold it off.[22] In Kuznetsk Okrug a large number of peasants sold off all their property before entering the kolkhoz, their attitude being 'I will be a worker in the kolkhoz and they will pay me two roubles per day'.[23] The pace of collectivization inevitably meant that many of the new kolkhozes were poorly organized, a fact that provoked one Kraikom official into saying that, for the peasants, 'the first experience of communism is that there is no pay'.[24] For example, the commune 'Red Proletarian' in Maslyanin raion was established in late 1929 with 349 members, overwhelmingly batraks and bedniaks. It had 58 workhorses and 48 cows, and was seriously short of fodder, despite the fact that there was hay in the fields. The commune was also faced with a severe seed shortage (only 19 per cent of its needs) for the spring sowing. It was recognized by the authorities that the commune was 'absolutely not economically viable' and the kolkhozniks 'did not know what to do'. Lack of food and fodder with starving peasants and livestock was a common problem faced by the new kolkhozes, which contributed to the mass exit of peasants from them in late March 1930. Of course, another explanation for the mass exit was the publication of Stalin's 'Dizzy with Success' article in *Sovet'skaia sibir'*, which itself recommended the creation of artels and tozi rather than communes.[25]

The flood of peasants from the communes may be illustrated by the following figures for Novosibirsk Okrug: on 20 March there were 74,622 peasant households in 641 kolkhozes (357 of which were communes), but by 10 April only 27,730 households remained collectivized in 368 kolkhozes (of which only 166 were communes).[26] At this point it appeared that the kolkhozes would be left as a rump in the countryside. It was the seredniaks that tended to leave first, while those who remained were overwhelmingly bedniaks and batraks. There was a chorus of self-interested protest from the remaining kolkhozniks about the party decision to transform the communes into artels. As the communard Kudrin, from Baksin raion explained:

'We the *bednota* do not agree with the changeover to agricultural artels, and if you insist, then it would be better for us to leave. There is no interest at all for us in an agricultural artel – none. We will not get any grain, no money either, we would be better off working for wages outside.' At the same time there was general mistrust of the party's decision to establish a series of financial privileges for kolkhozes, as the peasants tended to view these as a 'temporary' bait to lure them back which would be annulled at a later date.[27]

In many cases the raion authorities had appointed twenty-five thousander party activists from Leningrad, who were ignorant of agriculture, as the chairmen and deputy chairmen of the communes. These urban workers, far from home, were now being left bereft of the specialist agricultural skills, equipment, seed and livestock of the seredniak peasants. To a degree the twenty-five thousanders, and the attitude of local authorities to them, were part of the problem. The Kraikom chastised okruzhkoms for often ignoring the needs of the Leningraders: in Omsk, they were sent into the countryside without winter clothing; in Biisk, they were sent to sovkhozes without any preparation of living quarters and food supplies; in Kansk, Leningraders lived for four months on a commune without any instructions or definition of their role. Frequently, there was no liaison between these workers and the local authorities, and, most irritating for the workers, many of them did not receive any pay. This lack of control of the Leningraders must have been a contributory factor in the numerous cases where they were accused of misappropriating kolkhoz funds, getting drunk for days on end, raping the daughters of kulaks and terrorizing peasants. Some of them even abandoned their posts and returned to Leningrad.[28]

Attempts by the authorities to retain some of the property of peasants who left the kolkhozes, particularly seed grain stocks, or to redistribute them elsewhere, provoked *volynki* and instances of Luddism. On 8 April a *volynka* involving up to one hundred women erupted in the village of Nikonov, Maslyanin raion, Novosibirsk Okrug, when the rural soviet, acting on a decision of the raikom, deducted a 15 per cent tax when returning grain stocks to peasants. The peasants ransacked the barns where the grain was stored, beat up two store workers and destroyed equipment. Similar occurrences were reported in other villages of the raion as peasants went on the rampage to show the authorities 'how the people can steal'. Shortages of seed for sowing was not the only problem delaying the spring sowing. Shortages of fodder meant that many animals starved to death or were so seriously debilitated that they were too weak to do agricultural work. Faced with starving animals some communes took preemptory measures to slaughter livestock.[29]

Volynki involving hundreds, mostly women, also occurred in Achinsk Okrug in early April in response to attempts by the authorities to move seed grain to western okrugs of the krai which were short of supplies. In the village of El'nik, Berezov raion, a crowd forced the closure of state barns and after a meeting presented a list of demands to the soviet officials. The list illustrates the mixture of political, economic and cultural frustrations of the peasantry with the regime:

> 1. No grain is to be moved; 2. no more kulaks are to be resettled, because they are 'fellow-toilers' [*truzheniki*], and the exiled must be returned; 3. the teachers, Kiselev and Shvarts, must be removed because they made the students vote for the deportations; 4. religion is not to be infringed, services are not to be disrupted and the priest must be given a lodging; 5. give us goods from the consumer cooperative, especially leather, because we are all without shoes; 6. give us information on milling without delay, because we want to mill our surplus for sale; 7. immediately hold new elections for the whole administration of the consumer cooperative; 8. immediately remove from the kolkhoz the worker Kileev and his wife, because they fled from a collective in Minusinsk and have come here and acted like bandits.

In the village of Lebedinka, women cried: 'You will only take the seed when you bring in machine guns.'[30] In evaluating the implementation of the policy of accelerated mass collectivization, one can only draw the same conclusion as one speaker to the Kraiispolkom plenum in the middle of March: 'arrests and nagans' (revolvers) provided the impetus for peasants to enter the kolkhozes.[31]

DEKULAKIZATION AS *MARODERSTVO* (PILLAGING)

Dekulakized peasants were frequently at the mercy of the more criminal minded officials and fellow villagers, who regarded the new policy as an opportunity to pillage and rape. We should remember that local officials and peasant communities had already whetted their appetites for this kind of licentious behaviour during the mass confiscations and auctions of peasant property under Article 61 of the previous summer and autumn. Jealousy and hatred between village households and factions were unleashed by the opportunities to share in confiscated property and created a grassroots zeal for dekulakization. A Krai Procuracy report in late March listed 67 cases from across the krai to illustrate such 'distortions of the class line by lower authorities'. The policy of expropriating kulaks was taken by many local officials and activists as an injunction to 'take everything, even the shirts on their backs' (*do nitki*). Party reports noted that often all property, even porridge, loaves of bread and pots of butter, were seized. Confiscated property was often sold off at a pittance and local officials would reserve the best items for their own use. The pillaging was frequently accompanied by the rape of wives and daughters of dekulakized peasants, for which a handful of officials were tried and shot.[32] Not only means of production and arms were seized but also clothes and household articles, frequently without any kind of registration, were simply stolen by local officials, the brigades, peasants or kolkhozniks. This made the return of property to peasants wrongly dekulakized extremely difficult.[33]

To illustrate this tendency to pillage, and how it was instigated by newspaper statements by Stalin in preemption of authorization by party decrees, let us examine the case of Mariinsk raion, Tomsk Okrug. Here, six senior raiispolkom officials (the chairman, a member of the presidium and four plenipotentiaries) were charged and released on bail by the procuracy in late February 1930 for distortions of party directives in the implementation of dekulakization.[34] The affair began with the arrival of a telegram from the okrispolkom on 25 January which ordered the imposition of supplementary delivery quotas for seed grain on kulak farms. At the same time, the raion officials read Stalin's article in *Pravda* of 21 January 'On the Question of the Policy of Liquidating the Kulaks as a Class', which was an extract of Stalin's speech to the Congress of Agrarian Marxists on 27 December 1929. The following day the raiispolkom chairman, Gerasimov, convoked a secret plenary session of the raiispolkom to discuss Stalin's injunction and the new direction in party policy, to which he invited the town party actif and other key non-party raion officials. Gerasimov told the session that they must immediately go into the villages and liquidate the kulaks. No detailed operational instructions were issued as to how the dekulakization process was to be conducted. The activists were simply told that on arrival in the village, whether during the day or at night, they should draw up a list of kulak households and immediately register and seal up all kulak property. Following this they were to call together special meetings within one day to confirm the list of kulaks. In practice, village communists and seredniaks were not admitted to these meetings because they were regarded as untrustworthy. The confiscation of property was carried out within a 24-hour period from the confirmation of the list, concentrating in the first instance on those well-off kulaks who had consistently refused to fulfil plans and quotas, had slaughtered livestock or had otherwise resisted. Such kulaks were to be immediately detained by administrative order and sent into exile.

The only instruction given as regards the confiscation of kulak property was that livestock and machines were to be delivered to the raiispolkom, otherwise initially it was routine for property to be sold off by plenipotentiaries in the village, though a raiispolkom order on 29 January specified certain items of agricultural equipment and products (grain and seed) which were to be handed over to rural soviets until the raiispolkom decided what was to be done with them. This order came too late to save many kulak households from an orgy of pillaging in late January and early February. Such was the case with the dekulakization implemented by the raiispolkom plenipotentiary, and a leader of the town party actif, Malkov, on 27 January in the village of Novo-Aleksandrovka. Eight households were listed for dekulakization, but since Malkov refused to organize a *bednota* meeting to approve the list, six of the 'liquidated' households turned out to be seredniaks. There was no organized registration and confiscation of property. The Krai Procuracy report described the scene as follows: 'A tendency to pillage manifested itself in the population, property was dissipated, peasants and officials swiped everything for themselves, anything they could get their hands on, like the militiaman Zimin who took a featherbed, pillows and foodstuffs (meat, grain and honey).'[35]

Malkov even gave the chairman of the commune a list of names of workers and employees at a nearby grain elevator and leather factory, with the demand that they be given flour and meat taken from the confiscated property. The chairman refused, no doubt not for any ethical reason but because he wanted to keep as much as possible of the kulak booty for the commune. A similar pattern was repeated across the raion, as armed plenipotentiaries implemented dekulakization by day and night, in freezing weather, forcing kulaks, and many seredniaks wrongly listed as kulaks, out of their homes and stripping them of their property. According to the procuracy: 'The seredniak-bedniak mass was not organized for this campaign, neither the *bednota* nor the batraks in the villages knew why or on what grounds the "daylight robbery" was conducted, how or against whom dekulakization was to be applied.' Rather, raion officials pursued dekulakization on the basis of 'a system of administrative tyranny and work "by swoops" (*c naskoka*)'.[36] Zakovsky, the Krai OGPU Chief, later described how some kulaks were stripped naked and left in the open air, as plenipotentiaries ordered villagers not to take them in. In one instance a dekulakization actif robbed a priest of his cassock to sell to a trader, and left him out in the open during 30–40 degrees of frost. A seredniak took pity on the priest and gave him his sheepskin coat, but this was immediately seized by the actif and also sold to the trader.[37] In the village of N-Elovka, Barnaul Okrug, confiscated property was divided up among officials in front of onlooking villagers: the chairman of the rural soviet stole the priest's cross and gospels, while the secretary of the party cell took his eau-de-cologne, jam, children's toys, notepaper, pencils, a toothbrush and powder, and other belongings.[38]

The oral histories of many of the dekulakized families have only recently been collected in Russia.[39] The participation of the *bednota* in dekulakization is vividly portrayed in the oral history of Aleksandrovka in Slavgorod Okrug.[40] Here is how one villager remembered the episode:

> The raion demands more – give us kulaks. The bedniaks, that actif, went to the [soviet] office, planning who else would be denounced as kulaks. There was one Tarabrin, a shit, he had nothing – not even a chicken, he was coarse, rude, he says: 'Sorokalet – he's a kulak. I worked for him during sowing, he starved me' ...
>
> They estimated the worth of the house – immediately five roubles: 'Any more? Five and a half. Any more? Six roubles. Anyone else? Yours for six roubles.' The bedniaks became traders. Now a landed house, now some wreck of a house. Then they forced open chests: 'This thing – one rouble. Any more?' And so everything went down to the smallest thing.

The comprehensiveness of property confiscations during dekulakization is illustrated by an inventory detailed in a letter of complaint by the peasant Kos'ian, from the village of Khoroshem, in Novo-Alekseev raion, Slavgorod Okrug. Kos'ian was later excluded from the kulak list and obviously wanted to get his property back; the problem was that most of his household possessions had been taken away without any kind of registration, so he attached a list to his letter of complaint: 2 carpets, 4 handtowels, 4 shirts, 1 scroll, 3 children's shawls, 2 buckets (1 somebody else's), 1 glass lamp, 2 tin mugs, 3 teacups and saucers, 1 frying-pan, 2 table knives (1 somebody else's), 1 tub of cabbage (thrown on the floor), half a kilo of apricots (eaten on the spot), seven pounds of fat in pieces (put in pockets), crackling (also eaten), half a loaf of bread (also eaten), 2 kilos of flour, half a sheepskin, 3 pillows, 1 mirror, 4 plates, 2 bowls, 1 stool, a quarter of brick-tea (taken by the communard Aleksandr Tkach), 400 grams of soap, 1 stove, 1 sack of spinning wool, 3 spades, 1 pitchfork, 1 small saw, 1 tablecloth, personal papers (wife's).[41] A dekulakized peasant recalled to the author his despair on seeing, many years later, a *skatulka* decorated with a picture of the administration building of the commune 'First of May' in Yarki, Novosibirsk Okrug: for it was his former family home.[42]

Dekulakization provided a strong incentive for poor peasant participation in the form of virtually unrestrained pillaging of their wealthy neighbours. There were instances when the act of dekulakization was carried out by groups of bedniaks without the participation of party or soviet officials. On 27 January the bedniak actif in the village of Komar', Inderskoe raion, Novosibirsk Okrug, decided on its own initiative to expropriate 22 kulak households and elected a brigade for this purpose. The chairman of the rural soviet was powerless to stop them and went off to the raiispolkom to get instructions on how to deal with this peasant spontaneity.[43] Attempts to involve the mass of peasants in the dekulakization process met with mixed results. In Ust'-Uda, Irkutsk Okrug, peasants greeted dekulakization and participated in it 'mercilessly'. On the other hand, a plenipotentiary in Rubtsovsk Okrug, Zuev, wrote: 'Dekulakization is not coming from below, but as a result of the special plenipotentiaries sent from raion centres ... or the establishment of special teams.' Directives forbidding dekulakization of seredniaks were also ignored. In the village of Krest'iansk, Mamontev raion, Barnaul Okrug, the secretary of the party cell, Chernikov, threatened to shoot the seredniak Olennikov, if he did not vacate his home within 12 hours so that it could become a kolkhoz residence. In parts of Kuznetsk Okrug, seredniak farms were dekulakized despite the fact that they paid only four to 13 roubles in agricultural tax.[44] The involvement of peasants in the process could lead to perverse outcomes, as they gave vent to petty prejudices and the settling of old scores. In the village of Korostelevo, Kansk Okrug, the seredniak Antsiferov was dekulakized because he was denounced at the general meeting of peasants for 'riding around on his bicycle, and even wearing a tie'.[45]

According to the OGPU in many raions of Novosibirsk Okrug 'the mass of the *bednota* and batraks were not involved in the revealing of kulaks, the registering of their property or the practical implementation of expropriation', and consequently, 'the liquidation of the kulaks as a class and the expropriation of their property was carried out almost exclusively by administrative methods by rural soviets and raiispolkom plenipotentiaries.' This explained why so many (some 338 households – Novosibirsk raion alone accounted for about one-third of this total) seredniaks had been wrongly included in lists of kulaks. These seredniaks were picked out by the raion troiki at the collection points and and sent back to their villages.[46] In contrast, shortly after Stalin's retreat of early March, Eikhe continued to firmly assert that 'the general bedniak mass ... and the general mass of seredniaks' participated in dekulakization 'across the whole of Siberia'.[47] There were some cases of 'spontaneous' dekulakization in January, prior to the issuing of party and government decrees on the procedure. Zaitsev, the Novosibirsk Okruzhkom Secretary, informed a Kraikom conference of regional party leaders on 30 January: 'In Inderskoe raion they carried out a complete expropriation as a revolutionary act, regardless of the existing formal laws.' The OGPU report on dekulakization in the Siberian krai also claimed that prior to the elaboration of party directives on dekulakization in February: 'At the initiative of the batrak-bedniak actifs spontaneous dekulakization began.'[48]

The chances of the kulaks surviving in the areas of resettlement depended crucially on the fulfilment of Kraikom instructions that they be provided with basic foodstuffs and agricultural equipment. Yet, the OGPU observed many cases when local party organizations and kolkhozes had refused to deliver to the exiled kulaks the basic foods, means of production and clothes permitted by party decrees. When the supplies were handed over, they often failed to meet the minimum amounts or standards. In Novosibirsk raion, the kulaks were only given grain for 200 households instead of the 300 herded into the collection point; they were given the oldest and least healthy horses, and no fodder for the animals. In Kargat raion, the 180 exiled kulak families had to make do with food and seed supplies sufficient for only 95 families provided by the local authorities, and no fodder for their livestock.[49] Instead of providing the kulaks with food and equipment, some okrugs pushed them into neighbouring okrugs, thus Kamen' was accused by Novosibirsk, and Oirot by Biisk.[50]

Often last minute searches of kulak convoys before they left for collection centres provided an opportunity for local officials to confiscate property or replace serviceable goods, healthy livestock and so on with others of poor quality. To illustrate this abuse, the OGPU provided numerous cases, including that in the village of Kopylovo, Barnaul Okrug, where the kulak families of Vaskin and Smirnov were subjected to a final search by rural soviet officials prior to their departure. They had their best horses replaced by others which were in such a poor condition that they could not pull any loads, and other products, personal possessions and money were taken from them. By the time the first train load of Barnaul kulaks consisting of 199 kulak families (1,111 persons) arrived at their disembarkation point in Tomsk Okrug, the local OGPU chief reported that they had only 200 horses, 85 sleighs, 115 wagons (without wheels), only 20 harnesses, and poor quality agricultural implements. The second train shipment from Barnaul was in a similar state.[51] As the convoys of the dekulakized trekked north to the resettlement zones, peasants often sold anything of value that they had retained to buy food from the villages that they passed by.[52]

The dekulakized peasants did not always remain bystanders to their fate. In January alone in Novosibirsk Okrug, the OGPU reported that there were four 'mass *volynki*' in which upwards of 1,500 peasants took part, mainly women. The most serious incidents occurred in the above-mentioned village of Komar' and others in Inderskoe and Alekseev raions. When the bedniaks of Komar' attempted to dekulakize, and prepared to list property for confiscation, a crowd of some 500, mainly women and children, gathered and shouted anti-soviet slogans and called for raion and soviet officials to be beaten. To placate the crowd a village meeting was called, where again villagers shouted 'down with the communists, down with the tractors' and called for the return of kulak property and their right to vote. Usually, the OGPU reported that the mood of such peasants improved after 'kulaks' had been arrested and 'explanatory-agitational work' was carried out.[53]

The scale of peasant resistance can be deduced from the statistics on violent political crimes, which grew significantly in this period. Cases of 'banditism' grew from 67 in 1928 to 456 in 1929, and reached 880 in 1930. Similarly, cases of 'terrorism' involving killings shot up from 406 (14.25 per cent of krai killings) in 1928 to 756 (27.25 per cent) in 1929, and reached 624 (39 per cent) for the first nine months of 1930 (there were also 472 'terrorist' woundings in this period). Of course, the increase in these types of crimes was also a reflection of the growing use of Article 58, Clause 10 (against counter-revolutionary acts) against peasants who opposed collectivization and dekulakization.[54] At the same time the OGPU arrested thousands of peasants who opposed collectivization and dekulakization. OGPU reports for Novosibirsk Okrug from January to March 1930 reveal that in January 1930 107 kulaks were arrested under Article 58, but in the first three weeks of February the arrest rate dramatically increased to just under nine hundred, of which 138 were charged under Article 58.[55]

In Siberia as a whole, by 25 February, 4,442 persons had been arrested and charged with criminal acts during the agricultural campaigns, including 2,549 kulaks charged with slaughtering livestock and opposition. Krai Procuracy reports reveal that the sentences handed out to such peasants for their opposition to collectivization and dekulakization were exemplary and extremely harsh. The following cases are illustrative: the kulak S. Terskikh, from Biria, Minusinsk Okrug, was charged under article 58.10 and was sentenced to ten years in prison and five years of exile, plus a 1,000 rouble fine; the kulak Ryzhev, from the village of Tabat, for killing seven cows and selling three horses, was sentenced to two years in prison and three years of exile, plus the confiscation of all property; in the village of Bulatovka, Uzhur raion, Achinsk Okrug, the kulak Finiagin, for opposing the kolkhoz and organizing a band to make raids against it, received six years in a strict regime prison and confiscation of all his property, plus permanent exile.[56]

The process of rounding up kulak families for resettlement seems to have been conducted mainly in an atmosphere of peasant *pokornost'*, the fatalism which traditionally characterized the Russian peasant. The OGPU reported that the exile of kulaks from villages was conducted without any 'political difficulties', any 'excesses' or *volynki*. In Uzhanikhin raion, Novosibirsk Okrug, a crowd of about one hundred peasants, mainly women and children, gathered to watch the departure of a convoy of 576 (103 households) of their dispossessed kulak neighbours from the 'collection point': 'without any shouting, with absolutely no tears'. There had been, however, demands from some relatives who had not been dekulakized that they be allowed to join their kin and be resettled also.[57] Peasants from the village of Chemrovka, Biisk Okrug, on the other hand, attempted to prevent the shipment of a trainload of kulaks from Biisk to Tulun. As the train passed near the village, it slowed down to take a gradient on the line, and was met by a crowd of about one hundred men who pelted it with stones and opened doors in an attempt to free some of the 18 families from their village which were on board. The OGPU guards dispersed the crowd by firing into the air.[58]

The general passivity ensued from the fact that dekulakization was carried out suddenly, giving families little time to organize collective resistance. Moreover, many of the able-bodied men and youths (those most likely to resist) fled. Disorientation also followed from the fact that many heads of households were arrested in preliminary swoops as Category One kulaks. Zakovsky informed the Kraiispolkom: 'Some of the kulaks fled into the taiga with arms, without their families, some are hiding out in the hills . . . [some kulaks] want to engage in combat with us.' He spoke of 'numerous organized political *volynki*' and 'mass counter-revolutionary actions' against the party's measures, where the 'rural counter-revolution' was often organized by the many ex-White officers and soldiers who lived in the Siberian countryside.[59]

A member of a family dekulakized in the village of Yarki, Novosibirsk Okrug, told the author that socioeconomic differences within the village were a key factor in the dekulakization process. This was a large village of approximately 1,300 households. Intra-village enmities and jealousies were aroused. The 'poor', the 'shit of the village' were in the forefront: 'It was our activists, those who did not want to work, who drank all the time, they called themselves communists, but we only had a handful of communists in the village.' The actif met and listed about 100 households as kulaks. The dekulakized households were picked off individually by groups of officials and poor peasants to contain resistance:

> I was off ploughing. I came home late in the evening and everyone was crying. I asked what had happened and they said that early tomorrow

we would be forced to leave. My mother said that she would go to the raion because she thought that if there was no household head [the father had died some years before – author] then they would have no right to do it. She got up early in the morning and went to the raion. I did not stop her. I took the second horse and fled into the forest. I lived like that for a month.[60]

This peasant obtained false papers and made his way to Novokuznetsk where he found work as a fitter in a bakery – despite the fact that his fellow workers and management knew that he was a kulak: in fact, he was allowed to sleep in the workplace until he received a residency permit.

THE MUROMTSEVO REVOLT

Despite the universality of collectivization and dekulakization, there was only a handful of armed uprisings against the regime – an indication of the fragmentation of peasant solidarity that had been engineered by the social influence policy over the previous year. The most serious of four armed peasant revolts against collectivization and dekulakization in Siberia was centred on Muromtsevo raion of Barabinsk Okrug. A special investigatory commission of the okruzhkom, sent to the raion in March 1930, claimed that the organization of this 'kulak' group in opposition to the party's measures in the countryside dated back to 1927, but that it became more active from the summer of 1929 following the introduction of the new methods of grain procurement.[61] So-called 'counter revolutionary groupings' were apparently a common phenomenon in this area, and in the build up to collectivization the OGPU attempted to eliminate them; for example, a group of up to 24 persons were based in the villages of Kondrat'evo, headed by the priest Chuvinsky, and Bakmaska and Liapunovo, led by Andrei Sinitsin, who before the October revolution was a district representative and gendarme sergeant-major, and in the village of Taramaklinsko, a group ten strong was led by the peasant Kondakov, who had fought for Kolchak.[62]

During January and February 1930, at the height of the party's assault on the countryside, attempts by the local authorities to implement collectivization and dekulakization ran into trouble in the area. In many villages peasants were not intimidated by the presence of raion officials and militia officers, and when they attempted to address peasant meetings there were shouts of 'go away', 'shut up', and 'we're sick of you lot'. Faced with peasant opposition and indifference, the plenipotentiaries resorted to force and intimidation. In particular, in the village of Riazan, the raiispolkom plenipotentiary, Prokudin, arrested ten peasants and the priest. As one plenipotentiary put it: 'Either join us in the kolkhoz, or join the kulaks in the bog.' In a number of villages property was confiscated from kulaks and taken by rural soviet officials since there were no kolkhozes to deliver it to.[63] These excesses provoked a number of spontaneous peasant meetings in various villages to discuss how best to resist collectivization and dekulakization. At the initiative of the kulak Solomatov, at the beginning of February 1930, in the village of Viatska One, there was convened a meeting of a small group of peasants to discuss the organization of a larger opposition movement to the Bolsheviks. Subsequently, on 28 February, a meeting in the village of Riazan attracted many peasants and it was decided to organize resistance, in the first instance by appealing to the peasants' sense of community to halt the resettlement of local kulaks. At the same time, a core group was to prepare for armed resistance in the event that passive demonstrations failed to prevent deportations. Around this time, a similar pattern unfolded in the village of Taramaklinsko, where a band of 15 peasants led by Kondakov planned a raid to free kulaks held for resettlement at the nearby village of Kondrat'evo.[64]

On 1 March a force of 35–40 peasants arrived in Kondrat'evo but, failing to disarm and arrest the local militia chief and raiispolkom plenipotentiary, the peasants retreated. By now up to 150 peasants from surrounding villages had concentrated in Taramaklinsko. At that point, a gang of 'kulaks', led by a peasant named Sinaevsky, who that day had just returned from Kainsk (the okrug centre) having been released from prison for payment of a fine, went on a pogrom. Having failed to release the kulaks, a crowd of peasants proceeded to vent their anger, and no doubt settle old scores, on the local soviet officials, peasant actifs and kolkhozniks, who were all rounded up and beaten, the kolkhoz property was robbed and arms taken. This force now made a new advance on Kondrat'evo, which officials and militia seem to have deserted, and carried out more assaults, and seizure of arms and property from another kolkhoz. The peasant band advanced from village to village in the area (Bakmaska, Liapunovo) repeating and extending these tactics to burning soviet buildings and looting cooperatives, and growing stronger and more bold as the day went by. It was at this point that a decision was taken to try and spread the local conflict into a wider regional conflagration, as small bands from the core force were sent to neighbouring raions to rally peasant support. Once word spread of the activities of the band, however, not all villages welcomed them, and certainly local officials and kolkhozniks were bound to put up a fight. This was the case in the village of Tamochna, where the local soviet and actif fought off an attack by the main force of peasants.

By 2 March, the revolt had spread to 17 villages and, with its headquarters at Riazan where a force of some 500 peasants was concentrated, it began to move east towards the raion centre, Muromtsevo, where panic set in as raion party and soviet leaders fled. One of the leaders of the revolt, Guppel'ts, was a former Menshevik and Red Partisan. With such leaders the peasant force quickly began to assume a military structure, though most of their weapons were hunting rifles. Preparations were made to cut the telegraph line and road communications between Omsk and Tara, and plans were laid to attack OGPU units guarding kulak convoys heading north into the taiga in order to free the peasants. The revolt was quickly suppressed, however, as by 3 March government 'anti-banditry' units (probably OGPU) arrived in the area, and after armed clashes in Kondrat'evo where seven peasants were killed, and in Riazan where another 16 peasants died, the band dispersed, some dumping their arms, others fleeing into the forest, only to be hunted down. During the revolt, it was estimated that some 1,500 peasants were involved at one time or another, and their forces were blamed for the killing of six people (including a member of the okrispolkom) and assaults on more than 70. The band lost 25 dead and four wounded.[65]

OFFICIAL ASSESSMENTS

In a telegram to okruzhkoms on 19 February, the Kraikom itself recognized that in many areas 'the implementation of dekulakization amounts to pillaging, denuding and humiliation'. At the same time, the Kraikom warned local leaderships against 'weakening' dekulakization or any 'disruption of the plan of resettlement'.[66] The 'excesses' and confusion surrounding dekulakization was reflected in the content of Siberian party and OGPU reports on the campaign. In its assessment of the campaign, the Kraikom drew a sharp distinction between what it claimed was the active support of the 'batrak-bedniak-seredniak mass' and the 'rightist mood and rightist practice' of many rural party and soviet activists who opposed dekulakization and assisted kulaks with their 'tricks'. Top-secret party reports listed numerous representative examples of the latter tendency. In Uyar raion, Krasnoyarsk Okrug, rural soviet officials issued kulaks with certificates to exempt them from dekulakization. In many places no action was taken as kulaks sold up and moved out of the area.[67]

Belatedly, after Stalin's 'Dizzy with Success' article, the Siberian OGPU chief, Zakovsky, wrote a highly critical report to the Kraikombiuro in which he described the process of dekulakization in the krai as akin to:

'storming, a partisan raid verging on robbery, the expropriation of almost all kulaks, the seizure of all property down to underclothes, cooking utensils together with the last meal from the stove, expropriation not infrequently conducted at nighttime, with immediate ejection from homes, including women and babies, invalids, old people, without the arrangement of other shelter.'[68] He was adamant that the reason that the campaign had been problematic was that, unlike the grain procurement campaign of the previous year, the officials and activists on the ground had not targeted and isolated the kulaks as a social entity in the villages, and the use of force and intimidation had affected all sections of the peasantry, particularly the 'hundreds' of seredniaks that were wrongly dekulakized.[69] Concern about the effect of excesses on the army was voiced by Metsis, the head of the political department of the Siberian military district. He had been on manoeuvres with the 12th Rifle Division in Omsk Okrug, and reported how in every village the soldiers were bombarded by peasant complaints about the agricultural campaigns.[70] Fears that military discipline could be eroded if the Red Army was deployed against peasant disturbances were voiced by the Central Committee itself, and, some months later, Eikhe admitted that political work in the army had become 'extremely difficult' because of the rural campaigns.[71]

The main complaint of the Kraikom leadership, however, was that there had been insufficient linkage between dekulakization and collectivization. For example, in Suslov raion, Achinsk Okrug, only 8 per cent of households were collectivized yet the raikom directed that the 'liquidation of the kulaks' be carried out in 'all villages'. Biisk Okruzhkom confirmed that: 'Dekulakization is occurring without regard to the kolkhoz movement.' Kamensk Okruzhkom bluntly ordered: 'First liquidate and then carry out collectivization.' In fact, the Kraikom concluded that those okrugs that had a low rate of collectivization (Tomsk, Biisk, Kirensk), whether by plan or not, tended to liquidate kulaks by a form of 'naked dekulakization' at a very high tempo, and frequently reported back to the Kraikom that 'all have been dekulakized'. Maslyanin raion, Novosibirsk Okrug, which consistently had the highest levels of collectivization in February and March, was singled out as the worst area for abuses against peasants and 'distortions of the class line' of the party, and 18 local officials were arrested and charged with a variety of official misdemeanours.[72]

Kirensk Okruzhkom was criticized for permitting a rate of 20 per cent dekulakization by its raikoms and for 'mass cases' of threatening dekulakization on bedniaks and seredniaks if they did not join communes.[73] A clear breach of the strict instruction to exempt kulaks of foreign descent from dekulakization occurred in the German populated village of

Nikolaevka, Abakan raion, Minusinsk Okrug. The raion party organization gave this village a *tverdoe zadanie* to collectivize by no later than 20 March. The raion plenipotentiary threatened to exile anyone not entering the kolkhoz, and even forbade the peasants from speaking German at meetings.[74] The hysteria among local officials in over-fulfilling collectivization and dekulakization plans was such that it inevitably led to ridiculous situations. Krasnoyarsk Okruzhkom received the following telegram from a town in the Arctic region: 'Norilsk tribes have decided to go over to mass collectivization. We press you to allow us to implement dekulakization.' Even a Kraiispolkom meeting burst into laughter at the thought of conducting these policies among the indigenous nomadic minority peoples of the far north of Siberia, and Eikhe said that he 'nearly fell off his seat' when he read the telegram. One village in Irkutsk Okrug was divided along ethnic lines, with Russians residing in one half and Tatars in the other. Both groups protested to the plenipotentiary that they could not be put into the same kolkhoz, because the Russians kept and ate pigs (which offended the Tatar's Islamic beliefs), while the Tatars ate horsemeat which disgusted the Russians. Despite the protests, one kolkhoz was established for the whole village.[75]

'In some places', Eikhe observed, 'the distortions have assumed an objectively counter-revolutionary nature, for example, the confiscation of a six month old baby's dummy in Kansk Okrug [*sic*]'.[76] At the Kraiispolkom plenum in the middle of March, Eikhe poured scorn on these 'dummy heroes' and others of their ilk, ridiculing practices such as that in Shipunov raion, Barnaul Okrug, where gangs of bedniak children were organized to take the clothes of kulak children in the street, and the dekulakization of peasants for a variety of idiotic reasons: for marrying three times, for hiring a wet nurse, and so on. He also told of how Usol'e raion, Irkutsk Okrug, declared itself an area of 'comprehensive atheism', and closed churches and monasteries.[77] The Kraikom regarded all of these excesses as 'political hooliganism' and decided to tighten up discipline among rural officials by sending a further 6,000 town communists to the countryside.[78] On 3 March a Kraikom decree attempted to stamp out abuses by making okrug leaders personally responsible for 'distortions', and to illustrate the message, the Kamensk and Kansk okruzhkoms were singled out for reprimands for allowing dekulakization of seredniaks.[79]

Social tension mounted in the countryside in the wake of the retreat from mass collectivization, as peasants suspected that there might be a similar retreat on dekulakization. There was a flood of reports to the Kraikom from local party organizations complaining of how kulaks who had escaped dekulakization were slipping back into their villages and stirring up the peasants in the wake of Stalin's article and the party's U-turn. Sometimes peasants opposed to the party printed 'proclamations' or spread rumours in an attempt to rally opposition in the countryside. For example: 'Anyone entering the kolkhoz will be hung! Smash the Yids, Save Russia' (Irkutsk Okrug); 'Leave the kolkhoz immediately, 25 versts away there is a band which will slaughter all communards' (Barnaul Okrug).[80] In some villages in Omsk, after the publication of Stalin's article in the local press, kulaks declared 'We are for Stalin and the Central Committee', believing that over-zealous local officials were to blame for their plight.[81]

When a small number of kulaks escaped from the Shegarka river resettlement area and returned to their native villages to reclaim their property, they were met with a mixed reception. By 15 April some 75 kulak adults and about 150 young people fled from the Shegarka river, some into the taiga, but most back to their villages. In the village of B-Nikol', Uzhanikhin raion, on 7 April the wife of the exiled kulak Frolenko moved back into her home and took back the clothes and household goods which were being used by communards living in the house. When local officials attempted to send her back into exile, a large crowd gathered around the house to protect her, and there were shouts of 'kick them all out of other people's homes' and 'we must not allow the exiling'. Although the woman was eventually re-exiled two days later, the communards were frightened that they would be punished if kulaks returned to find them living in their houses. Thus, the battle lines were drawn between those peasants who had materially benefited from the dekulakization process, having sided with the state authorities, and those who had been victimized by the process and wanted revenge.[82]

9 The Great U-Turn

THE SEARCH FOR SCAPEGOATS

Despite mounting anxiety in the central leadership about the disastrous turn of events, with a few exceptions, there were virtually no public pronouncements on the effect of the party's new policies during February. Unease over the direction that dekulakization was taking on the ground was reflected in a *Pravda* editorial on 1 February 1930, which castigated officials who had allowed the policy to deteriorate into 'nothing but a division of the spoils'. Some days later, Stalin himself voiced his concern that there was insufficient linkage between the implementation of dekulakization and the development of collectivization. He feared that dekulakization had degenerated in practice from 'a policy of *socializing* in kolkhozes the confiscated kulak property to a policy of *share-outs* [*delezhki*] of this property for the personal enrichment of individual peasants'.[1] Of the key party leaders, only Syrtsov took an unqualified critical stance against the party's policy. Beginning with a press report of a session of Sovnarkom RSFSR on 11 February, he took the leading role in speaking out against the 'conveyor-belt of repressions' in the countryside and raising awareness of the negative consequences that abuses in collectivization and dekulakization would have for the spring sowing campaign.[2] He described the excesses of collectivization as the 'most shameful travesty of Soviet power' and spoke of the need to curb the zeal of dekulakizers – and this was almost two weeks before Stalin spoke out against excesses. In an oblique attack on Stalin's circle, he blamed the 'paper tempos' of comprehensive collectivization not on 'revolutionary enthusiasm' but on 'bureaucratic optimism'.[3]

Eventually, the prospect of massive disruption to the spring sowing campaign and the dire knock-on effect that this would have on the mood in the cities, the progress of industrialization and, perhaps even, the survival of the regime itself forced the Politburo to break its silence and enact a policy reversal. At its session on 25 February the Politburo appointed Rykov as head of a 'twenty-four hour' commission charged with drawing up revised statutes for kolkhozes to make them more palatable to the peasantry. The protocol of the session records the following item: 'to instruct [*poruchit'*] comrade Stalin to write a newspaper article'. The purpose of this, as we know, was to rein in the party in the countryside. This suggests that it was a collective decision taken by the Politburo and not a personal one made by Stalin, and supports rumours current at the time, originating from Italian diplomatic sources, which intimated that Stalin had been forced into the retreat by opposition from within the Politburo and the Soviet High Command.[4] Both the revised model statute, which allowed peasants to hold small private plots with livestock, and Stalin's article, under the famous heading 'Dizzy with Success', were published in *Pravda* on 2 March.[5] Stalin maintained that 'a fundamental turn of the countryside towards socialism can be considered already secured', and saw his article as a 'warning to comrades who were overstepping the mark'.[6]

Specific revisions of party policy were left to a Central Committee decree issued on 14 March which ordered the elimination of excesses in collectivization, particularly the violation of the 'voluntary principle' (sic). It spoke of the 'pillaging' (*maroderstvo*) of the peasantry and suggested that the high levels of collectivization had been achieved by a 'bureaucratic decree mania from above'. Party organizations were reminded that, as regards agricultural policy, the main problem facing the country was not a 'chicken' problem or a 'cucumber' problem, but the 'grain' problem, and collectivization should reflect this priority. In a belated attempt to calm peasant misgivings about collectivization, the party leadership claimed that it had never intended that the commune would be the model form of kolkhoz and ordered that the artel be reestablished as the primary form.[7]

The Kraikom quickly fell in behind Stalin's new turn and during March and April it issued many orders blaming 'Right' and 'Left' distortions of the party line for the chaos in the countryside.[8] In the same way that Stalin shifted the blame for the disastrous pace of collectivization and dekulakization on to lower party organizations, so regional leaderships reflected blame on to their subordinates in the search for scapegoats. The Kraikom singled out the hardline Biisk Okruzhkom Secretary, Spirov, for a reprimand on 6 March, accusing him of 'embarking on a road of bureaucratic orders' to increase collectivization, and encouraging 'a reckless dash for percentage rates of collectivization'. He had also published an article in the local newspaper *Zvezda altaia* announcing 'a day of liquidation of private agriculture', and stating that it was the duty of party organizations to complete collectivization 'within a few days'. The Kiren Okruzhkom Secretary, Shepot'ko, was similarly warned about excesses in collectivization.[9] For abuses committed by officials during collectivization and dekulakization in the Oirot national autonomous oblast, Eikhe ordered that the 'guilty be punished', but when this case attracted the attention of the centre the Kraikom disbanded the entire Oirot Oblast Party Committee.[10]

In the rush to 'socialize' property, little thought had been given to the collection of seed or the organization of sowing. During collectivization many peasants hid grain reserves and were reluctant to disclose these to the kolkhoz. There was also the problem of peasant incentives. Collectivization transformed the traditional link between the peasant, the land and the fruits of labour, in the process destroying the personal incentive to produce a marketable surplus. This was the key reason for turning the peasants' decision calculus against the policy. Collectivization madness had gone so far that in late February the Kraikom was forced to remind local party organizations that 'socialization' of agriculture did not apply to kitchen gardens, farmyard chickens, pigs and 'all minor spheres of farms of a clearly consumer kind'.[11] Indeed, some months later Mikoyan rebuked the Siberian party organization declaring that in other regions of the country, 'such socialization, as existed in Siberia, did not occur'.[12]

The party leadership was forced into retreat by the calamitous impact that collectivization and dekulakization was threatening on the spring sowing campaign. A Kraikombiuro decree on 25 February warned okruzhkoms about their failure to collect a seed reserve for the kolkhozes to the extent that they were supplied with only 40 per cent of their needs. Meanwhile, the concentration on dekulakization and collectivization meant that local party organizations had virtually ignored the problem of how to ensure that the individual peasant sector would be sufficiently stimulated to engage fully in the spring sowing. The spring sowing campaign was now to be intensified and the party was encouraged to apply various measures against peasant kolkhozniks who refused to contribute seed (social influence, fines, amnesties for those who voluntarily disclosed hidden stocks and even expulsion from the kolkhoz in the worst cases).[13]

On 5 March the Kraikombiuro attempted to stem the haemorrhage of peasants from the kolkhozes by quickly ratifying the signals from Moscow to establish the artel as the main form of collective, as opposed to the commune. Eikhe informed okrug party leaders on 10 March that in future the main form of kolkhoz was to be the artel, because 60 per cent of so-called communes lacked the facilities and means of production to make them a reality.[14] Later, he admitted that the 'wager on the commune' had been a costly mistake on the part of the Kraikom.[15] He also sought to instil in lower level officials the need to link dekulakization with the collectivization campaign, with the injunction that both campaigns be completed before the onset of the sowing season. It was recognized that the party had failed to carry the support of the mass of bedniak and seredniak peasants, and consequently a new emphasis was placed on the resuscitation of bedniak and batrak actifs, but within the kolkhozes, as an instrument for implementing party policy in the countryside. A Kraikombiuro decree of 16 March set a strict deadline for the completion of dekulakization of 20 March, by which date the exile of Category Two kulaks to northern regions and industrial areas was to be concluded. Furthermore, the resettlement of Category Three kulaks was strictly limited to those raions designated for comprehensive collectivization, and must be completed at least twenty days prior to the beginning of sowing. Raions of comprehensive collectivization were ordered to attain levels of 60 per cent completion by 1 April if they were in western okrugs, and 50 per cent if they were in eastern okrugs. Consequently, the Novosibirsk Okrug leadership restricted the resettlement of kulaks to those villages where collectivization was planned to reach a level of 60 per cent of households by 1 April. These new instructions threw the whole dekulakization campaign into chaos, for they came at the precise moment of a mass exodus from the kolkhozes which made a level of 60 per cent collectivization by 1 April appear a ludicrous prospect.[16]

When Eikhe warned one local party organization in late March that 'kolkhozes fall apart when they are established by force', it was already too late to rectify the damage done to relations between the party and the peasantry in many areas. In this case the Biisk Okrug party leadership had attempted to prevent peasants from leaving kolkhozes by applying judicial confiscation of the property which the peasants had contributed to the kolkhoz fund. In other words peasants in Biisk could leave kolkhozes but only if they left their property behind.[17] From 20–25 March special plenary meetings of okruzhkoms and okrispolkoms were held to discuss ways of combating excesses in compliance with directives from the Central Committee. A purge of rural party organizations followed in which 14 rural raikoms were dissolved, more then four hundred party members were expelled, twelve hundred others were reprimanded, and over one thousand party and non-party persons who had participated in the campaign were put on trial for offences.[18]

A PARTY DIVIDED

The Politburo was evidently seriously unnerved by numerous reports from around the country of sporadic peasant uprisings against the party. A secret letter from the Central Committee to all party organizations sent out on 2 April 1930, titled 'On the Tasks of the Kolkhoz Movement in Relation to the Struggle Against Distortions of the Party Line', reinforced the line pursued in Stalin's 'Dizzy with Success' article that local party officials were to blame for the disastrous outcome of forced mass collectivization and dekulakization through their 'distortions' of party policy. This apportionment of blame was, however, now considered secondary to a more worrying development facing the party in its struggle with the peasantry: an upsurge of 'mass uprisings' by armed peasants under 'kulak influence' which, unless speedily countered by political measures rather than repressed by the deployment of the Red Army, OGPU or militia units, threatened to destabilize large areas of the country (Central Black-Earth Region, North Caucasus, the Ukraine, Siberia, Kazakhstan, and even in the Moscow region).[19]

Nevertheless, the letter represented an attempt by the party leadership to get itself off the hook by selecting elements of the Central Committee decrees and orders on collectivization and dekulakization, and contrasting these with the reality of distorted 'anti-seredniak' implementation by lower level officials. This set a pattern which was to be replicated at the regional level, for blame was simply shunted downwards in the party apparatus as far as authority levels permitted. The regional party leaderships who had faithfully obeyed the centre's unremitting demands for 'over-fulfilment' in January and February now felt vulnerable under a barrage of attacks from central leaders for permitting an attitude of 'better to overdo than underdo'.[20]

In early April 1930, Kaganovich was sent to Siberia to temporarily replace Eikhe, who was taken ill with appendicitis. At a series of meetings with regional party leaders over the next few weeks Kaganovich attempted to balance the necessity to comply with Stalin's retreat from forced mass collectivization and the correction of excesses, with the ingrained instincts of the Stalinists for a hardline policy towards the peasantry, and the need to infuse a mood of confidence among the demoralized regional officials. It was only after his arrival, over one month after the publication of Stalin's 'Dizzy with Success' article, that the Kraikombiuro issued directives formally recognizing its mistakes in the drive for complete collectivization. The delay in formulating this *mea culpa* may well have been a reflection of the reluctance of Siberian party leaders to accept blame for an extremist policy forced on them by the centre.

Kaganovich attended his first session of the Kraikombiuro on 8 April, where Bazovsky delivered the main report on the spring sowing campaign and collectivization. Since Kaganovich was the *enfant terrible* of the Stalinist leadership, not surprisingly, many of the Siberian officials were intimidated by his presence and made formal, statistical reports. This infuriated Kaganovich, who constantly interrupted speakers demanding concrete facts, examples and interpretations of the situation in the countryside.[21] The session heard much evidence of reluctance on the part of local officials, who had been in the vanguard of the rural campaigns, to accept passively the blame that was now being shifted onto their shoulders. Kraikom officials who inspected okrug party organizations in late March 1930 reported that, whereas local communists were critical of Stalin and the party leadership for not giving them the appropriate directives sooner, peasants were saying that Stalin had been forced to publish his views in the press because of opposition to his line in the party leadership! The local party officials took the view that 'better Left excesses, than a Right deviation'.[22] At a conference some days later, the Slavgorod Okruzhkom Secretary, Klimenchuk, observed that lower level party officials were demoralized by Stalin's article and the new directives. Communists were refusing to take up posts saying that 'now it is dangerous to be elected, they can place you on a charge'. Stalin's article was denounced as a 'step backwards' by its opponents, while those who agreed with it felt it should have been published secretly and confined to party ranks, believing that it 'untied the hands of the kulaks'. The Omsk Okruzhkom Secretary, Alekseeva, revealed that in some raions newspapers containing Stalin's article were removed from sale by local officials.[23]

In a top secret resolution approved on 9 April 1930, the Kraikombiuro denounced as 'Leftists' those officials who criticized the change of policy initiated by Stalin.[24] The resolution signalled the Kraikombiuro's impatience with the obfuscation by lower level party organizations in dealing with peasant complaints and appeals against dekulakization. It seems that even when the courts ordered the return of peasant property for wrongful dekulakization, local authorities continued to delay. If peasant property could not be returned, then they could expect compensation to the full cost; however, the Kraikombiuro warned: 'At the same time when reviewing lists, it is not permitted to reimburse real kulaks.'[25] Once again a contradictory and ambivalent message was sent down the party hierarchy. A directive was issued the same day to okruzhkoms and raikoms, ordering them to review peasant complaints and to return property to those peasants declared as wrongfully dekulakized within three days of the review. Officials guilty of abuses were to be relocated to other areas. To drive home the point that excesses were being taken seriously, the Kansk Okruzhkom Secretary, Glukhov, was removed from his post.

The following day, 10 April, something akin to a formal apology was issued by the Kraikombiuro for its mistakes in the campaign. It made no reference to the decrees of the Central Committee or Sovnarkom forcing the pace of collectivization and dekulakization. Instead, it merely revoked the Kraikom decision of 2 February, that had been modelled on the secret Politbuiro instruction 'as a mistake'. At the same time, there was to be no retreat as regards the attainment of the collectivization of the 'main bedniak-seredniak mass' by the spring of 1932 – a target outlined in the Central Committee decision of 6 January. The artel was now established as the 'main form' of kolkhoz construction, while it was accepted that the creation of communes was 'mistaken in conditions of mass collectivization'.[26] To reinforce the decisions of the Kraikombiuro, an inter-okrug conference of party leaders and the Kraikom was held on 16 April 1930. Kuznetsov justified the criticisms of the lower apparatus by explaining that it was excesses against the seredniaks that concerned the party most, because 'colossal mistakes' in the 'chase for percentages' of collectivization had threatened the 'union with the seredniak'.[27] He also insisted that blame for excesses lay squarely with okruzhkoms and lower party organizations because they did not comply with the main Kraikom decree on collectivization and dekulakization of 2 February and later supplementary decrees.[28] Eikhe railed against the 'clumsy approach' of some officials who had presented collectivization to the peasants 'like manna from heaven', promising the immediate delivery of machines, tractors and other benefits which, in reality, would take years to materialize. He also attacked the 'parasitical line' of authorities in some areas which had been designated for comprehensive collectivization, who, understandably, had flooded the Kraikom with demands for tractors, credits, seed and so on to enable them to achieve the accelerated tempos of collectivization.[29]

Despite the U-turn by the party peasant complaints continued to flood into higher authorities, particularly to the procuracy whose job it was to investigate official abuses. The Krai Procuracy reported that local officials up to the okrug level disregarded complaints about dekulakization, disenfranchisement, agricultural tax supplements, the failure of kolkhozes to return peasant property and so on. In fact, local procuracy officials who attempted to investigate complaints found themselves being charged with 'sabotaging' collectivization.[30] A Sovnarkom RSFSR decree of 10 April had recommended that special commissions be established composed of senior representatives of okrispolkoms, okruzhkoms, the heads of okrug finance departments and okrug procurators to investigate peasant complaints arising from dekulakization and collectivization. It was only in the middle of May that the Kraikom issued a decree organizing these in Siberia.[31]

Reversing instances of incorrect dekulakization was not a straightforward operation since frequently the lists that had been used were inaccurate, retrieving persons from exile was laborious, and returning property was almost impossible given that it had been sold off and dispersed. Kaganovich attempted to expedite the review of peasant complaints in order to counter the 'anti-seredniak' abuses perpetrated by party and soviet officials during the agricultural campaigns. At special conferences held in the first weeks of April, presided over by Kaganovich, the party and soviet leaders from groups of okrugs were harangued for their failure to control subordinates. The outcome was an order to establish *troiki*, composed of one representative each from the OGPU, raiispolkoms and the procuracy, which had a five-day deadline to review peasant complaints of wrongful dekulakization. The okrispolkoms then had a three-day period to secure the return of property to those peasants successful in their complaints. Much as was the case with collectivization and dekulakization, the problem with this sort of hasty process of remedy was that the pressure of time on lower officials inevitably led to more mistakes.[32]

The rhetorical criticism of lower level communist officials in March and April was quickly translated into arrests and punishment. The Kraikombiuro session of 21 April (where both Eikhe and Kaganovich participated) heard reports from Krai Procuracy and Kraisud officials on legal redresses and punishments following the Kraikom decree of 9 April. A Krai Procuracy official, Meren, disclosed that 328 officials had been arrested and sentenced, mostly rural soviet officials (45 per cent), and raiispolkom officials (18 per cent). Eleven of them were shot (in five cases the sentence had been carried out), some (12 per cent) received more than three years in prison, but most (45 per cent) got less than three years. Another official disclosed that since the Kraikombiuro decree, the review of illegal cases against bedniaks and seredniaks arising from the collectivization and dekulakization campaigns generated the following results: 597 cases were abandoned, 1,613 peasants were released from detention, 257 were returned from exile, 3,272 were reenfranchised, and property was reimbursed to 2,088 bedniaks, 867 seredniaks, 94 batraks, and 153 ex-partisans. Reviews of cases under Articles 61, 79 and 107 led to the release from prison of some 1,600 persons.[33] By the beginning of June the OGPU estimated that 35,343 peasant complaints of wrongful dekulakization and loss of civic rights had been received. It appears that the vast majority of dekulakized households lodged an appeal. A large number of peasants were successful: 13,083 complaints were endorsed (a 44 per cent success rate) and 16,532 were rejected.[34] This suggests that: (a) dekulakization was highly excessive in the krai, or (b) that the authorities were over-fulfilling Stalin's injunction to correct abuses. While it was relatively easy to revoke the administrative decisions on dekulakization, it was extremely difficult to secure the return of peasant property which, in many cases, had been looted or otherwise dispersed (only 3,782 peasants had their property fully restored and 239 had part of it returned).[35]

Kaganovich took a noticeably much more hardline stance at the Kraikombiuro session of 21 April than he had previously revealed during his stay in Siberia, perhaps a warning sign of another change of policy direction in the top leadership. He demanded to know why the officials had been shot. Meren replied that the executions were for excesses in dekulakization, for pillaging (*maroderstvo*) and other 'humiliating acts', to which Kaganovich responded: 'Is this an excess?' Yes they were, affirmed Meren, standing his ground; moreover, they were 'of such a kind that . . . are in essence counter-revolutionary'. When Kaganovich asked, 'Exactly what kind of pillaging was it?' he was told matter-of-factly that these officials had stolen the property of kulaks: 'In Biisk Okrug, within a 24-hour period several villages of one raion were dekulakized and collectivized. During dekulakization [officials] took the property for themselves, they beat people, they stole their clothes and threw naked people out into the frost.' All of the cases, insisted Meren, had a 'disgusting, bandit-type, counter-revolutionary essence'. Like Kaganovich, Eikhe displayed an unusually keen interest in the personal details and social status of those who had been shot. The Siberian leaders must have been shocked by Kaganovich's next statement: 'I propose that comrade Meren and the Krai Procuror be designated to collect all information and figures for executions. The procuror and the Chairman of the Courts had better know this. In Siberia 21 communists have been sentenced by the courts – and you had better know these cases to the last detail and tell us about them.' Eikhe gave them one hour to produce the materials.[36]

Some Kraikombiuro members struck out against the empathy for communists guilty of such atrocious crimes. Vedeniapina, reporting for the Krai Judicial Department, began her address to the session with an ironical statement that the people she intended to talk about 'are already in their graves because they have already been shot'. She focused on the seven executions confirmed by the courts and carried out. In terms of social status: three were white-collar, two seredniaks, one bedniak, and one handicraftsman. They had been shot, she explained, 'not only for distortions of the party line', because that was an insufficient reason, but because of 'pillaging'. She gave the following example: 'The chairman of a rural soviet conducted an illegal search of a seredniak, and confiscated his property, taking it for his personal use . . . Very often the pillaging was accompanied by cases of rape of the wives of kulaks, on the pretext that they would not be resettled, on the pretext of sparing their husbands from exile and arrest etc.' This was a clear statement that dekulakization had been accompanied by systematic rape. It would appear that rape was used as an instrument of dekulakization, enforcing compliance by adding to the trauma of family breakup, social humiliation, isolation and dislocation.[37]

Vedeniapina provided Kaganovich with the details of the atrocities perpetrated by the communists who had been shot. In Biisk Okrug, the farm of a seredniak was searched and his wife and two daughters were threatened with knives, raped and tied to carts. In Minusinsk Okrug, two communists who had been mobilized to hunt down a band of armed kulaks, came to the cabin of a seredniak, an ex-partisan, got drunk, killed the peasant, raped his wife and daughter-in-law and killed them, and attempted to shoot his son. Kaganovich's only response to this atrocity was: 'Does this mean that they were shot for being drunk?' In Achinsk, the rural soviet secretary organized dekulakization by 'armed assault' and raped the wife of a kulak on the pretext that he would not harm her husband. In another case a deputy chairman of a raiispolkom and a member of a brigade came to the home of a kulak and attempted to rape his daughters. When the women resisted the communists fired shots and threatened them with knives. Both women were beaten and tied to carts. In this case the okrug court had sentenced both officials to be shot, but the Krai Judicial Department confirmed only one execution. Vedeniapina directly challenged the line being advanced by Kaganovich and Eikhe by accusing the courts of an 'excess' in the lenient treatment of a raiispolkom chairman in Irkutsk Okrug, a long-standing party member, who had a sentence of execution reduced to a prison term of two years. One Kraikombiuro member even complained that the communist had been sentenced to hard labour.[38]

It appears that Kaganovich was reflecting a change in Stalin's outlook when he expressed concern at the punishment of communists for actions committed during the rural campaigns. He lambasted the demoralized mood of the Siberian party organization, and in a speech in Krasnoyarsk he derided those party secretaries who spoke of 'retreats', 'defeats' and 'panic'. Eikhe also scoffed at the attitude of lower officials, and warned that in the rush to criticize party activists, work on the kolkhozes was being 'absolutely forgotten'. He quoted to the Kraikombiuro part of the text of a recent secret instruction from the Central Committee, which had insisted that an understanding view should be taken of the party activists guilty of excesses: 'They are good people, and they simply made mistakes; they exceeded some or other limit and in this instance found themselves in a more or less complicated and difficult situation.' In a move to reassure lower officals, Eikhe confimed that a 'massive reshuffle' would be too dangerous in West Siberian party organizations, but only because it would disrupt the sowing campaign.[39] The new Stalinist twist of policy was confidently asserted by the Second Secretary of the Kraikom, Kuznetsov, in the middle of May when he told the Omsk party organization conference: 'Many people want to draw the conclusion that the colossal tempo of collectivization which we had this year is the result of administrative pressure ... I ask you, can we permit such thinking? ... Only an enemy can support this, only an opportunist can support this.' He went on to assert that the great influx into the kolkhozes was a product of the 'increasing activism of the seredniak mass'.[40]

CONSEQUENCES

Demographic change

The increasing distress of the peasantry post-collectivization stimulated a flight from the countryside into the towns, as peasants fled state coercion and deteriorating living standards and sought employment in the new factories and projects created by the industrial expansion of the First Five Year Plan. The spring of 1930 saw the beginning of a large-scale demographic change in the country as a whole, and in Siberia in particular, as a result of this peasant flight. In Slavgorod alone by the summer the OGPU estimated that up to 400 peasants per day left the main grain producing area. The principal destinations of these migrants were the Ukraine, the Kuzbass and the Turksib railway project. The seredniak Gunbin from Omsk Okrug caught the distraught mood of the Siberian peasantry:

> They all bragged that agriculture will blossom. What the devil blossoms, when there is not a single pig left? Where there was one hundred cows, now there is ten. This year there will not be a sowing campaign, but woe, for the individual peasants do not want to sow anything at all because everything was taken from them. Never was there a sowing campaign like this year: they drove us and drove us, first into the kolkhoz, then out of the kolkhoz, everything was seized from the peasants, everyone was cleaned out. What do they think? The countryside gets poorer by the year, there is not enough grain, everyone is on rations, the horses have not seen any oats for a year, and how can we sow with them? Now the individual peasants have decided to sow only for themselves and if in the autumn they take away the grain, the peasants will all run off to work for wages [in industry].[41]

The regime was faced with a struggle on two fronts as the mounting peasant distress was matched by increasing worker militancy in the face of reductions in rations as a result of the food shortages: a militancy reinforced by the swelling numbers of dispossessed peasants eking out a living in the towns. Strikes by factory workers for this reason were reported in various places by the OGPU, but Barnaul, lying at the heart of the grain belt of south-west Siberia, was particularly affected, and there were frequent marches by demonstrators (mainly women demanding bread) on the office of the okrispolkom chairman.[42]

The exodus from the kolkhozes

A key element of Stalin's policy U-turn on collectivization was a ban on obstacles to peasant departures from the kolkhozes. Party reports described how the exit from the kolkhozes took on a 'mass character' from the second half of March. The exodus quickly gathered pace and like a chain reaction across the Siberian countryside, the mass kolkhoz movement that had been created in a matter of weeks was obliterated within the same timespan. The green light for the exodus was indicated by the Kraikom's vetoing of an attempt by Biisk Okruzhkom to put on trial peasants who wanted to leave the kolkhozes in late March.[43] Finally, the Kraikombiuro decree of 9 April emphasized that, henceforth, collectivization was to be regarded as a voluntary exercise. This opened the door for a mass exit from the kolkhozes, all of which had further disruptive effects on the spring sowing. The Kraikom notified Stalin that during these few weeks approximately 130,000 households of the estimated 771,000 collectivized departed.[44]

When Bazovsky informed the Kraikombiuro session of 8 April that collectivization had fallen from a level of 52 per cent in early March to a current level of 43.8 per cent, Kaganovich interjected 'it is very modest'. In fact, Bazovsky suggested, the real level of collectivization was even lower and falling rapidly.[45] By 10 April there had been a dramatic surge of peasants leaving the kolkhozes in Novosibirsk Okrug, with the number of collectivized farms slumping to less than half the peak figure, from 740,622 households (57.1 per cent of the total) to 270,730 (21.3 per cent). Analysing this exodus by raion, the OGPU observed that there was a clear link between the rate of departures and the use of force to collectivize. This was most obvious in the case of Maslyanin raion, which had been in the forefront of the drive for collectivization in the krai, but where by 10 April the level of collectivization had fallen to 17 per cent of households from a peak of 92.5 per cent on 20 March.[46]

By 20 April there had been almost a 50 per cent fall in the number of households collectivized in Siberia, and by this date only approximately 415,500 households (about 28 per cent of the krai total) remained in the kolkhozes (see Table 9.1). The figures for the decrease in some okrugs were astounding: almost 80 per cent in Oirot, 70 per cent in Barabinsk, over 68 per cent in Novosibirsk, 58 per cent in Krasnoyarsk. The fall

Table 9.1 The level of collectivization in Siberia, 1 July 1929 to 1 May 1930

Date	Number of kolkhozes	Number of households	% of total households
1 Jun 1929	3,303	50,000	3.7
20 Jan 1930	3,970	156,600	10.6
1 Feb 1930	5,422	282,000	19.1
10 Feb 1930	6,464	469,800	31.8
20 Feb 1930	7,394	624,600	42.3
1 Mar 1930	8,109	720,400	48.8
10 Mar 1930	8,548	781,800	52.9
20 Mar 1930	8,576	770,100	52.1
1 Apr 1930	8,170	648,000	43.8
10 Apr 1930	7,565	505,000	34.2
20 Apr 1930	7,014	415,500	28.7
1 May 1930	6,865	378,000	25.4

Source: GANO 2, f. 2, op. 1, d. 4095, 1. 140.

continued into the summer of 1930 when a low point of around 20 per cent of peasant households collectivized was reached before the situation stabilized. This figure was the second lowest of all the key grain areas in the country.[47] Typical of the absurdity which infected the party under Stalin's leadership, these figures were ludicrously trumpeted as an 'enormous success' in the resolutions of the Fifth Siberian Krai Party Conference held in June 1930. It was only from the beginning of 1931 that the level of collectivization began to rise significantly, and during that year the number of collectivized peasant households surged from a little over 22 to over 60 per cent.[48] It is this year that must be recognized as the beginning of a process of sustained transformation of Russian agriculture from individual to collective farming.

Famine in store

It quickly became clear that many peasants responded to the events of January–March 1930 by going over to consumption farming, especially in the grain belt of south-west Siberia. This lack of incentive to produce now posed a great danger not only for the regime's ability to secure the normal grain surplus needed for towns and other consumer areas and sectors, and for the new demands of industrialization in the First Five Year Plan, but also for agricultural needs. Fodder shortages, following in the wake of massive peasant slaughtering, threatened to further decimate livestock numbers. The concern at the faltering sowing campaign was clear from the Kraikombiuro decree of 9 April, which focused much more attention on this issue than on correcting previous mistakes in collectivization and dekulakization. Kaganovich was even persuaded to lobby the centre on the Siberian's behalf for emergency assistance in the form of additional grain supplies for the harvest failure stricken areas of south-west Siberia.[49]

The sowing campaign of 1930 was bound to encounter difficulties because of a harvest failure in Rubtsovsk, Slavgorod, Barnaul and Novosibirsk Okrugs in 1929. These okrugs lay at the heart of the main grain producing region of the krai, and, for example, whereas in 1928/9 Rubtsovsk and Slavgorod had provided approximately 440,000 tons, this year they had managed about one-quarter of this figure. There had been some state seed assistance to cushion the okrugs but not enough, and the Kraikombiuro requested aid of over 5,000 tons. The grain and fodder shortage, combined with protests against collectivization and dekulakization, caused an epidemic of mass slaughter of livestock in the period from January to March 1930 which resulted in a 17 per cent fall in horse numbers in the krai, and between 25 and 35 per cent in the worst affected okrugs, while cattle numbers fell even more sharply: 27 per cent for the krai, 37 per cent in the south-west region. Compared with 1928, by March 1930 the catastrophic plunge in livestock numbers was quantifiable as follows: horses 26 per cent, cattle 42 per cent, sheep 43 per cent and pigs 72 per cent. This decimation of livestock had major negative ramifications for livestock procurement and the processing of livestock products (meat and hides). Of more immediate concern for the authorities, it plunged the sowing campaign into crisis, placing a huge extra workload on the remaining working livestock. If in 1929 in Slavgorod and Rubtsovsk one horse had to plough about three hectares, then in 1930 it had to plough almost ten hectares. At the same time, the state had failed to deliver on its promises to facilitate collectivization by the massive provision of mechanized equipment, and Siberia was supplied with only 200 tractors for the 1930 sowing season.[50] This puts into perspective the reluctance of many raions to allow kulaks to depart for resettlement with working animals. In some areas it also gave rise to a further demonstration of the wiliness of the peasants, as they voluntarily left their livestock in the hands of the kolkhozes so that they would continue to be fed by the state until the spring.[51]

In April the Politburo turned its attention to clarifying the rules of administration of kolkhozes and the question of the scale of procurement from the new kolkhoz sector. A Politburo decision on 11 April established a kolkhoz grain procurement norm of one-quarter to one-third of the gross average harvest in grain producing areas, and one-eighth in non-grain areas.

All remaining grain surplus was supposedly placed at the disposal of the kolkhoz, though this was a somewhat fanciful proposition given the regime's clampdown on market relations.[52] While the Politburo considered how to extract as much grain as possible from the collective farm peasantry, a palpable fear gripped party leaders in Siberia that the poor harvest of 1929 compounded by the disaster of collectivization and dekulakization would rebound on the regime with a catastrophic decline in peasant production and a move to subsistence farming. In the first weeks of April 1930, Kaganovich and Eikhe repeatedly stressed the urgency for local party organizations to concentrate their energies on securing a good sowing campaign.[53] Given that for the 1930 sowing many individual peasant farms were drastically short of seed (there was a 20 per cent shortfall in Novosibirsk Okrug, while in Omsk it was estimated that the individual sector had only 33 per cent of its seed requirement), it was not clear how the party leaders' injunctions could be realized.[54] Meanwhile, telegrams arrived in the Kraikom from worried leaders of south-western okrugs warning that severe blizzards had taken a heavy toll in lost livestock, adding to the crisis of sowing in this crucial region.[55]

A combination of factors resulted in a disastrous sowing in early 1930: the poor weather, both in the summer of 1929 which reduced grain stocks, and the late winter of 1929/30 which obstructed work; the organizational chaos and exhaustion induced in party and soviet echelons by the successive waves of intense campaigning in the countryside; the lack of livestock for tilling due to the huge losses incurred as a consequence of both climatic conditions and party policies, while those that remained were seriously weakened by hunger; and peasant attempts to revive their uncaptured status by going over to subsistence agriculture as a reaction to collectivization, dekulakization and the the party's strangling of market relations. In many cases brand new agricultural equipment and the seed assistance provided by the centre lay unloaded and wasting away at railway stations in Slavgorod and Barnaul. By early June 1930, when work on the sowing campaign had been completed, the result was an almost 20 per cent drop in sown area compared with the previous year. While the sown area of the strengthened collective farm sector had increased significantly (by almost four times compared with 1929), this had barely any effect on the collapse in sowings by individual peasants (down by almost one-third).[56] The poor harvest of 1929 not only paved the way for a future calamity by the poor sowing of spring 1930, but also, according to the OGPU, resulted in peasant distress to the extent that 'beggary assumes a mass character'. The peasants often ate their seed stocks to survive the famine. Peasant *volynki* were more a reaction to the food shortages (in this sense they were food riots) than to collectivization and dekulakization. These *volynki* were characterized by crowds of peasants attempting to take seed stocks from state stores and prevent grain from leaving the locality. During the last three weeks of May there were over one hundred such *volynki*.[57]

Despite the poor sowing, the state grain procurement plan for Siberia in 1930/1 was increased to 1.5 million tons by a decision of the Politburo in early September 1930. As the party prepared itself for a new assault on the countryside, the Kraikom issued new guidelines which added a final Stalinist twist to the social influence method: where villages had already adopted delivery quotas, additional grain was to be collected by 'putting into practice the method of *voluntary over-fulfilment* of the plan' (sic). Similarly, while kolkhozes were not to be given delivery quotas in excess of norms established by the party, grain surpluses were to be taken 'by voluntary over-fulfilment of plans, including by krai and and intra-krai socialist competition between kolkhozes and individual households'.[58] All of this was against a background where the Politburo threatened to dismiss from their posts those officials who did not secure the necessary 'Bolshevik tempo'.[59]

The end of the kulaks

By 8 April 64,064 kulaks had been transported from across the USSR to the far north of Siberia. At this time the Siberian authorities were planning supplies for an estimated 142,811 persons in total, expecting the arrival of further shipments of 19,959 individuals and 58,788 family members from the west.[60] The taiga zones of Kansk and Achinsk Okrugs were selected as primary areas for the resettlement of kulaks, but no local preparations were made to receive this huge influx of people from west of the Urals. Consequently, the newly arrived kulaks were frequently kept in cattle cars at rail sidings and starved. As late as July, Achinsk Okrispolkom sent desperate telegrams to the Kraiispolkom requesting a meagre ton and a half of grain from reserves held at Tomsk to provide urgently needed food supplies for hundreds of sick and starving kulaks held at Tiazhin station, because there were 'absolutely no local reserves'. As kulaks began to arrive in these areas many of them were assigned to hard labour in industrial projects and resource extraction. OGPU officials frequently complained about the lack of preparations by the Committee for Northern Communications (*Komseveroput'*) and the Forestry Commission (*Leszag*), which between them took 3,546 kulak households for work but refused to house or supply them with provisions.[61]

There were nine major resettlement zones for kulaks, all of which were dispersed in areas of the Siberian taiga, mostly hundreds of kilometres from the nearest railway line, even further from the nearest town and often only reachable by rivers that were navigable in the summer months. The locations, with the number of Siberian kulak families held by April 1930 (a total of 12,479), were as follows: in Tomsk Okrug, on the basins of the rivers Lagyl-Lag (2,676), Chuzik (1,500), Toi and Nyursa (2,813), Galka (638); in Achinsk Okrug, on the basin of the river Chulym (1,898); in Krasnoyarsk Okrug, on the basin of the river Ket' (873); in Kansk Okrug, at Karabul' (1,033) and the basin of the river Angara at Kezhem (750); in Irkutsk Okrug, in Bratsk raion (298).[62]

What occurred in January–March 1930 was only a partial dekulakization. Instead of the planned 30,000 Category Two households, only 16,025 (53.4 per cent of the plan) consisting of a total of 82,922 persons were actually deported into resettlement zones. Men over 18 years old accounted for only about one-quarter (21,265), whereas the vast majority were women over eighteen (23,381) and children under eighteen (38,276) (see Table 9.2). Just over half of these families were moved by rail, the rest going by horse driven carts and sleighs and by foot. It required 40 convoys, organized by the OGPU on a strict military regime, to move all the kulaks from holding centres to the resettlement zones, and a variety of transportation was employed: by rail in 947 (supposedly) heated goods wagons, 124 open wagons and 40 passenger coaches; by road in 317 covered trucks and 601 covered horse-pulled wagons. Control of the operation was such that only three kulak men managed to escape. A further 1,000–1,500 Category Three kulaks were deported and settled apart from their villages. This left at least 60,000 kulak households (given official krai tax figures of over 76,000 kulaks) residing in their villages.[63] These figures did not, however, take account of the some 10,500 Category One kulaks who were shot or sent to concentration camps in the far north.[64]

Although they were not resettled, most of these kulak households had been dekulakized in the sense that their property had been confiscated. The Kraikom Information and Statistical Sector estimated that a total of 51,885 (3.4 per cent) of all peasant households had been dekulakized in Siberia by April 1930. In a later report the OGPU calculated that 59,062 households had been dekulakized in the sense that they had been expropriated of the following wealth: money (166,163 roubles), bonds (73,564), other valuables (2,332 roubles worth), cattle (60,698 head), horses (56,586), sheep (143,707), pigs (13,745), while some eleven million roubles worth of other kulak property was handed over to kolkhozes.[65] The value to the state of this confiscated property was that it mainly consisted of livestock, a productive factor essential to the success of the new kolkhoz movement.

Table 9.2 Siberian OGPU statistics on the deportation of Category Two kulaks, to 24 February 1930

Okrug	Krai control figure	Number of families	% of control figure	Exiled				Total persons
					of which			
				Men over 18 years	Women over 18	Children up to 18		
Omsk	4,630	3,176	68	3,412	3,448	4,563		11,423
Slavgorod	2,916	1,097	37	984	1,546	3,032		5,562
Barabinsk	1,532	1,371	89	2,180	2,182	3,243		7,605
Novosibirsk	2,964	501	17	730	735	825		2,340
Barnaul	3,291	1,617	50	1,958	2,751	4,234		8,943
Biisk	2,727	1,899	69	3,250	3,610	5,708		12,568
Rubtsovsk	2,702	1,667	61	2,477	2,551	5,539		10,467
Tomsk	1,022	255	22	291	262	431		984
Kuznetsk	725	632	87	857	794	1,089		2,740
Achinsk	848	447	52	730	832	2,309		3,921
Minusinsk	703	679	96	969	1,003	1,492		3,464
Khakassiya	354	354	100	548	555	858		1,961
Krasnoyarsk	857	426	50	566	702	899		2,167
Kansk	1,218	858	70	683	990	1,901		3,574
Irkutsk	1,264	298	23	413	330	654		1,397
Oirotiya	309	236	76	296	347	544		1,187
Kamensk	1,938	512	26	821	843	955		2,619
Total	30,000	16,025	53.4	21,265	23,381	38,276		82,922

Source: GANO 1, f. 47, op. 5, d. 103, 1. 66, Table no. 3.

On the whole, it seems that the dekulakization process was carried out in a targeted manner, with those defined as kulaks for taxation purposes, and therefore the most likely candidates for the peasant *verkhushka*, bearing the brunt of the onslaught. There is no indication from the author's investigations of Siberian archives to support the notion that 'any peasant whatever was liable to dekulakization'; indeed, the term of opprobrium 'sub-kulak' (*podkulachnik*), rather than being 'widely employed', was rarely referred to in official reports on the campaign.[66]

That many dekulakized peasants remained in their villages and continued to function as farmers is suggested by a questionnaire completed by the party secretary for the rural soviet of Verkh Kargatsky, Novosibirsk Okrug, on 17 May 1930. The questionnaire had a complicated format and contained 35 questions, many of which were left unanswered. In this village of 180 households, the activist element was reasonably strong: there were nine party members, eight komsomol members, and 13 members of the *bednota* actif. Yet, in the campaigns of 1929 and 1930 no kulaks had been prosecuted under Articles 61 and 58, none had been given multiple fines, and although 11 kulak households had been allocated compulsory delivery quotas, only two of these were given tax supplements. At the time that the questionnaire was completed, all the kulak households remained in the village, only three had lost their homes and two had had their property confiscated completely, and all of them continued to work the land. This practice seems to have been widespread, rather than an aberration.[67] This evidence and the above-mentioned official Kraikom figures on dekulakization in Siberia run counter to the argument that most kulaks were 'to be shot, imprisoned or deported' at this stage.[68]

The policy of using arrested peasants in forced labour camps was approved in July 1929 when the government ordered the OGPU to establish timber camps in remote regions, but the massive numbers of dekulakized peasants necessitated a huge expansion in the concentration camp system. Consequently, on 7 April 1930, a new agency was established within the OGPU to coordinate the camp system: the Main Administration of Corrective Labour Camps and Labour Settlements, otherwise known by its infamous abbreviated acronym, the GULag.[69] The huge influx of camp inmates was quickly exploited by the regime as labour reserves for the grand industrial projects of the First Five Year Plan, particularly in those remote areas of Siberia where free labour could not be attracted. By the summer, the Siberian OGPU organized the deportation of tens of thousands of kulaks on a more 'rational' basis for forced labour in the timber and gold industries. For the efficient 'administrative-economic' supervision of both groups of kulaks, those exiled and resettled in uninhabited areas and those left in the countryside, a special Command Department (*Komendantsky Otdel*) was created within the West Siberian Krai Administrative Affairs Department (ZSKAU), with subordinate sector commands (*komendatury*) determined by economic usage of each resettlement zone (agriculture, forestry, mining). A secret report from ZCKAU to the RSFSR Commissar of Internal Affairs, Tolmachev, in early July 1930 disclosed that by then, with regard to Category Two kulaks, 16,113 Siberian families (80,804 persons) and 19,958 persons from western parts of the country were settled in ten sectors operated by the Command Department, a total of 100,762 persons.[70] There were, of course, large numbers of Category One kulaks imprisoned in concentration camps in the far north.

In the absence of evidence to the contrary, Western historians have presumed that the Politburo targets for dekulakization in early 1930 were realized.[71] In fact, there are no statistics for camp inmates until 1933, by which time there were 800,000 prisoners.[72] The GULag estimated that 391,026 kulak families (1,803,392 persons) were deported to special settlements in 1930–31, the overwhelming majority of dekulakized peasants from European Russia being deported to the Urals, Western and Eastern Siberia (including the far north), and northern Kazakhstan.[73] According to this official tabulation, the Ukraine and Western Siberia accounted for by far the largest number of kulak deportations, with 67,817 and 52,091 families respectively. The evidence from Siberia, however, indicates that planned figures for deportations in early 1930 were greatly under-fulfilled. After a Sovnarkom decree of 15 August 1930 the use of kulaks as forced labour was regularized, with the majority of the single men placed at the disposal of industry, and even Category Three kulaks conscripted as forced labour. The major deportations followed in 1931 and 1932.[74] Similarly, in the neighbouring Urals Region the vast majority of deportations occurred in 1931 and 1932, with only 30,474 families resettled in 1930, over half of which came from other areas of the country.[75] Evidently, the great influx of peasants into concentration camps and resettlement zones occurred not in the first wave of dekulakization in late 1929–early 1930, but from the summer of 1930 and in the second and third waves of dekulakization in 1931 and 1932. Deportations of the remnants of Category Three kulaks continued until May 1933 when the party leadership decided that the kulaks had effectively been destroyed as a class.[76] The policy of collectivization and dekulakization, therefore, was a process which developed over several years. The practical experience and organizational mobilization of late 1929–early 1930 did not achieve the policy goals immediately, as was the intention of the Stalinists; rather they paved the way for their realization in subsequent years.

According to the most recent and informed Russian estimates of the numbers of victims of dekulakization, about one million peasant households were affected. In 1930 115,231 families were exiled and resettled, and a further 265,795 in 1931. These were drawn from Category One and Category Two kulaks. It is estimated that 200,000 to 250,000 managed to preempt this fate by self-dekulakization and flight to the cities or other areas. A further 100,000 families were exiled and resettled in 1932. Most of the approximately 400,000 to 450,000 Category Three kulaks, who were supposed to be settled apart within their local areas, were also deported or left the countryside for work in the cities and construction projects.[77] During the *Stalinshchina*, the great terror of the mid-to-late 1930s, the disastrous results of the mad rush into comprehensive collectivization and dekulakization were expunged from the official history, while most of the middle level party officials, and some of the top leaders like Syrtsov and Eikhe who had presided over the implementation of the policy, were executed. The orthodox party version that was propagated accorded with Stalin's aspirations of late 1929, at the time of his 'year of the great breakthrough' thesis: that a dynamic of social conflict within the peasantry itself would result in the destruction of the kulak 'class enemy'. The Stalinist *Short Course* history of the party described collectivization as 'a struggle of the peasant masses against the kulaks ... the peasants would expropriate them, driving them from the land, dispossessing them of their cattle and machinery and demanding their arrest and eviction from the district by the Soviet authorities.' These events were described as a 'revolution' equal to that of October 1917, 'accomplished *from above*, on the initiative of the state, and directly supported *from below* by the millions of peasants'.[78]

Whether Stalin himself believed this interpretation, had convinced himself over time of its accuracy, or simply adhered to it as part of the pretence of ideological conformity, we shall never know. When confronted by Churchill, however, at the height of the second World War in August 1942, about the fate of the Russian peasantry during collectivization, Stalin became agitated. He assured Churchill that there was no comparison between the World War currently being waged with Germany and the 'terrible' struggle against the Russian peasantry. Holding up all the fingers of both hands to stress that the conflict then had been with many millions, Stalin added: 'Some of them were given land of their own to cultivate in the province of Tomsk or the province of Irkutsk [i.e. Narym and Turukhansk: author] or farther north, but the great bulk were very unpopular and were wiped out by their labourers.'[79]

Conclusion

The Stalinist transformational project of the 'year of the great breakthrough' was shaped by the major political problem of the period: the nature of state–peasant relations. During the convoluted contingency of the year from mid-1928 to mid-1929 a Stalinist dynamic gained momentum in the communist party. It was a dynamic that drove policy towards the end goal of displacing the free peasantry, whose growth had been encouraged by NEP, and creating a captured peasantry. The idea was that a commandeered peasant economy could be directed towards developmental goals, namely the realization of Stalinist ideological aspirations for the construction of socialism through crash industrialization.

The grain crises in 1927 and 1928, primarily caused by harvest failures in the Ukraine and North Caucasus in two successive years, erupted at a critical juncture for the regime. The development of the country through industrialization, urbanization and demographic growth meant increased domestic consumer demand for agricultural produce. The demand of the state for agricultural commodities for export was also increasing, as the Stalinists placed their faith in the internal accumulation of resources from the peasantry in order to finance their increasingly ambitious industrialization plans. These demand pressures were accentuated by supply shortfalls. The above-mentioned harvest failures were one factor, over which the state had little control; however, other causative factors such as manufactured goods shortages, price differentials for agricultural products and swollen peasant monetary reserves (arising from a combination of a favourable balance of trade for agricultural commodities and low taxation) were a disincentive for the peasant marketing of grain, and were a reflection of poor state management of the economy. A small proportion of hard currency reserves was expended on grain imports in the spring and summer of 1928, but of more importance to the political psychology of the Stalinists was the fact that grain exports dwindled to a fraction of the levels of the mid-1920s, with a concomitant catastrophic fall in hard currency revenues from this source. The struggle for grain became emblematic of the state's struggle to capture the peasantry.

Bismarck claimed to have modernized Germany through 'blood and iron', but Keynes asserted that it had been achieved by 'coal and iron'. Stalin aimed to modernize the Soviet Union through 'grain and steel'. From October 1928 the Stalinist *dognat' i peregnat'* agenda of a crash programme of industrialization to create a 'metal-based' Russia militated against further grain imports to ease the social distress of food shortages and rationing. On the contrary, the Stalinist regime focused on the immediate maximum transfer and accumulation of resources for industrial investment from the peasantry. Rather than curtail industrial expansion, the Stalinists chose the option of exerting pressure on the new grain surplus areas in the East to make good the shortfalls in grain. The Siberian Krai, where NEP had propagated a 'green revolution' with a massive expansion in grain production, enjoyed three successive bumper harvests in 1927, 1928 and 1929, and was specially targeted by the regime for increased grain procurement. During this period the Siberian leadership assumed the role of the regime's 'breadwinners', becoming the biggest source for grain collections of all the regions in the USSR in 1928/9, and in the process boosting the confidence of the Stalinists in the dream of rapid modernization.

On the surface, it would appear that the conjuncture of events fostered the political environment where militant and radical solutions to the problem of 'taking grain' flourished. It could be argued that if there had been normal harvests in the Ukraine and North Caucasus, and these had been bolstered by the record harvests in Siberia, then there would have been favourable market conditions *within* NEP for state purchases and probably more than enough grain reserves to satisfy the needs of a 'great leap forward' by industrialization. Arguably, this scenario would have precluded Stalin's militant assault on the countryside in 1929, though, given the authoritarian and ideologically doctrinaire political direction in which he was pushing the regime, it seems doubtful that the attack on the independent peasantry would have been long postponed. Such a favourable combination of events was unlikely, however, given that the backwardness of agriculture was magnified by the unpredictability of climate and harvests in the Soviet Union – there being a one in three probability of a poor harvest in either of the eastern, central or southern grain producing regions in any given year. In view of this, perhaps, it is more useful to view the Stalin revolution as a product of the interface between ideology, personal ambition and *structure*, not only social but also geographic.

From the summer of 1928 the Bolshevik regime addressed the grain problem by abandoning the outright coercion of the *chrezvyshchaina* for a series of innovative measures designed to maximize 'social influence' and mobilize support from the *bednota* and seredniaks in the 'offensive against kulaks'. The policy was developed in three stages: stage one (summer–winter 1928/9), was the use of social influence as a mechanism to progressively redistribute the fiscal burdens imposed by the state on the peasantry so that the kulaks would pay more and the rest of the peasantry less or nothing; stage two (late winter–autumn 1929), was the application of the policy to grain collection; and stage three (winter–spring 1929–30) was the adoption of the policy as an instrument of dekulakization and collectivization. Having proved itself a success in less controversial areas such as taxation, social influence was extended to the problem of grain collection in March 1929. The 'Ural-Siberian method', as Stalin hailed the new method, consisted of a pseudo-democratic procedure for extracting grain for the state along the lines of that used for peasant self-taxation, utilizing the traditional legitimacy and authority of the *skhod*. The essence was to mobilize social pressure from *within* the village community to fulfil state tasks, as opposed to the reliance on coercion solely by outside agents of the party and state. This mobilization strategy entailed the recruitment of thousands of party officials and activists for work as plenipotentiaries in the countryside, whose work centred on the enlistment of the support of the mass of peasants or, in any event, ensuring their compliance.

The party's aim was to infiltrate and dominate the traditional governing institution of the peasantry, the *skhod*, by organizing a batrak-bedniak-seredniak caucus, and by excluding the kulaks. The mobilization of the 'rural proletariat' of poor peasants and the incorporation of *bednota* actifs and the *skhod* in the application of the new policy gave it a semblance of democratic legitimacy. The party aimed to rule the countryside by proxy, under the guise of the authority of the *skhod*. The policy transformed the way that the state applied economic exactions on the peasantry by shifting them on to a highly progressive basis. The kulaks and well-off households bore the brunt of tax surcharges and village grain delivery quotas, the middle peasants were intimidated but largely compliant, while the exemption of the poor peasants almost guaranteed their support. The refusal of kulaks to accept the process kindled social conflict in the villages, as plenipotentiaries and local officials organized social sanctions in the form of boycotts and applied *piatikratki* to combat non-compliance. State organized social sanctions also drew on the traditional forms and rituals of punishment applied in peasant society: charivari and *samosud*.

The Ural-Siberian method, so-called by Stalin because these were the regions where it was first applied, emerged as the result of a centre–regional–local dialogue. Its use was only endorsed in the middle of March 1929, after weeks of hesitation at the centre following exchanges with the Siberian Kraikombiuro, and after a broader discussion among the Siberian regional party elite. Once applied it produced a significant improvement in grain collections in the region. This success brought immediate political rewards for the Siberian party leader, Syrtsov, who was promoted to Chairman of Sovnarkom RSFSR in May 1929. The 'new method' was

Conclusion

established by the Politburo as the model for state grain procurement in the country from late March 1929 and was given legal authorization only on 28 June 1929 by amendments to Article 61 of the RSFSR Criminal Code. The party presented it as a more acceptable alternative to state coercion, emphasizing that it was a form of 'direct action' by the peasants themselves.

The evolution of the policy decisions on the Ural-Siberian method, collectivization and dekulakization, indicates that Stalinist policy formulation cannot be explained solely by a power concentration model which does not recognize the diffuse inputs and interactions of the various institutional actors and territorial levels of government. A radical upsurge 'from below', from the Siberian party, contributed to the dynamic that extended the social influence policy into grain collection. This first militant drive from the periphery on grain collection was followed in the autumn by a similar one from the Lower Volga for collectivization. These drives made a crucial impact in revolutionizing the thinking of the Stalinist wing of the party on the peasant question, encouraging a mode of thought which made forcible comprehensive collectivization and dekulakization of the countryside an immediate rather than a later prospect. The evidence from Siberia, with regard to the application of Article 61, followed by the conduct of dekulakization and collectivization, suggests that it is erroneous to assume that local authorities merely served as subordinate transmission belts for the implementation of orders from above. This study of policy-making in the emergent Stalinist state demonstrates that policies were not always vertically channelled 'from above' in the pure totalitarian fashion but often emerged from a complex bureaucratic interaction between the centre, regional and local tiers of government. To that extent, traditional approaches have overstated the informal side of politics and the 'hidden hand' of Stalin and understated the input side of the policy-making process. This is not to refute or preclude unrecorded collusion between Stalin and regional leaders in policy formation and implementation. Indeed, it was undoubtedly for this very reason that regional leaders were periodically recalled to Moscow for consultation.

The Stalinist attempt to capture the peasantry had powerful resonances, both in the practice and terminology, with previous patterns of state–peasant relations in Russia. In many fundamental aspects the policies of 1929–30 were inspired by the era of War Communism, and reached into the past to the traditions of Muscovite Russia. Stalin's notion of levying a tribute on the peasantry in order to finance a dash for industrial growth was a direct reference to the tax extracted by the Mongols from Muscovite Russia. Evidently, he regarded the social influence policy towards the countryside as nothing more than a tribute-collecting mechanism. Although the Stalinist leadership considered it to be grounded in the Bolshevik ideological dogma of class war, in fact the policy evolved from traditional Russian statist methods of dealing with an uncaptured peasantry. The method was evolutionary, a hybrid of past state practices. The idea of plenipotentiaries and worker brigades mobilizing the rural poor to assist the state in taking grain by planned compulsory delivery quotas has obvious parallels not only with the Kombedy and *razverstka* methods employed by the Bolsheviks during War Communism in 1918–19, but also with strategies used by both the tsarist regime and the Provisional Government. Like the Kombedy, the *bednota* actifs of 1929, formed under the guidance of plenipotentiaries and local party and soviet officials, were established to act as social and institutional agents of the state in grain collection.

This book has attempted to evaluate the usefulness of both moral economy and political economy concepts to understanding the development of Stalin's peasant policy in 1928–30, and peasant reactions to it. Stalin's peasant policy had two central goals: first, to limit (and ultimately eradicate) the economic power of the kulak stratum; second, to transform small-scale individual peasant holdings into large-scale collective farms. In the aftermath of the grain crisis of 1927/8, the Stalinist leadership synchronized its rejection of NEP with the implementation of a new strategy to mobilize social pressure within the peasantry in support of party policies. Beginning with Molotov's report 'On Work in the Countryside' to the Fifteenth Party Congress in December 1927, the Stalinists developed this strategy into a programme of policies designed to fracture potential peasant solidarity against the regime. The foundation on which this strategy rested was the enlistment, mobilization and organization of poor peasant support, and the neutralization of the middle peasant. The strategy was to be achieved by appeals both to customary peasant norms of equity and reciprocity which were threatened by commercialization under NEP (moral economy), and to the investment logic of the mass of peasants (political economy).

A key feature of the social influence policy, the notion of the collective responsibility (*poruka*) of the peasant community for material obligations to the state (in this case a grain plan), was deeply rooted in the 'embedded economy' of the peasant and a core principle of the Russian state tradition that can be traced back to Muscovite responses to the Mongol taxation system. The peasant custom law which evolved in response to *poruka* held that such responsibilities should be distributed fairly, according to a principle of proportionality. During the generation since Stolypin's reforms a market orientated kulak *verkhushka* farmer class had developed in the peasant economy. The economic liberalization of NEP had accelerated the

Conclusion

commercialization of agriculture, leading to an increase in socioeconomic differentiation in the countryside, and the disintegration of traditional peasant norms. The redistributional land commune was the cornerstone of the moral economy of the Russian peasant and its levelling principle was the bond which ultimately regulated peasant behaviour. Siberia was one of the leading regions in the country as regards the commercialization of agriculture, the emergence of a stratum of mechanized farmers and the disintegration of the redistributional commune during NEP.[1] The Stalinist social influence policy, and its reliance on the *skhod* for ratification and implementation, appealed to ancient peasant notions of a moral economy. Indeed, it was restorative, shoring up peasant norms that were being 'disembedded' by the commercialization of NEP and disregarded by the kulak farmer stratum. In this way the policy relied on a classic recipe of 'divide and conquer' to lever open social divisions in rural communities.

By applying political economy concepts to evaluate the peasant policy component of Stalin's 'revolution from above', I have attempted to shift attention away from the moral compulsion driving peasant opposition to it and focus more on the logic of collective action, the rational self-interest nexus between party, state and peasant, and the political and economic calculus that provided the dynamic for the whole process and motivated different strata of peasants. The political economy approach holds that participation in collective action is dependent on the inducement of benefits, particularly material benefits, that are excludable and selectively accessible through participation, that is to say that they are 'by-products' of participation over and above any collective good that may be achieved. Moreover, the mobilization of latent, rational group-oriented action is a function not simply of material incentives but can also be organized on the basis of 'social sanctions and social rewards', particularly where small groups are concerned. The Stalinist strategy organized small groups of poor and middle peasant *actifs* as caucuses to wrest the *skhod* from kulak hegemony and then use its legitimacy as the governing peasant institution to vote approval for party policies. Participation was secured by the provision of selective material incentives, including excludable benefits (from grain bounties, to free goods from cooperative stores and to a share of looted kulak property) for poor peasants who supported the state. Party and soviet officials also orchestrated social pressure as a device to control peasant behaviour and secure conformity by channelling it through traditional peasant rituals of social sanction. Peasants mobilized into *actifs* also had the incentive of an enhanced social status and power within the village. All of these factors were significant inducements for peasant participation.

Stalinist policy was geared to the provision of collective goods for the mass of middle and poor peasants. At first, these collective goods consisted of a progressive redistribution of the burdens of taxes and grain deliveries to the state so that the kulaks bore a disproportionate burden. The strategy was highly effective as an instrument for levying economic penalties on kulaks, because the rational self-interest decision calculus of the mass of peasants favoured such a policy of targeting: that is, if kulaks paid more, other peasants paid less. The strategy broke down in late 1929 and early 1930 when the Stalinists enforced a policy of comprehensive collectivization of the mass of peasants. In so doing, the regime abandoned its previous policy appeal to the rational behaviour and investment logic of the vast majority of peasants. The mass of peasants were quite willing to go along with the social influence policy because it offered the inducement of substantial material benefits, both selective for participation and collective in return for acquiescence in the targeting of kulaks. Communal approval for collectivization, which affected the private property of all, was less forthcoming because the cost-benefit analysis of the majority of peasants went against the party. Consequently, the Stalinists had to employ wholesale coercion to implement the policy. On the other hand, there is clear evidence that dekulakization was frequently enacted in a plebiscitary form by uncontrolled village activists and poor peasants. This was a logical outcome of the mobilization of latent poor peasant group-oriented action by the social influence policy. It released intra-village jealousies and rivalries, and proceeded quickly, and largely without disruption, because it extended the opportunities for even greater material incentives for peasant participation through the direct expropriation of kulak property.

The registration of property and people is a vital instrument of state control, resource mobilization and distribution in any society and this was one of the functions of the social influence policy. The success of this method in grain collection induced a rethink on other strategies towards the countryside. By empowering the poor and middle peasantry, isolating the kulaks and extending the party's organizational grip into the countryside, the Ural-Siberian method created the conditions for a captured peasantry. After the hiatus of NEP it was the central feature of the Bolshevik party's attempt to subjugate the countryside to the goal of rapid modernization. Stalin's speeches in late 1929 were littered with references to his belief that the success of the social influence policy meant that the peasant masses themselves were ready for collectivization and dekulakization. This belief might have been tinged by illusion but it was an instrumental factor in the policy shift to collectivization and dekulakization. The implementation of the social influence method had also entrenched the 'state-building'

Conclusion 211

organizational foundations, bureaucratic structures and institutional procedures which gave the party powerful levers to control the countryside. The Ural-Siberian method began the process of dekulakization: plenipotentiaries, local officials and village activists cooperated in the drawing up of lists of 'kulaks', registering their property and enacting their social isolation within the villages. The whole process disempowered and marginalized the targeted households, neutralizing their influence over their own communities and creating a 'little community' of social pariahs. All of this was a necessary prelude for the destructive finale of dekulakization.

The infiltration of party control into previously autonomous peasant institutions enabled the Bolshevik regime to achieve its policy goals, first in financially squeezing the kulak elite, then in the collection of grain surpluses, and was finally employed in the imposition of collectivization and dekulakization. Whereas the imposition of quotas and seizure of property under the social influence policy were merely adjuncts to the main intent of taking grain, the goal of collectivization was to consolidate state management of a captured peasantry, while dekulakization entailed the obliteration of the wealthy and most efficient peasant stratum as a social entity. The kulaks were to be 'liquidated as a class', as Stalin put it. Their dominating influence over village affairs was to be eradicated first by dispossessing them and then by physically eliminating or removing them from the countryside. We should also note the important role of dehumanizing pre-modern social rituals applied against kulaks during grain campaigns, for these mimicked by popular action the rhetorical demonizing propaganda of the party-controlled press. This demonizing was taken to its logical conclusion during dekulakization, when the humiliating ordeals of rape and torture were regularly perpetrated against victims. Kulaks were set apart from village society before being settled apart.

The study culminates in an analysis mapping the final stage in the development of the social influence policy – the destruction of the kulaks as a social entity, and the implementation of comprehensive collectivization in late 1929–early 1930. By the time that Stalin composed his 'year of the great breakthrough' article in November 1929, he had come to the conclusion that a maximalist project of dekulakization and collectivization was necessary to remove all obstacles to achieving the goal of modernization. I have offered a detailed explanation of what happened and how, by examining the pivotal decrees and decisions taken by the Politburo and their implementation by the Siberian party organization – a process of historical inquiry which hitherto has been obstructed by restricted access to Russian archives, and which previously could only be surmised from excerpts in the publications of collected documents selected and edited by

Russian historians working under the confines of the communist regime. In particular, the study is concerned with the constraints imposed on the Stalinist state in the implementation of its policies. Immense logistical tasks were involved in the dekulakization of hundreds of thousands of peasant households, composed of upwards of six million individuals, and the collectivization of 25 million peasant households, approaching 100 million individuals.

Many cases of mass peasant protests, particularly in areas of south-west Siberia, have been examined. Here, my analysis is situated within and influenced by the methodologies and techniques pioneered by social historians of peasant 'popular action' in other countries. It attempts to reconstruct the nature of the triangular relationship between party, state and peasant, which in many crucial aspects shaped the modernizing transformation of this period. I have tried to disembody the abstractions 'plenipotentiary' and 'muzhik', 'soviet official' and 'village crowd' and recreate the grassroots activities of party and state agents in the countryside, the peasant responses to them, and what shaped the relationships between different peasant strata. This has been made possible by the author's access to Siberian procuracy, judiciary, OGPU and party reports of investigations into official abuses and peasant protests (*volynki*), incidents which were not atypical but common occurrences. The availability of this new documentary evidence has allowed the author to recover something of the *mentalité* of these groups from *within*. This evidence reveals that peasant protests underwent a transition from the spontaneous, largely passive, or at least non-armed force, *volynki* form of resistance of 1929, to a few cases of organized armed uprisings during collectivization and dekulakization in early 1930. The typology of peasant protest against Stalinist policies was a complex and volatile amalgam of contradictory forms and motives, both the 'backward-looking' traditional – food-riots, Luddism, incendiarism, animal-maiming, assaults against peasant collaborators and agents of the state – and the 'forward-looking' modern – mass demonstrations, the use of human cordons, petitions, and the emergence of leaders who organized autonomous armed action across a wide area with declared political objectives. The rare evidence when peasants listed their demands illustrate this 'backwards-forwards' amalgam of the political (no dekulakization, the return of the exiled, new elections), the economic (no grain to be removed) and the traditional (churches to be reopened).

The policy of social influence has been widely misinterpreted by historians who, in my view, have tended to subsume it and other sophisticated measures of Stalinist management of state–peasant relations under one general heading: emergency measures. The classic orthodox interpretation of this period is generally dismissive of the notion that the countryside was amenable to Bolshevik attempts to incite social conflict, preferring to view the peasantry as a single social organism in which 'class struggle', as the party's Marxist-Leninist ideological paradigm termed it, was an artifice. The Bolshevik regime's mobilization of social pressure through poor peasant actifs has been ridiculed as a 'near-myth' by Moshe Lewin in his classic study of collectivization. He also dismissed poor peasant involvement in dekulakization as a 'mere formality'.[2] In his view the evolution of the regime's policy in this period can only be understood in terms of a bipolarized state–peasant conflict, where policy implementation relied on emergency methods of coercion. This interpretation is not sustained by the evidence presented in this book. My argument contends that one cannot fully comprehend the processes at work during this critical phase of Russian history unless one recognizes that socially variegated mobilization and social conflict within the peasantry were significant factors in the outcome.

Understanding Stalinist collectivization in terms of a simplistic state versus peasant dichotomy is a utopian view of the reality of social fragmentation within the Russian peasantry. It is the romanticized folk tradition within peasant studies which has helped to sustain the ubiquitous notion of the peasantry as a 'little community' prone to homogeneous 'collective action', as if peasant outbursts against perceived hostile political, economic and other stimuli could be understood as nothing other than unified acts of protest. This is an idealized picture of the reality of divided loyalties within peasant communities, and the diverse impact of outside agencies on different peasant groups. Villages, like cities, are socially stratified organisms. They are organized around vertical and horizontal divisions: clusters of kin ties, neighbourhood sectors, land distribution and patronage networks, with a high degree of overlap between kin, neighbourhood, landholding and social status. All things considered, they provide a fertile breeding ground for social conflicts which can be exploited by 'outside' state interests. The Stalinist regime acted precisely in this manner, exploiting peasant divisions, whether by appeals to moral economy or the provision of material incentives, to enhance the effectiveness of its agrarian policy implementation and successfully implant its agencies of control in the countryside.

What were the consequences of the policies of collectivization and dekulakization? By destroying the free peasantry, and physically eliminating the presence and influence of the kulak *verkhushka*, the Stalinists captured the countryside for the state, and eradicated its capacity to influence the pace and direction of the economic development of the country.

The process of capturing the peasantry required the penetration of party and state control into the villages, while the permanent mobilization of society, both city and countryside, became a hallmark of the Stalinist order. The policy of social influence, leading to collectivization and dekulakization, created a bureaucratic swell which sharply accelerated the *étatisation* of the Russian countryside, a process that had been evolving slowly under NEP. The Stalinists conceived of their modernizing revolution as a struggle to bridge the chasm between pre-modern and modern forms of social, economic and political organization in Russia, a conflict between the progressive forward-looking forces of party and state against the retarding, backward 'dark forces' of the countryside. In this sense it was a cultural and ideological struggle as much as a political and economic one. Stalin's speeches of late 1929 were a call-to-arms for the Bolshevik party, an appeal which fell on the fertile ground of Bolshevik millenarianism and found a ready response at all levels of the party. After all, extremist politics is about utopian visions and triumphalist idealism, and Stalin's oratory was masterful at capitalizing on both. The Bolsheviks wanted not merely to industrialize and modernize Russia, but to industrialize the *countryside*. The complex problems of state–peasant relations were reduced in Stalinist thinking to an iconographic 'backwards-forwards' juxtaposition of images: the muzhik with his wooden plough who represented Russia's backwardness, and the kolkhoznik on a tractor who represented modernity.

All the defining tasks intrinsic to the nature of a free peasantry, and central to the culture of the Russian village, were to be subjected to state regulation and control: ploughing, sowing, harvesting, reaping, binding, stacking, threshing and so on. Most of these operations were traditionally collectively organized, primarily on the basis of family labour, though the strengthening of a proprietorial kulak farmer stratum, the growth of peonage, and commercialization during NEP seriously weakened the communal roots of cultivation – a process which had begun well before the revolution, with Stolypin's reforms. Through collectivization the state had intervened and broken this very personal bond between the family unit and agriculture, replacing it with the notion of wage labour and nullifying the peasant's incentive to work efficiently. The social influence policy, collectivization and dekulakization stirred up social discord and unravelled the traditionally strong ties of community in peasant society. Taken together with the demolition, often literally, of the institutional structures and value system of the Orthodox Church which were the hub of the annual cycle of village life, the Stalin revolution effectively waged a cultural war against Russian peasant society.

Conclusion

Apart from the bond with the land and religion, there was one other keystone underpinning peasant society and culture: people. The year of the 'great breakthrough' initiated a massive demographic transfer in the Soviet Union. Dekulakization removed at least six million of, for the most part, the most technically advanced, economically progressive and innovative, and articulate peasants from the countryside. The comprehensiveness of the policy implementation meant that virtually every village in the country was affected. The destruction of the kulaks by shootings, concentration camps, resettlement in the inhospitable wilderness of the Siberian taiga, and settlements beyond the pale of collective farms, did not amount to a genocide, for it did not involve the annihilation of an ethnic group. There is no comparable word of opprobrium, however, to describe this systematic extermination of a socioeconomic stratum on the grounds of political expediency. In a more open society the Russian peasantry might well have responded to the appalling downturn in their living conditions by resorting to emigration as a remedy, perhaps to North America, much as the peasantries in other parts of Europe did in the nineteenth century. Trapped by closed borders, there was no deluge of external mass emigration; instead the peasants reacted by a massive internal shift of population from the countryside to the towns and newly industrializing areas of the country. The net effect of this demographic transfer was that it facilitated the mobilization of peasant labour for rapid industrialization. Furthermore, many kulaks were placed in forced labour colonies and deployed as expendable human resources in the harsh work of extractive and construction industry projects, often in inclement desolate areas of northern Siberia and the Far East.

The campaign of winter 1929/30 was only a partial success mainly because of constraints imposed by the sheer logistical difficulties of a rapid implementation of the policies. Moreover, these constraints were exacerbated by two complicating factors: pressure 'from above' from Stalin and his clique to over-fulfil tasks, and developments at the grassroots, where many local officials assumed that the injunctions of the Stalinist leadership were delivered to them *carte blanche* as regards implementation. Consequently, the whole campaign degenerated into an orgy of what was officially termed 'pillaging' of the kulaks and the coercion of the mass of peasants into collective farms. Whilst there was sporadic violent peasant resistance to the regime's policies, the predominant peasant response was a rational and passive one: the wholesale slaughtering of livestock and reduction in sowings for a marketable surplus. This was far more astute and devastating as regards its long-term economic consequences on the Stalinist developmental project, since it rendered the whole collectivization campaign counterproductive in its goal of raising agricultural efficiency. Testimony to the drawn-out backwardness of Russian agriculture, are the pictures viewed by the author in Siberian archives of kolkhozniks in the late 1940s using horses in ploughing teams, not the tractors promised by the Stalinists in 1930. While livestock numbers did not recover their pre-collectivization levels until the 1950s, that greatest agency of terror for the peasant, famine, ravaged the countryside in 1932–33, as a result of the combined effects of decreased sowings, poor harvests and inexorable state procurement, and perhaps also as a desired effect of revenge for Stalin.

The immediate political impact of the devastation of the countryside was such that the Stalin revolution was checked and the regime was forced into an embarrassing policy U-turn at the beginning of March 1930. Dekulakization was eased and, following the renewal of the 'voluntary' principle which frequently was a camouflage for coercion during the campaign, peasants were allowed to leave the collectives in a mass exodus. Even then, there is evidence that there was no peasant consensus as regards the welcome for the policy U-turn, as different peasant strata had diverse perceptions and reactions to it. The middle and well-off peasants hailed Stalin as a liberator; poor peasants felt betrayed and feared the wrath of their communities for their collaboration with the party. These reactions were shortlived, however, as after a hiatus of a few months the full-scale implementation of collectivization and dekulakization resumed in the winter of 1930–31. Only after this second projection of state power for a sustained surge in collectivization and dekulakization did the Stalin revolution permanently remake the Russian countryside, capturing the peasantry, eliminating individual farming and establishing the kolkhozes as a subordinate appendage of the state. The socialist reconfiguration of agriculture was, indeed, a veritable socioeconomic revolution. By 1930 all the essential features of the Stalinist order had been imprinted on Soviet society. The transition from emergency measures to the policy of social influence, and then to collectivization and dekulakization, was an intrinsic part of the regime transmutation. In this way Stalinism moulded the conflicting social pressures, created by tsarist industrialization and unleashed by the Russian revolution, into a modern authoritarian order.

Notes

INTRODUCTION

1. E.H. Carr argued that 'it would be far-fetched to suggest that it was dogma which drove the politicians to act as they did': 'Revolution from Above: Some Notes on the Decision to Collectivise Soviet Agriculture' in K.H. Wolff and Barrington Moore Jr (eds), *The Critical Spirit: Essays in Honour of Herbert Marcuse* (Boston, Beacon Press, 1967), p. 316. In contrast, R. Conquest affirmed that 'the communist ideology provided the motivation for an unprecedented massacre of men, women and children': *The Harvest of Sorrow: Soviet Collectivization and the Terror-Famine* (London, Arrow, 1988), p. 344. For the opposing viewpoints see the debate between A. Nove and J. Millar in 'A Debate on Collectivisation: Was Stalin Really Necessary?', *Problems of Communism*, Vol. 25, No. 4 (1976).
2. This interpretation is followed in recent publications by the leading Russian historians of collectivization: V.P. Danilov and N.V. Teptsov, '*Kollektivizatsiia: kak eto bylo*', Parts one and two, *Pravda*, 26 August and 16 September 1988; V.P. Danilov, *Kollektivizatsiia: kak eto bylo, stranitsy istorii sovetskogo obshchestva: fakty, problemy, liudi* (Moscow, Naukha, 1989); V.P. Danilov and N.A. Ivnitsky (eds), *Dokumenty svidetel'stvuiut, iz istorii derevni nakanune i v khode kollektivizatsii 1927–1932 gg.* (Moscow, Izdatel'stvo, 1989), p. 50.
3. This notion originated in the work of the Russian economic historian A.A. Barsov, who asserted that 'the majority of the accumulation needed for the implementation of socialist industrialisation . . . was created by the working class': *Balans stoimostnykh obmenov mezhdu gorodom i derevni* (Moscow, Nauka, 1969), p. 137. It was then developed in J. Millar, 'Mass Collectivization and the Contribution of Soviet Agriculture to the First Five Year Plan: A Review Article', *Slavic Review*, Vol. 33, No. 1, December 1974, pp. 750–66. See also H. Hunter, 'The Overambitious First Soviet Five Year Plan', *Slavic Review*, Vol. 32, No. 2, June 1974.
4. In the summer of 1929, Trotsky wrote: 'Finding themselves in an economic cul-de-sac, the Stalinist cadres, against their will, are conducting a leftward zig-zag, which in the process of struggle has taken them further to the left than they wanted': *Biulleten' oppozitsii*, No. 1–2, July 1929, p. 9.
5. I. Deutscher proposed that Stalin's 'second revolution' was initiated in an 'unpremeditated, pragmatic manner' and was 'precipitated' by events in 1928–29: *Stalin, A Political Biography* (London, Oxford University Press, 1949), pp. 318, 322. E.H. Carr rather contradictorily argued that the decisions were ideologically motivated, 'dictated by the dynamic force inherent in the revolution itself', in *Socialism in One Country, 1924–1926, Vol. 1* (London, Macmillan, 1958), pp. 174–86; and that they were 'precipitately adopted' and 'something of a puzzle', in *The Critical Spirit*, p. 313. M. Lewin held that Stalin's concern for a 'short-term policy of moderate aims' was pushed to extreme solutions by the grain crisis, and that 'events drove the Communist Party leadership to embark upon mass collectivization': 'The

Immediate Background to Soviet Collectivization', an article of 1965 republished in *The Making of the Soviet System* (London, Methuen, 1985), pp. 98–100, 110, and his *Russian Peasants and Soviet Power, A Study of Collectivization* (London, Allen & Unwin, 1968), p. 20. O. Narkiewicz argued that the decisions were taken on 'the spur of the moment': 'Soviet Administration and the Grain Crisis of 1927–28', *Soviet Studies*, Vol. 20, No. 4, October 1968, p. 235. For a Russian version of this analysis see N.A. Ivnitsky, *Klassovaia bor'ba v derevne i likvidatsiia kulachestva kak klassa* (1929–1932 gg.) (Moscow, Nauka, 1972).

6. R.W. Davies, *The Socialist Offensive: The Collectivisation of Soviet Agriculture, 1929–1930* (London, Macmillan, 1980), pp. 116–37; L. Viola, *Best Sons of the Fatherland, Workers in the Vanguard of Soviet Collectivization* (Oxford, Oxford University Press, 1987).

7. Carr held that Stalinist policy was 'essentially impersonal': *Socialism in One Country, Vol. 1*, p. 174. Nove argued that the policy of collectivization 'cannot be attributed to Stalin personally, and therefore the consequences which flowed from its adoption must be a matter of more than personal responsibility': *Was Stalin Really Necessary? Some Problems of Soviet Political Economy* (London, Allen & Unwin, 1965), p. 24.

8. For a recent collection of essays representing this *oeuvre* see W.G. Rosenberg and L.H. Siegelbaum (eds), *Social Dimensions of Industrialization* (Bloomington, Indiana University Press, 1993).

9. See H. Kuromiya, *Stalin's Industrial Revolution, Politics and Workers, 1928–1932* (Cambridge, Cambridge University Press, 1988); S. Fitzpatrick (ed.), *Cultural Revolution in Russia, 1928–1931* (Bloomington, Indiana University Press, 1978), pp. 17–18, 133–4. Fitzpatrick's hypothesis is that the Stalin revolution was 'the period in which the social and generational tensions of NEP came to a climax in an onslaught... on privilege and established authority': ibid., p. 11. A recent study suggested that generational conflict between peasant migrant workers (*otkhodniki*) and village elders was a more useful explanation of peasant conflict during collectivization. This study was, however, based on the Moscow Region, which was significantly untypical in terms of the close interaction of the peasant economy with the metropolitan economy: David L. Hoffman, 'Land, Freedom and Discontent: Russian Peasants of the Central Industrial Region Prior to Collectivisation', *Europe–Asia Studies*, Vol. 46, No. 4, 1994, pp. 579–96.

10. J. Arch Getty, 'The Politics of Stalinism' in Alec Nove (ed.), *The Stalin Phenomenon* (London, Wiedenfield & Nicholson, 1993), p. 132.

11. R. Tucker pointed to the 'system of obligatory labour and the immobilisation of the peasant' as the key institutional developments under collectivization which reverted to serfdom: 'A Choice of Lenin's' in G.R. Urban (ed.), *Stalinism, Its Impact on Russia and the World* (London, St Martin's Press, 1982), pp. 157–8.

12. N. Mandelstam, *Hope Against Hope: A Memoir*, trans. M. Hayward (London, Collins and Harvill Press, 1970), p. 13.

13. S. Johnson and P. Temin, 'The Macroeconomics of NEP', *Economic History Review*, Vol. XLVI, No. 4, 1993, pp. 750–67.

14. The exception is M. Fainsod, *Smolensk Under Soviet Rule* (London, Unwin Hyman, 1958, repr. 1989). Fainsod drew on the materials of the Smolensk

Oblast party archive captured by the US army from the Germans in 1945. Fainsod devoted only one chapter of twenty-three to collectivization and dekulakization, and, besides, Smolensk was a minor agricultural area: it was neither a grain producing region, nor an area of comprehensive collectivization or mass dekulakization.
15. For the alternate viewpoints see E.P. Thompson, 'The Moral Economy of the English Crowd in the Eighteenth Century' and 'The Moral Economy Reviewed', Chapters 4 and 5 respectively of his *Customs in Common*, (London, Penguin, 1993). Chapter 4 is a reprint of an article first published in *Past and Present* in 1971; James C. Scott, *The Moral Economy of the Peasant: Rebellion and Subsistence in Southeast Asia* (London, Yale University Press, 1976); Samuel L. Popkin, *The Rational Peasant: The Political Economy of Rural Society in Vietnam* (Berkeley, University of California Press, 1979). For a critique see William J. Booth, 'On the Idea of the Moral Economy', *American Political Science Review*, Vol. 88, No. 3, September 1994, pp. 653–67.
16. Thompson, p. 188.
17. Scott (1976), p. vii.
18. Barrington Moore, Jr, *Social Origins of Dictatorship and Democracy: Lord and Peasant in the Making of the Modern World* (Harmondsworth, Peregrine, 1969), pp. 453–83.
19. Eric Wolf 'On Peasant Rebellions' in Teodor Shanin (ed.), *Peasants and Peasant Societies* (Harmondsworth, Penguin, 1971), p. 272.
20. Theda Skocpol, *States and Social Revolutions: A Comparative Analysis of France, Russia, and China* (Cambridge, Cambridge University Press, 1979), pp. 114–15. The leverage was determined by three factors: the solidarity of peasant communities, peasant autonomy and state coercive sanctions.
21. For these classic forms of peasant resistance see James C. Scott, *Weapons of the Weak: Everyday Forms of Peasant Resistance* (London, Yale University Press, 1985).
22. Karl Marx, *The Class Struggles in France 1848–1850* (London, Lawrence and Wishart, 1990), pp. 159, 302–8; *The Eighteenth Brumaire of Louis Bonaparte* (Moscow, Progress, 1967), p. 106.
23. Robert Redfield, *The Little Community and Peasant Society and Culture*, (Chicago, University of Chicago Press, 1971).
24. Eric Wolf, *Peasant Wars of the Twentieth Century* (New York, Harper Row, 1969), p. 282; Henry A. Landsberger, *Rural Protest: Peasant Movements and Social Change* (London, Macmillan, 1974), pp. 21–2, 49–51.
25. See Teodor Shanin, *The Awkward Class: Political Sociology of Peasantry in a Developing Society: Russia 1910–1925* (Oxford, Clarendon Press, 1972).
26. The concept was first applied by Mancur Olson, *The Logic of Collective Action: Public Goods and the Theory of Groups* (Cambridge, Harvard University Press, 1965). A detailed treatment of peasant collective action was provided by Popkin, especially Chapters 1, 2 and 6.
27. Ibid., pp. 20–3.
28. Ibid., pp. 24–7. The significance of selective incentives in peasant collective action is discussed in Mark Lichbach, 'What Makes Rational Peasants Revolutionary? Dilemma, Paradox, and Irony in Peasant Collective Action', *World Politics*, Vol. 46, No. 3, April 1994, pp. 383–418.

29. Olson, pp. 1–2, 48, 53–4, 60–5. Olson has applied his ideas to contemporary Soviet-type societies but not to the historical context of Stalinism: 'The Logic of Collective Action in Soviet-type Societies', *Journal of Soviet Nationalities*, No. 1, 1990, pp. 8–27.
30. Ibid., p. 245.

CHAPTER 1   CAPTURING THE PEASANTRY

1. For the growth of grain production in Siberia and the causes of the grain crisis see James Hughes, *Stalin, Siberia and the Crisis of the New Economic Policy* (Cambridge, Cambridge University Press, 1991), pp. 19–25, and Chapter 4.
2. Here, I have inverted Goran Hyden's concept of a 'captured' peasantry, by which he meant the incorporation of peasant producers into a regulated market economy. The 'uncaptured' status of the peasantry referred to its ability to opt out of the state and revert to independent subsistence agriculture. See his *Beyond Ujamaa in Tanzania: Under-Development and an Uncaptured Peasantry* (Berkeley, University of California Press, 1980).
3. F. Chueva, *Sto sorok besed c Molotovym* (Moscow, Terra-Terra, 1991), p. 377. A conversation of 21 June 1972.
4. From a speech to the Urals Obkom in early 1928, cited in a letter of M. Frumkin of 15 June 1928: Iu. G. Fel'shtinsky, *Razgovory c Bukharinym*, (Moscow, *Izdatel'stvo gumanitarnoi literatury*, 1993), Appendix 4, pp. 47–53.
5. Lewin (1968), Chapter 11 title; Lewin (1985), p. 100.
6. I.V. Stalin, *Sochineniia, Vols 1–13* (Moscow, Gosudartsvennoe izdatel'stvo politicheskoi literatury, 1946–52), Vol. 11, pp. 5–9, 40–2, 88–97; *IS*, No. 5, 15 March 1928, pp. 7–11; *KPSS v rezoliutsiiakh i resheniiakh s"ezdov, konferentsii i plenumov Ts. K. (1898–1986), Vols 1–9*, 9th edn (Moscow, Izdatel'stvo politicheskoi literatury, 1983–86), Vol. 4, pp. 350–5.
7. Lewin (1968), p. 252. The author's views on the 'kulak' issue and peasant differentiation generally are set out in Hughes (1991), Chapter 3. For the debate among Russian historians see the articles by V. Tikhonov and V. Danilov in *Istoriia SSSR*, No. 3, 1989.
8. For example, Molotov spoke of 'poor peasant illusions about the collectivization of the broad peasant masses', *Pravda*, 9 May 1925.
9. *(XV) Piatnadtsatyi s"ezd VKP (b), 2–19 dekabria 1927 g., stenograficheskii otchet, 2 Vols* (Moscow, Gosudarstvennoe izdatel'stvo politicheskoi literatury, 1962), Vol. 1, p. 63, and Vol. 2, pp. 1419–21; Stalin, *Sochineniia*, Vol. 11, pp. 5–9, 40–2, 88–97; 'Rezoliutsii IV plenuma sibkraikoma VKP(b) o blizhaishikh khoziaistvenno-politicheskikh zadachakh', *IS*, No. 5 (15 March 1928), pp. 7–11; *KPSS v rezoliutsiiakh*, op. cit., Vol. 4, pp. 354–5.
10. *Sibirskaia sel'sko-khoziaistvennaia kooperatsiia*, No. 3–4, 1928, p. 31 (Kraiispolkom decree); *IS*, No. 7–8, 27 April 1928, pp. 1–2 (Kraikom directive).
11. The practice of excluding kulaks was formalized by the Fourth Siberian Party Conference; *Sovetskaia sibir'*, 21 March 1929. See also *(XVI) Shestnadtsataia konferentsiia vkp (b), aprel' 1929, stenograficheskii otchet* (Moscow,

Gosudartsvennoe izdat'elstvo politicheskoe literatury, 1962), pp. 312 (Lominadze), 325 (Syrtsov).
12. *KPSS v rezoliutsiiakh*, Vol. 4, p. 372 (November 1928 plenum); *Istoriia sibiri c drevneishikh vremen do nashikh dnei*, 5 vols, Vol. 4 (Leningrad, Naukha, 1968), p. 232; *IS*, No. 16, 15 September 1928, p. 3 (Kraikombiuro decree); *GANO* 1, f. r-47, op. 1, d. 696, l. 45, Eikhe's letter.
13. This obstructionism is discussed in *ZS*, No. 3–4, March–April 1928, pp. 5–14.
14. Cited in V.N. Burkov, '*Deiatel'nost' KPSS po ukrepleniia derevneskikh partiinikh organizatsii zapadnoi sibiri v usloviiakh podgotovki i provedeniia massovoi kollektivizatsii, 1927–1932 gg.*', *dissertatsiia kandidat istorii nauka* (Tomsk, *Tomskii gos. univ.*, 1966), p. 162.
15. *GANO* 2, f. 2, op. 2, d. 373, l. 247–50, letter from the Kraikom to all okruzhkoms, signed Kisis and Komarov, 23 November 1929.
16. See Hughes (1991), pp. 146–8.
17. *XVI konf.*, pp. 792–3 note 128; *KPSS v rezoliutsiiakh*, Vol. 4, pp. 354–5; *RTsKhIDNI*, f. 17, op. 2, d. 375, p. 51, stenogram of the July 1928 plenum.
18. *IS*, No. 17, 30 September 1928, p. 5, Kraikombiuro decision on 'Construction of New Grain Sovkhozes' of 4 September 1928; ibid., No. 22, 20 December 1928, p. 4, Kraikombiuro decree on the spring agricultural campaign of 12 December 1928; *XVI konf.*, p. 89 (Eikhe); *NLP*, No. 22, 15 November 1928, p. 4.
19. *GANO* 1, f. 2, op. 1, d. 3449, l. 28.
20. '*Rezoliutsii IV plenuma Sibkraikoma VKP(b)*', *IS*, No. 5, 15 March 1928, pp. 7–11; *KPSS v rezoliutsiiakh*, Vol. 4, pp. 322–3.
21. For the twenty-five thousanders see Viola.
22. '*O meropriiatiiakh po ukrepleniiu nizovykh derevneskikh organizatsii*', *IS*, No. 13, 25 July 1928, p. 6; ibid., No. 16, 15 September 1928, p. 5; *Kollektivizatsiia sel'skogo khoziaistvo zapadnoi sibiri (1927–1937 gg.)*, (Tomsk, *Tomskii gos. univ.*, 1972), pp. 44, 322 note 12; Burkov (1966), pp. 127, 130–1.
23. *GANO* 1, f. r-47, op. 1, d. 696, l. 53, a letter dated 24 October 1928.
24. Burkov, p. 198; *Sovetskaia sibir'*, 15 January 1929, p. 4.
25. *GANO* 2, f. 2, op. 2, d. 386, l. 8–14, Report No. 5 on Soviet elections, from the Organization Department of the Kraiispolkom, 10 January 1929.
26. E.A. Preobrazhensky, *Novaya ekonomika. Opyt analiza sovetskogo khozyaistva, Vol. 1, Part 1*, Moscow 1926, trans. by Brian Pearce: *The New Economics* (Oxford, Oxford University Press, 1965).
27. See John Salter, 'On the Interpretation of Bukharin's Economic Ideas', *Soviet Studies*, Vol. 44, No. 4, 1992, pp. 563–79.
28. Stalin, *Sochineniia*, Vol. 11, pp. 157–9, 168–70. The actual stenogram records critical interruptions from Bukharin: *RTsKhIDNI*, f. 17, op. 2, d. 375, pp. 98–106.
29. *Sotsialisticheskii vestnik*, No. 6 (196), 22 March 1929, p. 10; 'Bukharin–Kamenev conversation', ibid., No. 9 (199), 4 May 1929, p. 10; *XVI konf.*, pp. 806–7. See also p. 228, note 6.
30. N. Valentinov, 'Iz proshlogo', *Sotsialisticheskii vestnik*, No. 4 (752) April 1961, p. 72.
31. *KPSS v rezoliutsiiakh*, Vol. 4, pp. 285, 305, 311.

32. For the tax reforms in 1926–7 see E.H. Carr and R.W. Davies, *Foundations of a Planned Economy, Vol. 1, 1926–1929* (Harmondsworth, Penguin, 1974), pp. 800–5.
33. *Krasnaia sibiriachka*, No. 5 (1928), p. 3; ibid., No. 6, 1928, p. 2; *ZS*, No. 6, June 1928, pp. 32–5; *Za chetkuiu klassovuiu liniiu. Sbornik dokumentov kraikoma vkp (b) i vystuplenii rukovodiashchikh rabotnikov kraia* (Novosibirsk, *Kraiizdat*, 1929), pp. 231–2.
34. *Krasnaia sibiriachka*, No. 4, 1928, p. 5.
35. Cases of this kind of self-dekulakization in Slavgorod Okrug are described in M. Lukashin, *Kratkie itogi raboty slavgorodsk okruzhkoma vkp (b)* (Slavgorod, *Partizdat*, 1928), pp. 21–2.
36. '*Pervye itogi zagotovitel'noi kampanii i dal'neishie zadachi partii*', Stalin, *Sochineniia*, Vol. 11, pp. 18–19; *NLP*, No. 3, 15 February 1928, p. 4.
37. The Joint Plenum of the Central Committee and Central Control Commission, 6–11 April 1928, Stenographic Report: *RTsKhIDNI*, f. 17, op. 2, d. 354, Vol. 1, pp. 55 (Lepa), 63 (Mikoyan).
38. John Maynard, *The Russian Peasant and Other Studies* (London, Victor Gollancz, 1942), p. 284.
39. Stalin, *Sochineniia*, Vol. 11, pp. 10–19.
40. Cited in Fel'shtinsky, pp. 49, 51.
41. N. Ya Gushchin, *Sibirskaia derevnia na puti k sotsialismu* (Novosibirsk, *Nauka*, 1973), pp. 97, 102; *Pravda*, 27 March 1928, p. 5. At the Sixteenth Party Conference Eikhe spoke of kulaks decreasing their sown area but that of seredniaks and bedniaks expanding by 9 per cent; *XVI konf.*, p. 91. He based this on figures provided by Kavraisky and Nusinov for whose work see Hughes (1991), pp. 88–96.
42. *GANO* 1, f. 288, op. 1, d. 502, l. 122–128*ob*, Kraitorg report from Zlobin and Shibailo (August 1928) 'On the results of grain procurement in 1927/28 and the organization of the grain procurement campaign of 1928/29'.
43. *GANO* 2, f. 2, op. 2, d. 373, l. 206, telegram from Kisis to all okruzhkoms, 3 August 1928.
44. *GANO* 2, f. 2, op. 2, d. 373, l. 176, telegram from Kisis to all okruzhkoms, 24 August 1928.
45. *GANO* 2, f. 2, op. 2, d. 373, l. 169–70, letter from the Kraikom Secretariat to all okruzhkoms (undated, probably early September 1929).
46. *KPSS v rezoliutsiiakh*, Vol. 4, pp. 351–2, 371; A. Briukhanov, 'Itogi khlebnoi kampanii 1928/29 goda', *Ekonomicheskoe obozrenie*, No. 11, November 1929, pp. 129–30.
47. *KPSS v rezoliutsiiakh*, Vol. 4, p. 370; *XVI konf.*, p. 32 (Krzhizhanovsky); Stalin, *Sochineniia*, Vol. 12, p. 86.
48. *KPSS v rezoliutsiiakh*, Vol. 4, p. 371. See also *GANO* 2, f. 2, op. 7, d. 485, *Chetvertaia sibirskaia konferentsiia vkp (b), 25 fevralia–4 marta 1929, stenograficheskii otchet, Vols 1–3* (Novosibirsk, *Kraiizdat*, 1929), Vol. 1, p. 4 (Syrtsov).
49. *GANO* 2, f. 2, op. 2, d. 373, l. 189–91, directive no. 461/c from Zaitsev and Eikhe to secretaries of okruzhkoms and chairmen of okrispolkoms, 18 September 1928.
50. *GANO* 2, f. 2, op. 2, d. 294a, l. 98, telegram from Syrtsov to Stalin and Mikoyan, 27 October 1928 (via the OGPU).

51. See the resolutions of the plenum and extracts of speeches in *IS*, No. 20–21, 23 November 1929, pp. 10–14.
52. *Pravda*, 27 March 1928, p. 5; Gushchin (1973), pp. 97 (Table 12), 102 (Table 16), 105 (Table 18); *Chetvertaia sib. part. konf.*, p. 315 (Syrtsov); *GANO* 1, f. r-47, op. 1, d. 696, l. 38, Siberian procurement plan as of 16 October 1928.
53. *RTsKhIDNI*, f. 17, op. 2, d. 375, l. 67, 155, stenogram of the July 1928 Central Committee plenum; ibid., d. 397, l. 54, stenogramme of the November 1928 Central Committee plenum.
54. Yu. A. Moshkov, *Zernovaia problema v gody sploshnoi kollektivizatsii sel'skogo khoziaistva SSSR (1929–1932 gg.)* (Moscow, *Moskovskii gos. univ.*, 1966), pp. 49–51. See also Mikoyan's speech p. 40. More details of price differentials between high free market and low state prices are provided at *XVI konf.*, 20 (Rykov). For example, he quotes the price differential for a tsentner of rye flour in consumer areas of RSFSR as 4 roubles 44 kopecks on 1 March 1928, soaring to 26 roubles 64 kopecks by 1 March 1929 (a more than five times increase).
55. *GANO* 1, f. r-47, op. 1, d. 696, l. 5–6, report by Zlobin to the Sibkraikombiuro of 19 November 1928.
56. *GANO* 1, f. r-47, op. 1, d. 696, l. 144–6, report of Zlobin and Shibailo to the Kraiispolkom on 21 November 1928.
57. GANO 1, f. r-47, op. 1, d. 696, l. 28–30, report from Myshkin to Syrtsov of 20 October 1928.
58. For the report see: *GANO* 1, f. r-47, op. 1, d. 696, l. 92–4. For the letter see ibid., l. 45.
59. *GANO* 1, f. r-47, op. 1, d. 696, l. 34–6, protocol No. 1, Presidium Rubtsovsk Okruzhkom, 3 October 1928; ibid., l. 33, telegram from Head of Rubtsovsk Okrtorg of 1 November. For the Kraiispolkom's opposition to emergency measures see ibid., l. 31, telegram from Voronin, Deputy Chairman of Kraiispolkom, and Reshchikov, Secretary of Kraiispolkom, of 16 November, and Eikhe's report cited at note 58 above.
60. *GANO* 1, f. r-47, op. 1, d. 696, l. 52, letter from the Chairman of the Siberian Cultivators Union, Strelkov, and the Chairman of the Siberian Cooperative Union, Strikovsky, to Eikhe on 23 October 1928.
61. *GANO* 1, f. r-47, op. 1, d. 696, l. 80, report from Kupryanov, Krai Procurator, of October 1928 to Eikhe; ibid., l. 81–2, report from Leonidov, Assistant Krai Procurator, of 29 October 1928 to Kavraisky. For the Stalin slogan see the Report 'On Excesses Occurring in the Post-April Period of 1928' by Kupryanov and Leonidov of 5 October 1928 to Eikhe at ibid., l. 107.
62. *IS*, No. 20–21, 23 November 1928, p. 8 (Kraikombiuro directives); *GANO* 1, f. r-47, op. 4a, d. 232 'b', l. 185, a report on self-taxation from the Kraikom Political Department of 10 May 1929.
63. *GANO* 1, f. r-47, op. 1, d. 696, l. 55–60, report of Khristal' to the Kraikom of 18 October 1928; ibid., l. 74–6, report of Antipov to Eikhe of 20 October 1928; *GAAK*, f. 917, op. 1, d. 10, l. 10–12, Bulletin 1/7, 15 October 1928 of Biisk Okrug Procuracy; *GANO* 1, f. r-47, op. 1, d. 697, l. 67–8 (Turukhansk).
64. A.B. Lunacharsky, *Mesiats po sibiri* (Moscow, *izdat'elstvo krasnaia gazeta*, 1929), pp. 30–1.

65. *RTsKhIDNI*, f. 17, op. 2, d. 397, l. 70, stenogram of the November 1928 Central Committee plenum; *XVI konf.*, pp. 286–7, 747. The tax total for 1928–29 was reduced from 400 million roubles to 375 million.
66. Stalin, *Sochineniia*, Vol. 11, p. 248.
67. *GANO* 1, f. r-47, op. 1, d. 696, l. 140–3, telegram from Stalin and Rykov to Syrtsov, Eikhe, Klokov (Novosibirsk Okruzhkom Secretary) and Zaitsev (Novosibirsk Okrispolkom Chairman) of 29 November 1928.
68. For the Eikhe/Syrtsov telegrams see *GANO* 1, f. r-47, op. 1, d. 696, l. 159–60 (2 December), 164 (5 December), 172 (20 December), 175 (28 December); *IS*, No. 23–24, 30 December 1928, p. 1 (Kraikombiuro directive of 27 December).
69. *GANO* 1, f. r-47, op. 1, d. 696, l. 193, Report of Biisk Okruzhkom and Okrispolkom to the Kraiispolkom, 17 December 1928; *GANO* 2, f. 2, op. 2, d. 3128, l. 79, a report on grain procurement by Krasnoyarsk Okruzhkom, 25 December 1928; ibid., f. 2, op. 1, d. 3563, l. 11, supplement to protocol no. 1 of Kuznetsk Okruzhkombiuro, 30 December 1928.
70. *Otchet iv okruzhnoi partiinoi konferentsii, 25–30 Noiabria 1928* (Barnaul, *Izdat'elstvo krasnyi altai*, 1928), p. 3.
71. *GANO* 1, f. r-47, op. 1, d. 696, l. 169, report from Levin, Deputy Head of People's Commissariat of Finance RSFSR, of 12 December 1928 to Eikhe.
72. See, for example, *GANO* 1, f. r-47, op. 1, d. 696, l. 43, a letter from Rubtsovsk Okruzhkom and Okrispolkom to the Kraiispolkom of 26 September 1928 (on the ongoing problem of price differentials between Siberia and neighbouring northern Kazakhstan); ibid., l. 186–93, report from Biisk Okruzhkom and Okrispolkom to the Kraiispolkom of 17 December 1928. Railway wagon shortages in Siberia were such that in early November an estimated 31,424 tons of grain were stockpiled at Semipalatinsk station and surrounding areas, see ibid., l. 11–12, Narkomtorg Circular of 13 November 1928. For rail transport shortages in south-west Siberia see, ibid., l. 35 (Rubtsovk), 99 (Barnaul), 190 (Biisk).
73. *GANO* 1, f. r-47, op. 1, d. 696, l. 174, a letter from Zlobin to Zaitsev, Chairman of Novosibirsk Okrispolkom, of 21 December 1928. For working-class discontent in the country during the Soviet elections see Viola, p. 223 note 64. The introduction of rationing in late 1928 is mentioned at *XVI konf.*, pp. 21 (Rykov), 772, note 12.
74. *RTsKhIDNI*, f. 17, op. 3, d. 726, l. 3–4, Protocol No. 64 of Politburo session of 14 February 1929; *GANO* 1, f. r-47, op. 1, d. 697, l. 206–8, Protocol No. 22/a of Sovnarkom RSFSR session of 15 February 1929 (amending a decree of 2 February 1929). Rationing in Moscow and Leningrad was tightened further by the Politburo in early March: *RTsKhIDNI*, f. 17, op. 3, d. 729, l. 1, 4, Protocol No. 67 of 7 March 1929.

CHAPTER 2   MOBILIZING SOCIAL INFLUENCE

1. *GAAK*, f. 917, op. 1, d. 10, l. 99, joint circular of OGPU, Krai Judiciary and Krai Procuracy, 22 December 1928.
2. *GANO* 1, f. r-47, op. 1, d. 593, l. 1, Protocol of Kraikombiuro session of 14 January 1929; ibid., l. 2–4, 6–7 (OGPU reports); *GANO* 1, f. r-47, op.

1, d. 696, l. 204, a letter from Eikhe to Kraitorg of 5 March 1929 on railway disruption.
3. Kraikom instructions on the conduct of the soviet elections made it clear that the aim was to destroy kulak authority in the countryside as much as possible; see *GANO* 2, f. 2, op. 2, d. 373, l. 255, telegram from the Kraikom (Kisis), to all okruzhkoms, 27 December 1928 (via GPU). The purge of party members continued well into 1929 and resulted in the expulsion of 4,635 members (18.2 per cent of the total); see *GANO*, f. 7, op. 1, d. 102, l. 153. For hostility to ex-partisans see *GANO* 2, f. 2, op. 2, d. 373, l. 291, telegram no. 616/c from the Kraikom (Kisis) and Head of the Department for Work in the Countryside (Komarov) to all okruzhkoms, 25 January 1929.
4. For the renewed focus on organizing the *bednota* see *Pravda*, 25 October 1928; *KPSS v rezoliutsiiakh*, Vol. 4, p. 395; *IS*, No. 1–2, 25 January 1929, pp. 8–9; *GANO* 2, f. 2, op. 2, d. 373, l. 261–2, unsigned letter from Secretary of the Sibkraikom and Department for Work in the Countryside to all obkoms, okruzhkoms, raikoms, rural cells, undated (December 1928?).
5. More than 1,000 were already in the countryside in January to assist with the organization of the soviet elections: B. Kavraisky, '*Podkhod rabochikh na kulaka*', *NLP*, No. 3, 15 February 1929, pp. 44–7.
6. *Sovetskaia sibir'*, 3 and 4 January 1929, p. 1. See also note ? above.
7. N. Ya. Gushchin, *Sibirskaia derevnia na puti k sotsializmu* (Novosibirsk, *Nauka*, 1973), pp. 195–6, 198–200; V.A. Kavraisky and P. Khamarmer, *Uroki klassovoi bor'by. Itogi vyborov v sovety sibiri. 1928–1929 gg.*, (Novosibirsk, *Kraiizdat*, 1929), pp. 6, 10, 17; *Sibirskii krai statisticheskii spravochnik* (Novosibirsk, *Kraiizdat*, 1930), pp. 60–1; *GANO* 1, f. r-47, op. 1, d. 697, l. 76–9.
8. *Pravda*, 5 December 1928; 10 and 26 January 1929.
9. *GANO* 2, f. 2, op. 4, d. 33, l. 34, Protocol No. 128/b of Kraikombiuro session of 11 January 1929.
10. *GANO* 2, f. 2, op. 2, d. 373, l. 265, directive from Syrtsov to okruzhkoms, undated (probably early January 1929).
11. *GANO* 2, f. 2, op. 4, d. 33, l. 36, Protocol No. 129/b of Kraikombiuro session of 17 January 1929. For the decree see *GANO* 1, f. r-47, op. 1, d. 697, telegram from the Kraikom (Kisis) and Kraiispolkom (Eikhe) to secretaries of okruzhkoms and chairmen of okrispolkoms, 18 January 1929 (via OGPU). See also *GANO* 1, f. r-47, op. 1, d. 697, letter telegram from the Kraikom (Kuznetsov) and Kraiispolkom (Eikhe) to all okruzhkoms and okrispolkoms, 17 January 1929, also on collection of payments.
12. *RTsKhIDNI*, f. 17, op. 3, d. 722, l. 1, Protocol No. 60 of Politburo session of 17 January 1929. This may have been the proposal that Vaganov refers to – see p. 64.
13. *GANO* 2, f. 2, op. 4, d. 33, l. 46, Protocol No. 130/b of Kraikombiuro session of 18 January 1929. For Mikoyan's telegram see ibid., l. 21, Protocol No. 127/b of 8 January 1928.
14. For documents relating to this affair see *GANO* 1, f. r-47, op. 4a, d. 218, l. 23–9.
15. *GANO* 1, f. 288, op. 1, d. 536, l. 16–18; *Sovetskaia sibir'*, 22 February 1929; *GANO* 1, f. r-47, op. 1, d. 697, l. 80.

16. *GANO* 2, f. 2, op. 2, d. 373, l. 272, letter-telegram from the Kraikom (Kisis) to all okruzhkoms, 19 January 1929; *GANO* 2, f. 2, op. 4, d. 33, l. 48, Protocol No. 131/b of Kraikombiuro session of 20 January 1929.
17. For Eikhe's speech see *GANO* 2, f. 2, op. 1, d. 3449, l. 4–6. The slogan was that of I.A. Vyshnegradsky (Minister of Finance 1886–92), who aimed to squeeze peasant consumption in order to boost grain exports and thereby eliminate the Russian balance of payments deficit; see O. Crisp, *Studies in the Russian Economy before 1914* (London, Macmillan, 1976), Chapter 4.
18. *GANO* 2, f. 2, op. 1, d. 3449, l. 144–5.
19. *GANO* 2, f. 1, op. 1, d. 3448, l. 182–4 (Mikoyan's speech). See also *Sovetskaia sibir'*, 26 January 1929.
20. *GANO* 2, f. 2, op. 1, d. 3072, l. 116, report of Achinsk Okruzhkom on grain procurement, 10 February 1929.
21. *GANO* 1, f. r. 47, op. 1, d. 696, l. 195, extract of Protocol No. 118 of Novosibirsk Okrispolkom, 24 January 1929, signed by the Head of the Secret Section, A. Bykov. Further details are in the supplement to the above; ibid., l. 194, telegram to raikoms from Novosibirsk Okrispolkom of 25 January 1929. Syrtsov's report is mentioned at *GANO* 2, f. 2, op. 4, d. 33, l. 55, Protocol No. 132/b Kraikombiuro of 24 January 1929.
22. For the use of Article 107 and Stalin's role in its application see Hughes (1991), pp. 141–2, 151–9.
23. *GANO* 2, f. 2, op. 4, d. 33a, l. 3–4, supplement to Protocol No. 133/b of Kraikombiuro session of 28 January 1929 (special reprimand). For Stalin's telegram to all party organizations of 6 January 1928 see *GANO* 1, f. r-47, op. 4a, d. 119, l. 153–153a (Document 1).
24. Ibid., f. 2, op. 4, d. 33, l. 81, Protocol No. 137/b of Kraikombiuro session of 2 February 1929.
25. *GANO* 2, f. 2, op. 4, d. 33, l. 91–2, Protocol No. 139/b of Kraikombiuro session of 12 February 1929; ibid., l. 93–6, Supplement to Protocol No. 139/b (a draft of the decree); *GANO* 1, f. r-47, op. 1, d. 697, l. 218, telegram from Kraikom (Kuznetsov) and Kraiispolkom (Voronin) to okruzhkoms and okrispolkoms of 6 February 1929. Siberia received about 1,200 railway wagons of manufactured goods between October 1928 and the end of March 1929, and by late March 82 of every 100 were directed into the countryside; *Sovetskaia sibir'*, 31 March 1929.
26. The Sovnarkom decree was incorporated into a revised decree issued by the Presidium of the Kraiispolkom on 18 February; see *GANO* 1, f. r. 47, d. 696, l. 205. For Eikhe's anti-kulak views see Hughes (1991), pp. 46, 49, 100–1, 186.
27. *RTsKhIDNI*, f. 17, op. 3, d. 729, l. 6, item 30 of Protocol No. 67 of Politburo session of 7 March 1929; ibid., l. 10, Supplement No. 2, telegram from Sibkraikom of 27 February 1929.
28. *Sobranie zakonov i rasporiazhenii*, No. 12, 1929, pp. 102–3. On the same day another decree further tightened restrictions on the hiring of labour in agriculture; ibid., No. 14, 1929, p. 117.
29. *Chetvertaia sib. part. konf.*, p. 167 (Kuznetsova reporting on events in Minusinsk Okrug).
30. Ibid., p. 289 (Maimin).
31. See P. Semenikhin, '*O propushchennykh kulak i nevycishchennykh kommunistakh*', *NLP*, No. 5–6, 30 March 1929, pp. 51–5.

32. *GANO* 1, f. 1570, op. 1, d. 35, l. 62, Protocol No. 2 of Kraikombiuro session of 3 February 1929.
33. See *Sovetskaia sibir'*, 20 February 1929, p. 1; ibid., 23 March 1929, p. 1; *GANO* 1, f. r-47, op. 1, d. 696, l. 198–203, report on the grain procurement situation in Slavgorod Okrug, 16 March 1929.
34. *GANO* 2, f. 2, op. 2, d. 355, l. 1–33, 'Stenogram of Kraikombiuro session (14 March 1929)'. Parts of this document were doctored for political correctness, but the original stenogram is still discernable. For the Krai Procuracy report on these events see *GANO* 1, f. r-47, op. 4a, d. 218, l. 31–4, report of Rubtsovsk Procuracy of 14 March 1929.
35. *GANO* 2, f. 2, op. 2, d. 355, l. 1.
36. For a discussion of *samosud* and charivari see Stephen P. Frank, 'Popular Justice, Community and Culture among the Russian Peasantry, 1870–1900', in Ben Eklof and Stephen P. Frank (eds), *The World of the Russian Peasant, Post-Emancipation Culture and Society* (London, Unwin Hyman, 1990), pp. 133–53.
37. Author's interview with Yegor Efimovich Mikhailov, Novosibirsk, 29 January 1995.
38. *GANO* 2, f. 2, op. 2, d. 355, l. 3.
39. Ibid., l. 5–8. A special letter instructing that Article 58 was not to be used for grain procurement was also sent out by the Kraikom in the middle of February; see ibid., l. 30.
40. *GANO* 1, f. r-47, op. 4a, d. 218, l. 31–4, report from Rubtsovsk Okrug Procuracy on the kulak band '*trudguzh*', 15 March 1929.
41. Ibid., l. 33.
42. Ibid., l. 9.
43. *GANO* 1, f. r. 47, op. 4a, d. 218, l. 35–35ab, a report note from Krai Procurator, D.A. Lisin, to Syrtsov of 19 March 1929.
44. Ibid., l. 10–11.
45. *GANO* 1, f. r-47, op. 4a, d. 218, l. 32.
46. Ibid., l. 12–13 (Komarov).
47. Ibid., l. 15–18 (Ksenofontov).
48. Ibid., l. 21–2 (Lyaksutkin).
49. Ibid., l. 23–6 (Eikhe), 27–8 (Kisis), 29–32 (Syrtsov). For the full Kraikombiuro decision on this affair see ibid., f. 2, op. 4, d. 34, l. 9, Supplement to Protocol No. 3/b. A Kraikombiuro statement on the matter was published in *IS*, No. 8, 30 April 1929, p. 4.
50. *Pravda*, 16 and 24 February 1929.
51. Y. Taniuchi, 'A Note on the Ural-Siberian Method', *Soviet Studies*, Vol. 33, No. 4, October 1981, pp. 519–21. See also J. Hughes, 'Capturing the Russian Peasantry: Stalinist Grain Procurement Policy and the "Ural-Siberian Method"', *Slavic Review*, Vol. 53, No. 1, Spring 1994, p. 77.

CHAPTER 3   THE SEARCH FOR A NEW METHOD

1. *Pravda*, 19 July 1929.
2. *Chetvertaia sib. part. konf.*, pp. 25, 29 (Syrtsov), 158 (Eikhe), 185 (Kuznetsov), 263 (Zlobin).
3. Ibid., p. 168 (Krylov).

4. Ibid., pp. 28–9.
5. Ibid., p. 29.
6. For the Right's critique on 'military-feudal exploitation' see pp. 81, 231 note 21.
7. *Chetvertaia sib. part. konf.*, pp. 46–8. Much of this is repeated verbatim in his speech to the Sixteenth Party Conference, see *XVI konf.*, pp. 319–26.
8. Ibid., p. 83 (Bezhanova from Novosibirsk).
9. *Chetvertaia sib. part. konf.*, pp. 117–18.
10. Ibid., pp. 136–7.
11. Ibid., pp. 270–1 (Kavraisky), and see also p. 263 (Zlobin).
12. Ibid., pp. 140–1 (Nusinov).
13. Ibid., pp. 158–9.
14. For support of the grain loan and attacks on the 'Right deviation' see Ibid., pp. 192–3 (Buzov), 166–7 (Kuznetsova, Minusinsk Okruzhkom Secretary), 169–90 (Ksenofontov), 182–3 (Kuznetsov).
15. Ibid., pp. 167–9. See also his article, '*Za planovost' khlebozagotovkakh*', *NLP*, No. 10, 31 May 1929, pp. 23–9.
16. Ibid., pp. 184–5.
17. Ibid., p. 252. In the 'Platform of the Left' of September 1927 Trotsky had proposed a forced grain loan from the wealthiest 10 per cent of the peasantry, amounting to 150–200 million puds: L.D. Trotsky, *The Real Situation in Russia*, trans. Max Eastman (London, Allen Lane, 1928).
18. *Chetvertaia sib. part. konf.*, pp. 210–11.
19. Ibid., pp. 238–9. Zakovsky was also a reluctant supporter of the grain loan, see Ibid., 252–3.
20. V.A. Kavraisky and I.I. Nusinov, *Klassy i klassovye otnosheniia v sovremmennoi sovetskoi derevne* (Novosibirsk, *Kraiizdat*, 1929). For a discussion of this study and the peasant differentiation debate in Siberia see Hughes (1991), pp. 88–96.
21. See *Chetvertaia sib. part. konf.*, pp. 251 (Lyapin, Barabinsk Okruzhkom Secretary), 253–4 (Zakovsky), 271 (Kavraisky).
22. Ibid., pp. 314–23 (Syrtsov's speech of 1 March 1929).
23. *IS*, No. 5–6, 25 March 1929, p. 5.
24. *GANO* 2, f. 2, op. 4, d. 34, l. 5, Protocol No. 2/b of Kraikombiuro session of 9 March 1929; *Pravda*, 9 March 1929.
25. *GANO* 2, f. 2, op. 4, d. 34, l. 5, Protocol No. 2/b, part 3.
26. *Itogi IV sibirskoi kraevoi partiinoi konferentsii* (Novosibirsk, *Kraiizdat*, 1929), p. 28.
27. *GANO* 2, f. 2, op. 2, d. 432, l. 79.
28. Stalin, *Sochineniia*, Vol. 12, p. 88.
29. *RTsKhIDNI*, f. 17, op. 3, d. 731, l. 4–5, Protocol No. 69 of Politburo session of 21 March 1929, approving its decision of 20 March on grain procurement. The decision was signed by Stalin. For Tomsky's comment see *RTsKhIDNI*, f. 17, op. 2, d. 417, p. 36.
30. Taniuchi (1981), especially pp. 521–4; Lewin (1968), pp. 388–95.
31. Tanuichi (1981), p. 518.
32. Moshkov, pp. 52–3. The Central Committee plenum did not meet until 16–23 April. The discussions at the Politburo sessions on 30 January and 9 February predated the adoption of the measure known as the 'Ural-Siberian

method' on 20 March. The main agenda at these sessions focused on statements by the Right (Bukharin, Rykov, Tomsky) complaining about overtaxation of peasants and claiming that party policy in the countryside represented a 'military-feudal exploitation of the peasantry': *XVI konf.*, pp. 745, 806–7.
33. F.M. Vaganov, *Pravyi uklon v vkp (b) i ego razgrom (1928–1930 gg.)*, (Moscow, *Politizdat*, 1970), p. 154. The author has only found one joint proposal to the Politburo from the Siberian and Urals party committees around this time, and it concerned reductions in grain procurement plans, see note 12, p. 000 above. Taniuchi (1981), p. 521 and Lewin (1968), pp. 388–9, misconstrue the new method for the measures of social influence applied in the first months of 1929.
34. *RTsKhIDNI*, f. 17, op. 3, d. 732, l. 5, Protocol No. 70 of Politburo session of 28 March, including notes of Politburo session of 25 March. The speakers were listed in the following order: Bukharin, Voroshilov, Kuibyshev, Molotov, Rykov, Stalin, Tomsky, Mikoyan, Chubar', Yaroslavsky, Smirnov, Kubyak, Skiryatov, Bauman, Yakovlev, Litvinov, Rukhimovich, Briukhanov, Krzhizhanovsky, Sokol'nikov, Pyatikov, Kamenev, Trilisser.
35. Vaganov, p. 234; Stalin, *Sochineniia*, Vol. 12, pp. 92–5; *Pravda*, 19 July 1929 (Kalinin); *XVI konf.*, p. 780 note 56.
36. *KPSS v rezoliutsiiakh*, Vol. 4, pp. 449–54.
37. *Sovetskaia sibir'*, 22 March 1929.
38. *GANO* 2, f. 2, op. 4, d. 34, l. 13, Protocol No. 4/b of Kraikombiuro session of 21 March 1929. See also Ibid., f. 2, op. 1, d. 2597, l. 890, an instruction letter from Kavraisky to all okruzhkoms of 2 April 1929.
39. *GANO* 2, f. 2, op. 4, d. 34, l. 17–18, supplement to Protocol No. 4/b of 21 March 1929.
40. *GANO* 2, f. 2, op. 2, d. 351, l. 171, from his speech to the joint plenum of the Kraikom and Kraiispolkom in early June.
41. *GANO* 1, f. r-47, op. 4a, d. 218, l. 35–35ab. For the Kraikom directive of 12 February see p. 00 above. See also the decree of Novosibirsk Okrispolkom of 24 January on self taxation discussed on p. 00 above.
42. *GANO* 1, f. r-47, op. 1, d. 696, l. 203, a short report on the grain procurement situation in Slavgorod Okrug, 16 March 1929.
43. *GANO* 2, f. 1570, op. 1, d. 34, l. 27.
44. Lars T. Lih, *Bread and Authority in Russia, 1914–1921* (Oxford, Oxford University Press, 1990), pp. 10–12, 33, 59–61.
45. Lih, pp. 128–36, 188, note 48. Lih cites Soviet estimates of 20,000 Bolshevik casualties from rural duties in 1918. For the decrees establishing the Kombedy and grain requisition detachments in 1918 see Martin McCauley (ed.), *The Russian Revolution and the Soviet State 1917–1921, Documents* (London, Macmillan, 1975), pp. 247–50.
46. Lih, pp. 169–84.
47. The reference to the 'Chinese–Mongol system' is in Richard Pipes, *The Russian Revolution, 1899–1919* (London, Collins Harvill, 1990), p. 742; see also his *Russia Under the Old Regime* (Harmondsworth, Penguin, 1979), pp. 55–6, 74–6. Collective responsibility for taxation and the origins of peasant egalitarianism is discussed in Dorothy Atkinson, 'Egalitarianism and the Commune' in Roger Bartlett (ed.), *Land Commune and Peasant Community in Russia* (London, Macmillan, 1990), pp. 7–19. As early as

1423 Royal estate peasants were assessed for tax 'according to their ability' to pay: see R.E.F. Smith (ed.), *The Enserfment of the Russian Peasantry* (Cambridge, Cambridge University Press, 1968), p. 48, and his *Peasant Farming in Muscovy* (London, Cambridge University Press, 1977), pp. 224–30.

48. For the persistence of the authority of the commune in the 1920s see the studies by Y. Taniuchi, *The Village Gathering in Russia in the Mid-1920s* (Birmingham, Birmingham University Press, 1968), and D.J. Male, *Russian Peasant Organisation Before Collectivisation: A Study of Commune and Gathering, 1925–30* (Cambridge, Cambridge University Press, 1971).

49. A.M. Bol'shakov, *The Soviet Countryside 1917–1924, Its Economics and Life* (Leningrad, *Priboi*, 1924), in R.E.F. Smith (ed. and trans.), *The Russian Peasant* (London, Frank Cass, 1974), pp. 29–61 at p. 48.

CHAPTER 4   THE URAL-SIBERIAN METHOD

1. *Sovetskaia sibir'*, 22 March 1929, p. 1. There are, in fact, two villages with this name in Novosibirsk Okrug, one in Berdsk raion and the other in Gutovsk raion. That it was a propaganda exercise is suggested also by the lack of detail in O. Barabashev, '*Nekotorye itogi "zav'ialovskogo opyta"*', *NLP*, No. 10, 31 May 1929, pp. 30–3.
2. *GANO* 2, f. 64, op. 1, d. 16, Protocol No. 2 of Kamensk Raikom plenum, 22–23 March 1929; ibid., f. 2, op. 1, d. 2597, l. 899–901. The 'service note' is unsigned and the name of the raikom is illegible.
3. *Sobranie zakonov i rasporiazhenii*, 1928, No. 3, Article 29.
4. *GANO* 1, f. 1570, op. 1, d. 34, l. 36, Protocol No. 6 of a general meeting, 30 March 1929; ibid., l. 70–2, Protocol No. 4 of a rural soviet meeting, undated (late March 1929?); ibid., l. 77, Protocol No. 1 of a *bednota* group meeting, 28 March 1929; ibid., l. 79, Protocol No. 1 of a village *troika* meeting, 31 March 1929.
5. Gushchin (1973), pp. 192–3.
6. *GANO* 2, f. 2, op. 1, d. 2597, l. 922–6, secret telegram from Mikoyan to Syrtsov, Eikhe and Zlobin, received on 25 March 1929.
7. *GANO* 2, f. 2, op. 4, d. 33, l. 183, Protocol No. 7/b of Kraikombiuro session of 27 March 1929. For an example of how the Kraikombiuro decree and Kaganovich's amendments were translated into action by Tulun Okruzhkom see *GANO* 2, f. 2, op. 1, d. 3862, l. 144, 148, 151. For Article 61 see *Sobranie uzakonenie i rasporiazhenii raboche-krest'ianskogo pravitel'stva*, No. 60, 1929, Articles 589, 590, 591.
8. *GANO* 2, f. 2, op. 2, d. 378, l. 22–3a. Kaganovich proceeded on to Sverdlovsk in the Urals Oblast where he presumably ordered the adoption of the measures taken by the Siberians. For the instruction-letter see ibid., f. 2, op. 1, d. 2597, l. 890.
9. *GANO* 1, f. 288, op. 1, d. 536, l. 24–4ob.
10. *GAAK*, f. 917, op. 1, d. 10, l. 222, directive from Vranetsky (Krai Judicial Department) and Kupryanov (Krai Procurator) to Chairmen of Okrug Judicial Departments and Okrug Procurators, 5 April 1929. For mention of the Kraikom directive of 9 April see *GANO* 1, f. r. 47, op. 1, d. 697, l. 31.

Notes 231

11. *GANO* 2, f. 2, op. 21, d. 4099, l. 92–104, Krai Finance Department Instruction, 'On revealing clear-kulak households and levying the richest part of kulak households with individual supplements under the Agricultural Tax' (undated), April 1929.
12. Ibid., l. 93, 97.
13. *Sotsialisticheskii vestnik*, No. 6 (196), 22 March 1929, p. 11; ibid., No. 9 (199), 4 May 1929, p. 10.
14. *RTsKhIDNI*, f. 17, op. 2, d. 417, pp. 73–98, Bukharin's speech of 18 April.
15. Stalin, *Sochineniia*, Vol. 12, pp. 86–92, 374 note 1, his speech of 22 April 1929. Also at *RTsKhIDNI*, f. 17, op. 2, d. 417, pp. 236–63.
16. For a discussion of Stalin's militancy during the grain crisis of 1927/8 see Hughes (1991), pp. 137–48, 152–3.
17. Central Committee decrees of 15 June and 20 October 1929 organized the mobilizing of poor and middle peasants as social bases of support in the countryside: see pp. 129–30.
18. *XVI konf.*, pp. 83 note 215, 806 note 236.
19. *RTsKhIDNI*, f. 17, op. 2, d. 375, p. 115.
20. Stalin, *Sochineniia*, Vol. 11, p. 256, a speech of 19 November 1928.
21. At the Politburo session on 9 February, Bukharin, Rykov and Tomsky had issued a written declaration to this effect: *RTsKhIDNI*, f. 17, op. 2, d. 417, p. 12.
22. Ibid., p. 35.
23. Stalin, *Sochineniia*, Vol. 11, p. 48.
24. The personalized nature of the breach between Stalin and the Right was revealed by Bukharin in his secret conversations with Kamenev in July 1928: see p. 221, note 29.
25. *RTsKhIDNI*, f. 17, op. 2, d. 417, pp. 50–3, stenogram of the April 1929 Central Committee plenum.
26. *XVI konf.*, pp. 780, note 57, 781 note 63, 76 (Kuibyshev), 174 (Khloplyankin).
27. Ibid., p. 387 (Sheboldaev). Lewin (1968), p. 390 takes the reference to 'community' as meaning 'the party cell, if there was one, the local officials, and the local bednyak group, or simply a number of bednyaks with no group organisation'.
28. *XVI konf.*, pp. 91–2.
29. Ibid., pp. 319–26.
30. The Siberian Kraikom was the first regional party committee in the country to take a decision to exclude kulaks from joining kolkhozes, at its Fourth Conference in late February–early March. The centre did not reach a decision on this until the November 1929 plenum.
31. *XVI konf.*, p. 86.
32. N. Briukhanov, 'Itogi khlebnoi kampanii 1928/29 goda', *Ekonomicheskoe obozrenie*, No. 11, November 1929, p. 133.
33. Moshkov, pp. 50, 53; *IS*, No. 11, 15 June 1929, pp. 4–5.
34. See Davies (1980), Table 8, pp. 430–1. Siberia (including the Far East and Buryat-Mongolia ASSR) contributed over 1.9 million tons against the Ukraine's 1.8 million tons.
35. For Syrtsov's career see Hughes (1991), pp. 31–3, 202–3, and S.A. Kislitsyn, *Variant Syrtsova: iz istorii formirovaniya antistalinskogo soprotivleniya v sovetskom obshchestve v 20–30-e gg.* (Rostov-on-Don, *Nauchno-*

metodicheskii tsentr 'Logos', 1992), especially pp. 67–8, 74–6, 127–8. For the promotions see *RTsKhIDNI*, f. 17, op. 3, d. 741, l. 2, Protocol No. 81 of Politburo session of 23 May 1929, items 10 and 11; ibid., d. 745, l. 2, Protocol No. 85 of Politburo session of 20 June 1929, decisions of Politburo of 17 June 1929, item 26; *Pravda*, 5 June 1929.

36. *RTsKhIDNI*, f. 17, op. 3, d. 738, l. 1, Protocol No. 78 of the Politburo session of 3 May 1929 (and its supplement No. 1); ibid., d. 741, l. 2, Protocol No. 81 of Politburo session of 23 May 1929, item 7.
37. *GANO* 1, f. r-47, op. 1, d. 697, l. 84–5, situation reports on grain procurement to the Kraiispolkom, 10 June 1929.
38. *GANO* 2, f. 2, op. 2, d. 351, l. 137–8, stenogram of the joint plenum of the Kraikom and Krai Control Commission, 1–3 June 1929; *GANO* 1, f. r-47, op. 1, d. 697, l. 34, telegram from Chernov (Moscow) to Kraitorg, Zlobin, 29 May 1929.
39. *GANO* 1, f. r. 47, op. 1, d. 697, l. 35, Circular No. 11 of 17 May 1929, from the Deputy Chief of the Krai Militia, Makarov, to all okrug militia chiefs; *GANO* 2, f. 2, op. 2, d. 351, l. 229, speech of Larin to the July joint plenum of the Kraikom and Kraiispolkom.
40. *GANO* 2, f. 2, op. 2, d. 351, l. 155, 172.
41. *GANO* 2, f. 2, op. 2, d. 351, l. 145–50 (Zlobin), 178 (Gordienko).
42. Ibid., l. 154–9.
43. Ibid., l. 161–3.
44. A. Zlobin, '*Vypolnim plan zagotovok*', *NLP*, No. 8, 30 April 1929, p. 26.
45. Ibid., l. 173 (Kavraisky), 179 (Voronin), 198 (Eikhe), 224–5 (Spirov). For Eikhe's appointment see *IS*, No. 11, 15 June 1929, p. 9.
46. A. Redfield, *The Little Community and Peasant Society and Culture*. Chicago: University of Chicago Press, 1971.

CHAPTER 5 *VOLYNKI*: THE RUSSIAN *JACQUERIE*

1. G. Rudé, *Ideology and Popular Protest* (London, Lawrence and Wishart, 1980).
2. John Bohstedt, *Riots and Community Politics in England and Wales, 1790–1810* (Cambridge, Mass., Cambridge University Press, 1989), p. 27.
3. For these categories of peasant action see T. Shanin (1972), pp. 215–16.
4. See note 7, p. 220.
5. Hughes (1991), pp. 10–11.
6. E.J. Hobsbawm and G. Rude, *Captain Swing* (London, Lawrence and Wishart, 1969), p. 176.
7. A. Zlobin, '*Vypolnim plan khlebozagotovok!*', *NLP*, No. 8, 30 April 1929, pp. 23–7 at p. 25.
8. E.H. Carr, *The Bolshevik Revolution 1917–1923*, Vol. 2 (Harmondsworth, Penguin, 1972), p. 154.
9. *GANO* 2, f. 2, op. 2, d. 386, l. 281; ibid., f. 4, op. 2, d. 374, l. 109, decree of Slavgorod Okruzhkom on grain procurement of 23 June 1929; Gushchin (1973), p. 194; *XVI konf.*, p. 322 (Syrtsov).
10. *GANO* 2, f. 2, op. 2, d. 3128, l. 102–3; ibid., d. 386, l. 281–2; *GANO* 1, f. r-47, op. 1, d. 697, l. 72.

11. See, for example, the situation reports on grain procurement to the Kraiispolkom for May–June 1929: *GANO* 1, f. r. 47, op. 1, d. 697, 1. 82–90.
12. *GANO* 2, f. 2, op. 2, d. 386, 1. 249, Kraikom information report, 12 April 1929.
13. The following examples are taken from *GANO* 2, f. 2, op. 2, d. 386, 1. 288–91, Supplement no. 2, Kraikom information report, 30 May 1929: 'Incidents of the use of women by kulaks against grain procurement'; and *GANO* 1, f. r-47, op. 1, d. 697, 1. 73–5, Bulletin No. 14/15 of the Krai Procuracy to the Kraiispolkom, 12 June 1929.
14. For a detailed report of this incident see: *GANO* 2, f. 2, op. 1, d. 2866, 1. 144–5.
15. *GANO* 1, f. 1228, op. 3, d. 14, 1. 708–13, based on OGPU investigations up to 1 July 1929.
16. *GANO* 2, f. 2, op. 1, d. 2866, 1. 142–6, 'On Mass Protests Against Grain Procurement', from materials of the Information-Political Department of Biisk Okruzhkom, 7 May 1929.
17. *GANO* 2, f. 2, op. 7, d. 520, 1. 5–6: *Rezoliutsii ob'edinennogo plenuma biiskogo okruzhnogo komiteta i kontrol'noi komissii vkp (b), iv sozyva (12–17 maya 1929)*.
18. *GANO* 2, f. 2, op. 1, d. 2866, 1. 142ob, 145ob. For this incident see also: *GANO* 2, f. 2, op. 2–1, d. 3506, 1. 3–4, report of Biisk Okruzhkom, 21 April 1929.
19. I. Gladkov, '*Verkh-Chumysh urok*', *NLP*, No. 1–2, 15 January 1929, pp. 74–83.
20. *GANO* 2, f. 2, op. 2, d. 386, 1. 282–4, Kraikom information report, 30 May 1929. For Kaganovich's tour see p. 000. Civil war abuses perpetrated by the Siberian peasantry are reported in Maxim Gorky, 'On the Russian Peasantry' in Smith (1977), p. 17.
21. *GANO* 2, f. 2, op. 2, d. 429, 1. 5, letter from Kovalev to Eikhe (undated, mid-July 1929).
22. *XVI konf.*, p. 323.
23. For types of peasant protest see Landsberger, pp. 21–2, 49–51.
24. *GANO* 2, f. 2, op. 2, d. 351, 1. 166, stenogram of the Joint Plenum of the Kraikom and Kraiispolkom, 1–3 June 1929 (Sergeeva).
25. *GANO* 2, f. 2, op. 2, d. 386, 1. 243, 247, from a Kraikom report of 12 April 1929.
26. A. Chekhov, '*Muzhiki*', *Izbrannoe* (Leningrad, *Lenizdat*, 1982), p. 432.
27. *GANO* 2, f. 2, op. 2, d. 386, 1. 244, 248, 278–9.
28. *GANO* 1, f. 1570, op. 1, d. 34, 1. 27, Protocol of general meeting, 13 March 1929.
29. *GANO* 2, f. 1570, op. 1, d. 34, 1. 50, Protocol of general meeting of Ust'-Insk, 22 September 1929.
30. *GANO* 1, f. r-47, op. 1, d. 697, 1. 72, Bulletin No. 14/15 of the Krai Procuracy to the Kraiispolkom, 12 June 1929.
31. *Sovetskaia sibir'*, 10 April 1929.
32. *GANO* 2, f. 2, op. 2, d. 386, 1. 242, report of the Kraikom Information-Statistical Political Department, 12 April 1929.
33. *GANO* 1, f. r-47, op. 1, d. 697, 1. 212, telegram from Eikhe and Kavraisky to all okruzhkoms, 17 April 1929.

34. *GANO* 2, f. 2, op. 2, d. 393, l. 35, telegram from Shibailo in Sibkraikom to Syrtsov (his hands only), Siberian delegation, Moscow, 13 April 1929 (via OGPU); ibid., d. 386, l. 273, Kraikom information report, 30 May 1929.
35. *GANO* 2, f. 2, op. 2, d. 386, l. 274–5, Kraikom information report, 30 May 1929.
36. *GANO* 1, f. r. 47, op. 1, d. 697, l. 204–5, telegram from Kamensk Okruzhkom (Kandeev) and Okriispolkom (Uzlikov) to Eikhe, 22 April 1929.
37. *GANO* 2, f. 2, op. 1, d. 2597, l. 863–4, letter from P. Nekrasov of 3 April 1929.
38. *GANO* 2, f. 2, op. 2–1, d. 3506, l. 2, report of Biisk Okruzhkom of 21 April 1929.
39. *GANO* 2, f. 2, op. 2, d. 3443, l. 333, a letter of a peasant woman from the village of Karatuz, 14 April 1929.
40. *GANO* 1, f. r. 47, op. 1, d. 697, l. 114, information report from the Assistant Krai Procurator, Staroshcuk (date illegible, July–August 1929?). Such practices were a repeat of those in a notorious case from Kamensk Okrug during grain collection the previous year which had been sharply criticized by the Kraiispolkom in January 1929: ibid., l. 93–110.
41. *GANO* 2, f. 2, op. 2, d. 421, l. 93–6.
42. *GANO* 2, f. 2, op. 2, d. 366, l. 188 and 200.
43. Gushchin (1973), p. 192. For example, official figures for 14 raions of Omsk Okrug claimed that of those farms auctioned off 367 were kulak and 33 seredniak. In Barnaul Okrug, of 697 auctions, 639 were kulak and well-off and 21 were seredniak, and in Biisk, of 630 auctions, 609 were kulak and well-off and 21 seredniak; *NLP*, No. 8, 30 April 1929, p. 26.
44. *XVI konf.*, p. 388 (Sheboldaev, party secretary for Lower Volga).
45. *GANO* 1, f. r-47, op. 1, d. 697, l. 17–18, telegrams to okruzhkoms and okrispolkoms from Eikhe and Kavraisky, undated (after 9 April–before 20 April 1929).
46. Ibid., l. 19. For other examples see *GANO* 1, f. r-47, op. 1, d. 697, l. 17–19. The telegrams had a standard format.
47. *GANO* 1, f. r-47, op. 1, d. 697, l. 30.
48. Ibid., l. 29, telegram from Terikhov, Head of Secretariat of Chairman of VTsIK RSFSR, to Eikhe and Syrtsov, 1 April 1929; ibid., l. 20, letter to Secretariat of Chairman of VTsIK RSFSR, copy to Kraiispolkom, from Presidium Achinsk Okrispolkom, 22 April 1929.
49. *GANO* 1, f. r-47, op. 1, d. 697, l. 25, a telegram from Reshchikov (Kraiispolkom) to Chairman of Tomsk Okrispolkom, undated (probably mid-April 1929).
50. *GANO* 1, f. r-47, op. 1, d. 697, l. 31–31*ob*, Circular No. 10, from Krai Procurator Lisin to all Okrug Procurators, 30 April 1929.
51. *GANO* 1, f. r-47, op. 1, d. 697, l. 53–6, 60–5.
52. *GANO* 2, f. 2, op. 1, d. 2597, l. 510–12, report from Kovalev, Kamensk Okruzhkom Secretary to Kuznetsov, 25 September 1929.
53. *GANO* 1, f. r-47, op. 1, d. 697, l. 116, telegram from Kisis to all okruzhkoms, 17 August 1929.
54. *GANO* 2, f. 2, op. 1, d. 2597, l. 697, letter from Biisk Okruzhkom Secretary, Gredel', to the Kraikom, 26 June 1929.
55. *GANO* 2, f. 2, op. 4, d. 40, l. 94, letter from Burmistrov to Eikhe, 26 October

1929; ibid., l. 95–6, report of the Assistant Krai Procurator, Sadkovsky, on the Shipunovo case (undated).
56. *GANO* 2, f. 2, op. 2, d. 366, l. 189–98. For a similar case of scapegoating of a plenipotentiary in Novosibirsk Okrug see *GANO* 1, f. 1228, op. 3, d. 14. Concern about the numerous cases when property confiscated under Article 61 was auctioned of too cheaply was also raised at a meeting of Biisk Okrug Procuracy officials and OGPU representatives on 28 May 1929: *GAAK*, f. 917, op. 1, d. 10, l. 244–5.

CHAPTER 6 A PROLOGUE OF REPRESSION

1. *GANO* 1, f. r-47, op. 1, d. 697, l. 69, Sovnarkom RSFSR Circular No. 321.29/cc, signed A. Smirnov, 3 June 1929.
2. *RTsKhIDNI*, f. 17, op. 3, d. 744, l. 2, Protocol No. 84 of Politburo session of 13 June 1929, item 10 (b); ibid., d. 746, l. 1–2, 10, Protocol No. 86 of Politburo session of 27 June 1929, items 1 and 10, and Supplement No. 2 (for the draft decree).
3. *Sobranie uzakonenii i rasporiashenii*, 1929, Part 1, No. 60, Articles 589 and 591.
4. Ibid., Article 590. For Stalin's grain bounty see Hughes (1991), p. 142.
5. *Sovetskaia sibir'*, 4 July 1929. For an example of a local directive on the use of Article 61 see *GANO* 1, f. 1570, op. 1, d. 32, l. 151, a directive to rural soviet and consumer cooperatives from Kamensk Raiispolkom, Novosibirsk Okrug, 9 July 1929.
6. *GANO* 2, f. r-47, op. 4a, d. 218, l. 39–39*ob*, letter from Krai Procurator to Kraikom Secretary, 2 August 1929.
7. *GAAK*, f. 917, op. 1, d. 10, l. 253, Circular of the Krai Judicial Department and Krai Procuracy, 22 July 1929.
8. *GAAK*, f. 917, op. 1, d. 10, l. 257–8.
9. *GANO* 1, f. r-47, op. 4 a, d. 260 'a', l. 1–26 at l. 2–2*ob*, 7: 'Report of the Siberian Krai Procuracy on the Grain Procurement Campaign of 1929', signed Burmistrov, 3 February 1930. (NB: This was forwarded to the Kraiispolkom at the height of forced mass collectivization.)
10. Ibid., l. 38–38*ob*, Kraiispolkom decree, signed by Kuznetsov, to all okrispolkom chairmen, 17 August 1929.
11. *GANO* 2, f. 2, op. 1, d. 2597, l. 631, telegram from Eikhe to Zlobin, 31 July 1929.
12. A. Mikoyan, '*Novaia khlebozagotovitel'naia kampaniia i zadachi partii*', *Bol'shevik*, No. 15, 15 August 1929, pp. 15–24 at pp. 23–4.
13. Moshkov, pp. 63–4; V.P. Danilov, '*K kharakteristike obshchestvenno-politicheskoi obstanovki v sovetskoi derevne nakanune kollektivizatsii*', *Istoricheskie zapiski*, No. 79, 1967, p. 44.
14. *IS*, No. 11, 15 June 1929, p. 1.
15. Ibid., p. 5.
16. A. Zlobin, '*K novoi khlebozagotovitel'noi kampanii*', *NLP*, No. 13–14, 31 July 1929, pp. 59–68.
17. *KPSS v rezoliutsiiakh*, Vol. 4, pp. 515–22, especially pp. 521–2.
18. *GANO* 2, f. 2, op. 2, d. 351, l. 70 (Reznichenko), 96 (Kutyavin).

19. *IS*, No. 12, 15 July 1929, pp. 12-13.
20. *GANO* 1, f. r-47, op. 1, d. 697, l. 111-12, Narkomtorg Directive No. 63122/65c, signed Mikoyan and Stepanov, received by the Kraiispolkom on 10 July 1929.
21. *GANO* 1, f. r-47, op. 4a, d. 260 'a', l. 2-3.
22. *GANO* 1, f. r-47, op. 4a, d. 232 'b', l. 20-1, resolutions of a conference of heads of okrug militia on fulfilling grain procurement, 31 August 1929.
23. *NLP*, No. 13-14, 11 July 1929, pp. 48, 66.
24. Ibid., pp. 46-8, 53, 55.
25. *IS*, No. 12, 15 July 1929, p. 7; *NLP*, No. 17, 15 September 1929, p. 3.
26. *Pravda*, 12 September 1929.
27. Davies (1980), pp. 116-37.
28. Ibid., pp. 63-7.
29. *NLP*, No. 13-14, 31 July 1929, p. 44; Ibid., No. 17, 15 September 1929, p. 7; *GANO* 2, f. 2, op. 2, d. 467, l. 543, telegram from Krylov (Sibkraikom) to Eikhe (in Moscow), 25 June 1930.
30. *RTsKhIDNI*, f. 17, op. 3, d. 754, l. 9, Supplement to Protocol No. 94 of Politburo session of 22 August 1929; ibid., d. 755, l. 3, Protocol No. 95 of Politburo session of 29 August 1929, item 16 (d); ibid., d. 757, l. 2-4, Protocol No. 97 of Politburo session of 12 September 1929, items 13, 20; ibid., d. 758, l. 14-15, Supplement No. 3 to Protocol No. 98 of Politburo session of 19 September 1929.
31. *GANO* 1, f. r-47, op. 1, d. 697, l. 117-118, letter-directive of 9 September 1929.
32. *GANO* 1, f. 1570, op. 1, d. 32, l. 184-5.
33. C.B. Hoover, *The Economic Life of Soviet Russia* (London, Macmillan, 1931), pp. 95-6.
34. This bureaucratization is evident in the protocols of rural soviet meetings held in September-October 1929: *GANO* 1, f. 1570, op. 1, d. 53 (Ust' Insk rural soviet); ibid., 1356, op. 1, d. 106 (Berdsk raiispolkom).
35. *GANO* 1, f. r-47, op. 1, d. 697, l. 121-3, report of Kisis and Kuznetsov to Molotov, 16-17 September 1929.
36. *GANO* 1, f. r-47, op. 4a, d. 260 'a', l. 3ob-4.
37. *GANO* 2, f. 2, op. 2, d. 432, l. 5-7, letter from Khalatov to Eikhe, 20 November 1929.
38. *RTsKhIDNI*, f. 17, op. 3, d. 759, l. 10, Supplement No. 3 (affirmed 20 September 1929) to item 27 of Politburo session of 26 September 1929; ibid., d. 760, l. 3, item 15 of Protocol No. 100 of Politburo session of 28 September 1929; ibid., d. 761, l. 17, supplement Nos 3-4 to item 62 of Protocol No. 101 of Politburo session of 5 October 1929.
39. N. Zlobin, '*Bor'ba za khleb*', *ZS*, No. 11-12, November-December 1929, p. 24; *IS*, No. 19, 15 October 1929, pp. 1-2, 8-9; *NLP*, No. 18, 30 September 1929, pp. 3-4; *GANO* 1, f. r-47, op. 4 a, d. 260 'a', l. 3.
40. '*Raz"iasnenie kraevoi procurora*', *Sovetskaia sibir'*, 25 September 1929; *GANO* 2, f. 2, op. 4, d. 44a, l. 61, Order No. 2 of Krai Judicial Department and Krai Procuracy, 23 October 1929.
41. *RTsKhIDNI*, f. 17, op. 3, d. 761, l. 4, item 19 of Protocol No. 101 of Politburo session of 5 October 1929.
42. For this instruction see p. 78.

43. *GANO* 2, f. 2, op. 21, d. 4099, l. 9–10, report from the head of the Krai Financial Administrtion, Maimin, and the head of the Taxation Department, Zhavrin, to Eikhe, 14 December 1929.
44. *GANO* 1, f. r-47, op. 4 a, d. 260 'a', l. 1–26, Burmistrov's report of 3 February 1930.
45. *GANO* 1, f. r-47, op. 4a, d. 260 'a', l. 5–5ob.
46. Ibid., l. 5ob.
47. Ibid., l. 6ob–7ob.
48. Ibid., l. 8. Five to six million roubles had been raised by the sale of confiscated kulak property by December 1929, but the Krai Financial Department was concerned that much of it was being sold off too cheaply: *GANO* 2, f. 2, op. 21, d. 4099, l. 11–12, Protocol of a conference to discuss the sale of kulak property held by the Krai Financial Administration on 13 December 1929.
49. Ibid., l. 8–9.
50. Ibid., l. 10–15.
51. Ibid., l. 15–18, 25ob. The 525 cases compares with 681 for the nine months to September 1929.
52. M. Chernov, 'Na khlebnom fronte', *Bol'shevik*, No. 19, 15 October 1929, pp. 8–18 at p. 12.
53. For numerous cases of such abuses see *GANO* 1, f. r-47, op. 4a, d. 260 'a', l. 18–20ob.
54. *GANO* 1, f. 1570, op. 1, d. 53, l. 37, instruction from Novosibirsk Raiispolkom, 11 December 1929.
55. *GANO* 1, f. r-47, op. 4a, d. 260 'a', l. 21ob–22.
56. Ibid., l. 22ob. Based on figures from Omsk Okrug Procuracy for cases to 5 December 1929.
57. *KPSS v rezoliutsiiakh*, Vol. 4, pp. 567–70.
58. *GANO* 2, f. 2, op. 2, d. 432, l. 72.
59. *RTsKhIDNI*, f. 17, op. 3, d. 764, l. 3, item 17 of Protocol No. 105 of Politburo session of 25 October 1929; *GANO* 1, f. r-47, op. 4a, d. 260, l. 4–4ob.
60. Stalin, *Sochineniia*, Vol. 11, pp. 248–9, from his speech of 19 November 1928.
61. Ibid., Vol. 12, pp. 118–35 at p. 118.
62. Ibid., Vol. 12, p. 181, from his article, 'On the Question of the Policy of Liquidating the Kulaks as a Class', 21 January 1930.
63. Ibid., Vol. 12, pp. 125, 127–8, 131–2, 135.
64. For a discussion of the debates at the plenum see Davies (1980), pp. 159–69; *RTsKhIDNI*, f. 17, op. 2, d. 441, stenogram of the November 1929 Central Committee plenum.
65. *RTsKhIDNI*, ibid., addendum 'On the Results and Further Tasks of Kolkhoz Construction, pp. 50–1.
66. *KPSS v rezoliutsiiakh*, Vol. 5, pp. 17, 29, 31.
67. The declaration was published in Danilov and Ivnitsky (eds), (1989), pp. 274–82.
68. *RTsKhIDNI*, f. 17, op. 2, d. 441, l. 51, stenogram of the November 1929 Central Committee plenum.
69. Eikhe, 'On the Situation and Tasks of Constructing Kolkhozes and Sovkhozes',

238 Notes

from a speech of 18 February 1929 published in *Materialy k IV sibirskoi kraevoi partkonferentsii* (Novosibirsk, *Kraiizdat*, 1929), pp. 2, 20.
70. *RTsKhIDNI*, f. 17, op. 2, d. 397, l. 53–4 (Eikhe), 67–8 (Syrtsov), stenogram of the November 1928 plenum.
71. *RTsKhIDNI*, f. 17, op. 2, d. 441, l. 50–1.
72. Kislitsyn, p. 128.
73. *RTsKhIDNI*, f. 17, op. 2, d. 441, l. 68–71.
74. In October 1929, the area had been visited by a government commission headed by the arch-collectivizer Ryskulov, Syrtsov's deputy at Sovnarkom RSFSR, after which restraints on an accelerated tempo of collectivization were removed: Davies (1980), pp. 154–5.
75. *RTsKhIDNI*, f. 17, op. 2, d. 441, l. 70.

CHAPTER 7 STALIN'S FINAL SOLUTION

1. For a discussion of the work of this commission and its subcommissions see Davies (1980), pp. 185–202.
2. *RTsKhIDNI*, f. 17, op. 3, d. 765, l. 11, Supplement No. 1 to Protocol No. 106 of Politburo session of 5 November 1929; ibid., d. 769, l. 3, item 8 of Protocol No. 110 of Politburo session of 20 December 1929.
3. Davies (1980), pp. 388–90.
4. *GANO* 2, f. 2, op. 2, d. 1824, l. 208, telegram from Eikhe to Vetrov (Siberian representative in Moscow), 11 December 1929; ibid., l. 209, telegram from Vetrov to Eikhe, undated. For Ryskulov's role in the drive for collectivization see Davies (1980), pp. 154, 178–80, 186–8, 190.
5. *GANO* 2, f. 2, op. 2, d. 1824, l. 210, copy of a draft Kraikom decree; *RTsKhIDNI*, f. 17, op. 21, d. 3097, l. 134.
6. See Gushchin (1973), p. 284.
7. *GANO* 2, f. 2, op. 2, d. 3468, l. 34.
8. *GANO* 2, f. 2, op. 4, d. 41, l. 15, Kraikombiuro decree 'On the Construction of Large-Scale Kolkhozes and the Supervision of Collectivization', 5 January 1930.
9. *Za sotsialisticheskoe zemledelie*, No. 1, 15 January 1930, p. 3.
10. *RTsKhIDNI*, f. 17, op. 3, d. 771, l. 3, 21–3, item 13 of Protocol No. 112 of Politburo session of 5 January 1930 and its supplement No. 2; *KPSS v rezoliutsiiakh*, Vol. 5, pp. 72–5.
11. From a discussion in Sovnarkom RSFSR in early January 1930, cited in Davies (1980), p. 213.
12. *GANO* 2, f. 2, op. 2, d. 450, l. 1, stenogram of a Kraikom conference on the spring sowing campaign and collectivization, 23–24 January 1930; ibid., d. 451, l. 193 (Eikhe), stenogram of a Kraikom conference on the spring sowing campaign and collectivization, 30–31 January 1930.
13. *GANO* 2, f. p-2, op. 2, d. 444, l. 34, Protocol No. 30/c of Kraikombiuro session of 11 January 1930; ibid., l. 60–5, Supplement to Protocol No. 30/c, Kraikom Decree on the distribution of Leningrad officials; *IS*, No. 4, 15 February 1930, p. 22; Gushchin (1973), p. 285.
14. *GANO* 2, f. 2, op. 2, d. 466, l. 83, Report No. 23 of Barnaul Okruzhkom Information Sector, 28 February 1930; *GANO* 2, f. 2, op. 1, d. 4117, l. 475–81, Kraikom Information Report No. 7 on the work of twenty-five thousanders.

15. Alexander Chayanov, *The Theory of Peasant Cooperatives*, trans. David Wedgwood Benn (London, I.B. Tauris, 1991), p. 1.
16. *GANO* 1, f. 1228, op. 3, d. 17, l. 290–1.
17. *GANO* 1, f. 1228, op. 3, d. 17, l. 625, OGPU Special Report for Novosibirsk Okrug, 16 April 1930.
18. *GANO* 1, f. 1228, op. 3, d. 17, l. 293.
19. *GANO* 2, f. 2, op. 2, d. 451, l. 144.
20. *GANO* 2, f. 2, op. 2, d. 450, l. 2 (Bazovsky), 10 (Eikhe), Kraikom conference, 23 January 1930.
21. R.I. Eikhe, *Likvidatsiia kulachestva kak klassa (doklad tov. R.I. Eikhe na sobranii novosibirskogo gorodskogo partaktiva, 27 ianvaria 1930 g.)* (Novosibirsk, *Kraiizdat*, 1930), p. 4.
22. *GANO* 2, f. 3, op. 2, d. 92, l. 83; ibid., d. 41, l. 1; *Sovetskaia sibir'*, 14 February 1930, p. 1.
23. *GANO* 2, f. 2, op. 2, d. 451, Kraikom conference of 30–31 January 1930; *GANO* 2, f. 2, op. 2, d. 467, l. 158–61, Kraikom decree of 16 February 1930.
24. *GANO* 1, f. 1228, op. 3, d. 17, l. 241–2.
25. *RTsKhIDNI*, f. 17, op. 3, d. 772, l. 14, Supplement No. 1 to Protocol No. 113 of Politburo session of 15 January 1930 (confirming a decree of TsIK and STO USSR); *GANO* 2, f. 2, op. 2, d. 3468, l. 37, telegram from Kisis to okruzhkoms, 14 January 1930; ibid., l. 38, telegram from Eikhe to okruzhkoms 11 February 1930.
26. *GANO* 2, f. 2, op. 2, d. 450, l. 16.
27. See the Krai Procuracy reports at *GANO* 1, f. 47, op. 5, d. 114, l. 10, 12, January 1930; ibid., l. 18, February 1930; ibid., l. 73, 91, March 1930.
28. *GANO* 2, f. 2, op. 2, d. 3468, l. 40, telegram from Eikhe and Klimenko to all okruzhkoms and okrispolkoms, 26 February 1930.
29. *GANO* 2, f. 2, op. 2, d. 3468, l. 55–7, telegram from Kuznetsov to Stalin, undated (mid-April 1930). See also Gushchin (1973), Table 68, p. 291.
30. *GANO* 1, f. 1228, op. 3, d. 17, l. 290–1, 352, 614.
31. *RTsKhIDNI*, f. 17, op. 3, d. 771, l. 22–3, Protocol No. 112 of Politburo session of 5 January 1930.
32. *RTsKhIDNI*, f. 17, op. 3, d.774, l. 10, Supplement No. 1 to Protocol No. 115 of Politburo session of 25 January 1930: 'On the New Tasks of Soviets with regard to the Wide Development of Collectivization in the Countryside'.
33. Stalin, *Sochineniia*, Vol. 12, pp. 141–72, at 141, 145–6, 166–9, 170. The speech was first published in *Pravda*, 29 December 1929. For Stalin's speeches in Siberia see Hughes (1991), pp. 137–48.
34. Stalin, *Sochineniia*, Vol. 12, pp. 178–83.
35. *RTsKhIDNI*, f. 17, op. 3, d. 775, l. 10, 14, Protocol No. 116 of 5 February 1930. Soviet scholars have failed to find any copies of these newspapers in central or local archives. The decree has still not been published in Russia.
36. 'On Measures for the Strengthening of Socialist Reconstruction of Agriculture in Areas of Total Collectivization and for the Struggle against the Kulak', *Sobranie zakonov*, 1930, No. 9, Article 105 (signed by Kalinin, Rykov and Enukidze); *Izvestiia*, 2 February 1930.
37. *GANO*, f. 47, op. 5, d. 104, l. 32–4*ob*. The text is also available in V.P. Danilov and S.A. Krasil'nikov (eds), *Spetspereselentsy v zapadnoi sibiri, 1930–vesna 1931 g.* (Novosibirsk, *Nauka*, 1992), pp. 21–5.

38. This secret order has remained unpublished even after the opening of archives. It was not included in the glasnost era collection of documents, many published from party archives for the first time, edited by two leading Soviet revisionist historians, Danilov and Ivnitsky. It was also absent from the most recent collection of archival documents by Danilov and Krasil'nikov. Extracts of a resolution of Western Oblast of 2 February 1930, based on the Politburo order, were published in a collection of regional documents on collectivization in 1968 and cited in Davies (1980), p. 234, note 151.
39. Eikhe, *Likvidatsiia kulachestva kak klassa*, pp. 7–10.
40. *GANO* 2, f. 2, op. 2, d. 451, l. 200, 205–6.
41. *GANO* 2, f. 2, op. 2, d. 451, l. 226–7.
42. For the commission and discussion of its resolutions see *GANO* 2, f. 2, op. 2, d. 451, l. 235–7 (Kavraisky), 239–41 (Sharangovich), 243 (Kuznetsov).
43. For the decree see *GANO* 2, f. 2, op. 2, d. 3468, l. 22–9, and ibid., f. 3, op. 2, d. 41, l. 1.
44. See, for example, the decree of Achinsk Okruzhkom, 10 February 1930: *GANO* 2, f. 2, op. 2-1, d. 4142, l. 82–5, and Slavgorod Okruzhkom, 8 February 1930: *GANO* 2, f. 2, op. 2, d. 440, l. 65–6. For the Kraiispolkom decree see '*Kak nado raskulachivat*', *Za sotsialisticheskoe zemledelie*, No. 4, 30 February 1930, pp. 11–12.
45. *RTsKhIDNI*, f. 17, op. 3, d. 777, l. 8, item 41 of Protocol No. 118 of 25 February 1930.
46. Maynard, p. 288.
47. At the November 1928 Central Committee plenum Syrtsov suggested that the number of kulak households in the krai was 'in excess of 6 per cent' compared with the 3 per cent assessment for the country as a whole: *RTsKhIDNI*, f. 17, op. 2, d. 397, l. 70.
48. The linkage between dekulakization and agricultural taxation assessments was stated in the Kraiispolkom decree of 12 February.
49. *GANO* 2, f. 2, op. 2, d. 451, l. 229 (Garin), secret report of OGPU to Kraikom conference on collectivization, 30–31 January 1930.
50. *GANO* 2, f. 2, op. 2, d. 3468, l. 25. The Kraiispolkom decree of 12 February only referred to two categories: the first was 'the kulak actif' and the rich; all others were placed in the second category.
51. Danilov and Krasil'nikov (1992), p. 273, note 3.
52. Warnings about the disgruntled mood of peasant officers and soldiers in the Siberian military districts were given by Metsis, the head of the Krai Political Department of the Red Army, at the Kraikom conference on collectivization, 31 January 1930: *GANO* 2, f. 2, op. 2, d. 451, l. 231–4.
53. *RTsKhIDNI*, f. 17 op. 3, d. 775, l. 4, item 13 of Protocol No. 116 of 5 February 1930.
54. *RTsKhIDNI*, f. 17, op. 3, d. 775, l. 15, items 70–1 of Protocol No. 116 of 5 February 1930.
55. *RTsKhIDNI*, f. 17, op. 3, d. 775, l. 16, item 72 of Protocol No. 116 of 5 February 1930.
56. Estimates of about one million victims of dekulakization are found in: Lewin (1968), p. 507; Davies (1980), p. 236, note 153; Conquest 1988, pp. 120–1; V.P. Danilov, *Kollektivizatsiia: kak eto bylo* (1989), p. 244.
57. Davies (1980), p. 235.

58. *GANO* 1, f. 1228, op. 1, d. 848, l. 1–2*ob*, top secret Kraiispolkom decree to chairmen of okrispolkoms only, 1 March 1930. Unless otherwise stated the following details are derived from this decree.
59. *GANO* 1, f. 47, op. 1, d. 921, l. 42–8 (telegrams from Tomsk, Irkutsk and Kiren okrispolkoms).
60. *GANO* 1, f. 1228, op. 3, d. 17, l. 772, OGPU Special Report, 1 March 1930: 'Facts on the Practical Implementation of the Resettlement of Category Two Kulaks in Novosibirsk Okrug'; ibid., l. 489, OGPU report for 10 March 1930.
61. *GANO* 1, f. 47, op. 5, d. 103, l. 35, OGPU report, 'On the Expropriation of the Kulaks in Siberia', April 1930; ibid., l. 64, 'Distribution: Places of Resettlement, Loading, Unloading and Control-Holding Centres', Table No. 1, 24 February 1930, approved by Zakovsky, Lipekhin (head of UCHOSO OGPU Sibkrai), Khvalensky (head 1st Department UCHOSO OGPU Sibkrai).
62. *GANO* 1, f. 1228, op. 1, d. 848, l. 1–2*ob* (Kraiispolkom decree): *GANO* 1, f. 47, op. 5, d. 103, l. 46.
63. *GANO* 1, f. 47, op. 5, d. 103, l. 33.
64. Ibid., l. 36–7 (no date for this decree was given).
65. See, for example, ibid., l. 145–9, the report of Krasnoyarsk Okrispolkom on dekulakization, 8 May 1930.
66. Novosibirsk Regional Museum, No. 17289 *osn*. and No. 17173 *osn*. The notes date from May 1931. See also ibid., No. 17341 for a pencilled note on the transfer of kulak property to a kolkhoz, dated 27 June 1931.
67. *GANO* 1, f. 1228, op. 1, d. 848, l. 10–11*ob*, Decree No. 2 of the Presidium of Novosibirsk Okrispolkom, 6 March 1930 (Top Secret); GANO 1, f. 1228, op. 3, d. 17, l. 488–90, OGPU Special Report for Novosibirsk Okrug, 10 March 1930, 'On the Process of Resettlement and Exile of Category Two and Three Kulaks'.
68. *GANO* 1, f. 1228, op. 3, d. 17, l. 493; *GANO* 1, f. 1228, op. 1, d. 848, l. 10*ob*.
69. *GANO* 1, f. 47, op. 5, d. 103, l. 42.
70. *GANO* 1, f. 47, op. 5, d. 103, l. 33, 40.
71. *GANO* 2, f. 2, op. 2, d. 451, l. 227, secret report of an OGPU official, Garin, to the Kraikom conference on collectivization, 31 January 1930.
72. *GANO* 1, f. 1228, op. 3, d. 17, l. 243, 363; *GANO* 2, f. 2, op. 2, d. 450, l. 28.
73. *GANO* 2, f. 2, op. 2, d. 3468, l. 54–9, Kraikom Information Report No. 3, 1 March 1930, 'On the Course of the Liquidation of the Kulaks as a Class'.
74. *GANO* 1, f. 1228, op. 3, d. 17, l. 494, OGPU Report for Novosibirsk Okrug, 10 March 1930.
75. *GANO* 1, f. 47, op. 5, d. 103, l. 54–7.

CHAPTER 8 *BARSHCHINA* AND *MARODERSTVO*

1. Copies of the letters may be found at *GANO* 2, f. 2, op. 21, d. 4104, l. 4–12. Two letters are dated (29 December 1929, 4 January 1930), others are undated, but the editor's letter to the Kraikom is dated 11 January 1930.
2. Ibid., l. 5.

3. Ibid., l. 6.
4. Ibid., l. 8.
5. Ibid., l. 9.
6. Ibid., l. 10.
7. Pierre Dominique, *Secrets of Siberia*, trans. W.B. Wells (London, Hutchinson, 1934), p. 225.
8. For procuracy reports see *GANO* 1, f. 47, op. 5, d. 114. The OGPU reports for Novosibirsk Okrug are at *GANO* 1, f. 1228, op. 3, d. 17.
9. *GANO* 1, f. 47, op. 5, d. 114, l. 6.
10. *GANO* 2, f. 2, op. 2, d. 3608, l. 4, report No. 2 of the Information-Political Department of Novosibirsk Okruzhkom, 20–31 December 1929.
11. *GANO* 2, f. 2, op. 4, d. 44a, l. 34, Kraikom decree of 24 November 1929.
12. *GANO* 1, f. 1228, op. 3, d. 17, l. 230–4, OGPU Special Report, 'On the Political Mood of Peasants in Novosibirsk Okrug in Relation to the Implementation of Mass Collectivization', 5 January 1930.
13. See the OGPU reports on this case at *GANO* 2, f. 2, op. 2, d. 471, l. 1; *GANO* 1, f. 47, op. 5, d. 114, l. 14, 50–50*ob*. The Krai Court ordered a review of his case.
14. *GANO* 2, f. 2, op. 2, d. 471, l. 59, Siberian OGPU Report, 20 February 1930.
15. *GANO* 1, f. 1228, op. 3, d. 17, l. 291.
16. *GANO* 1, f. 47, op. 4 'a', d. 245 'a', l. 46–46*ob*, an appeal (*zaiavlenie*) registered by the Kraiispolkom on 11 April 1930.
17. *GANO* 1, f. 1228, op. 3, d. 17, l. 296–8, OGPU Report for Novosibirsk Okrug, 28 January 1930.
18. *GANO* 1, f. 1228, op. 3, d. 17, l. 373.
19. *GANO* 1, f. 1228, op. 3, d. 17, l. 491–2. For examples of excesses against seredniaks and bedniaks see ibid., l. 542.
20. *GANO* 2, f. 2, op. 2, d. 450, l. 2–3, 12.
21. Interview conducted by V.A. Il'ynikh, 29 November 1990.
22. *GANO* 2, f. 2, op. 2, d. 450, l. 12.
23. *GANO* 2, f. 2, op. 2, d. 451, l. 77 (Skripkin), Kraikom conference on collectivization, 30 January 1930.
24. *GANO* 2, f. 2, op. 2, d. 450, l. 5 (Bazovsky).
25. *GANO* 1, f. 1228, op. 3, d. 17, l. 543–6.
26. *GANO* 1, f. 1228, op. 3, d. 17, l. 614, OGPU Special Report for Novosibirsk Okrug, 16 April 1930, 'On the Course of Collectivization and Preparatory Work for the Spring Agricultural Campaign'.
27. *GANO* 1, f. 1228, op. 3, d. 17, l. 617.
28. *GANO* 1, f. 1228, op. 3, d. 17, l. 620; *GANO* 2, f. 2, op. 2, d. 467, l. 427–8, Kraikom decree, undated (April 1930).
29. *GANO* 1, f. 1228, op. 3, d. 17, l. 621. For a literary description of this type of women's *volynka* see Mikhail Sholokov, *Virgin Soil Upturned* (Harmondsworth, Penguin, 1977), Chapter 33, 'A Fight for Grain'.
30. *GANO* 2, f. 2, op. 2-1, d. 4142, l. 235–7, Report of the Kraikom Information Sector, 'On Mass *Volynki* in Achinsk Okrug', 2 April 1930.
31. *GANO* 2, f. 2, op. 2, d. 449, l. 12.
32. See pp. 190–3.
33. *GANO* 1, f. 47, op. 5, d. 114, l. 73ob, 81, 97–106*ob*; *GANO*, 2, f. 2, op. 2,

d. 3468, l. 46, telegram from Eikhe to all okruzhkoms (except Kirensk), 3 March 1930; *GANO* 2, f. 2, op. 2, d. 3468, l. 58–9. Cases resulting in the execution of officials for pillaging are discussed in Chapter 9.
34. The details of this case may be found at *GANO* 1, f. 47, op. 5, d. 103, l. 3–6, short survey by the Krai Procurator, Burmistrov, to Eikhe, Klimenko and Lyaksutkin, 25 February 1930.
35. *GANO* 1, f. 47, op. 5, d. 103, l. 4.
36. *GANO* 1, f. 47, op. 5, d. 103, l. 4ob, 6.
37. *GANO* 2, f. 2, op. 2, d. 449, l. 48, speech to Kraiispolkom plenum, 14 March 1930.
38. See *GANO* 2, f. 2, op. 2, d. 472, l. 106–10, report of Barnaul Okruzhkom, 1 April 1930, for this and other examples.
39. For two family histories see Irina V. Pavlova (ed.), *Vozvrashchenie pamiati* (Novosibirsk, *Novosibirskoe knizhnoe izdatel'stvo*, 1991), pp. 191–210.
40. The author would like to thank V.A. Il'ynkh for making these interviews available.
41. *GANO* 2, f. 2, op. 2, d. 440, l. 109. For a similar list from another village see *GANO* 2, f. 2, op. 2, d. 472, l. 124, Barnaul Okruzhkom Information Sector, Report No. 10, 5 March 1930.
42. Author's interview with Yegor Efimovich Mikhailov, Novosibirsk, 29 January 1995.
43. *GANO* 1, f. 1228, op. 3, d. 17, l. 355, OGPU Report for Novosibirsk Okrug, 3 February 1930.
44. *GANO* 2, f. 2, op. 2, d. 3468, l. 56–9.
45. *GANO* 2, f. 2, op. 2, d. 474, l. 4, Krai OGPU report, 1 June 1930.
46. *GANO* 1, f. 1228, op. 3, d. 17, l. 490.
47. *GANO* 2, f. 2, op. 2, d. 449, l. 9, from his speech to the Kraiispolkom Plenum on 14 March 1930.
48. *GANO* 2, f. 2, op. 2, d. 451, l. 8, stenogram of a conference of okruzhkom secretaries held by the Kraikom on 30 January 1930; *GANO* 1, f. 47, op. 5, d. 103, l. 31–63, at l. 31, report of Zakovsky, OGPU Plenipotentiary for Siberia, 'On the Expropriation of the Kulaks in Siberia', April 1930.
49. *GANO* 1, f. 1228, op. 3, d. 17, l. 475, 477.
50. *GANO* 1, f. 2, op. 2, d. 449, l. 50.
51. *GANO* 1, f. 47, op. 5, d. 103, l. 41.
52. Pavlova, (1991) p. 193.
53. *GANO* 1, f. 1228, op. 3, d. 17, l. 358–60, OGPU Report for Novosibirsk Okrug, 3 February 1930.
54. *GANO* 1, f. 47, op. 5, d. 112, l. 1–41 at 1–2, Report of Head of the West Siberian Krai Administrative Affairs Department, Skripko, 6 December 1930. For details of cases see the procuracy reports at *GANO* 1, f. 47, op. 5, d. 114.
55. *GANO* 1, f. 1228, op. 3, d. 17, l. 300, 443.
56. *GANO* 2, f. 2, op. 1, d. 4118, l. 27–8, information report of the Krai Procuracy, 25 February 1930.
57. *GANO* 1, f. 1228, op. 3, d. 17, l. 473.
58. *GANO* 1, f. 47, op. 5, d. 103, l. 47.
59. *GANO* 2, f. 2, op. 2, d. 449, l. 46, 51–3 from his speech to the Kraiispolkom plenum of 14 March 1930.
60. Author's interview with Yegor Efimovich Mikhailov, Novosibirsk, 29

January 1995. This household was a wealthy one, owning a large number of animals, with a large sown area, equipment and a mill.
61. *GANO* 2, f. 2, op. 2-1, d. 4224, l. 2–66, at l. 46, 'A Report into the State of Work of Muremtsevo Party Organization by the Investigatory Commission of the Okruzhkom', March 1930. Similar 'kulak' uprisings involving large bands of armed peasants, occurred in Uch-Pristan' raion of Biisk Okrug in the middle of March, in Karatuz raion, Minusinsk Okrug in late June, and Karasuk raion, Slavgorod Okrug in the summer of 1930: Gushchin (1973), pp. 428–9.
62. *GANO* 2, f. 2, op. 2-1, d. 4224, l. 47.
63. Ibid., l. 60–1*ob*.
64. Ibid., l. 48–50.
65. Ibid., l. 50–6.
66. *GANO* 2, f. 2, op. 2, d. 3468, l. 39.
67. *GANO* 2, f. 2, op. 2, d. 3468, l. 54, Kraikom Information Report No. 3, 1 March 1930, 'On the Course of the Liquidation of the Kulaks as a Class'.
68. *GANO* 1, f. 47, op. 5, d. 103, l. 32, OGPU report of April 1930.
69. *GANO* 2, f. 2, op. 2, d. 449, l. 48–50, speech to the Kraiispolkom plenum of 14 March 1930.
70. Ibid., l. 60–3. During 1930, 155 soldiers were dismissed from Siberian Red Army units for their 'kulak origins': *GANO* 2, f. 2, op. 1, d. 3567, l. 148.
71. The secret letter of the Central Committee to party organizations, 2 April 1930, is discussed on p. 000. *Sovetskaia sibir'*, 11 June 1930, p. 1, from Eikhe's speech to the Fifth Siberian Party Conference.
72. *GANO* 1, f. 1228, op. 3, d. 17, l. 543.
73. *GANO* 2, f. 2, op. 2, d. 3468, l. 50, telegram from Eikhe to Shepot'ko, 13 March 1930; ibid., l. 52–3, telegram from Eikhe, 27 March 1930.
74. *GANO* 2, f. 2, op. 2, d. 467, l. 230, telegram from Kuznetsov to Minusinsk Okruzhkom, 14 March 1930.
75. *GANO* 2, f. 2, op. 2, d. 449, l. 14, 18, from the Kraiispolkom plenum of 14 March 1930.
76. *GANO*, 2, f. 2, op. 2, d. 3468, l. 46, telegram from Eikhe to all Okruzhkoms (except Kiren), 3 March 1930.
77. *GANO* 2, f. 2, op. 2, d. 449, l. 26, 29, 32.
78. *GANO* 2, f. 2, op. 2, d. 3468, l. 58–9.
79. *GANO* 2, f. 2, op. 2, d. 3468, l. 46.
80. *GANO* 2, f. 2, op. 2, d. 465, l. 122–3.
81. *GANO* 2, f. 2, op. 2, d. 467, l. 266, telegram from Eikhe and Kuznetsov to Omsk Okruzhkom, 23 March 1930.
82. *GANO* 1, f. 1228, op. 3, d. 17, l. 624.

CHAPTER 9 THE GREAT U-TURN

1. *Pravda*, 1 February 1930; Stalin, *Sochineniia*, Vol. 12, p. 188, an article of 9 February (also published in *Pravda*, 10 February 1930).
2. Davies (1980), pp. 255, 261, 266.
3. S.I. Syrtsov, *'Zadachi partii v derevne'*, *Bol'shevik*, No. 5, 15 March 1930, pp. 41–59 at pp. 54–5. This was an edited version of his speech to the Institute of Red Professors on 20 February 1930.

Notes 245

4. See Jonathan Haslam, *Soviet Foreign Policy, 1930–33, The Impact of the Depression* (London, Macmillan, 1983), Appendix 1, pp. 121–2.
5. *RTsKhIDNI*, f. 17, op. 3, d. 778, l. 5–6, item 33 of Protocol No. 119, decisions of Politburo session of 25 February 1930; *Pravda*, 2 March 1930, and Stalin, *Sochineniia*, Vol. 12, pp. 191–9.
6. Stalin, *Sochineniia*, Vol. 12, pp. 191, 212–13.
7. *KPSS v rezoliutsiiakh*, Vol. 5, pp. 101–4.
8. See, for example, *GANO* 2, f. 2, op. 2, d. 465, l. 91–103, Kraikom Information Report No. 5, 29 March 1930.
9. *GANO* 2, f. 2, op. 2, d. 467, l. 210, telegram from Eikhe to Spirov, 6 March 1930; ibid., l. 228, telegram from Eikhe to Shepot'ko, 13 March 1930. These cases are also mentioned at *GANO* 2, f. 2, op. 2, d. 3468, l. 47.
10. *RTsKhIDNI*, f. 17, op. 21, d. 3099, l. 15–16; *GANO* 2, f. 3, op. 2, d. 416, l. 19.
11. *GANO* 2, f. 2, op. 2, d. 3468, l. 44–5, telegram from Eikhe to all okruzhkoms, undated (*c.* 25 February 1930).
12. From his speech to the Fifth Siberian Krai Party Conference in June 1930, cited in Gushchin (1973), p. 292.
13. *GANO* 2, f. 2, op. 4, d. 41, l. 158–61, Resolution of Kraikombiuro, 'On the Course of Preparations for the Spring Sowing Campaign', 25 February 1930.
14. *GANO* 2, f. 2, op. 4, d. 41, l. 195–6, Kraikombiuro decree, 5 March 1930; ibid., op. 2, d. 3468, l. 42–3.
15. *GANO* 2, f. 2, op. 2, d. 460, l. 34, speech to Kraikombiuro session of 21 April 1930.
16. *GANO* 2, f. 2, op. 4, d. 41, l. 209–10, Kraikombiuro decree 16 March 1930; ibid., f. 2, op. 2, d. 467, l. 231, telegram from Kisis to all okruzhkoms, 16 March 1930; *GANO* 1, f. 1228, op. 1, d. 848, l. 54–54*ob*, Decree of Novosibirsk Okruzhkom and Okrispolkom to all raikoms and chairmen of raiispolkoms (except Baksin), 17 March 1930.
17. *GANO* 2, f. 2, op. 2, d. 3468, l. 51, telegram from Eikhe to Biisk Okruzhkom, 26 March 1930; ibid., l. 54, telegram from Kavraisky to all okruzhkoms, 31 March 1930.
18. *GANO* 2, f. 2, op. 2, d. 3468, l. 56.
19. The letter was published in Danilov and Ivnitsky, pp. 387–94.
20. For example, when Rykov made a critical address at the Tenth Urals Obkom Conference in June 1930, the regional party secretary, I.D. Kabakov, attacked him for undermining the party secretaries and wanting them removed from their posts: *X (Des'iataia) ural'skaia oblastnaia konferentsiiavkp (b), biulleten' no. 2-a* (Sverdlovsk, Ural'komizdat, 1930), pp. 11–18.
21. *GANO* 2, f. 2, op. 2, d. 459, l. 30–1, stenogram of Kraikombiuro Session of 8 April 1930.
22. *GANO* 2, f. 2, op. 2, d. 459, l. 19–20 (Barabinsk), 32 (Rubtsovsk), 40 (Minusinsk).
23. *GANO* 2, f. 2, op. 2, d. 464, l. 144–5 (Klimenchuk), 154 (Alekseeva), speeches to an inter-okrug party conference, 16 April 1930.
24. *GANO* 2, f. 2, op. 2, d. 465, l. 104–9, Supplement to Protocol No. 78/c, Resolution of the Kraikombiuro, 9 April 1930.
25. Ibid., l. 104.
26. *GANO* 2, f. 2, op. 2, d. 465, l. 104–5, Supplement to Protocol No. 78/c, Kraikombiuro Resolution, 9 April 1930; ibid., d. 3468, l. 58, extract from

Protocol No. 79/b, Kraikombiuro, 10 April 1930; *Sovetskaia sibir'*, 12 April 1930.
27. *GANO* 2, f. 2, op. 2, d. 464, l. 116–17, 119.
28. Ibid., l. 120–6.
29. Eikhe, *Likvidatsiia kulachestva kak klassa*, p. 11.
30. *GANO* 1, f. 47, op. 4 'a', d. 245 'a', l. 8–9*ob*, report of the Krai Procuracy to Kraikom and Kraiispolkom, 7 May 1930.
31. Ibid., l. 9–10*ob*.
32. *GANO* 2, f. 2, op. 2, d. 467, l. 390–2, Protocol of conference held at Omsk, 16 April 1930.
33. *GANO* 2, f. 2, op. 2, d. 460, l. 10 (Meren), 31 (Arsen'ev), stenogram of the Kraikombiuro session of 21 April 1930.
34. For rehabilitations in other areas see Davies (1980), pp. 280–1.
35. *GANO* 2, f. 2, op. 2, d. 474, l. 4, Krai OGPU report, 1 June 1930.
36. *GANO* 2, f. 2, op. 2, d. 460, l. 10–11, stenogram of the Kraikombiuro session of 21 April 1930.
37. *GANO* 2, f. 2, op. 2, d. 460, l. 28–30.
38. Ibid., l. 30.
39. *GANO* 2, f. 2, op. 2, d. 460, l. 35–6.
40. *GANO* 2, f. 2, op. 1, d. 4231, l. 21, from Kuznetsov's speech to the Fifth Omsk Okrug Party Organization Conference, 19 May 1930.
41. *GANO* 2, f. 2, op. 2, d. 474, l. 7, Krai OGPU report, 1 June 1930.
42. Ibid., l. 11–13.
43. *GANO* 2, f. 2, op. 2, d. 467, l. 304, telegram from Kavraisky to all okruzhkoms, 31 March 1930.
44. Ibid., l. 105; GANO 2, f. 2, op. 2, d. 3468, l. 57, telegram from Kuznetsov to Stalin, undated (on or after 9 April 1930).
45. *GANO* 2, f. 2, op. 2, d. 459, l. 2.
46. *GANO* 1, f. 1228, op. 3, d. 17, l. 614, OGPU Special Report for Novosibirsk Okrug, 16 April 1930.
47. Davies (1980), Table 17, pp. 442–3. Only the Central Black-Earth region had a lower decline in the level of collectivization.
48. *GANO* 2, f. 2, op. 2, d. 465, l. 110–25, at l. 110, top-secret Report No. 9 of the Information-Statistical Sector of the Kraikom, 28 April 1930; Gushchin (1973), pp. 299 (Table 69), 305, 306, 308. Davies (1980), pp. 286–7, based on inexact central data, stated that Siberia was one of two regions (the other being the Ukraine) which 'retained a substantial proportion of those who joined in January and February'.
49. *GANO* 2, f. 2, op. 2, d. 467, l. 348, telegram from Kaganovich to Stalin, 9 April 1930. On 5 May the Politburo released 150,000 puds of grain seed from regional procurements for use in the sowing campaign in Siberian kolkhozes: *RTsKhIDNI*, f. 17, op. 3, d. 784, l. 11. See also ibid., d. 786, l. 5.
50. *GANO* 2, f. 2, op. 2, d. 459, l. 2–5, 7, Bazovsky speech to Kraikombiuro session of 8 April 1930. For a breakdown of the fall in livestock numbers see Gushchin (1973), p. 289, Table 67.
51. *GANO* 2, f. 2, op. 2, d. 459, l. 16–17.
52. *RTsKhIDNI*, f. 17, op. 3, d. 782, l. 5, 11, 13, 34: items 20, 61, 62 and 75 of Protocol No. 123 of Politburo Session of 15 April, and its Supplement No. 8. A corresponding decree was issued by the Kraikombiuro on 13 April 1930: *GANO* 2, f. 2, op. 2, d. 467, l. 360–1.

53. *GANO* 2, f. 2, op. 2, d. 467, l. 393–6, telegram from Eikhe to all okruzhkoms, 23 April 1930. See also ibid., l. 504, telegram from Kuznetsov and Klimenko, 10 June 1930.
54. *GANO* 1, f. 1228, op. 3, d. 17, l. 620; *GANO* 2, f. 2, op. 2, d. 474, l. 2*ob.*
55. *GANO* 2, f. 2, op. 1, d. 4095, l. 156, 160.
56. *GANO* 2, f. 2, op. 5a, d. 80, l. 91, 93; ibid., f. 3, op. 3, d. 75, l. 14.
57. *GANO* 2, f. 2, op. 2, d. 474, l. 1–13, OGPU Report, 'On the Political Attitude of the Population of Siberia in Connection with the Conduct of Campaigns', 1 June 1930.
58. *GANO* 2, f. 3, op. 3, d. 11, l. 163, Protocol No. 18/b of Kraikombiuro session of 16 September 1930; ibid., l. 169, Protocol No. 19/b of Kraikombiuro session of 21 September 1930.
59. *RTsKhIDNI*, f. 17, op. 3, d. 796, l. 24, Supplement No. 1 to Protocol No. 8 of Politburo session of 15 September 1930.
60. *GANO* 1, f. 47, op. 1, d. 921, l. 131, telegram from Baryshev, head of Sibkraiispolkom Administrative Affairs Department, to Vetrov, Sibkraiispolkom plenipotentiary in Moscow, 14 May 1930.
61. *GANO* 1, f. 47, op. 5, d. 103, l. 43, 48, report from Siberian OGPU on dekulakization, April 1930; GANO 1, f. 47, op. 1, d. 921, l. 127, telegram to the Kraiispolkom from the head of *SibULON* (the OGPU Special Camp Administration), Chuntov, 22 April 1930; *ibid.*, l. 169–70, 237–8.
62. *GANO* 1, f. 47, op. 5, d. 103, l. 48.
63. *GANO* 1, f. 47, op. 5, d. 103, l. 44–6, 62, 66.
64. *GANO* 2, f. 3, op. 2, d. 105, l. 83, 246. The actual figure for Category One kulaks was more than double the original OGPU estimate of 5,000 given in early February – see p. 147. A Krai Procuracy report at the end of March 1930 stated that approximately 9,757 'kulaks' had been convicted in Siberia on charges of 'agitation' and killing of livestock. It is not clear whether these were in addition to or part of the Category One contingent: *GANO* 1, f. 47, op. 5, d. 114, l. 73.
65. *GANO* 2, f. 2, op. 2, d. 465, l. 121, Kraikom Information Report No. 9, 28 April 1930; *GANO* 2, f. 2, op. 1, d. 4095, l. 136–43, Kraikom Information-Statistical Sector Report, undated (May 1930).
66. For these views see Conquest (1988), p. 119.
67. *GANO* 2, f. 2, op. 2-1, d. 4181, l. 13. A Russian-American journalist visiting his native village in central Russia in the summer of 1930 reported that dekulakized peasants were allowed to remain in the locale, some even within the village: Maurice Hindus, *Red Bread: Collectivization in a Russian Village* (London, Allen Unwin, 1931), Chapter 13.
68. Conquest (1988), p. 122, based on figures from Western Oblast in Fainsod (1958), pp. 241–4, 259.
69. See John L. Schere and Michael Jakobsen, 'Collectivization and the Prison Camp System', *Europe–Asia Studies*, Vol. 45, No. 3, 1993, pp. 533–46.
70. *GANO* 1, f. 47, d. 106, l. 45–6. This report is also published in Danilov and Krasil'nikov (1992), pp. 186–98. See also a report of August 1930 at *GANO* 1, f. 47, op. 5, d. 112, l. 8–12.
71. See Davies (1980), pp. 247–8.
72. Schere and Jakobsen (1993), p. 539.
73. 'Information on the Deportation of Kulaks in 1930–1931', GULAG OGPU, *GARF*, f. 9479, op. 1, d. 89, l. 204, cited in V.N. Zemskov, '*Sud'ba "Kulatskoi*

ssylki" (1930–1954 gg.)', *Otechestvennaia istoriia*, No. 1, January–February 1994, pp. 118–47 at pp. 119–20.
74. For these deportations see the documents in V.P. Danilov and S.A. Krasil'nikov (eds), *Spetspereselentsy v zapadnoi sibiri, vesna 1931–nachalo 1933 goda* (Novosibirsk, *Ekor*, 1993).
75. See I.E. Plotnikov, '*Kak likvidorivali kulachestvo na urale*', *Otechestvennaia istoriia*, No. 4, July–August 1994, pp. 159–67 at p. 162.
76. Conquest (1988), pp. 125–6.
77. V.P. Danilov and N.V. Teptsov, '*Kollektivizatsiia: kak eto byla*', Part two, *Pravda*, 16 September 1988.
78. Anon., *History of the Communist Party of the Soviet Union (Bolsheviks), Short Course* (Moscow, Foreign Languages Publishing House, 1939), pp. 303, 305.
79. W.S. Churchill, *The Second World War, Vols 1–6* (London, Cassell, 1948–54), *Vol. 4: The Hinge of Fate*, pp. 447–8. Churchill quotes Stalin as stating that the struggle was with 'ten million', which would be an appropriate figure for kulaks. From the context it is possible that Stalin was emphasizing that the struggle had been with 'tens of millions' of peasants, and Churchill misquoted the remark.

CONCLUSION

1. Hughes (1991), especially Chapters 1 and 3.
2. Lewin (1968), pp. 391, 501. Some have reluctantly accepted that the policy worked 'to a certain degree': Conquest (1988), p. 129.

Appendix: Documents

LIST OF DOCUMENTS

1. Telegram from Stalin to all party organizations, 6 January 1928
2. (a) Telegram from the Sibkraikombiuro to the Politburo, 27 February 1929, On Grain Procurement
   (b) Protocol 67 of Politburo Session, 4 March 1929
3. Protocol 69 of Politburo Session, 21 March 1929, and the decision of the Politburo of 20 March 1929
4. Telegram to Kraikom, Syrtsov, copy to Eikhe and Zlobin from Mikoyan, 25 March 1929
5. Protocol of the General Meeting of Citizens of the Village of Mikhailovka, Mikhailovka raion, Biisk Okrug, 11 April 1929
6. Protocol 86 of Politburo Session, 27 June 1929, Supplement No. 2: 'On Extending the Rights of Local Soviets in the Assistance of the Fulfilment of State Duties and Plans'
7. Extracts from the Sibkraikombiuro Decree of 2 February 1930: On measures towards the fulfilment of the decision of the Central Committee VKP (b): 'On Tempos of Collectivization and the Liquidation of the Kulaks as a Class'
8. Extract from the Protocol of the General Meeting in the Village of Mochishe, Novosibirsk raion, Novosibirsk Okrug, on the Dekulakization of the Sizov family, 10 May 1931

Documents

1. TELEGRAM FROM STALIN TO ALL PARTY ORGANIZATIONS, 6 JANUARY 1928, ON GRAIN PROCUREMENT

To Klokov Novosibirsk Okruzhkom and for the attention of Syrtsov, Dogadov

Copies to Zlobin, Pankratov, Sakharov, Zykov, Strikovsky

Despite two successive strict directives from the Central Committee on increasing grain procurement, there has still been no breakthrough in the level of grain procurement ... All of this speaks of your absolutely intolerable slackness as regards this fundamental revolutionary duty before the party and proletariat. Given these facts the Central Committee demands that you secure a decisive breakthrough in grain procurement within the one week period of receipt of this directive, without any excuses whatsoever or references to the holidays and so on. The Central Committee will consider that a gross breach of party discipline. The Central Committee instructs:

1. Adopt the *compulsory [tverdiie]* fulfilment of annual and monthly *tasks [zadaniia]* of grain procurement set by Narkomtorg for your guberniia/okrug. Fulfil all the current directives from Narkomtorg without delay.

2. Fulfil all the orders from Narkomtorg on the shipment of grain with strict exactitude and on time.

3. Implement all previous directives by the Central Committee regarding the collection of monetary reserves in the countryside and impose on the peasants the maximum reduction in periods of payments ... and immediately institute supplementary local collections on the basis of the law on self-taxation.

4. In punishing arrears of any type of payments, immediately apply severe penalties, in the first instance in relation to the kulak; special repressive measures are essential against the kulaks and speculators who are disrupting agricultural prices.

5. Mobilize all the best forces of the party – without delay – including members of Gubkombiuros, Okruzhkoms and Raikoms, as well as the Presidiums of Ispolkoms to achieve the utmost increase in grain procurement and keep them in areas of procurement until there is a decisive breakthrough.

6. Impose personal responsibility on leaders of party, soviet and cooperative organizations for the fulfilment of procurement tasks given to them, immediately dismissing those of them who do not display the capacity and skill to secure the success of the grain procurements.

7. Organize an extensive press campaign around the grain procurements ...

The Central Committee warns you that delays in the implementation of this directive and failures to achieve real successes by a decisive breakthrough in grain procurement within a one week period will raise before the Central Committee the need to change the current leaderships of party organizations ...

Secretary of the Central Committee I. Stalin

Source: GANO 1, f. r-47, op. 4a, d. 119, l. 153–153ob. (The italics are mine – author.)

2. (A) TELEGRAM FROM THE SIBKRAIKOMBIURO TO THE POLITBURO, 27 FEBRUARY 1929, ON GRAIN PROCUREMENT

By 25 February 86 million puds were delivered, 32 million remain, the current rate of procurement is such that with the existing methods of procurement a decline will be inevitable. At best there will be 100 million puds by the end of the year. Having thoroughly consulted about this situation at a special meeting with secretaries of okruzhkoms and chairmen of okrispolkoms, we consider it necessary and most acceptable to implement on the territory of Siberia the compulsory alienation of grain surpluses in the form of a loan from grain holders who are sabotaging grain procurement. The quota of farms in this category is 6 to 8 per cent, the amount of the loan is 15–18 million puds. The terms of payment for alienated grain, in form of money after one year, in form of grain after two or three years. In the case of refusal there will be a punishment of a multiple fine equal to five times the amount of grain not delivered and in certain cases confiscation of all property and exile for three years. Ten per cent of alienated grain is to be left in the village for the supply of bedniaks with food and seed. This is absolutely necessary to carry out the loan. We regard this procedure as a stimulus for revitalizing and increasing grain procurement and we consider it necessary to issue immediately a decree in Siberia and to implement it steadily according to the procurement rate. We ask the Politburo for direction in this question. In the event of a positive response, the krai conference gives us the opportunity to immediately mobilize the energy of the Siberian organization around this procedure.

Syrtsov, Eikhe, Lyaksutkin, Kisis

PROTOCOL 67 OF POLITBURO SESSION, 4 MARCH 1929

Item 3: The suggestion of the Sibkraikom to implement a compulsory grain loan.
Decided: The Central Committee flatly rejects the decision of the Sibkraikom to apply the grain loan.

Source: RTsKhIDNI, f. 17, op. 3, d. 729, l. 9.

3. PROTOCOL 69 OF POLITBURO SESSION, 21 MARCH 1929

Attended: Voroshilov, Kalinin, Kuibyshev, Molotov, Rykov, Tomsky, Stalin. Cands: Mikoyan; plus 29 others.

Decided: To approve decision of Politburo of 20 March on grain procurement and apply this method in Kazakhstan, Urals, Siberia.

Decision of Politburo, 20 March 1929
To adopt the suggestion of comrade Kaganovich on measures for improving grain procurement.

(a) The decision to use compulsory quotas [*tverdiie zadaniia*] to fulfil the grain plan in villages should be an open initiative not of grain procurement representatives or organs of power but of social organizations (bednota groups and actifs) and then promulgated by the general meeting of citizens.

(b) In fulfilling the grain plan adopted by the general meeting it is necessary to separate out the kulak *verkhushka* in the village from the mass of peasants in order to apply against them the fixed compulsory duties to sell grain to the state from their surpluses, either through the general meeting or by special commissions acting on its decisions.

(c) The remainder of the grain plan, after kulaks have fulfilled their duties, is to be divided up among the peasantry according to self-taxation rates. The whole process should be conducted with active agitational work and the mobilization of proletarian social influence on the peasant masses.

Signed: Stalin

Source: RTsKhIDNI, f. 17, op. 3, d. 731, l. 4–5.

4. TELEGRAM TO KRAIKOM, SYRTSOV, COPY TO EIKHE AND ZLOBIN, FROM MIKOYAN, 25 MARCH 1929

To main procurement agencies, not for publication, with the aim of improving grain procurement STOP to guarantee the fulfilment of the annual plan of grain procurement in your krai I propose the immediate implementation of the following STOP FIRST, relying on the initiative of rural communal organizations, allocate plan tasks to villages in order to fulfil the remainder of the grain procurement plan, from such plan tasks your krai can guarantee the complete fulfilment of the remainder of the annual grain procurement plan plus we propose procurement for the month of July to an amount of 3.5 million puds, SECOND, in the adopting by general meetings of citizens of resolutions on the fulfilment of the village plan, the general meeting of citizens is to impose on the kulak *verkhushka* of the village a compulsory quota to sell grain to the state STOP this apportionment onto individual kulak households may be applied by either the general meeting of citizens or a special commission assigned for this purpose by the general meeting, THIRD, the quantity of grain due in the plan of a given village over and above the compulsory quotas on the kulak *verkhushka* is to be distributed among the remaining mass of peasants by the general meeting of citizens or the above mentioned special commission, FOURTH, it may be explained to the villages that the fulfilment of the stated village plan tasks of grain procurement will conclude the grain procurement campaign for this year, FIFTH, to supervise the practical implementation of the decisions of the general meeting on the fulfilment of plan tasks in a given village, the general meeting is to elect a special commission STOP it is essential to secure a proper representation on these commissions of the bedniak-seredniak actifs STOP SIXTH, Given the advance of the bad roads season, it is essential to organize in particular the direct intake of grain in villages and settlements either by means of special leased barns or by leaving it with peasants on a reserved receipt basis with the duty to transport it within a specified time and on collection of an appropiate written undertaking STOP we propose the implementation of this within the shortest time possible STOP mobilize for this purpose a sufficient number of officials, secure the implementation of the relevant decisions of the general meetings of citizens and conduct widespread agitation in the countryside to mobilize poor peasant groups, coop actifs, soviet and party actifs STOP telegraph confirmation of receipt.

Source: GANO 2, f. 2, op. 1, d. 2597, l. 922–6.

5. PROTOCOL OF THE GENERAL MEETING OF CITIZENS OF THE VILLAGE OF MIKHAILOVKA, MIKHAILOVKA RAION, BIISK OKRUG, 11 APRIL 1929

PARTICIPATED: 200 men, 100 women

11 April 1929

PRESIDIUM: Bol'shakova (ex-kulak), Glotova Anna (wife of a Kolchak militiaman), Shishkina Varvara (husband killed by Reds), Serediaeva Anna (disenfranchised), Pakhov Trofim (disenfranchised), Pechenkina Evdokiia (bandit)

Agenda

The solution of misunderstandings that have arisen from the selling off of property and the delivery of seed and other matters.

DECIDED:
1. To return auctioned property, livestock and buildings with the exception of surpluses.
2. To lift the boycott.
3. To restore voting rights to all.
4. To elect a commission to investigate the activities of the commission for revealing surpluses.
5. To [dole out] seed and food grain to the poor ...
6. To restore mills to all millers.
7. To regulate and lower [dues] in consumer cooperatives.
8. ... point to elect a commission of the following citizens, Chesovkikh Aleksandra, Saprin Mikhail, Bol'shakova Mariia, Pashkov Trofim, Ryzhikh Matrena, Koshkarev Matvei, Akim Dem'ianov, Illarionov, Shibaev Anisim.

... to the Ok[r]ispolkom with this protocol Kupavin Nikita, Saprin Mikhail and Dem'ianov Ul'ian.

PRESIDIUM: Pashkov, Bol'shakov and Penkina
Secretary: [unreadable] (ex-policeman).

Source: GANO 2, f. 2, op. 2-1, d. 3506, l. 4. This document was at some time in the past retyped by archivists. The derogatory insertions on social origins were added at a later date. Words in square brackets have been added by me – author.

6. PROTOCOL 86 OF POLITBURO SESSION, 27 JUNE 1929, SUPPLEMENT NO. 2

On Extending the Rights of Local Soviets in the Assistance of the Fulfilment of State Duties and Plans

Complying with numerous petitions from the bedniak-seredniak masses in grain producing areas, and to restrain kulak and speculant elements, TsIK and SNK order:

1) in cases when the decisions of citizens [the village *skhod*] to adopt resolutions for the fulfilment by the whole village of grain collections in the form of self-taxation were approved, and according to the decisions the distribution of plans to different farms was approved, the local soviet will have the right to apply the following under Article 61:
a) to exact by an administrative process an amount exceeding by five times the duties imposed by the general meeting or rural soviet commission, and to carry out the sale of property in cases of non-compliance.
b) in cases of non-compliance by different groups of farms and their opposition to the sale of grain, subject these cases to criminal prosecution on grounds of opposition to the authorities according to clause 3 of Article 61.
2) to allot 25 per cent of the fines and sums from auctions, accruing under the above from malicious kulaks, to the bedniak assistant fund of the village or raion.
3) in accordance with point one of this decision to change Article 61 of the Criminal Code RSFSR with the following form: 'Refusal to fulfil duties, general state tasks or productive work, having a general state importance incurs:
> For a first offence – administrative penalty by means of a fine from the responsible authorities of up to five times the amount of the imposed duty or task. For a second offence – imprisonment or forced labour for up to one year. Actions perpetrated by groups of individuals on a conspiratorial basis resulting in active opposition incurs imprisonment for up to two years with confiscation of property and exile from the locality.

Source: RTsKhIDNI, f. 17, op. 3, d. 746, l. 10.

7. EXTRACTS FROM THE SIBKRAIKOMBIURO DECREE OF 2 FEBRUARY 1930

Strictly-secret

On measures towards the fulfilment of the decision of the Central Committee VKP (b): 'On Tempos of Collectivization and the Liquidation of the Kulaks as a Class'

The wide development of the kolkhoz movement, the quickening tempo of construction of new collective farms, bringing into the movement millions of the mass of *bednota* and seredniaks – has laid an essential foundation for a fundamental turning-point from the policy of limiting and displacing the kulak to a policy of its (the kulak) liquidation as a class. Thus, the carrying out of dekulakization is a component part and result of the development of the kolkhoz movement, it must be directly linked with the construction of new kolkhozes, uniting in their membership the real wide mass of batraks, *bednota* and seredniaks.

Consequently, the most important task of the Siberian party organization is to achieve a further acceleration in the tempo of development of the kolkhoz movement through a drive to fully include the basic mass of batraks, bednota and seredniaks in kolkhoz construction in time for the spring agricultural campaign of 1930.

The Siberian party organization must build all of its measures for liquidating the kulak on the basis of a direct linkage with the growth of the kolkhoz movement . . .

The Siberian Krai Committee VKP (b) decrees:

. . .

4. It is suggested that in the implementation of measures for the liquidation of the kulak all okruzhkoms be guided by the following:

A. The expropriation of the kulak must be a consequence of the spread of comprehensive collectivization of okrug, raion and village in accordance with rates of growth of kolkhoz construction. Naked dekulakization, without bringing into the kolkhozes the basic mass of the batraks, *bednota* and seredniaks in this or that village or raion – is not permitted.

B. Expropriation is to be applied to all kulak farms of a given village or raion going over to comprehensive collectivization. The number of kulak farms to be liquidated must be strictly differentiated by raion, so that the general number of kulak farms to be liquidated in all the main raions of the krai is on average approximately 4 per cent–5 per cent . . . The basis for defining the farms to be subjected to expropriation is the indicators of clear-kulak farms established for the tax campaign of 1929/30 . . .

C. For the aim of decisively undermining the influence of the kulak on some elements of the bedniak-seredniak peasantry and guaranteeing the suppression of any attempts at counter-revolutionary opposition from the side of the kulak against the measures implemented by soviet power and kolkhozes, apply the following measures to kulaks:

a) first category – the counter-revolutionary kulak actif is to be immediately liquidated by means of imprisonment in concentration camps, not hesitating to impose the severest measures of repression [execution – author] on organizers of terrorist acts, counter-revolutionary demonstrations and insurgency organizations.

b) the second category should consist of the remaining elements of the kulak actif, especially from the wealthiest kulaks and quasi-landlords, who are to be sent into exile to remote parts of the USSR and to remote areas of the krai.

c) the third category includes the kulaks remaining within the boundaries of the raion, who are to be resettled in new zones outside of the boundaries of kolkhoz farms.

D. ... Exiled and resettled kulaks, having their *property confiscated* must be left with only the most essential household articles, some elementary means of production in accordance with the character of their work in the new place, and a minimum of food stocks essential for an initial period. Money is also to be confiscated from exiled kulaks leaving, however, in the hands of kulaks a certain minimal sum (up to 500 roubles per family) essential for travel and construction in the place.

E. In relation to kulak households who are to be left in the locality and taken away to new zones beyond kolkhoz fields, be guided by the following:

a) Okrispolkams must be instructed about the place of resettlement so that only small village settlements in the assigned areas are permitted, the administration of which will be by special committees [*troiki*], or plenipotentiaries appointed by raiispolkoms and confirmed by okrispolkoms ...

F. *Lists* of kulak farms (second category) to be sent into exile to remote areas are to be compiled by raiispolkoms on the basis of decisions of meetings of kolkhozniks, and batrak-bedniak meetings, and confirmed by okrispolkoms. The order of resettlement of the remaining kulak farms (third category) will be decided by okrispolkoms ...

5. ... In their work of expropriating the kulak rural soviets must institute the following procedure:

At first the general question is to be discussed by batrak-bedniak meetings, with the participation of representatives of local social organizations (party cells, komsomol, peasant committees of mutual aid, kolkhozes, cooperatives and others), and also by the seredniak actif. At these meetings, kulak farms that have slipped through the tax lists are to be noted, while at the same time correcting mistakes committed in relation to individual seredniak farms ...

The decisions of bedniak-batrak meetings are to be brought for discussion to the general meetings of citizens in each village, those who have the right to vote, after which it is for the rural soviet to confirm, with the participation of the representatives of the Raiispolkom and OGPU.

Source: GANO 2, f. 2, op. 2, d. 3468, l. 22–9.

8. EXTRACT FROM THE PROTOCOL OF THE GENERAL MEETING IN THE VILLAGE OF MOCHISHE, NOVOSIBIRSK RAION, NOVOSIBIRSK OKRUG, ON THE DEKULAKIZATION OF THE SIZOV FAMILY, 10 MAY 1931

Extract

From the protocol of the general meeting of members of the agricultural artel 'OGPU', Mochishe rural soviet, Novosibirsk raion, together with the *bednota* group and bedniak-seredniak actif on 10 May 1931.

Participated: 77 kolkhozniks and 25 individual peasants
Chairman: Bochkarev
Secretary: Myrenov

Agenda: On the kulak Sizov, Yacov Nikolaevich

Discussion
Shchanova, A: Sizov employed a batrak woman, Glukova, in 1926.
Aganov: comrade [unreadable] confirms this and adds that he hired another batrak in 1927, Laptev. In 1928 Solov'ev and Kharlamov lived there, Kharlamova from 1927.
Decided: the household of Sizov, Yacov Nikolaevich is a clear kulak, having hired batraks: from 1926 to 1927, Glukova. In 1928 Solov'ev, Kharlamov and Kharlamova, and Laptev right up to 1931. In 1928 he owned – 3 horses, 5 cows, 10.05 hectares of sown area. He was taxed 107 roubles 87 kopecks. He owned a repair workshop. He rented out a house.
In 1929 he owned 3 horses, 3 cows, a sown area of 7.54 hectares: his tax was 488-70. In 1930 he owned 2 horses, 2 cows, 5 calves, a sown area of 3.76 hectares, and was taxed 173r-93k.
For this reason the household Sizov, Yacov Nikolaevich is expropriated and sent off into exile to uninhabited areas beyond the borders of the West Siberian Krai.

Approved: Chairman Bochkarev, Secretary Myrenov

Source: Novosibirsk Regional Museum, No. 17289 osobyi fond.

Bibliography

ARCHIVES

(GAAK) State Archive of Altai Krai
(GANO 1) State Archive of Novosibirsk Oblast
(GANO 2) State Archive of Novosibirsk Oblast Corpus 2 (ex regional party archive)
(RTsKhIDNI) Russian Centre for the Preservation and Study of Documents of Modern History (former CPSU central archive)

NEWSPAPERS, JOURNALS AND PERIODICALS

American Political Science Review
Biulleten' oppozitsii,
Bol'shevik
Economic History Review
Ekonomicheskoe obozrenie
Europe-Asia Studies
Istoriia SSSR
Izvestiia
Izvestiia sibkraikoma vkp(b)
Journal of Soviet Nationalities
Krasnaia sibiriachka
Na leninskom puti
Otechestvennaia istoriia
Pravda
Problems of Communism
Sibirskaia sel'sko-khoziaistvennaia kooperatsiia
Slavic Review
Sobranie uzakonenie i rasporiazhenii raboche-krest'ianskogo pravitel'stva
Sobranie zakonov i rasporiazhenii SSSR
Sotsialisticheskii vestnik
Sovetskaia sibir'
World Politics
Za sotsialisticheskoe zemledelie
Zhizn' sibiri

BOOKS, THESES, ARTICLES, ETC. IN RUSSIAN

Barsov, A.A., *Balans stoimostnykh obmenov mezhdu gorodom i derevni*. Moscow: Nauka, 1969.
Burkov, V.N., 'Deiatel'nost' KPSS po ukrepleniia derevenskikh partiinikh organizatsii zapadnoi sibiri v usloviiakh podgotovki i provedeniia massovoi

kollektivizatsii, 1927-1932 gg.', Kandidatskaia dissertatsiia. Tomsk: Tomskii gosudartsvennyi universitet, 1966.
Chekhov, A., *Izbrannoe*. Leningrad: Lenizdat, 1982.
(IV) Chetvertaia sibirskaia kraevaia konferentsiia VKP (b), 25 fevralia-4 marta 1929, stenograficheskii otchet, Vols 1-3. Novosibirsk: Kraiizdat, 1929.
Chueva, F., *Sto sorok besed c Molotovym*. Moscow: 'Terra'-'Terra', 1991.
Danilov, V.P., *'K kharakteristike obshchestvenno-politicheskoi obstanovki v sovetskoi derevne nakanune kollektivizatsii'*, Istoricheskie zapiski, No. 79, 1967.
Danilov, V.P., *Kollektivizatsiia: kak eto bylo, stranitsy istorii sovetskogo obshchestva: fakty, problemy, liudi*. Moscow, 1989.
Danilov, V.P. and Ivnitsky, N.A. (eds), *Dokumenty svidetel'stvuiut, iz istorii derevni nakanune i v khode kollektivizatsii 1927-1932 gg*. Moscow: Izdatel'stvo politicheskoi literatury, 1989.
Danilov, V.P. and Krasil'nikov, S.A. (eds), *Spetspereselentsy v zapadnoi sibiri, 1930-vesna 1931 g*. Novosibirsk: Nauka, 1992.
Danilov, V.P. and Krasil'nikov, S.A. (eds), *Spetspereselentsy v zapadnoi sibiri, vesna 1931-nachalo 1933 goda*. Novosibirsk: Ekor, 1993.
X (Des'iataia) ural'skaia oblastnaia konferentsiiavkp (b), biulleten' no. 2-a. Sverdlovsk: Ural'komizdat, 1930.
Eikhe, R.I., *Likvidatsiia kulachestva kak klassa (doklad tov. R.I. Eikhe na sobranii novosibirskogo gorodskogo partaktiva, 27 ianvaria 1930 g.)*. Novosibirsk: Kraiizdat, 1930.
Fel'shtinsky, Yu. G., *Razgovory c Bukharinym*. Moscow: Izdatel'stvo gumanitarnoi literatury, 1993.
Gushchin, N.Ya., *Sibirskaia derevnia na puti k sotsialismu*. Novosibirsk, Nauka, 1973.
Istoriia sibiri c drevneishikh vremen do nashikh dnei, 5 vols, Vol. 4. Leningrad: Nauka, 1968.
Itogi IV sibirskoi kraevoi partiinoi konferentsii. Novosibirsk: Kraiizdat, 1929.
Ivnitsky, N.A., *Klassovaia bor'ba v derevne i likvidatsiia kulachestva kak klassa (1929-1932 gg.)*. Moscow: Nauka, 1972.
Kavraisky, V.A. and Khamarmer, P., *Uroki klassovoi bor'by. Itogi vyborov v sovety sibiri. 1928-1929 gg*. Novosibirsk: Kraiizdat, 1929.
Kavraisky, V.A. and Nusinov, I.I., *Klassy i klassovye otnosheniia v sovremmennoi sovetskoi derevne*. Novosibirsk: Kraiizdat, 1929.
Kislitsyn, S.A., *Variant Syrtsova: iz istorii formirovaniya antistalinskogo soprotivleniya v sovetskom obshchestve v 20-30-e gg*. Rostov-on-Don: Nauchno-metodicheskii tsentr 'logos', 1992.
Kollektivizatsiia sel'skogo khoziaistvo zapadnoi sibiri (1927-1937 gg.). Tomsk: Tomskii gosudarstvennyi universitet, 1972.
KPSS v rezoliutsiiakh i resheniiakh s"ezdov, konferentsii i plenumov Ts. K. (1898-1986), Vols 1-9. 9th edn. Moscow: Izdatel'stvo politicheskoi literatury, 1983-6.
Lukashin, M., *Kratkie itogi raboty slavgorodsk okruzhkoma vkp (b)*, Slavgorod: Partizdat, 1928.
Lunacharsky, A.B., *Mesiats po sibiri*. Moscow: Izdat'elstvo krasnaia gazeta, 1929.
Materialy k IV sibirskoi kraevoi partkonferentsii. Novosibirsk: Kraiizdat, 1929.
Moshkov, Yu.A., *Zernovaia problema v gody sploshnoi kollektivizatsii sel'skogo khoziaistva SSSR (1929-1932 gg.)*. Moscow: Moskovskii-gosudarstvennyi universitet, 1966.

Otchet iv okruzhnoi partiinoi konferentsii, 25–30 Noiabria 1928. Barnaul: Izdat'elstvo krasnyi altai, 1928.

Pavlova, I.V. (ed.), *Vozvrashchenie pamiati*. Novosibirsk: Novosibirskoe knizhnoe izdatel'stvo, 1991.

(XV) Piatnadtsatyi s"ezd VKP (b), 2–19 dekabria 1927 g., stenograficheskii otchet, 2 Vols. Moscow: Gosudarstvennoe izdatel'stvo politicheskoi literatury, 1962.

Plotnikov, I.E., 'Kak likvidorivali kulachestvo na urale', *Otechestvennaia istoriia*, No. 4, 1994.

(XVI) Shestnadtsataia konferentsiia vkp (b), aprel' 1929, stenograficheskii otchet. Moscow: Gosudartsvennoe izdat'elstvo politicheskoe literatury, 1962.

Sibirskii krai statisticheskii spravochnik. Novosibirsk: Kraiizdat, 1930.

Stalin, I.V., *Sochineniia, Vols 1–13*. Moscow: Gosudartsvennoe izdatel'stvo politicheskoi literatury, 1946–52.

Vaganov, F.M., *Pravyi uklon v vkp (b) i ego razgrom (1928–1930 gg.)*. Moscow: Politizdat, 1970.

Za chetkuiu klassovuiu liniiu. Sbornik dokumentov kraikoma vkp (b) i vystuplenii rukovodiashchikh rabotnikov kraia. Novosibirsk: Kraiizdat, 1929.

Zemskov, V.N., 'Sud'ba "Kulatskoi ssylki" (1930–1954 gg.)', *Otechestvennaia istoriia*, No. 1, 1994.

BOOKS ETC. IN OTHER LANGUAGES

Bartlett, R. (ed.), *Land Commune and Peasant Community in Russia*. London: Macmillan, 1990.

Bohstedt, J., *Riots and Community Politics in England and Wales, 1790–1810*. Cambridge, Mass.: Cambridge University Press, 1989.

Booth, W.J., 'On the Idea of the Moral Economy', *American Political Science Review*, Vol. 88, No. 3, 1994.

Carr, E.H., *Socialism in One Country, 1924–1926, Vol. 1*. London: Macmillan, 1958.

Carr, E.H., 'Revolution from Above: Some Notes on the Decision to Collectivise Soviet Agriculture', in Wolff, K. and Moore, B. Jr (eds), *The Critical Spirit: Essays in Honour of Herbert Marcuse*. Boston: Beacon Press, 1967.

Carr, E.H., *The Bolshevik Revolution 1917–1923, Vol. 2*. Harmondsworth: Penguin, 1972.

Carr, E.H. and Davies, R.W., *Foundations of a Planned Economy, Vol. 1, 1926–1929*. London: Macmillan, 1974.

Chayanov, A., *The Theory of Peasant Cooperatives*, trans. David Wedgwood Benn. London: I.B. Tauris, 1991.

Churchill, W.S., *The Second World War, Vols 1–6, Vol. 4: The Hinge of Fate*. London: Cassell, 1948–54.

Conquest, R., *The Harvest of Sorrow: Soviet Collectivization and the Terror-Famine*. London: Arrow, 1988.

Crisp, O., *Studies in the Russian Economy before 1914*. London: Macmillan, 1976.

Davies, R.W., *The Socialist Offensive: The Collectivisation of Soviet Agriculture, 1929–1930*. London: Macmillan, 1980.

Deutscher, I., *Stalin, A Political Biography*. London: Oxford University Press, 1949.

Dominique, P., *Secrets of Siberia*, trans. W.B. Wells. London: Hutchinson, 1934.
Eklof, B. and Frank, S.P. (eds), *The World of the Russian Peasant, Post-Emancipation Culture and Society*. London: Unwin Hyman, 1990.
Fainsod, M., *Smolensk Under Soviet Rule*. London: Unwin Hyman, 1958, repr. 1989.
Fitzpatrick, S. (ed.), *Cultural Revolution in Russia, 1928-1931*. Bloomington: Indiana University Press, 1978.
Haslam, J., *Soviet Foreign Policy, 1930-33, The Impact of the Depression*. London: Macmillan, 1983.
Hindus, M., *Red Bread: Collectivization in a Russian Village*. London: Allen & Unwin, 1931.
History of the Communist Party of the Soviet Union (Bolsheviks), Short Course. Moscow: Foreign Languages Publishing House, 1939.
Hobsbawm, E.J. and Rudé, G., *Captain Swing*. London: Lawrence & Wishart, 1969.
Hoffman, D.L., 'Land, Freedom and Discontent: Russian Peasants of the Central Industrial Region prior to Collectivisation', *Europe-Asia Studies*, Vol. 46, No. 4, 1994.
Hoover, C.B., *The Economic Life of Soviet Russia*. London: Macmillan, 1931.
Hughes, J., *Stalin, Siberia and the Crisis of the New Economic Policy*. Cambridge: Cambridge University Press, 1991.
Hughes, J., 'Capturing the Russian Peasantry: Stalinist Grain Procurement Policy and the "Ural-Siberian Method" ', *Slavic Review*, Vol. 53, No. 1, 1994.
Hunter, H., 'The Overambitious First Soviet Five Year Plan', *Slavic Review*, Vol. 32, No. 2, 1974.
Hyden, G., *Beyond Ujamaa in Tanzania: Under-Development and an Uncaptured Peasantry*. Berkeley: University of California Press, 1980.
Johnson, S. and Temin, P., 'The Macroeconomics of NEP', *Economic History Review*, Vol. XLVI, No. 4, 1993.
Kuromiya, H., *Stalin's Industrial Revolution, Politics and Workers, 1928-1932*. Cambridge: Cambridge University Press, 1988.
Landsberger, H.A., *Rural Protest: Peasant Movements and Social Change*. London: Macmillan, 1974.
Lewin, M., *Russian Peasants and Soviet Power, A Study of Collectivization*. London: Allen & Unwin, 1968.
Lewin, M., *The Making of the Soviet System*. London: Methuen, 1985.
Lichbach, M., 'What Makes Rational Peasants Revolutionary? Dilemma, Paradox, and Irony in Peasant Collective Action', *World Politics*, Vol. 46, No. 3, 1994.
Lih, L.T., *Bread and Authority in Russia, 1914-1921*. Oxford: Oxford University Press, 1990.
McCauley, M. (ed.), *The Russian Revolution and the Soviet State 1917-1921, Documents*. London: Macmillan, 1975.
Male, D.J., *Russian Peasant Organisation Before Collectivisation: A Study of Commune and Gathering, 1925-30*. Cambridge: Cambridge University Press, 1971.
Mandelstam, N., *Hope Against Hope: A Memoir*, trans. M. Hayward. London: Collins & Harvill Press, 1970.
Marx, K., *The Eighteenth Brumaire of Louis Bonaparte*. Moscow: Progress, 1967.
Marx, K., *The Class Struggles in France 1848-1850*. London, Lawrence and Wishart, 1990.

Maynard, J., *The Russian Peasant and Other Studies*. London: Victor Gollancz, 1942.

Millar, J., 'Mass Collectivization and the Contribution of Soviet Agriculture to the First Five Year Plan: A Review Article', *Slavic Review*, Vol. 33, No. 1, 1974.

Moore, B., Jr, *Social Origins of Dictatorship and Democracy: Lord and Peasant in the Making of the Modern World*. Harmondsworth: Peregrine, 1969.

Narkiewicz, O., 'Soviet Administration and the Grain Crisis of 1927–28', *Soviet Studies*, Vol. 20, No. 4, 1968.

Nove, A., *Was Stalin Really Necessary? Some Problems of Soviet Political Economy*. London: Allen & Unwin, 1965.

Nove, A. (ed.), *The Stalin Phenomenon*. London: Wiedenfield & Nicholson, 1993.

Nove, A. and Millar, J., 'A Debate on Collectivisation: Was Stalin Really Necessary?', *Problems of Communism*, Vol. 25, No. 4, 1976.

Olson, M., *The Logic of Collective Action: Public Goods and the Theory of Groups*. Cambridge, Mass.: Harvard University Press, 1965.

Olson, M., 'The Logic of Collective Action in Soviet-type Societies', *Journal of Soviet Nationalities*, No. 1, 1990.

Pipes, R., *Russia Under the Old Regime*. Harmondsworth: Penguin, 1979.

Pipes, R., *The Russian Revolution, 1899–1919*. London: Collins Harvill, 1990.

Popkin, S., *The Rational Peasant: The Political Economy of Rural Society in Vietnam*. Berkeley: University of California Press, 1979.

Preobrazhensky, E.A., *Novaya ekonomika. Opyt analiza sovetskogo khozyaistva, Vol. 1, part 1*, Moscow 1926, trans. by Brian Pearce: *The New Economics*. Oxford: Oxford University Press, 1965.

Redfield, R., *The Little Community and Peasant Society and Culture*. Chicago: University of Chicago Press, 1971.

Rosenberg, W.G. and Siegelbaum, L.H. (eds), *Social Dimensions of Industrialization*. Bloomington: Indiana University Press, 1993.

Rudé, G., *Ideology and Popular Protest*. London: Lawrence & Wishart, 1980.

Salter, J., 'On the Interpretation of Bukharin's Economic Ideas', *Soviet Studies*, Vol. 44, No. 4, 1992.

Schere, J.L. and Jakobsen, M., 'Collectivisation and the Prison Camp System', *Europe–Asia Studies*, Vol. 45, No. 3, 1993.

Scott, J.C., *The Moral Economy of the Peasant: Rebellion and Subsistence in Southeast Asia*. London: Yale University Press, 1976.

Scott, J.C., *Weapons of the Weak: Everyday Forms of Peasant Resistance*. London: Yale University Press, 1985.

Shanin, T. (ed.), *Peasants and Peasant Societies*. Harmondsworth: Penguin, 1971.

Shanin, T., *The Awkward Class: Political Sociology of Peasantry in a Developing Society: Russia 1910–1925*. Oxford: Clarendon Press, 1972.

Sholokov, M., *Virgin Soil Upturned*. Harmondsworth: Penguin, 1977.

Skocpol, T., *States and Social Revolutions: A Comparative Analysis of France, Russia, and China*. Cambridge: Cambridge University Press, 1979.

Smith, R.E.F. (ed.), *The Enserfment of the Russian Peasantry*. Cambridge: Cambridge University Press, 1968.

Smith, R.E.F. (ed. and trans.), *The Russian Peasant*. London: Frank Cass, 1974.

Smith, R.E.F., *Peasant Farming in Muscovy*. London: Cambridge University Press, 1977.

Bibliography

Taniuchi, Y., *The Village Gathering in Russia in the Mid-1920s*. Birmingham: Birmingham University Press, 1968.

Taniuchi, Y., 'A Note on the Ural-Siberian Method', *Soviet Studies*, Vol. 33, No. 4, 1981.

Thompson, E.P., *Customs in Common*. London: Penguin, 1993.

Trotsky, L.D., *The Real Situation in Russia*, trans. Max Eastman. London: Allen Lane, 1928.

Urban, G.R. (ed.), *Stalinism, Its Impact on Russia and the World*. London: St. Martin's Press, 1982.

Viola, L., *Best Sons of the Fatherland, Workers in the Vanguard of Soviet Collectivization*. Oxford: Oxford University Press, 1987.

Wolf, E., *Peasant Wars of the Twentieth Century*. New York: Harper & Row, 1969.

Glossary

Barshchina — The requisitioned labour of a vassal for a feudal lord, or *corveé* under serfdom.

Bednota — The poor peasantry, both landed and landless.

Bedniak — A poor peasant, usually with a smallholding.

Chrezvyshchaina — A wave of excessive use of emergency measures.

Desiatin — Land measure equivalent to slightly less than one hectare.

Kombedy — Committees of poor peasants, first organized in 1918 to assist the Bolshevik regime in controlling the countryside.

Kraikom (biuro) — Krai party committee, with subordinate territorial committees in regions (*okruzhkomi*) and areas (*raikomi*).

Kraiispolkom — Krai Soviet Executive Committee, with subordinate committees in regions (*okrispolkomi*) and areas (*raiispolkomi*).

Kraisud — Krai Judicial Department.

Kulak — Literally 'fist': a wealthy peasant, rural trader or entrepreneur, defined by the party as a 'petty-capitalist'. From 1928, the term was increasingly used by the party as a shorthand definition of any peasant opponent. Poor peasants who opposed the state were often refered to as *podkulachniki* (kulak lackeys).

Narkomprod — *Narodnyi kommissariat prodovol'stvie* (People's Commissariat of Food Supplies).

Narkomtorg — *Narodnyi kommissariat vneshnei i vnutrennoi torgovli* (People's Commissariat of Foreign and Domestic Trade of USSR).

OGPU — *Ob"edinennoe gosudarstvennoe politicheskoe upravlenie* (United State Political Administration: the secret police, 1922–34).

Piatikratniki — Peasants who refused to comply with compulsory delivery plans levied by the state, with the result that they were exemplarily punished with fines (*piatikratki*) equivalent to five times the original amount.

Pud — A weight equivalent to 16.38 kilograms.

Razverstka — State requisitioning of goods and products by plan allocations distributed to areas, villages and households.

Seredniak — The 'middle peasant': a broad categorization applied by party and state to peasants falling into the middle income stratum.

Skhod — Village assembly of peasants, generally composed of male heads of landed households.

Smychka — Party slogan for the political alliance between workers and peasants.

Sovnarkom — *Sovet narodnykh komissarov* (Council of People's Commissars, of the USSR unless otherwise stated).

Soiuzkhleb — 'Union Grain': a grain procurement organization under Narkomtorg.

TOZ — *Tovarishchestvo po sovmestnoi obrabotke zemli* (Association for the Joint Cultivation of Land).

Troika	Committee of three persons, often created by the party for speedy implementation of decisions in a crisis.
Tverdiie Zadaniia	Compulsory delivery plans for agricultural produce levied by the state on peasant households and villages.
Verkhushka	Party term for the peasant elite or wealthiest stratum.
Volynka	A generic term for peasant civil disobedience and collective protest, often degenerating into violence.

Index

Article 58, 30, 44, 48, 104, 128, 175
Article 61,
   in grain campaigns, 77–8, 104, 111–16, 121–9, 207
   in collectivization, 142–3, 169
   see procuracy, Ural-Siberian method
Article 107,
   1927–8 grain campaign, 17, 23, 31, 34, 36, 39, 42, 53, 77
   1928–9 grain campaign, 56, 59–60, 67, 83–4, 104, 112, 125
Article 271, 78

Bauman, K. Ya, 136
Bol'shakov, A.M., 72
Bukharin, N.I.,
   attacks Stalin's notion of tribute, 8, 14–15, 24, 79–82
   military-feudal exploitation, 53, 81
   opposes Ural-Siberian method, 63, 65
   capitulation of, 133

carnivals, *see* social influence policy
charivari, *see* social influence policy
Chayanov, A.V., 5, 140
Chukhrit, G.A., 17
collective farms,
   actifs, 130
   exodus from in early 1930, 194–5
   grain quotas, 127, 196–7
   increase in numbers, 116–17, 143
   role of communes in collectivization, 165–6
   role of communes in dekulakization, 171–2, 182
   size, 134
   sowing campaign 1930, 185, 193, 195–8
   statutes revised, 183–4
   types, 138–9, 143, 167–8, 184–5, 189
collectivization,
   agricultural surplus, 1
   anti-religion campaign, 181
   Article 61, 112
   consequences, 193–203, 213–14
   dekulakization link, 147–8, 180, 199
   development, 9–12, 134
   ethnic factor, 181
   excesses, 137–8, 141–3
   interpretations of reasons, 1–2
   kraiispolkom investigates excesses, 165, 181, 187
   levels, 194–5
   livestock slaughtering, 142–3, 164, 168, 170, 175, 195–6, 215
   mobilization of *bednota*, 129–30
   organization and implementation, 162–9
   party decisions, 136–9, 141, 183–4, 187, 216
   peasant attitudes, 142, 160–2, 163, 166
   quotas, 181
   reasons for initial failure, 185, 210
   'spontaneous', 117, 132–3, 207
   Stalinist drive, 121, 131–5
   see Communist Party of the Soviet Union (Bolsheviks); Siberian Party Organization
Committee for Northern Communications (*Komseveroput*'), 198
Communist Party of the Soviet Union (Bolsheviks),
   Central Committee plenum November 1929, 132–5
   decisions on collectivization, 115, 137–9, 183–4, 186–8, 192, 198
   Fifteenth Party Congress, 10, 15, 18, 34, 44, 208
   Left Opposition, 61
   militarization of grain procurement, 129–31
   organization of *bednota*, 129
   Politburo Commission on revision of Article 61, 111
   Politburo Commission on collectivization, 136–8, 141
   Politburo Commission on dekulakization, 145–7
   Politburo decisions on grain campaign 1929–30, 118, 121
   Politburo decision on procurement from kolkhozes, 196–7
   Sixteenth Party Conference, 11, 28, 53, 64, 66, 83–6, 100, 102, 104
   see Siberian Party Organization
contracts system, 8–10, 22, 43, 114, 116
cooperatives, 37, 44, 46, 48, 51, 55, 56, 91, 95–102 passim, 104, 115, 169

Index

Danilov, V.P., 114
Dekulakization,
  Article 61, 114, 124
  excesses punished, 170, 180, 190–1
  exemptions, 152–3
  exile and resettlement, 157–8, 174–6, 178, 182, 186, 196, 198–203
  family Syzov, 155–6
  forced labour, 200–2, 215
  Kraikom decrees, 147–51, 254–6
  Kraiispolkom decrees, 151–9
  mobilization of *bednota*, 130
  Molotov Commission, 144–6
  numbers of victims, 203, 215
  organization and implementation, 169–77
  peasant opposition, 169, 175–9
  'pillaging' during, 160, 169–72, 184, 191, 215
  Politburo decision, 145–7
  rape, 168–70, 191–2
  reversal of cases, 189–90
  role of *skhod*, 149–50, 173
  self-dekulakization, 16, 203
  social influence, 206, 210–11
  Stalinist drive, 121, 131, 139
  state-building, 113
  tax lists, 148, 153
  see Communist Party of the Soviet Union (Bolsheviks); Siberian Party Organization

Eikhe, R.I.,
  analysis of crisis of NEP, 39
  anti-kulak stance, 44, 90, 133–4
  collectivization, 134, 139, 141–2, 181, 185–6, 189
  dekulakization, 146–8, 153, 173, 180–1, 184, 191–2
  excesses, 50, 106, 108, 191–2
  emergency measures, 24, 30
  grain campaign 1928–9, 22–6 passim, 30, 56–7
  promoted to Kraikom Secretaryship, 90
  support for social influence policy, 83–5, 87–8
  Ural-Siberian method, 114, 119
emergency measures,
  abandonment summer 1928, 8, 205
  during collectivization, 137
  local party attitudes, 26–7, 43, 46, 66, 74
  party bans use, 23, 30, 36
  party confusion, 74, 84–5

historians' confusion, 212
  peasant attitudes, 73
  Siberian leadership proposes reapplication, 36, 54, 61
  see Bukharin, Eikhe, Stalin

Five Year Plan,
  significance of peasant policy for, 65–6, 132–3
  link with mass collectivization, 137, 193, 195, 201, 204
Frumkin, M.I., 19

grain,
  imports, 65
  production, 7
grain procurement,
  biological yield method, 120
  campaign 1927–8, ix, 1–2, 7, 11, 15, 16, 22, 30, 33, 38, 42, 45, 61, 80, 83, 102, 204, 208
  campaign 1928–9, 20–32, 35–51 passim, 52–9 passim, 66, 76, 80, 84–91, 111, 204, 206
  campaign 1929–30, 114–35 passim
  campaign 1930–1, 195–8
  famine 1932–3, 216
  'loan' proposal of Siberian party, 54–63, 67
  quota system, 16–17, 41, 44, 48, 54, 56–8, 61–2, 64, 67, 69–72, 73–9, 85, 89–92, 94, 97, 100–16 passim, 123–31, 143, 170, 198, 208, 211
  reorganization 1928, 12–14
  speculators, 29, 31, 43, 69, 81–2, 104
  state tradition, 67–72
  village commissions, 64, 73, 75–7, 89, 95, 97, 99, 106–7, 120, 128–9
GULag, 201
Gushchin, N. Ya., 76

Kabakov, I.D., 37
Kaganovich, L.M.,
  advocates use of Article 61, 100, 111
  opposes punishment of communist excesses, 187–92, 194, 196–7
  proposes Ural-Siberian method, 63, 76–9
  visits Siberia, 100, 187
Kalinin, M.I., 11, 28, 105, 107
Kamenev, L.B., 79
Kaminsky, G.N., 136
Kavraisky, B., 42, 66, 78, 90, 142
Kavraisky, V.A., 54, 58, 60, 62, 124

Khleboprodukt, 12
Khlopyankin, M.M., 83–4
Kisis, R. Ya., 10, 20–1, 42, 59, 108, 137
Kombedy, 68–70, 72, 82, 208
Komsomol,
  mass collectivization, 147, 149, 164
  organizational work in countryside, 13, 129–30
  self-taxation campaign, 19
  Ural-Siberian Method, 75
Krai Financial Department, 45, 59, 78, 122, 148
Krai Judicial Department,
  application of Article 61, 122, 125–7
  cases arising from mass collectivization, 142–3, 190, 192, 212
  'kulak terror' cases, 34
  opposes repression of peasants, 78, 112, 129
  party attacks moderation, 38–9, 62
Krai Procuracy,
  Article 61, 78
  excesses in collectivization, 162–3, 189–90
  excesses in dekulakisation, 169–71, 190–2
  excesses in grain procurement, 26–8, 30, 48–9, 66, 104, 106–10
  purged, 61–2
  reports, 49, 96, 113, 175
Krai Statistical Department, 62, 199
Kraikom Agriculture Department, 62
Kraisoiuz, 56, 62
Kraitorg, 12, 20, 24, 31, 123
Krai Trades Unions Organization, 43
Krivoshein, A., 68
Kuibyshev, V., 83
Kulikov, N.I., 13
Kunov, I.D. (Kraikom Procurator 1928–9), 38, 62, 106
kulaks,
  estimates of numbers in Siberia, 122, 148
  'kulak terror', 34
  party 'offensive' against, 15–16, 20, 36
  see dekulakization, OGPU
Kuznetsk industrial complex, 133, 158, 177

Lenin, V.I., 13, 28, 79, 82, 86, 131, 147, 162
Lepa, A.K., 17
Lewin, M., 8, 213
Lih, L.T., 68
Lisin, D.A. (Krai Procurator, 1929–30), 65, 67, 106–7

Litvinov, M.M., 150
Lunacharsky, A.B., 28

Machine Tractor Stations, 117, 139
Marx, K., 5
Maynard, J., 148
Mikoyan, A.I.,
  collectivization, 134, 185
  emergency measures, 17–18
  grain campaign 1928–9, 23, 24, 37, 39, 40, 43, 48, 62, 65
  grain campaign 1929–30, 117–18, 130
  instruction on Ural-Siberian method, 76–7
  revision of Article 61, 111, 114
Molodoi rabochii affair, 38–9
Molotov, V.M.,
  anti-kulak policy, 7
  heads Politburo Commission on dekulakization, 144–7
  report to Fifteenth Party Congress, 9, 15, 18, 208
  supports rapid collectivization, 132
Moshkov, Yu. A., 64
multiple fines,
  Siberian party first proposes, 61
  first use of, 73–4, 77, 102
  peasant reaction, 91, 97
  regularized by courts, 77
  after revision of Article 61, 111–12, 122, 126–7
  reviewed by procuracy, 107, 129
Muromtsevo revolt, 177–9

Narkomfin, 31
Narkomprod, 13, 69
Narkomtorg,
  condones emergency measures, 17–18
  coordinates grain procurement, 12, 20, 23, 31, 118
  inspects use of social influence, 51
  pressurizes Siberian leadership, 25, 29, 35–6, 116, 120
Narkomzem RSFSR, 11
Narkomzem USSR, 136, 138
New Economic Policy,
  breakdown of commune during, 5, 71
  commercialization, 6, 204, 208–9, 214
  party commitment to, 21, 131
  peasant differentiation, 18, 72
  peasant attitudes, 94
  reasons for end, ix, 1, 7, 14, 32
  support of Siberian party, 10
  see Bukharin, Eikhe, Syrtsov, Stalin

Nusinov, I.I., 54, 58, 60
Nusinov, I.S., 31, 56, 77, 100, 124

OGPU,
  investigates peasant complaints, 190
  organization of dekulakization, 145–51, 153–9, 175–7
  reports on collectivization, 162, 194–5, 197
  reports on dekulakization, 171, 173–6, 179–80, 193, 199–200
  reports on grain procurement, 46–51, 73, 96, 110, 118
  repression of kulaks, 30, 34, 36, 38, 121–2, 177, 179, 187
Olson, M., 5
Ordzhonikidze, G.K., 79
Orthodox Church, 47–8, 171–2, 214
Osinsky, N., 24

partisans, 34, 100, 150, 152, 163, 179
Peasant Committees of Mutual Aid, 115, 149
peasant actifs,
  collectivization, 130, 141, 145
  dekulakization, 172–4, 176–8, 185
  grain campaigns 15–16, 18, 23, 39, 64, 66, 72, 75–6, 91
  Ural-Siberian method, 102, 107, 115, 206, 209, 213
peasantry
  complaints against party policies, 105–7, 162, 172, 189, 190
  demographic change, 193–4, 215
  development of party policy, 68–72, 92–3, 143, 204, 207, 210, 213–14, 216
  emigration, 93–4, 120, 215
  étatisation, 214–15
  mentalité, 160–9, 188, 193, 196, 197
  moral and political economy, 3–6, 67–72, 92–3, 112, 125, 141–2, 182, 185, 208–9, 213
  protests, 4–5, 6, 46–51, 83, 88, 92–6, 101, 104, 177–9, 186, 212
  serfdom, 2, 14, 70
  social conditions in Siberia, 19
  social differentiation, 5, 8, 18, 60, 78–9, 93, 208
  see contracts system; skhod; volynki;
Plenipotentiaries,
  role in collectivization, 139–40, 162–9, 181
  role in dekulakization, 146, 157, 171, 173, 177–8
  excesses in grain procurement, 17, 26–7, 46–50, 66, 89, 119–20, 124, 128–9
  party mobilization, 12–13, 21
  organization of rural actifs, 72
  self-taxation campaign, 19, 41
  Siberian party criticism, 44
  under tsarist regime, 68
  Ural-Siberian Method, 74–5, 95–110 passim, 206, 212
  see twenty-five thousanders
Pokrovsk affair, 46–51
Popkin, S., 5
Preobrazhensky, E.A.,
  'thesis', 14–15
Prices policy, 15, 40, 65, 95, 134

rationing, 24, 31–2, 193, 205
razverstka, see grain procurement, quota system
Red Army,
  discharging of 'kulaks', 36,
  exempted from dekulakization, 150
  peasant unrest, 88, 180, 184, 187
  soldiers' attitudes, 100, 161–2
Redfield, R., 91
Rettel', I. Ya., 11
Right Opposition,
  capitulation, 133
  Eikhe's position, 24
  emergence, 8
  opposition to emergency measures, 14, 19
  opposition to Ural-Sibcrian Method, 65–6, 79–83
  used as scapegoat, 129
Rudé, G., 92
Rykov, A.I.,
  attacked by Stalinists, 84
  conflict with Siberians, 133
  grain campaign 1928–9, 29–30
  opposes Ural-Siberian method, 63, 65
  replaced as Chairman of Sovnarkom RSFSR, 87
  heads Politburo Commission to revise kolkhoz statutes, 183
Ryskulov, T.R., 136–7

samosud, 47, 96, 206
Scott, J., 4
Sheboldaev, B.P., 84
shevtsvo movement, 13, 35

Siberia,
  commercial farming, 209
  demographic change, 193
  'green revolution' in 1920s, 7, 20, 205
  industrial development, 133
Siberian Party Organization,
  collectivization, 117, 137–8, 140–2, 168–9, 185
  dekulakization, 149–50, 170–94 passim, 181–2, 201, 255–6
  execution of officials for excesses, 190–1
  proposal for grain 'loan', 52–62, 251
  purges, 142, 186
  recruitment of poor peasants, 35
Skocpol, T., 4
skhod,
  Article 61, 111–13
  dekulakization, 149–50, 173, 256–7
  erosion of traditions, 71, 92–3, 101
  social influence policy, 40–1, 57
  taxation, 36–7
  see Ural-Siberian method
smychka, 16, 45, 53, 76, 82, 86
social influence policy,
  boycotts, 33, 39, 40, 42, 44–8 passim, 51, 53, 62, 63, 76, 91, 97, 99, 106, 206
  carnivals, 46–7, 99, 102
  charivari, 47, 206
  collectivization, 136, 141
  dekulakization, 146, 149–50, 177
  development, 8–9, 16–20, 205–6, 208, 211–14
  excesses in use, 47–8, 106–8
  as grain procurement method, 53–72 passim, 73–6, 88, 94–6, 198
  introduction, 16–20
  lower party confusion, 26–7
  moral and political economy, 6, 93
  Stalin, 81–3, 90–1
  tax campaigns, 36–7, 45, 51
Soiuzkhleb, 12, 24
Sokol'nikov, G., 11
soviets,
  collectivization, 143
  dekulakization, 149
  elections, 34–5, 57
  focal point for peasant anger, 96–8, 100, 169
  intimidation of peasants, 48
  lists of grain holders, 40, 45–6, 61
  powers under Article 6, 111–12, 127, 254
  Ural-Siberian method, 75, 89, 102

Sovnarkom RSFSR,
  grain campaign 1928–9, 23, 25, 29, 43–4
  promotion of Syrtsov as chairman, 87
  amendment of Article 61, 111
  criticism of collectivization, 183, 189
  decree on kulak forced labour, 202
Sovnarkom USSR, 145
Stalin, J.V.,
  attacks Syrtsov's moderation, 135
  attitudes of peasants, 161, 188
  bureaucratization under, 120
  'catch up and overtake' slogan, 28, 131, 204
  conversation with Churchill on kulaks, 203
  criticizes implementation of dekulakization, 183, 190
  decision-making under, 33–4, 52
  dekulakization as 'revolution from below', 203
  'dizzy with success' article, 167, 173, 179, 182–4, 186–8
  emergency measures, 27, 63, 80–3, 250–1
  encourages overfulfilment, 215
  evolution of peasant policy, 80–3, 204–5, 208, 210–16
  'liquidation of the kulaks as a class' policy, 144–5, 170, 211
  mobilization of poor peasants, 6, 18–19, 112, 130, 132
  modernization project, ix, xvi, 2–4, 28–9, 131–2, 204–5, 214
  opposes grain 'loan', 62–3
  opposes punishment of communist excesses, 192
  pressurizes Siberian party for grain, 29–32
  promotes Syrtsov, 87
  rapid collectivization, 9, 11
  reorganizes state management of countryside, 7
  'revolution from above', 131, 207, 209
  Siberian tour January 1928, 37, 42, 133
  social influence policy, 16, 18–20
  speech to April 1929 plenum, 80–3
  tax reductions for seredniaks, 28
  tribute, 14–15, 71
  Ural-Siberian method, 16–17, 67, 76, 119, 131, 206
  'Year of the Great Breakthrough' article, 131–2, 203, 204, 211
Stetsky, A., 24

Stolypin, P.A., 71, 72, 93, 208, 214
strikes, 193
Strikovsky, L.S., 56–7, 60, 62
supriaga (sharecropping), 19
Syrtsov, S.I.,
   criticizes collectivization, 133–5, 139
   criticizes dekulakization, 183
   excesses, 50, 106
   grain campaign 1928–9, 22–6 passim, 30, 95, 100
   grain campaign 1929–30, 117–18
   NEP, 61, 83
   promotes Kavraisky, 62
   promotion to Sovnarkom RSFSR chairmanship, 87, 206
   proposes grain 'loan', 54, 60–1, 251
   revision of Article 61, 111
   social influence policy, 19, 53, 83–8
   sowing campaign 1930, 197
   speech to Sixteenth Party Conference, 85–6, 102–3, 106
   support for Stalin against Right, 53–4, 85–6
   temporarily replaced by Kaganovich, 187
   visits Moscow for consultations, 36–7, 39, 41

Taniuchi, Y., 64
taxation policy,
   food tax, 70
   individual supplements, 27–9, 33, 41–6, 49, 53, 122, 148
   social targeting of payments, 35, 78–9, 92, 106, 110, 173, 201, 210
   milling tax, 25
   reform of April 1928, 15–16
   self-taxation, 19, 36, 51, 73, 127
   role of *skhod*, 36–7
   social influence policy, 62–4, 66–7, 76, 91, 205–6
   tribute, 14–15, 70–1
Thompson, E.P., 4
Tomsky, M.P., 63, 65, 82, 133
Toz, 116, 143
tractors,
   production, 136
   supplies to Siberian kolkhozes, 134, 196, 216
tribute, 8, 14–15, 53, 70, 79–80, 207
transport, 31, 34, 43, 52, 133, 199
troiki, 12, 46, 74, 75, 156, 173
Trotskyism, 24, 58
Turk-Sib railway, 11, 193
twenty-five thousanders, 12, 13, 21, 35, 65, 68–9, 97, 140–1, 147, 168, 181, 192
   see plenipotentiaries

Ural-Siberian method,
   application, 101–16
   collectivization, 117
   dekulakization, 211
   development, 33, 55, 62–7, 73, 76–8, 251–3
   distinct from social influence, 51
   role of *skhod*, 64, 73, 76, 97–8, 102, 115, 119, 128, 206, 209, 252–4
   Stalin, 16, 80–1, 83, 90–1
   see Article 61

Vaganov, F.M., 64, 65
volynki,
   against collectivization, 168–9
   against dekulakization, 174–6
   against grain procurement, 92–3, 96–100, 197–8

War Communism, 62, 67, 69, 79, 207
West Siberian Krai Administrative Affairs Department (ZSKAU), 202
women's riots, *see volynki*
worker brigades, *see* twenty-five thousanders

Yakovlev, Ya. A., 136
Yanson, Ya., 111

Zakovsky, L.M., 34, 46–8, 50, 60, 171, 176, 179
Zav'ialovo experiment, 73–6, 112
Zernotrest, 11
Zlobin, A.N., 25, 88–90, 114, 116, 123, 130